3.12

The Rhizome and the Flower

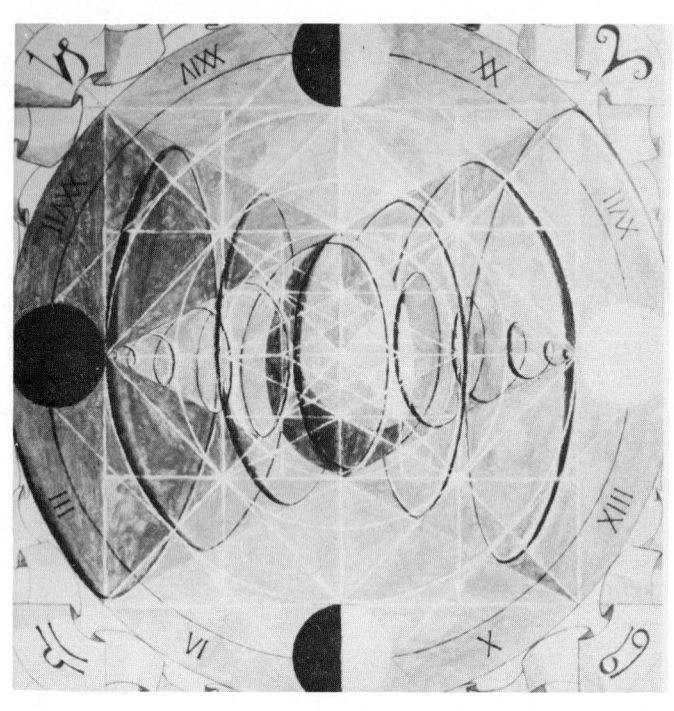

James Olney
The Rhizome and the Flower
The Perennial Philosophy—
Yeats and Jung

UNIVERSITY OF CALIFORNIA PRESS

Berkeley / Los Angeles / London

University of California Press
Berkeley and Los Angeles, California
University of California Press, Ltd.
London, England
© 1980 by The Regents of the University of California
ISBN 0-520-03748-0
Library of Congress Catalog Card Number: 78-62834
Printed in the United States of America

1 2 3 4 5 6 7 8 9

This book, from its inception,
has been for
KATHLEEN RAINE

and now, at its completion,
it is also for
NATHAN

CONTENTS

Note to the Reader   ix

Acknowledgments   xi

On Abbreviations and Citations   xiv

Prolegomena   3

I. The *Rhizōmata*, Plato, and Platonism   24

II. Numbers, Harmony, and Metempsychosis   54

III. *Logos* and the Sensible Flux   86

IV. The One Being   125

V. Gyres and Cycles, the Quaternity and the Sphere   150

VI. *Mythos*, *Eidos*, and the *Daimon*   184

VII. The Poetics of Mummy Wheat   234

VIII. Psychology of the Pleroma   288

IX. System   346

Index   371

NOTE TO THE READER

This book is not a study of the poetry or the poetics of W. B. Yeats; it is not a study of the psychology of C. G. Jung; it is not a study of the Pre-Socratic philosophers; and it is not a study of Platonism. Neither is it a study of the similarities between Yeats and Jung. I say this at the outset merely to discourage certain conventional (but perhaps natural) expectations. The book is a study of what I have chosen to call "The Rhizome and the Flower," or, in other words, a study of "the Perennial Philosophy" and of "Yeats-and-Jung." *The Rhizome and the Flower* is of course concerned in part with the poetics of Yeats, in part with the psychology of Jung, in part with the manifold similarities between Yeatsian poetics and Jungian psychology, and in part with that Perennial Philosophy that in ancient Greece spoke the language of the Pre-Socratics, Plato, and Platonism; but in the end the various subjects merge and interpenetrate to that degree that they cannot be set off and apart from one another. Hence the unconventional shape of the book and hence this request: that readers approach this book on its own terms, not on any others (those terms being described fully in the "Prolegomena"), and that they not expect the conventional in a book that in plan, in purpose, and in structure is designedly and necessarily unconventional.

While it may seem that *The Rhizome and the Flower* takes a long time to get to Yeats and Jung, it should be observed that the intellectual history of the West also took a long time to reach them, and a book like the present one, which is not a comparative study but an exercise in the history and psychology of ideas, owes first loyalty to its subject. However, readers who are initially interested only in Yeats, the poet, or only in Jung, the psychologist, may, of course, proceed directly from the "Prolegomena" to Chapter 7 or Chapter 8. Those chapters do not contain anything like the entire argument of the book, but I believe that they can stand on their own as essays on the poetics of Yeats and the psychology of Jung; they may also, I hope, spark an interest in the real subject of the book and so lead the specialized reader back to preceding chapters.

ACKNOWLEDGMENTS

Research on this book was begun with a grant from the Frances G. Wickes Foundation and was concluded with a fellowship from the National Endowment for the Humanities. I could never have written the book without this generous support, and I am deeply grateful to both the Wickes Foundation and the NEH for their faith in the work.

Miss Anne Yeats and Mr. Franz Jung opened their fathers' libraries to me, and both of them, with the kindest hospitality and generosity, spent hours talking with me about their fathers. Any sense of humanity in this book is largely owing to these two remarkable children of remarkable parents.

Students of Yeats will perhaps remark and be surprised by a general absence of reference to Yeats criticism. This is not to be ascribed to any lack of respect nor (I trust) to ignorance on my part. On the contrary, I think Yeats has been singularly fortunate in his critics, and what I know about reading him is due in large measure to what I have learned from such excellent critics as Denis Donoghue, Richard Ellmann, Edward Engelberg, T. R. Henn, A. Norman Jeffares,

Frank Kermode, Thomas Parkinson, B. L. Reid, Jon Stallworthy, John Unterecker, Helen Vendler, and Thomas Whitaker. That these names seldom occur in my text is because I had absorbed, so far as I was capable, the body of criticism that they represent before I set about my study. In other words, Yeats criticism is a sort of *a priori* "given" for this study, and *The Rhizome and the Flower* could not exist in anything like its present form without that criticism. I can only express my general gratitude here.

A number of friends and colleagues have read parts of the book (or closely related pieces) in manuscript and have greatly assisted me with comments: James Gardner, William Howarth, Richard Hughes, Lawrence Lipking, A. Walton Litz, E. M. Manasse, Ernest Mason, Thomas Parkinson, Roger Rosenblatt, Carol H. Smith, and Alan Weinblatt. I am grateful to all these friendly critics both for the advice that I accepted, thereby strengthening the manuscript, and for the advice that I rejected—which, together with the certain knowledge that some of them would not approve of all the book says, makes me insist on full responsibility for it. To Doris Kretschmer and Paul Weisser I am deeply grateful for the care they gave to the manuscript at the University of California Press.

To the following people I am grateful for various kinds of information and assistance: Mrs. Anne Baynes, Mrs. Sybille Bedford, Thomas Blanding, W. K. C. Guthrie, George Mills Harper, Mrs. Joanna Hitchcock, John S. Kelly, William and Paula McGuire, Geoffrey Watkins, and E. H. Herndon (who found me an office when I needed one).

Three of my brothers—Byron, John, and Richard—have read parts or all of the manuscript and have kept my spirits up with positive responses while improving the text with questions and criticisms. To Richard I owe the fine painting of schemes Yeatsian and Jungian which appears on the dust cover and as frontispiece; that painting faced me constantly as I wrote the book—which at times has seemed to me little more than a gloss (very extended to be sure) on the painting. My wife Judith has sustained me throughout. Every page of this book is indebted to Kathleen Raine in complex and manifold ways, and I offer it to her in gratitude and affection.

Grateful acknowledgment is made to Miss Anne Yeats, Mr. M. B. Yeats, the Macmillan Co. of London and Basingstoke, and the Macmillan Publishing Co., Inc., of New York for permission to quote from *The Variorum Edition of the Poems of W. B. Yeats*, edited by Peter Allt and Russell K. Alspach, including poems copyright © 1924, 1928, 1933, 1934 by Macmillan Publishing Co., Inc., renewed 1952, 1956, 1961, 1962 by Bertha Georgie Yeats; poems copyright © 1940 by Georgie Yeats, renewed 1968 by Bertha Georgie Yeats, Michael Butler Yeats, and Anne Yeats; and a poem copyright © 1957 by Macmillan Publishing Co., Inc.

A part of Chapter VII originally appeared in "W. B. Yeats's Daimonic Memory," *Sewanee Review* 85 (1977). Copyright © 1977 by the University of the South. Reprinted by permission of the editor.

ON ABBREVIATIONS AND CITATIONS

References to Plato are given in the conventional way, by page number and by subsection on each page (a through e), as established in the edition of Stephanus (1578).

Fragments of the Pre-Socratics are cited by their numbers in *Die Fragmente der Vorsokratiker*, by Hermann Diels, revised by Walther Kranz.

W. B. YEATS

Auto. = *Autobiographies* (London: Macmillan, 1955)
E. & I. = *Essays and Introductions* (London and New York: Macmillan, 1961)
Ex. = *Explorations*, selected by Mrs. W. B. Yeats (London and New York: Macmillan, 1962)
Letters = *The Letters of W. B. Yeats*, ed. Allan Wade (London: Rupert Hart-Davis, 1954)
Memoirs = *Memoirs*, transcribed and edited by Denis Donoghue (London: Macmillan, 1972) [Includes "Autobiography—First Draft" and "Journal"]

On Abbreviations and Citations   xv

Myth. = *Mythologies* (London and New York: Macmillan, 1959) [Includes *Per Amica Silentia Lunae*, which consists of two parts: "Anima Hominis" and "Anima Mundi"]

On the Boiler = *On the Boiler* (Dublin: The Cuala Press, 1939)

Poems = *The Variorum Edition of the Poems of W. B. Yeats*, ed. Peter Allt and Russell K. Alspach (New York: Macmillan, 1957)

1925 *Vision* = *A Vision* (London: privately published by T. Werner Laurie, 1925)

Vision, or *A Vision* = *A Vision* (London and New York: Macmillan, 1937)

Yeats/Moore *Correspondence* = *W. B. Yeats and T. Sturge Moore: Their Correspondence 1901–1937*, ed. Ursula Bridge (New York: Oxford University Press, 1953)

Hone = Joseph Hone, *W. B. Yeats, 1865–1939* (London: Macmillan, 1962)

Parrish/Painter = *A Concordance to the Poems of W. B. Yeats*, ed. by Stephen Maxfield Parrish, programmed by James Allan Painter (Ithaca: Cornell University Press, 1963)

Other works are given full citations on first occurrence.

C. G. JUNG

CW = *The Collected Works of C. G. Jung*, trans. R. F. C. Hull (Princeton: Princeton University Press [Bollingen Series XX]; London: Routledge & Kegan Paul, 1953–1978) [Citations are made by volume and paragraph: e.g., *CW*, VIII, par. 421]

Freud/Jung Letters = *The Freud/Jung Letters: The Correspondence between Sigmund Freud and C. G. Jung*, ed. William McGuire, trans. Ralph Manheim and R. F. C. Hull (Princeton: Princeton University Press/Bollingen, 1974)

Letters = *C. G. Jung: Letters*, 2 vols., ed. Gerhard Adler, in collaboration with Aniela Jaffé, trans. from German by R. F. C. Hull (Princeton: Princeton University Press/Bollingen, 1973 and 1976)

Memories = *Memories, Dreams, Reflections*, recorded and edited by Aniela Jaffé, trans. Richard and Clara Winston (New York: Pantheon Books [Random House], copyright 1961, 1962, 1963; London: Collins and Routledge & Kegan Paul, 1963) [Page citations are first to the American edition, then to the British edition: e.g., *Memories*, p. 75/82]

Other works are given full citations on first occurrence.

rhizōma, noun (plural, rhizōmata) — 1. a root, a mass of roots, a root system 2. an element, or the four elements, as the root or roots of physical nature and the world-system: Pythagoras—"the *tetraktys* is the fount and root [*rhizōma*] of eternal nature"; Empedocles—"hear first the four roots [*rhizōmata*] of all things."

adapted from the *Greek-English Lexicon* of Lidell and Scott

rhizome, noun (anglicized from *rhizōma* and now more usual) — a prostrate or subterranean rootlike stem emitting roots and usually producing leaves at its apex; a rootstock.

Oxford English Dictionary

As to the most lordly kind of soul in us we must think thus: that the god has given to each of us as his own *daimon* that soul which we say dwells at the top of the body and which raises us from earth toward our kindred in heaven (for we are indeed a plant sprung not from the earth but from heaven). And this is a most true account—for it is to heaven, whence the soul first grew, that the divine part attaches the head and rhizome-root of us and keeps the whole body upright.

Plato

The shapes of beauty haunting our moments of inspiration . . . [are] a people older than the world, citizens of eternity, appearing and reappearing in the minds of artists and of poets . . . ; and because beings, none the less symbols, blossoms, as it were, growing from invisible immortal roots, hands, as it were, pointing the way into some divine labyrinth.

W. B. Yeats

Life has always seemed to me like a plant that lives on its rhizome. Its true life is invisible, hidden in the rhizome. The part that appears above ground lasts only a single summer. Then it withers away—an ephemeral apparition. . . . I have never lost a sense of something that lives and endures underneath the eternal flux. What we see is the blossom, which passes. The rhizome remains.

C. G. Jung

PROLEGOMENA

"Yeats and Jung—what a marvellous idea!" The friend who said this when I proposed a study of W. B. Yeats and C. G. Jung in tandem echoed quite nicely what was at that time my own thought, for the subject seemed a natural and obvious one—so natural, indeed, and so much *there* as to be almost easy. I recognized, of course, even in those days that now seem so long ago, that there would be a good deal of reading to be done and that it would be necessary to sort out my attitude toward the two men and to maintain the proper tone; yet . . . almost easy. . . . As Heraclitus might put it, however, different and different waters have flowed over me, around Yeats and Jung, and under the bridge since the study that produced the present book seemed an obvious, natural, and almost easy one. Indeed, in working it out, my very conception of the subject has been "transformed utterly," to the point that I would now be disinclined to call it a comparative study of Yeats and Jung at all. Yet it did start from a conjunction of those two great creative minds.

Thinking about the strange similarities between Yeats and Jung and the magnetic field of force in which they seem drawn together, I have at times entertained the fantasy that the two men might have bumped into one another at Watkins' Bookshop in Cecil Court, for both of them were friends of John Watkins and regular patrons of his bookshop. If they did collide as my imagination has sometimes suggested to me, then I am sure that they did no more than murmur their mutual apologies and go on their different ways, for each was —and remained—pretty much ignorant of the other's existence. In one of the more or less jokey prefaces to the first version of *A Vision* (1925), Yeats has Michael Robartes asking Owen Aherne, "Where is Yeats? I want his address," and Aherne responding, "I did not know where Mr Yeats lived, but said that we could find out from Mr Watkins the book-seller in Cecil's Court. . . ." This "Mr Watkins the book-seller in Cecil's Court" is also the John Watkins who, in 1925, privately published a small booklet called *Septem Sermones ad Mortuos* that claimed to be by Basilides of Alexandria— but was in fact by C. G. Jung of Zurich. When and how Jung arranged that publication I am not certain (though Mr. Geoffrey Watkins assures me that it could not have been in "the spring of 1917," when Robartes and Aherne made their fictional jaunt to the bookshop in search of Yeats's address[1]), but it is certain that Jung called in at Watkins' Bookshop whenever he was in London.

Now this tale of Yeats and Jung that revolves around Cecil Court becomes more tangled. In Jung's magnificent library, which is still intact in Küsnacht, there is a copy of a book bearing this title page:

A VISION

AN EXPLANATION OF LIFE
FOUNDED UPON THE WRITINGS
OF GIRALDUS AND UPON CER-
TAIN DOCTRINES ATTRIBUTED
TO KUSTA BEN LUKA

By

WILLIAM
BUTLER
YEATS

LONDON
Privately Printed for Subscribers only by
T. WERNER LAURIE, LTD.
1925

---

1. In a private communication, Mr. Watkins pointed out that Jung obviously could not have crossed to England during the first World War.

And on a later page we find:

> A VISION
>
> *This edition consists of six hundred
> copies numbered and signed.*
>
> *This is No.....* 139 ...
>
> W B Yeats [signature]

Whether Jung acquired his autographed copy of *A Vision* from John Watkins I do not know,[2] but whatever the source of No. 139, I am quite sure that Jung never read it; in fact, he seems to have opened it in Küsnacht just long enough to decide that it should be shelved with his alchemical texts[3] and then left it untouched for the rest of his life, for in response to a question from two inquirers, Jung wrote, "Your remarks about Yeats have interested me very much. As you rightly surmise, I am not acquainted with his work at all. I have never read a line of his."[4]

Meanwhile, back in London and in Ireland, the mystery is no less piquant, but the crossed paths are no clearer either. The journalist H. W. Nevinson reports that when he called on Yeats in October 1916, "he talked of Freud and Jung and the Subconscious Self, applying the doctrine to art."[5] I think, however, that Jung would

2. A number of books in Jung's library are from Watkins, among them Shri Purohit Swami's *An Indian Monk: His Life and Adventures* (London: Macmillan, 1932), which has an introduction by Yeats and an acknowledgment from the author that begins: "Dr. W. B. Yeats said he wanted from me a 'concrete life, not an abstract philosophy'; here is the result. . . . If any readers find enlightenment in the following pages, let them join me in thanking the greatest living Irish poet" (p. vii). According to Geoffrey Watkins, in an article on "Yeats and Mr. Watkins' Bookshop" in *Yeats and the Occult*, ed. George Mills Harper (Toronto: Macmillan of Canada, 1975), "It was my father who was responsible for introducing Yeats . . . to Shri Purohit Swami" (p. 309). All the pages of Jung's copy of *An Indian Monk* are cut (but a foreign signature—"H. F. Zinno"—is on the flyleaf); a label on the flyleaf reads "John M. Watkins, Publisher and Bookseller, 21 Cecil Court, London WC2."

3. It was Mr. Franz Jung who remarked this curious fact when he took the book down from the shelf for me to look at.

4. Richard J. Wall and Roger Fitzgerald, "Yeats and Jung: An Ideological Comparison," *Literature and Psychology*, 13, No. 2 (Spring 1963), p. 52, n. 8. According to Wall and Fitzgerald, this remark occurred "in private correspondence with the authors, dated January 28, 1960"—i.e., a little over a year before Jung's death.

5. H. W. Nevinson, *Last Changes Last Chances* (London: Nisbet, 1928), p. 123. As far as I know, Thomas Whitaker first pointed out the passage in Nevinson. Whitaker's *Swan and Shadow* has excellent observations on the similarities in thought existing between Yeats and Jung.

In an interview with Yeats that appeared over the initials "F. H." (i.e., Francis

have failed to recognize any of his own distinctive ideas in what Nevinson goes on to report of Yeats's conversation, so that this unique recorded instance of Jung's name on Yeats's lips must be treated as a simple dead end. In Virginia Moore's *The Unicorn* we are offered another tantalizing tidbit when we are told (p. 300) that "Yeats's unpublished journal contains Jung's name and address"— but George Mills Harper disposes of this item with the information (privately communicated) that, while Jung's name and address are indeed there, they are written in an unknown hand, certainly not Yeats's. In *Wheels and Butterflies*, Yeats remarks, very much in passing, that "a German psycho-analyst has traced the 'mother complex' back to our mother the sea" (*Ex.*, p. 378); and while Jung was neither German nor (by 1934) a "psycho-analyst," I am confident that Yeats was referring to Jung—but I am equally confident that he only half understood what he was talking about and that Yeats's information came from what someone told him rather than from a reading of Jung.[6] At any rate, it is certain that Yeats never mentions Jung in anything he ever published, and according to John S. Kelly there are no references to Jung in any as yet unpublished letters of Yeats. Yeats and Jung were strangers.

This, however, only makes the question the more interesting, for while one spoke the language of poetry and the other the language of psychology, Yeats and Jung are nevertheless in astonishing agreement on all the following concepts, doctrines, and beliefs:

> The relation between the collective unconscious (Jung) and *Anima Mundi* (Yeats) on the one hand and the personal unconscious and *anima hominis* on the other hand.

Hackett) in *The New Republic* of 24 November 1917 (p. 100), the interviewer writes, "I spoke of Jung's belief in England's national complex. He [Yeats] was greatly interested." "F. H." does not reveal the form that Yeats's great interest took; indeed, these two sentences are his entire account of the matter.

6. As to Yeats's reading of Jung: there is one volume of Jung in Yeats's library— *Collected Papers on Analytical Psychology* (London: Bailliere, Tindall & Cox, 1916)—but the essays in that volume can hardly be taken as very revealing about Jung's mature ideas. Virginia Moore and T. R. Henn suggest that certain elements in Yeats show a remarkable consonance with the ideas expressed by Jung in his commentary on *The Secret of the Golden Flower*, and from Yeats's *Letters* (pp. 786 and 788) it would appear that he borrowed Olivia Shakespear's copy of the book, though whether he actually read it remains very uncertain; in any case, Jung's commentary could hardly have been formative as far as Yeats's ideas or his poetry are concerned, for he encountered the book only in 1931/32.

Jung's concept of the archetype and Yeats's theories of the archetypal symbol in life, in magic, and in poetry.

Their ideas on Unity of Being (Yeats's term), on individuation (Jung's term), and on the nature of the self (a shared term).

Jung's theories of "synchronicity" and Yeats's of minds flowing into one another, their shared feeling that both time and space may be relative when psychic phenomena are in question, and their joint belief in prevision, precognition, and extrasensory perception.

The division and unification of human types and of humanity in *Psychological Types* and in *A Vision*.

Their schematic representations (drawings of antinomies, circles, and quaternities in Jung's "Red Book" and in Yeats's *Vision*) of psychological and cultural processes.

Their notion that all energy and all creativity is from a conflict of opposites and that human history itself moves in perpetual cycles that oppose, reverse, and complement one another.

Jung's theory of shadow figures and of anima and animus and Yeats's theory of masks and images.

Their shared idea that tradition—familial, cultural, national, and intellectual—finds its culmination in present creativity.

Their beliefs about the relation of the living to the dead and about the relation of emotions and instincts.

A belief in what both of them called "the *daimon*."

Their concepts of symbolism as a creative transformation of psychic and spiritualistic energy.

The symbolic significance (psychological and poetic) of their towers in Bollingen and Gort.

While this list by no means exhausts the number of points at which Yeats and Jung touch and merge, it does at least demonstrate that it is not at all out of poverty that one would decline to accept simple—or complex—comparison as a sufficient subject. Who cares simply that Yeats and Jung were in some ways alike—of course they were—if there is no more to it than that? If the only conclusion to which we can come is that they had similar thoughts, then this is more than unfortunate because it is not a conclusion at all: it is instead the accepted *premise*, the *donnée* from which the study would properly start.

The wrong way to begin, I am thoroughly convinced, would be by reading Yeats through Jungian spectacles or Jung through Yeatsian spectacles. Yeats had no great love for psychology; Jung had even less for what he called "modern art," and modern poetry he found especially offensive. To adopt either literary criticism or psychology as a discipline and an exclusive mode for approaching the subject would be to murder the one man in order to dissect the other. Not that literary criticism and psychology should be abandoned altogether: Yeats demands to be approached as a poet, and in ways appropriate to poetry; Jung demands to be approached as a psychologist. What is necessary is to discover—while not altogether abandoning literary criticism or psychology—a *tertium quid*, as Jung might call it, or a *tertium comparationis*: a third language that displays a syntax and grammar similar to the syntax and grammar of Yeats's poetics and at the same time similar to the syntax and grammar of Jung's psychology. Refusing the language of psychology or the language of literary criticism as our sole speech, what we must attempt is to find a *tertium* between the two conflicting opposites that would integrate them at a higher level and provide the grounds for a valid comparison between them if and because they both share, through the uniting third, in a similar underlying structural configuration. Moreover, this *tertium* must be a twofold "higher third," comprehending both historical and psychical origins of an idea, an image, or an expression.

If we must give up literary criticism as an exclusive discipline, if we must abandon psychology as an exclusive analytical tool, and if there are no direct, lateral ties to be discovered between Yeats and Jung, then where do we stand? There still remain, it seems to me, various ways in which to account for the many similarities in thought, image, expression, and intention discoverable in the works of the two men. It could be, for example, that (1) the personal and cultural circumstances in which the bodies of work were produced caused them to be alike—that the works were, in a manner of speaking, precipitated out by the times; or (2) it could be argued that Jung's notion of "synchronicity" was a valid one and in this case potently operative; again, (3) it might be that the systems implicit in

Yeats and Jung answer to some basic configuration and archetypal need of the human mind and at the same time, perhaps, to an ontological and metaphysical reality outside the mind; and finally, (4) it is possible that the two men participated in and were to a large extent shaped by the same philosophical tradition—behind the systems, in other words, was what might be called "The System," an historically evolved, humanly articulated structure of thought and feeling. Moreover, if (3) and (4) were joined, it might be that the systems/System would bear legitimate reference not only within to the structure of the mind that shaped it but outside itself as well to the structure of the cosmos. I think it best not to reject out of hand either of the first two possible explanations, but there can be no doubt that the latter two explanations, especially if seen as corollaries that serve to extend one another, provide a far richer subject for our consideration. There is no lateral or temporal line that connects Yeats with Jung, but there are parallel lines which one could demonstrate and retrace, stretching back from both so far into the past of human history that as they reach the limits of our vision and our historical perspective they cease to be parallel and come together on the horizon of human thought in such primal figures as Plato first, and then, beyond Plato (in the order in which we meet them as we trace our lines back into the past), Empedocles, Parmenides, Heraclitus, and Pythagoras. Seen in this light, the works of Yeats and Jung are present moments of a long past, a creative surfacing in geographically discrete places of a continuous and unbroken, though sometimes chthonic and subterranean, body of slowly developed and developing human thought and performance. Thus a great tradition is discoverable behind these two very individual talents, and here is the first face of our *tertium quid*: the Platonic system, shaped by Plato himself out of his four great predecessors and issuing in that immense tradition called Platonism.

"I ceased to read modern books that were not books of imagination," Yeats tells us in a volume of his *Autobiographies*, "and if some philosophic idea interested me, I tried to trace it back to its earliest use, believing that there must be a tradition of belief older than any European Church, and founded upon the experience of the world before the modern bias" (*Auto.*, p. 265). Thus also the intention and the mode of the present book: to trace back to their earliest use, many centuries before Yeats and Jung, those ideas, images, figures, and expressions that the poet and psychologist shared so lavishly, but unknowingly, with one another. Having observed the two contemporaneous flowers, so strikingly alike in form and structure but growing in different gardens and alien soils, I should like to examine the rhizome from which they have grown and blossomed and to which they return. As to the antiquity of the tradition that I would outline, Yeats's intuition was right: unless there are still European worshippers in a Church of the Orphic Mysteries, then the "tradition of belief" traceable back from Yeats and Jung is certainly "older than any European Church," and it was indeed "founded upon the experience of the world before the modern bias." Jung imagined, too, in a very Yeatsian manner, that the history of philosophy could be seen as something like a preparation and prologue for his own thought—as it were a series of analogues politely provided by intellectual history to confirm thoughts he would pursue in Basel and Zurich. "I read a brief introduction to the history of philosophy," Jung says in his autobiography, "and in this way gained a bird's-eye view of everything that had been thought in this field. I found to my gratification that many of my intuitions had historical analogues. Above all I was attracted to the thought of Pythagoras, Heraclitus, Empedocles, and Plato . . . " (*Memories*, p. 68/76). And according to C. M. Bowra, when Yeats "read the Greek philosophers in the translations of Thomas Taylor, what he looked for in them was examples and images to confirm his own beliefs."[7] I should imagine that it would provide a very considerable gratification to discover that philosophic history has all along been preparing the way for one's own advent—ever since Pythagoras, Heraclitus, Empedocles, and Plato and the tradition of belief that commenced with those great ancients.

But did that tradition really commence with Pythagoras, his confrères, and successors? Of course it did not, but if we are to begin we must begin somewhere. I can do no better in this matter of origins than to quote, with gratitude and admiration, the very first sentence of Pierre Duhem's great and monumental ten-volume treatise, *Le Système du monde: Histoire des doctrines cosmologiques de Platon à Copernic*—and I would suggest that for "une doctrine scientifique" one could substitute "une idée archétype" without essential change

---

7. Bowra, *Memories: 1898-1939* (Cambridge, Mass.: Harvard University Press, 1967), p. 234.

in Duhem's meaning: "En la genèse d'une doctrine scientifique, il n'est pas de commencement absolu; si haut que l'on remonte la lignée des pensées qui ont préparé, suggéré, annoncé cette doctrine, on parvient toujours à des opinions qui, à leur tour, ont été préparées, suggérées et annoncées; et si l'on cesse de suivre cet enchaînement d'idées qui ont procédé les unes des autres, ce n'est pas qu'on ait mis la main sur le maillon initial, mais c'est que la chaîne s'enfonce et disparaît dans les profondeurs d'un insondable passé" ["In the generation of a scientific doctrine, there is no absolute beginning; no matter how far one retraces the line of thoughts which led up to this doctrine and suggested and hinted at it, one is always coming on ideas which, in their turn, have been led up to, suggested and hinted at; and if one ceases to follow the chain of ideas which have given rise to one another, it is not because one has laid one's hand on the very first link, but because the chain sinks down and disappears in the depths of an unfathomable past"]. It would be very foolish to put one's finger on some one text or to point to some one thinker and argue that here, just here and nowhere else, the tradition commenced. This is not the way a scientific doctrine or an archetypal idea is generated, nor the way that either of them takes shape; and there are unquestionably roots and influences much deeper down and further back than we can ever hope to see. When, having retraced link after link, however, we arrive back at Pythagoras, we find the past pretty murky and the depth pretty unfathomable (though there is also a certain advantage in that murkiness, as I shall point out later), and it will profit us little to try to push back beyond Pythagoras. Let us call Pythagoras the first link in the chain —the *aurea catena* of the Hermetists—all the while acknowledging that this is only a manner of speaking and that certainly Pythagoras had his predecessors, who had their predecessors, who had *their* predecessors, etc. But for those others we have no names; and while much is uncertain about the historicity of Pythagoras, we do at least have a name for him and a grand one at that.

To go behind the similarities of thought, image, and expression in Yeats and Jung and so to discover the tradition that issued in their works (and in many another man's work also, of course) is only one step of the way, however; for that merely leaves us with the perception of multiplied similarities: Yeats is like Jung is like Blake is like Swedenborg is like Boehme is like Paracelsus is like Nicholas of

Cusa is like St. Augustine is like Plotinus is like Plato is like Pythagoras . . . almost to that infinity which we cannot reach only because our vision cannot extend indefinitely into the past. This tradition has been developing for so long and in so many places that it seems never to have begun, to have almost no limits, and to be the natural and necessary creation of a corporate human consciousness: the intellectual/emotional complement of human life as such. The other necessary step of the way, then, beyond the first step of delineating a tradition, is to abandon historical and chronological order and to go not only behind the surface similarities between Yeats and Jung but also behind the tradition. What is it, not in history but in the human mind—what creative forces, what inner impulses or structures or necessities—what is it that impels these individual creations, all established, as it would appear, on the one essential ground plan?

Writing of his and Lady Gregory's experience in collecting stories from peasants in the West of Ireland—stories in which he discovered precisely that same ancient "tradition of belief" mentioned in the *Autobiographies*—Yeats says, "Again and again, she and I felt that we had got down, as it were, into some fibrous darkness, into some matrix out of which everything has come . . . " (*E. & I.*, p. 429). Let it be noted that though Yeats felt that in the stories he had discovered the same ancient tradition of belief as he could find by tracing a philosophic idea back to its earliest use, he specifically describes himself as going *down* rather than *back* into a "fibrous darkness," and his choice of adverb clearly indicates that the journey in this case was psychic rather than historic. What is that "matrix out of which everything has come"? Jung gave it a name—a name not lovelier but perhaps more scientific than "fibrous darkness"—for Yeats's matrix is the unconscious (or subconscious, as Yeats called it: "down" beneath consciousness), which is a dark, teeming, creative matrix that is also, in one of its aspects, collective. "The unconscious is the matrix of all metaphysical statements, of all mythology, of all philosophy," according to Jung (*CW*, XI, par. 899). Elsewhere in the same volume of the *Collected Works*, Jung writes, "Because the unconscious is the matrix mind, the quality of creativeness attaches to it. It is the birthplace of thought-forms such as our text considers the Universal Mind to be. . . . In so far as the forms or patterns of the unconscious belong to no time in particular, being seemingly eternal, they convey a peculiar feeling of timelessness when consciously realized" (par. 782). If this is true (and Yeats certainly would have found himself in passionate agreement with what Jung says), then the ideas that we give Pythagoras credit for are products of the human psyche—of the unconscious and especially the collective unconscious—and in that "fibrous darkness," the "matrix out of which everything has come," we can expect to find still in our time, as in any time, a shadowy Pythagoras, Heraclitus, Parmenides, and Empedocles, all of them known to us and yet unknown, all of them unconscious but forever rising into consciousness. This necessitates, as I earlier remarked, that our *tertium* be twofold. The Yeatsian and Jungian blossoms that we now observe are of the present and of consciousness, but there is both an historical rhizome and a psychical rhizome from which they draw their life, for those two momentary flowers have their roots, alike and together, in ancient Greece and in the collective depths of the unconscious. This is the other, the second face of our *tertium comparationis*, to be made out not on the surface level, not even on the first subsurface level, not so much in history nor in written texts, but further down in that "fibrous darkness" that is the emotional and mental makeup of humanity itself. This may seem very like saying that Yeats and Jung will serve as little more than pretexts for unfolding a drama of the human mind and of human creativity, a drama that is not, at least not in any limiting sense, Jungian or Yeatsian. Against such a charge—that I have "used" Yeats and Jung for my own purposes—I have no defense to offer, nor any apology—unless it be apology to remark that both Yeats and Jung did the same thing in their works and in their days and so gave the example for our work and our day.

Yeats and Jung, with their different, nearly parallel lines that converge on the one source, drew on the Platonic tradition for a number of their phrases and notions ("archetypes" and "Anima Mundi," to choose two major examples), and this unquestionably has much to do with their systematizing in similar ways. All the same, a careful balance must be struck so that neither the Platonic tradition nor any other will be made uniquely responsible for an independent recurrence of images and expression, for the truth is that Yeats claimed no more than confirmation and Jung no more than amplification from any philosophic tradition. Neither one acknowledged the Platonic tradition as the ultimate source of his ideas or his images. Yeats derived his system, according to his own testimony, from Celtic mythology, from other poets, and from occult experiences (his wife's automatic writing, his own visions and voices in the night, and certain group efforts in spiritualism). Jung was even more insistent: the writings of the ancients might serve to amplify his patients' (and his own) dreams, visions, and fantasies, but it was in these latter products of the human psyche—products that he observed, recorded, and claimed as empirical evidence—that Jung discovered (but, he stoutly maintained, did *not* invent) a coherent system created apparently by the collective unconscious of mankind. The Yeats/Jung correspondences thus carry one very far away from themselves as mere curiosities—to a remove of twenty-five centuries into the past and to a penetration far down deep into the human psyche, both individual and collective.

With Yeats and Jung and all the swarming, buzzing, proliferating implications generated by their conjunction for subject, where does one begin? For some months past I have felt compelled, as it were from beyond my own will and in order to escape sole domination by either the poet or the psychologist, to read and reread all of Plato and the Pre-Socratics and a good part of the scholarship on ancient Greek philosophy; yet at the same time a quiet but insistent voice has told me that if I were going to spend so much time looking into dark and distant corners of scholarship, I should have to acknowledge that Yeats, after all, was at best an indifferent scholar and was not really concerned to be a better one; and while Jung was a man of very great erudition and extremely wide reading (I have seen a copy of the *Timaeus* that he annotated now in Latin and now in Greek, now in German and now in English), he nevertheless always claimed to be an empirical scientist rather than, in the ancient Greek manner, a philosopher who loved wisdom and pursued it far beyond the doors of any laboratory or clinic. It was precisely that realm far above, or far beneath, the touch of modern science that was the special concern of the Greek philosopher; but Jung regularly maintained that the modern psychologist, in contrast to the ancient philosopher, had no business making metaphysical statements of any kind or asserting anything at all about Truth. Now certainly the poet should be read as a poet, the psychologist as a psychologist; and yet, while we should honor (at least to a degree) Jung's disclaimers and while we must acknowledge Yeats's limitations as a scholar, there still remain good and justifiable reasons—reasons both of structure and of content—for carrying a study of Yeats and Jung back to Greek philosophy, which is to say back to the most ancient Western thinkers of whom we have a record. In those antique philosophers we discover sharper outlines and simpler designs than we will find in the system after it developed for twenty-five centuries; but those outlines, easier to discern because of their cleaner, bolder clarity, have the same schematic form as the basic ground plan informing the much more complex elaborations of Yeats's poetics and Jung's psychology.

Platonism has been traced a number of times in Yeats's works;[8] there has been no need, on the other hand, to perform the same service for Jung, since he cites the texts of the Platonic tradition frequently and quotes from them copiously himself. This is not enough, however, for Platonism did not spring full-blown from the forehead of Plato, nor was it the immaculate conception of his brain alone: a good deal of mental intercourse went on—among the Pre-Socratics and between Plato and his predecessors—before the Platonic system was conceived and before it was brought to birth in a very slow delivery. I freely admit that we cannot expect to get back to a very first ancestor—a single Adam in whom the entire race originated—nor can we expect to come up with the first link in the chain and prove it to be first. But we *can*, all the same, and with great profit in my judgment, push the limits of our vision back earlier than Plato to the Pre-Socratics on whom he constructed his system. Approaching, as nearly as we can, the beginning of the Western construct, we come to those men who contributed one or two main insights, one or two elements in the system; with Plato,

---

8. To mention the most stimulating critics who have pointed out Platonic elements in Yeats: Kathleen Raine, very much a Platonist herself, has produced a pair of monographs (*Yeats, the Tarot, and the Golden Dawn* and *Death-in-Life and Life-in-Death: "Cuchulain Comforted" and "News for the Delphic Oracle"*) and several articles ("Yeats and Platonism," "A Traditional Language of Symbols," and "Yeats's Debt to William Blake"); Virginia Moore's *The Unicorn* touches on the Platonic influence, as does T. R. Henn's *The Lonely Tower*; Morton Irving Seiden's *The Poet as Mythmaker* attempts to come to terms with Yeats's system, especially as that system was drawn out of occult traditions bearing close ties to the Platonic tradition; and F. A. C. Wilson's two books (*W. B. Yeats and Tradition* and *Yeats's Iconography*) are the standards by which Yeats's debt to Neoplatonism must be measured. Wilson, like Seiden, is stronger on the successors to Plato than on his predecessors or on Plato himself, and it is this latter ground that the present volume intends to explore.

however—myriad-minded Plato—and much more with Plotinus or St. Augustine, we have to do not with a man of a single truth or two but with a full-blown synthesizer and systematizer. Heraclitus, for example, is subtle enough, but primarily he stands for only one or two great truths, and he has not anything like the knotted complexity of Plato. Pushing further back in time has much the same strategy about it and the same effect as descending deeper into the human mind: in either case we find bolder outlines, a scheme that is simpler in its nature, more basic and primitive in its appeal.

In "Leda and the Swan"—which began as a political poem, "but as I wrote, bird and lady took such possession of the scene that all politics went out of it"—Yeats tells us that he imagined "the annunciation that founded Greece as made to Leda. . . . But all things are from antithesis," he continues, "and when in my ignorance I try to imagine what older civilisation that annunciation rejected I can but see bird and woman blotting out some corner of the Babylonian mathematical starlight" (*Vision*, p. 268). Much the same thing happens to the explorer who goes far back in Western thought and deep down in the human psyche toward beginnings. Like Yeats, he discovers the same basic configurations realized again and again until finally the contours of specific civilizations, like politics, disappear, as do also the distinguishing features of individualized men, leaving those primordial images (bird and woman) and those generalized patterns (mathematical starlight) according to which human behavior shapes itself and has always shaped itself. There, approaching as near to the ground and beginning as he can, the investigator finds images with a high degree of internal organization but with, as yet, little or no realized, individualized content: beyond Zeus and Leda there is bird and woman; beyond bird and woman there is masculine and feminine, divine and human; beyond these, once more, there are, in Yeats's terms, images of sphere (divine) and gyre (human), and there are, in Jung's terms, the numbers three and four—the ultimate abstractions from the concrete realities of history. For four, according to the discoveries of Jung's science, is not only the number of wholeness but also the feminine number, and three is not only an incomplete quaternity but also the masculine number.

We can, if we like, call this ultimate abstraction of the image and the numerical pattern from the confusion of experience "number mysticism" and thus go a certain distance toward dismissing it; but it would be as well to observe at the same time that men, apparently everywhere and at all times, have felt numbers to possess arcane properties prior to and quite outside human imaginings. Numbers, that is, or so men have always believed, were there in the structure of reality before the human mind existed to observe the fact; indeed, the human mind, according to such a belief, is itself a part of that structure of reality that is determined by number and number relations, and numbers therefore have not been shaped or invented by the human mind but, on the contrary, have shaped and invented it. To Philip Wylie, who had offered an objection to something in Jung's numerology, Jung wrote (in 1957), "Don't worry about my mathematics. I never dreamt of adding anything to mathematics, being myself utterly 'amathematikós.' My affiliation to it consists only in the equation $3 + 1 = 4$, which is a psychological fact indicating the fundamental relation between psychology and mathematics" (*Letters*, II, 404). This, which is Jung's equation for wholeness, is simple enough in mathematical terms; simple though it be, however, in Jung's view it also represents the most profound mystery— it is, he says, "the mystery of the psychologist" (ibid.)—for just such a simple equation as this is the bond that joins mind and nature, *psychē* and *physis*, and makes them a single, indissoluble unity beyond our capacity to see or to conceptualize. It was on this ground that Jung could say (quoting the mathematician Leopold Kronecker), "Man created mathematics, but God created whole numbers: ὁ θεὸς ἀριθμητίζει ['God arithmetizes']" (*Letters*, II, 23). This god that arithmetizes, as Plato argued in the *Timaeus*, to the entire satisfaction and agreement of Yeats and Jung, does so throughout his creation both physical and psychic. How exquisitely the mind is fitted to nature, with number as the pre-existent, analogical, and informing bond, was Platonic doctrine (and before Plato it was Pythagorean) that Wordsworth turned into Romantic psychology and poetry and that Yeats and Jung embraced heart and soul; nor could they do otherwise, since heart and soul are themselves numerically, rhythmically organized.[9]

9. That psyche (like the cosmos) is numerically and rhythmically organized is one of the principal tenets of the *Timaeus*; that the heart too is so organized we learn from ancient medical writers—cf. W. B. Stanford, *The Sound of Greek* (Berkeley: University of California Press, 1967), pp. 36–37: "Galen, quoting an earlier medical writer,

Pythagoreans (and neo-Pythagoreans of all times and places) consider numbers to be archaic in the most literal sense: for such *mathematici*, numbers are the *archai*, the primordial principles, the generative source of all created beings, and as such they provide a formal replacement for the physical *archai* of the Ionian philosophers. That is to say, according to Pythagoreans, the cosmos had its beginning in numbers and in the formal relations of numbers rather than in some such substance as water, air, etc. Given the fact that he wanted to be taken for an empirical scientist, it was rather daring of Jung—but as Pythagorean as daring—to write that "Whole numbers may well be the discovery of God's 'primal thoughts' " (*Letters*, II, 302). It is not the higher mathematics, as Jung saw it—and so also the ancients—but simple number that rules throughout the cosmos, both micro- and macro-. "Thus Number," the Pythagorizing Plotinus tells us, "the primal and true, is Principle and source of actuality to the Beings." In Jung's terminology, numbers would be said to be archetypal, and it is certainly true that schematic representations of Jungian archetypal figures (e.g., mandalas) display a very great instress of numerical organization. Bringing the question back to a psychological focus, one might take numbers to be the structural dominants of the psyche and, going a step further, take the procession and recession of numbers (that is, the multiplying of numbers out of oneness and the return of multiplicity to original unity) to be the twofold analogue to the intricate, double movement of the mind in its typical mode of operation: analyzing and synthesizing, dividing and unifying. This would be to suggest the possibility that there is a configurational correlation between typical thought patterns and basic mental structure determined on a simple mathematical ground.

While other numbers may have equal potency in certain regards, the human mind has repeatedly viewed reality, in the schematizing light of the first four integers, as being monadic, dyadic, triadic, or quaternal—or sometimes, and this is perhaps more interesting as well as more complex, as alternating between the monadic and one or more of the other three. Greek philosophic history, conveniently enough, provides the prototypes for each of these readings of the

---

says that there is a similarity between the systolic and diastolic beats of the pulse and the arsis and thesis of a metrical foot. . . .[W]hatever Galen's exact meaning may be, his statement emphasizes the fact that even in our blood stream there is both stress and time. Our pulse beat is a built-in measure of rhythm."

way things really are. Parmenides' poem stands as the great statement in antiquity of an uncompromising philosophical monism; Heraclitus is the primal antinomist; Pythagoras apparently reverenced various numbers (one, four, and ten, for example), but it could well be argued that three had a special force for him (Aristotle: "As the Pythagoreans say, the whole world and all things in it are summed up in the number three; for end, middle and beginning give the number of the whole, and their number is the triad. Hence we have taken this number from nature, as it were one of her laws, and make use of it even for the worship of the gods" [*De Caelo*, 268a10]); and Empedocles was the stoutest exponent of quaternal arrangements (albeit with occasional glances toward monism and dualism) until Jung came along twenty-three or twenty-four centuries later as champion of the number four. So these four Pre-Socratics, individually and in sum, offer us a story occurring in time that is nicely parallel in its character, its plot, and its structure—and ultimately parallel also in its significance—to the nontemporal story of the human psyche in its efforts, conscious and unconscious, to analyze and synthesize all the experience that it encounters.

Late in his life, Jung was moved to an unusual excitement by the report that (as Jung phrases it in a paragraph in the *Collected Works* that he revised so as to reveal some of his intense interest in the discovery) "two American investigators [have] succeeded in evoking an hallucinatory vision of coloured squares and circles by stimulating the occipital cortex" (*CW*, III, par. 582). At first this may not seem such a very thrilling discovery, but on second thought one would have to agree that Jung had good reason for his excitement, for "coloured squares and circles" is another way of saying "mandalas," which is another way of saying "archetypes," and what had been reported thus seemed to Jung to provide a localization and a physiology for the phenomenon of archetypes. "I have long thought," Jung says, "that, if there is any analogy between psychic and physiological processes, the organizing system of the brain must lie subcortically in the brain-stem."[10] In a later publication

10. Ibid. Cf. Jung's letter to the man who sent him news of the investigators' findings: "Thank you very much for your really interesting letter! The physiological approach to the most frequent and the most important archetype is indeed a major discovery, confirming in a way my suspicion that its localization could have to do with the brain-stem. But since my work is all on the biological and psychological side, I did not dare to speculate, having already the greatest trouble in convincing my contemporaries of the existence of original and basic patterns of behaviour, i.e., of archetypes" (*Letters*, II, 256).

(*The Mystery of the Mind*), one of the "two American investigators," the neurosurgeon Wilder Penfield, came to very much the same conclusion as Jung: that the phenomenon that Jung calls "psyche" and that Penfield calls "mind" is not, as Jung says elsewhere, an "epiphenomenon" of the brain (though it operates in tandem with the brain—the latter being, as it were, the mechanism of mind); and that for the creation of such archaic, primal forms as archetypes we must look not to the cortex (here Penfield agrees precisely with Jung) but "subcortically in the brain-stem"—i.e., to the most archaic, the most ancient part of the brain ("the old brain"). When positive responses were elicited (and Jung would think the formation of an archetypal figure very positive indeed) by stimulating the cortex, the response came, according to Penfield's later book, not from the cortex but from activation set off in the distant subcortex: "If there is . . . a positive response, it is due to functional activation of distant gray matter. Consequently, when the electrode is applied to the hand area of the motor cortex, the delicate movements of the hand, which the cortex makes possible, are paralyzed, but the secondary station of gray matter in the spinal cord is activated, and crude movements, such as clutching, movements of which an infant is capable, are carried out."[11] At this deep level of the brain and the mind, where we are returned to the infancy of the individual and the race, physiology and psychology appear to merge —*physis* and *psychē* become indistinguishably united—and archetypes, with their potent numerical organization, rule over all. "I would conjecture that such a subcortical system might somehow reflect characteristics of the archetypal forms in the unconscious," Jung writes in the revised essay on "Schizophrenia" cited earlier. "Mandala symbols appear very frequently in moments of psychic disorientation as compensatory ordering factors. This aspect is expressed above all in their mathematical structure. . . . " I have no more intention of dissecting a brain[12] than I would have competence

11. Wilder Penfield, *The Mystery of the Mind* (Princeton: Princeton University Press, 1975), p. 29.
12. Were one a competent neurophysiologist and capable of metaphysical brain surgery as well, one might find something interesting at the base of that organ—at least according to Voltaire: "Ce monde, suivant Platon, était composé d'idées archétypes qui demeuraient toujours au fond du cerveau" ["This world, according to Plato, was composed of archetypal ideas which still dwell at the bottom of the brain"]. This quotation (for which I am indebted to my brother Richard) came to hand synchronistically at the moment that I was writing the above. I am not sure

to do it, but the distinction and marriage that Penfield (like Jung) sets forth between mind (or psyche) and brain offers a very convenient analogy and metaphor in working out our duplex *tertium quid*, since, as Penfield demonstrates, all the higher, more developed, refined, and elaborate mental functions are rooted in a much more ancient, undifferentiated, archaic, and primitive organizing system, a sort of rhizome far down in the "fibrous darkness"—that "matrix out of which everything has come"—just as Jung's elaborate psychology and Yeats's elaborate poetics are rooted far back in the first, archetypal thinkers of the Western world who sometimes hesitantly, sometimes boldly (as the infant will do) put forth their simple, grand, primitive, and always number-organized truths. In them, as in whole numbers, and as in the creations of the unconscious, we discover what we might call (in Jung's words) "God's 'primal thoughts' "—also the primal thoughts of Yeats and the primal thoughts of Jung.

To describe the way in which the mind has countless times over set about dividing and unifying experience—for the division and unification of experience is what the thought of mankind has always been about: the systole and diastole of human creativity—is in effect to perform that division and unification once again. The most compelling description of human performance will always be found in reperformance, and this is one way of stating what the present book proposes: a creative reenactment that would hope to be more meaningful and persuasive than any mere stitching or pasting can ever be. What I intend, after the manner of the Aristotelian imitation of an action, is an imitation of the subject—which is the action of the mind in ancient Greece and the action of the mind in the contemporary West. Not that the great predecessors, Yeats and Jung, Heraclitus and Empedocles, have failed, leaving their job yet to be done. On the contrary, precisely because they have done their job, we are obliged to do ours. What Yeats does in *A Vision* and Jung in *Psychological Types* is different of course from what Empedocles does in his two poems or Heraclitus in his dark and riddling aphorisms; but it is different only as to the superficial content on which their minds operated, not as to the way the mind operates and the patterns it seems to discover simultaneously within itself and in the

---

where Voltaire finds this in Plato, but I could give a string of references where it could be found in Jung.

universe without. This is the same difference and the same similarity that Yeats discovered existing between Greek and Christian annunciations: on the one hand, Leda and Swan are unquestionably different from Mary and the Holy Ghost, just as the two civilizations they heralded were opposites; on the other hand, however, in both cases, and at deeper levels of image, pattern, and meaning, we have woman and bird, human and divine, sphere and gyre, female and male, four and three. And just so too with Yeats and Jung, Heraclitus and Empedocles, who differ one from another on the surface but not at all on deeper levels of the psyche where archaic ideas, primal patterns, and the passion to divide and unify experience have their origins. At that deep level, we discover archetypal "images that yet/Fresh images beget," and as they are archetypal they can scarce be distinguished and differentiated individually. One might well suppose, as I have implied, that this virtually instinctive urge to division and unification—a double movement compounded of halves opposed and complementary—is somehow a reflection, an analogy, and a consequence of a deep, inner life-rhythm: something in the structure of the brain and the central nervous system, something also in unconscious imitation of the flow out and back of blood from the heart, or of breath, *pneuma*, taken in and out of the lungs, and in imitation of a cosmic system as well, for *pneuma* is not only breath but also the wind that "bloweth where it listeth" and that moves all things in rhythm and pattern throughout the cosmos.

This, however, carries us all the way forward to the end of the book, and perhaps it would be as well to leave conclusions such as these until premises have been stated and demonstrations offered. The plan of the book, which would deliver us to these conclusions, is like this: Chapter 1 tells the Pre-Socratic and Platonic story as a narrative both of history and of the human psyche—the making of the Platonic system and the making of the mind of the West. Chapters 2 through 5 are given over to (in order) Pythagoras, Heraclitus, Parmenides, and Empedocles—their individual roles in the Pre-Socratic drama, their place in the development of Western thought and the Western psyche, and their pervasive, primal presence in Yeatsian poetics and Jungian psychology; and these chapters also develop, respectively, a theory of aesthetics (Chapter 2), an account of process philosophy (Chapter 3), a theory of the symbolic mode (Chapter 4), and a thesis on time and history in Western thought

(Chapter 5). Chapter 6 treats Plato, the culmination, the synthesizer and systematizer of what went before him, as the preceding four chapters treated his predecessors, and it also takes up the question of myth and the whole man (Yeats's Unity of Being, Jung's individuation) in terms of poetry, psychology, philosophy, and biography/autobiography. Chapter 7 reads Yeats's poetry as an expression of ancient truths revealed to him by spirits of the past and spirits of the unconscious, and it argues that his poetics are determined by concepts that are Pythagorean, Heraclitean, Parmenidean, Empedoclean, and Platonic. Chapter 8 maintains the same basic components for Jung's psychology and demonstrates that psyche is for Jung a natural system and his psychology, therefore, a natural science. Chapter 9[13] concerns itself with systems—poetic system, psychic system, philosophic system, cosmic system—how they determine and reflect one another and what they have to do with what Socrates calls "no light matter: it is the question, what is the right way to live?" Arriving at "System," we arrive at the end of our quest—which is also its beginning.

13. Here mention should be made of two chapters—the first planned but never executed, the second executed but now omitted—the absence of which might seem to leave gaps in the treatment as a whole. A chapter to have been called "The Rhizome" was originally to have come between "*Mythos, Eidos,* and the *Daimon*" and "The Poetics of Mummy Wheat"; this chapter would have traced the long tradition of Platonism from the fourth century B.C. down to Yeats and Jung. Merely to mention the plan will give some idea of why there is no such chapter in the book: it would require another five hundred pages to deal with the historical rhizome (and then quite inadequately). Moreover, to treat of such figures in the tradition as Hermes Trismegistus, Philo Judaeus, the Gnostics, the various Neoplatonists, St. Augustine, Pseudo-Dionysius, Paracelsus, Boehme, Swedenborg, the Cambridge Platonists, and Blake would merely obscure the clarity of the lines so painstakingly sought out by a return to antiquity. The second chapter, originally coming between "The Psychology of the Pleroma" and "System" and titled "The Esoteric Flower," intended to demonstrate that there is an esoteric or occult component in the Platonic tradition—a dark twin, as it were—that has grown alongside the exoteric philosophic tradition. This chapter has been excluded, partly because I have published some of the same material elsewhere (*Yeats and the Occult*), and partly because that material is touched on in other chapters of this book.

CHAPTER I

The *Rhizōmata,* Plato, and Platonism

τέσσαρα γὰρ πάντων ῥιζώματα πρῶτον ἄκουε
Then hear first the four roots of all things

Empedocles

Pythagoras, Heraclitus, Parmenides, and Empedocles, these four: not that Plato had no other debts and Platonism no other roots; but everything that we call "Platonic" can be deduced, and was by Plato deduced, from the archetypal doctrines associated with these four semilegendary figures. Once their work was accomplished, Plato himself became virtually inevitable—the necessary conclusion to a series of premises: Pythagoras, Heraclitus, Parmenides, and Empedocles, *therefore* Plato. If St. Augustine could write as if Plato had been a Christian unawares, then Pythagoras, Heraclitus, Parmenides, and Empedocles, seen as a contentiously cooperative quaternity (producing out of themselves the *quinta essentia* that was Plato's doctrine),[1] might equally well be called pre-Platonic, unconscious Platonists. These four Pre-Socratics are the elements, the roots, the

1. Jung's phrasing in the *Mysterium Coniunctionis*, though intended to describe the four elements and the goal of alchemy rather than the four elements and the history of philosophy, is too felicitous to forego: "As the square represents the quaternio of mutually hostile elements, the circle indicates their reduction to unity. The One born of the Four is the Quinta Essentia" (*CW*, XIV, par. 439).

rhizōmata of the *Philosophia Perennis*, that organic body of thought which never really had any beginning but to which, in the Western world, Plato was the first to give a full and distinctive articulation. Viewing the four Pre-Socratics through the spectacles of Platonism and describing ancient Greek philosophy as if it were more a story than history (a procedure which textual and critical scholarship would no doubt regard with a good deal of suspicion) offers some very distinct advantages. A story, unlike history, is committed more to meaning than to time. Any story that would be a coherent tale, even though it be composed of several parts, must nevertheless be the imitation of a single action with (to continue Aristotle's terminology) a beginning, a middle, and an end; indeed, it is the pattern of beginning, middle, and end that creates what we feel to be meaning. The course of Pre-Socratic thought, when viewed in a post-Platonic retrospect, assumes a definite shape, which is something it could not possess otherwise, and it appears as just such a story—a Platonic μῦθος, a teleological tale—fitted out with characters and themes, with a prevailing pattern, and with a consequent meaning. Wherever we set its beginning, that tale, because it is seen through the focus of Plato's achievement, becomes possessed of a logical, inherent, inevitable end—Socrates and Plato—the climax and culmination of those philosophers called "Pre-Socratics." Approached in this way, the philosophic activity of the (approximately) two hundred years between Pythagoras' *floruit* and Plato's death displays very clearly what might be called its *logos* (in a Heraclitean sense): an internal balance or proportion, composed of conflicting opposites, that functions as the principle of its being and the law of its becoming.

Ever since Aristotle showed himself so reluctant to have to do with any man named "Pythagoras" (he much preferred to describe the beliefs of "those who are called Pythagoreans" and to leave Pythagoras the man to fend for his own historicity), scholars have been plagued by doubt about that unquestionably powerful but frustratingly insubstantial figure. Was he, like Plato, a real, historic man; or was he, like Orpheus, more legend than man, more myth than legend? History, like Aristotle—who in these matters is usually our first, best historian—presents us with almost no Pythagoras at all. Tradition, on the other hand, generously compensating for the paucity of historic fact, supplies a very rich and grand figure indeed under that name. For Pythagoras was, as Yeats says, "world-famous" and at the same time—which is another order of fact altogether—"golden-thighed." And the case is very similar with Heraclitus and with Empedocles, if not with Parmenides, a strict logician about whom there are few biographical details at all. Even Parmenides, however, though not by an inflation of biographical anecdote, assumes a certain mythic quality and a more than individual significance in the evolution of Greek philosophy.

Anticipating the rationalistic and dismissive answer of the historically minded, we should be clear that it is not because Pythagoras and his three antagonistic confrères lived in prehistory that they have become mythic, legendary figures. Chronological distance may *allow* myth and legend to accumulate about a name, a life, and a doctrine, but it does not *cause* that accumulation. The cause lies not in history but in the human psyche. Human psychology, human thought, human self-awareness has required such figures to express itself, understand itself, and become conscious of itself. They are archetypal figures in the realm of thought as Oedipus, for example, is a mythic and archetypal figure in the realm of emotion and in the complex relationship of the family constellation. And like Oedipus, their lives are not less but more real to us for being mythic. Few people since Freud would care to say that Oedipus was not real; or, more accurately, few would say that he *is* not real, since he lives among us now. So also Heraclitus, who has the power to change our lives because he dwells among us and within us. Like Oedipus at the end of *Oedipus at Colonus*, Heraclitus and Pythagoras are become mighty *daimones*—spirits of the ancestors, tutelary beings, great indwelling powers of psyche.

"Pythagoras," according to Diogenes Laertius, "was the first person who invented the term Philosophy, and who called himself a philosopher" (*Lives of Famous Philosophers*, I, 12). There is little reason to trouble history to discover if this is so or not, just as there is no point in asking about Pythagoras' golden thigh: history, on such matters, remains silent. Tradition, however, affirms the truth not only of these things but of many other useful things about Pythagoras as well. He was a divine god-man, for Pythagoreans a true *daimon*, who was capable of hearing that marvellous harmony of the spheres inaudible to ordinary men; he was able in memory to leap barriers of birth and death and could recall having been incarnated as Æthalides, Euphorbus, Hermotimus, and Pyrrhus, and now, in the body of Pythagoras, "he still recollected everything, how he had been formerly Æthalides, then Euphorbus, then Hermotimus, and then Pyrrhus" (DK 14, 8). Pythagoras' traditional character (perhaps the name should be written PYTHAGORAS to indicate that he was more archetype than man), like the philosophy ascribed to him, was one of great mystery, with both the character and the philosophy testifying to the considerable power of the mysterious and the arcane in compelling belief. Thus one of the roots of the Platonic system, by way of the god-man Pythagoras, reached deep down into the chthonic mysteries and thence derived vital nourishment for the flower that blossomed two centuries later.

If tradition has gathered together under the name of Pythagoras a character that is worthy of reverence, it has treated Heraclitus rather differently. Heraclitus was imperious and haughty, tradition tells us, and so say the extant fragments also; he was proud and disdainful, contentious and quarrelsome, a scornful elitist and the bitter antagonist of οἱ πολλοί, "the many," who are despised for nothing more than being the many, and who in English are burdened with the derisory appellation (*hoi polloi*) borrowed from the term which in Greek is neutral except in the mouth of someone as proudly isolated and scornful as Heraclitus himself. Yet, so far at least as Plato was concerned, Heraclitus was par excellence the philosopher not of some transcendent realm to which so proud a spirit might be supposed to aspire, but the philosopher precisely of this world all about us of process and change and perpetual instability.

"My mind," Yeats wrote on the endleaf of Bertrand Russell's *Outline of Philosophy*, "follows abstraction with difficulty," and that is no doubt one reason why Yeats made so little use of Parmenides in his systematic construction. While Yeats seized eagerly on the chthonic mysteries of Pythagoras and quoted delightedly and often the antinomic aphorisms of Heraclitus, he could find nothing more in Parmenides than the image of the sphere that is so perfect and so divine that it can never enter into human experience. Though his philosophy is cast as a verse and though Plato could never have done without him, Parmenides is the John Stuart Mill of the Pre-Socratic brotherhood: the complete type, or the Idea, of the abstract logician. Fittingly, tradition has not a single tale to tell us about Parmenides, nor is Parmenides himself more forthcoming than tradition. The frame "story" of his poem (the steeds, the goddess, the gates of Night and Day, etc.) is all plainly an allegory—which is not, however, to say that the meaning of the allegory is plain. What must be said of Parmenides is said as if of a mind rather than of a man: the mind of Parmenides is stubborn, intransigent, uncompromising, determined, logical, intellectual; it is also not quite human. Yet, in the history of developing thought, Parmenides is no less an archetypal figure than Pythagoras or Heraclitus, his philosophic opponents, or than Empedocles, his philosophic heir apparent. The cloudless, pure logic of Parmenides, training itself on a perfect, changeless state not of this world, was as indispensable to the Platonic system as the divine mathematics of Pythagoras or the ceaseless flow of Heraclitus.

For the anecdotal reticence surrounding Parmenides there is more than sufficient compensation in the excited, tale-telling impetuosity of Empedocles. Parmenides may talk of his goddess and may claim inspiration from her, but it sounds like nothing more than literary convention. Empedocles, on the other hand, strikes one as a true and literal enthusiast: it is the god inside him that impels Empedocles to his excited, breathless, visionary utterance. There is something of the Ancient Mariner about Empedocles, something of the sense of a possessed man who must tell his story again and again; and the reader, though he may have a wedding to go to, when fixed by that glittering eye has little choice but to listen. It requires a considerable oracular assurance (which Yeats also affected: "I the poet William Yeats") to seize the reader by his lapel and demand that he "hear first the four roots of all things." The account of creation and of the nature of reality in the *Timaeus* is presented as "a likely story"; yet apart from that preliminary qualification, the myth that Timaeus narrates, like myths elsewhere in Plato, is notably Empedoclean—as marvellously assured in the completeness of its vision as in the firmness of its details—and so the rhapsodic utterance of divine myth specific to Empedocles assumes its needful place as one *rhizōma* nourishing the total Platonic organism.

But what of the systematizer himself? What of Plato's personality and his psychology? From documentary history (The Platonic epistles, for example) we know more about Plato than about the other four put together; yet, paradoxically, Plato's personality remains dimmer than any of the others. A reasonable explanation for this dimness would be that Plato's personality recedes from the foreground of philosophic statement and doctrine into the hazy background of tone and implied attitude because he chose to write for the most part in the dramatic form of dialogue. Thus Socrates' personality is sharper and clearer than Plato's. There is more to it than this, however. Plato was not only describing other men's conversation, he was receiving and molding other men's insights and ideas. These other men were the great Originals; they were the archetypal giants. Plato stood on the shoulders of his predecessors, he extended and qualified their primal perceptions, but those figures of towering originality, who correspond individually to various components of our own psychic makeup, are naturally clearer to our sight and imagination, as they are closer to basic constituents of our minds, than the figure on their shoulders.

Commentators have remarked that the Eleatic Stranger in the *Sophist* is, on the one hand, a representative of the best in Parmenides' philosophy and, on the other hand, a spokesman for Plato himself, a sort of alter ego of the author, who thus recreates his predecessor for his own artistic and philosophic purposes. This has led to the conclusion that (as F. M. Cornford put it) "Plato claimed to be the true heir of Parmenides."[2] Nor is this a unique instance in Plato, for elsewhere, by his performance, he is to be found implicitly claiming to be the true heir of Pythagoras, of Heraclitus, and of Empedocles. Or perhaps it would be more accurate to say that in various places he presents himself as the perfector of the best elements in the doctrines of each of the four men. A large part of the intention of the *Phaedo*, according to another commentator, is to criticize early Pythagoreanism and "to show how Plato's own εἴδη is the right conclusion to Pythagorean premises."[3] This is the line Plato takes with all his predecessors: a criticism of their doctrines and a demonstration that his own theory of Forms is the proper conclusion to their thoughts and their discoveries, to their insights and their *logoi*. This is how he treats Pythagoras not only in the *Phaedo* but in the *Republic*, the *Laws*, and the *Epinomis*; this is the use he

---

2. *Plato's Theory of Knowledge* (London: Routledge & Kegan Paul, 1960), p. 170. Cf. Burnet to the same effect in *Greek Philosophy: Thales to Plato*, 2d ed. (London: Macmillan, 1914), pp. 236-37 and 274, and W. D. Ross, *Plato's Theory of Ideas* (Oxford: Oxford Univeristy Press, 1951), p. 105: in the *Sophist*, Ross says, Plato "hints that he is himself in some sense an heir to the philosophy of Parmenides."
3. Alister Cameron, *The Pythagorean Background of the Theory of Recollection* (Menasha, Wisconsin: George Banta, 1938), p. 46, n. 29.

makes of Parmenides not only in the *Sophist* and the *Statesman* but in the *Parmenides* and the *Theaetetus*; this is what he makes of Heraclitus in the *Cratylus*, the *Theaetetus*, and the *Sophist*; this is the treatment he gives to Empedocles in the *Phaedrus*, in the Myth of Er in the *Republic*, and in the *Statesman*; this, finally, is the attitude he adopts toward all of them in the *Timaeus*, that central document in the Platonic corpus in which nearly everything from the four Pre-Socratics is drawn together, purged of its one-sidedness, and transformed into the "likely story" that Timaeus tells about cosmogony and cosmology and that was to have such endless echoings and reechoings in the epistemology, the metaphysics, and the ethics of the Platonic-Neoplatonic tradition.

The central and most characteristic doctrine of Platonism, which Plato's predecessors approached, hinted at, and half stated but which he was the first to articulate fully, I take to be this: that there are two realms or modes of existence—one of being, the other of becoming, one of Forms, the other of sensibles—that are distinct from one another and even, at times, in opposition but that are not absolutely and irrevocably sundered or unrelated. From this, everything else in Platonism proceeded, and by this, everything else in Platonism was philosophically justified. "Everything else" means such typical, essential beliefs of Platonism (and of Plato's predecessors) as these: that the human soul is immortal and, by nature, divine and is reincarnated in a series of bodies; that as soul is prior, in origin and in kind, to body, so is spirit prior to matter in general and understanding of the mind superior to evidence of the senses, which are in any case highly fallible witnesses; that cognition is really recognition of what we have always known or what we learned between incarnations; that the vital and ordering principle in human beings is identical with the vital and ordering principle in the universe; that the cosmos is based on formal rather than physical or material principles; that the most perfect of solid bodies is the sphere and of plane figures the circle, and from that one perfect sphere (i.e., the transcendent Form of circularity) all things derive their order and to it they all continually aspire; and that philosophy is a divine activity, it is its own end and justification, and it performs a cathartic service for the philosopher, enabling him to reattain the status of a god. None of the Pre-Socratics held all of these complexly interrelated ideas (nor did Yeats or Jung unfailingly and invariably subscribe to them all); nevertheless, every one of the four pointed the way to the central doctrine and each contributed in some unique and characteristic manner to Plato's eventual formulation of the whole lot (as, also, more than twenty centuries later, Yeats renewed their vitality in his poetry and Jung in his psychology). Indeed, we can see from after the fact that it was only as a result of the intellectual and linguistic efforts of Pythagoras, Heraclitus, Parmenides, and Empedocles that Plato was himself finally able to draw and to state the conclusions to which their thoughts had all along been tending, guided—or so it seems after more than two thousand years—by a will or an intention beyond the consciousness of any one of them alone, including Plato. Such is the teleology of Platonism.

None of the Pre-Socratics taught everything that is to be found in Platonism, but Pythagoras came close, in some ways very close. What exactly "the master himself said" is not certain, primarily because the Pythagoreans had the reverential but troublesome habit of buttressing all their discoveries and beliefs with αὐτὸς ἔφα, "himself said," thus delighting the mythographer but confounding the historian. "None the less," according to Porphyry in his *Vita Pythagorae*, "the following became universally known: first, that he maintains that the soul is immortal; next, that it changes into other kinds of living things; also that events recur in certain cycles, and that nothing is ever absolutely new; and finally, that all living things should be regarded as akin. Pythagoras seems to have been the first to bring these beliefs into Greece."[4] These beliefs are all compatible with Platonism, or can easily enough be made so, but Porphyry is notably silent both on Pythagoras' hint at the central doctrine of Platonism (i.e., the two separable but related modes of being) and on the teaching for which Pythagoras is best known by tradition. With his attention fixed on the "religious" aspects of Pythagoras' teaching, Porphyry says little of Pythagorean "science," but in Pythagoras, more than in any other philosopher, the two are of major and equal importance and cannot be separated one from the other nor either of them from the close-knit, unified, and organic system which represents the single whole that is Pythagoras' vision.

4. DK 14, 8a; trans. by J. E. Raven, from Kirk and Raven, *The Presocratic Philosophers* (Cambridge: Cambridge University Press, 1957), p. 223.

The fact that Pythagoras "Fingered upon a fiddle-stick or strings/ What a star sang and careless Muses heard," is not mentioned in the Porphyrian passage, yet Pythagoras is no doubt best known to tradition (as to Yeats) for his discovery, by sounds from a fiddlestick and tightened strings, that simple numerical ratios determine the harmony of human music and the corresponding order of the cosmos: the Music of the Spheres. After this awesome discovery, Pythagoras justifiably went on to conclude that number is the organizing principle of all reality; and then, taking an incautious leap into a dark both physical and metaphysical, he declared (or his followers declared in his name) that physical things *are* numbers, as are all qualities both physical and moral, indeed that everything is number and number is everything. One has only to glance at Aristotle on the Pythagoreans or at Parmenides on "The Way of Truth" to see what that bit of Pythagorean mysticism could do to a rationalistic mind. "What do they *mean*?" Aristotle angrily demands time and again, as if this were a personal affront as well as a logical one. "How can a number be a thing?" How can the One—which is, according to the logic of Parmenides' vision, so perfect that nothing can be said of it except that nothing can be said of it—how can that One become all the fish in the seas, all the hyenas and the Yahoos (not to mention the lower orders) of this hopelessly pluralistic world? For himself, turning away from his former teacher, Parmenides found it more logical and more satisfying to deny reality to the hyenas and the Yahoos (and in effect to himself) than to agree that the One could have any connection at all with such impure things. Whether Parmenides' solution commends itself to us or not, the question he put was a necessary one: How does a single form become a myriad substances if form and substances are of the same order of being?

While he was never solely committed to rationalistic logic, Plato nevertheless saw the Parmenidean-Aristotelian objection to Pythagorean cosmogony, he concurred in it, and therefore—because he was unwilling to surrender the emotional satisfaction of Pythagorean mysticism—he sought a way out of the dilemma that would maintain the reality, if not glorify the existence, of the Yahoos while ascribing a superior reality to the numbers that somehow lay behind the Yahoos. The error of the Pythagoreans was to say that things are numbers and thereby to suggest that numbers, pure, perfect, and formal, can have physical existence in this world which is so plainly not pure, not perfect, and, at best, only partly formal. If they have physical existence, then numbers are not purely formal, they are not perfect, they are, simply, not numbers. One is equal to one—perfectly, unchangingly, and forever—but one apple is not equal to another apple, much less to a pear. Just as the ideal Triangle, as soon as it is committed to paper and extended in space becomes impure and ceases to be ideal or to be a Form, so the number one becomes imperfect and ceases to be itself by its attachment to apple or pear. Numbers were for Pythagoras divine, with all the glorious mystery and perfection of the divine about them, but they were also, he said—and here he brought Parmenides and Aristotle down on his head—the essence of the physical world. If Plato saw the logical error in Pythagoreanism, however, he also saw how to set it right without losing any of the beauty of that music that "a star sang and careless Muses heard."

Plato's prevenient response, disarming the criticism in advance, to Aristotle's complaint that the Pythagoreans "thought things must be numbers—not separately existing numbers, but numbers of which things are made,"[5] was precisely to separate the two, numbers in an eternal world of transcendent Forms on the one hand, things in a temporal world of physical matter on the other hand. Plato was the first to disentangle the confusion of the two realms, the first to push those realms apart, and the first to state clearly the conditions dividing them, but he would never have done so, or been able to do so, without his Pythagorean heritage. There were some, indeed, who felt that the Pythagoreans had implied, or perhaps even accomplished, what Plato was later given credit for—i.e., the conceptual separation (*chōrismos*) of Forms, particularly mathematical Forms, from the physical universe. Thus Syrianus, commenting in the fifth century A.D. on Aristotle's version of the Pythagoreans in his *Metaphysics*, asks: "But how is it possible they [the Pythagoreans] could have spoken thus sublimely of number, unless they had considered it as possessing an essence separate from sensibles, and a transcendency fabricative, and at the same time paradigmatic?"[6] Syrianus' language had no doubt been influenced by the whole tradition of

---

5. *Metaphysics*, N3 1090a20; trans. John Warrington (London: Everyman, 1961), p. 287.
6. Quoted by Thomas Taylor in his translation of Iamblichus' *Life of Pythagoras* (London: John M. Watkins, 1965), p. 78 n. The fine but obscurantist phrasing is probably as much owing to Thomas Taylor as to Syrianus.

Platonism intervening between the fifth century B.C. and the fifth century A.D.; yet, if one considers what the Pythagoreans said about numbers and mathematical porportion and, even more, how they said it, one can see that Syrianus' hesitant claim for the Pythagoreans is not without foundation and that Plato's theory of Forms is there—perhaps only implicitly or embryonically there, but there all the same—in Pythagorean number doctrine.

In the last dialogues especially (the *Laws*, the *Epinomis*, and the *Timaeus*), Plato happily adopted Pythagoras' divine numbers and projected them into a conceptual perfection beyond the mortal realm; but then, with a characteristic turn of the wrist, after separating and distinguishing the two realms, he introduced, midway between sensibles and Forms, a third mode of being which serves to unify them even while separating them. Mathematical objects, insofar as they are "mathematical" are formal, insofar as they are "objects" are sensible, and being somewhat of each, they mediate between the two realms, dividing Forms and sensibles by drawing them together. Thus there are in the end three kinds of beings: the mortal, the immortal, and that intermediate one of mathematical objects, of *daimones*, of spirits, of symbolic/archetypal images which have something of substance but more of spirit and so are able to exercise powerful spiritual effects in a physical realm.

The account of the creation in the *Timaeus* is not only mature Platonic doctrine but is Pythagorean through and through, but Pythagoras' influence is by no means confined to the mystical numerology in that dialogue or in the *Laws* and the *Epinomis*. The theory of anamnesis and metempsychosis worked out in the *Meno* (especially 81b-d) is notably Pythagorean both in content and in expression, and as early as the *Gorgias* (493a) and the *Cratylus* (400c), Socrates draws on Pythagoras in his suggestion that the pun of the ascetics that equates σῶμα (body) and σῆμα (tomb) is a legitimate one both etymologically and philosophically. Again in the *Gorgias* (507e-508a), Socrates rounds on the "rugged individualist" Callicles with the Pythagorean observation that his faulty moral views are due to his ignorance of geometry. In the *Republic*, Plato's warm tribute to Pythagoras (600b) follows soon after a curriculum devoted to such Pythagorean studies as arithmetic, geometry, astronomy, and music —subjects first conceived as being essentially the same by Pythagoras himself. In the *Philebus* (16d), Socrates refers to a "Prometheus, or one like him," who brought to men "a gift of the gods" which was nothing other than the first pair of Pythagorean opposites, "Limit and Unlimitedness." In the *Laws* (771) and in the *Republic* (587), Pythagorean numerology determines the number of citizens in the ideal state (5040) and the degree to which the just man is happier than the unjust (he is precisely 729 times as happy because 729 is the divine number three squared and the product raised to the third power). Finally, in the *Phaedo* and the *Republic*, in the *Phaedrus* and the *Philebus*, in the *Symposium* and the *Theaetetus*, Socrates proclaims, as insistently as Pythagoras himself appears to have done, that the philosophical life is the only way to reestablish in ourselves that same immortal harmony that obtains among the heavenly spheres and that reigns in the entire universe. This is all, from beginning to end, Pythagorean doctrine in Platonic dress—which brings one near to imagining that Pythagoras, having been in turn Æthalides, Euphorbus, Hermotimus, and Pyrrhus in the past, was born as Plato after his incarnation as Pythagoras. Without insisting on reincarnation as the explanation, one could fairly say that Plato Pythagorized and Pythagoras Platonized, and one might imagine that both were unconsciously doing the bidding of a Mind beyond either of them.

Plato obviously had a very considerable respect and admiration for Pythagoras and, after Pythagoras, for Parmenides; on the other hand, I think it would be fair to judge that he did not have any great temperamental affinity with Heraclitus. Nevertheless, in spite of any coolness Plato may have felt for the doctrines of the "Weeping Philosopher," a Heraclitean stream flows through all the Platonic dialogues from the early *Cratylus* to the late *Timaeus*. Wherever Plato comes out—whether with Pythagoras, with Parmenides, or with Empedocles—he always goes in with Heraclitus, the Platonic effort invariably commencing with the felt need to build a system that will not deny, but that will somehow accommodate and answer, yet go beyond, his great truth of ceaseless, sensible flux.

Moreover, in spite of the fact that Heraclitus is seldom mentioned in the dialogues except as the champion of the doctrine that everything is in process and therefore not a possible object of knowledge, a strong case could be made for the view that the Heraclitean Logos is as adequate a formal explanation of cosmic order as Pythagoras' numbers, and that his Logos, being in creation and abstracted therefrom, anticipates, though no doubt gnomically and cryptically, the entire logic of Plato's theory of Forms. For while everything in the world changes, according to Heraclitus, and nothing remains itself, the measure or the rule according to which all things change is universal and constant. Heraclitus can be as absolute as Parmenides or anyone else when it comes to asserting the invariability of his Logos: "this Logos exists (or is true) for ever"[7] and "all things come to pass in accordance with this Logos." Of the universal order established by the Logos, Heraclitus declares: "This world-order [*kosmos*], the same for all, none of the gods nor of men has made, but it was always and is and shall be: an ever-living fire, which is being kindled in measures and extinguished in measures" (Fr. 30). Nature is indeed, as G. M. Hopkins said, "a Heraclitean Fire," but it burns by a very regular law which is the Logos that it exhibits even as it burns. This being so, one could well argue that, as Clement of Alexandria put it in introducing this fragment of Heraclitus, "the world of this world-order is none other than a modification of the eternal world."[8] Thus the light of the sun, on which our eyes cannot bear to look directly, and the fire of the Logos which is itself invisible, are somehow reflected, albeit imperfectly and at times glaringly, in the flow of the stream.

Nevertheless, however much of Plato's transcendence we may be able to squeeze from Heraclitus' immanence, it remains true that Plato's references are nearly always to a very different Heraclitus—to the Heraclitus who said (in the version of Simplicius) ὅτι ἀεὶ πάντα ῥεῖ: "that all things are always in flux." Heraclitus' absoluteness is again to be remarked: he does not say "some things" or "sometimes" but "all things" and "always," which is doubtless why Plato takes Heraclitus to speak for the "fluxionists" in the quarrel with Parmenides and the Eleatic "antifluxionists." There were, however, those of his followers who went further even than Heraclitus himself in asserting universal inconstancy, in proclaiming complete relativity, and in declaring that human knowledge is flatly impossible. It

---

7. This is W. K. C. Guthrie's translation (*Hist. of Gr. Phil.*, I, 424–25) of a much disputed passage from DK Fr. 1; G. S. Kirk gives the other logical translation in *Heraclitus: The Cosmic Fragments* (Cambridge: Cambridge University Press, 1954), pp. 33 ff., and in Kirk-Raven, *The Presocratic Philosophers*, p. 187. The translation of Fr. 30 that follows ("This world-order," etc.) is also by Guthrie, op. cit., p. 454.

8. Kirk, *The Cosmic Fragments*, p. 307.

was from one of these Heraclitean extremists that Plato, according to Aristotle, learned his doctrine: "From his early years Plato was familiar with the Heraclitean doctrine of Cratylus, that all sensible things are in a constant state of flux and that we can have no knowledge of them. To the end of his life Plato remained loyal to those tenets . . ." (*Metaphysics*, A6, 987a32; trans. Warrington).

If, as Heraclitus asserted and Plato was compelled to agree, everything is always changing into something else ("Fire lives the death of earth and *aer* lives the death of fire, water lives the death of *aer*, earth that of water"), if everything is ceaselessly becoming that which it was not a moment since and will no longer be a moment hence, if there is no way to stay the stream or to get out of it—then how can we know anything at all about anything at all? The conclusion that Plato was forced to draw from the doctrine that all sensible things are in process and cannot be stayed long enough to be fixed with a definition, is that anything which is to be taken for an object of knowledge must be of some realm other than the sensible realm: it must have an existence that contrasts with the state of material phenomena, flowing hither and thither, ἄνω κάτω, up and down, now this, now that, nonexistent because always between existences, always giving one form up to become another. Aristotle, immediately after describing Plato's lifelong adherence to the Heraclitean doctrine of ceaseless flux, says that Plato, perceiving that an object of knowledge must always be what it is and not in the continual process of becoming something else, accepted Socrates' method of defining universals "and argued that definition is properly concerned with something other than sensibles; for he realized that there can be no permanent definition of sensibles if they are always changing. He described these non-sensibles as 'Ideas' or 'Forms,' with reference to and in respect of which sensibles exist."

"The perfectly real is perfectly knowable," Socrates declares in the *Republic*, "and the utterly unreal is entirely unknowable" (477a; trans. Cornford), which is another way of expressing the dilemma that Heraclitus presented to Plato at the very beginning of his epistemological quest. You cannot know that which is perpetually changing, as everything in this world is doing, because it is not *real*, or it *is* not, and even to say that it is unreal is to falsify the ceaseless flux by predicating of the unpredicable. Nevertheless, however thorny the epistemological difficulty, Plato was unwilling to retire into silence with his mentor Cratylus (who was said to have abandoned speech altogether in favor of waggling his finger in silent imitation of the flux); hence, he postulated a sensible realm where everything is Heraclitean and "in process of becoming" and, separated from this, an intelligible realm where nothing is becoming but all *is* and is *one*. "Once more, then," Socrates asks Theaetetus (157d; trans. Cornford), "tell me whether you like this notion that nothing is, but is always becoming, good or beautiful or any of the other things we mentioned?" Plato, we know, continued to "like this notion" throughout his life—or I should say, rather, that temperamentally he disliked it very much indeed, but that philosophically he was forced to accept it, like it or not—but only in respect of the sensible world, not in respect of the intelligible world, where "the Good" and "the Beautiful" and all the other Forms remain at rest, "perfectly real" and "perfectly knowable," entirely unaffected by the many sensible opposites continually flowing into and out of one another, perpetually abandoning what they are to become something else with a new form, a transient identity, and an already false name—false because it is as wrong to call a thing earth now as it was to call the same thing water a moment ago.

The instance most often chosen by Plato to illustrate the Heraclitean πάντα ῥεῖ in the sensible realm is, very properly, the human body itself with its faulty senses and its internal-external experience of perpetual flux. In the *Phaedo*, Cebes, worrying that the soul, though it is capable of outliving many bodies yet in the end may itself be worn out, employs a language and an imagery that are distinctly Heraclitean: "the body may stream and waste away while its owner still lives, yet the soul will always replace the worn-out tissue with new-woven material" (87d-e); and Socrates not only agrees with him—"of course the body is incessantly and always perishing" (91d)—but, ascribing the doctrine to a group of unnamed philosophers who are unquestionably of Heraclitean persuasion, he elevates the particular instance of the human body to a general principle of physical existence: "everything in existence . . . is fluctuating this way and that just like the tide in the Euripus: nothing abides for a moment in one stay" (90c; trans. Hackforth). Timaeus, likewise, when he describes how the lesser gods—those gods created directly by the Demiurge—performed their appointed task of placing immortal souls in physical bodies, borrows his thought, his phrasing, and his imagery from Heraclitus. The Demiurge's command to the lower gods, his children, is that they shall, "weaving mortal to immortal, make living beings," and so commanding, he brings into existence that same double, endlessly interconnected, ironic and human-divine state described by Heraclitus: "Immortal mortals, mortal immortals, living the others' death, dying the others' life."[9] Once created, Timaeus' immortal mortals/mortal immortals live—and simultaneously die—in a perfectly imperfect Heraclitean world, in-flowing and out-flowing without end. "And they confined the circuits of the immortal soul within the flowing and ebbing tide of the body. These circuits, being thus confined in a strong river, neither controlled it nor were controlled, but caused and suffered violent motions; so that the whole creature moved . . . forward and backward, and again to right and left, and up and down. . . . For strong as was the tide that brought them nourishment, flooding them and ebbing them away, a yet greater tumult was caused . . . when some creature's body chanced to encounter alien fire from outside . . . joining with that perpetually streaming current in stirring and violently shaking the circuits of the soul . . ." (43a–d). There are other evident echoes and recalls of Heraclitus in the dialogues—for example, the *daimon* that is said to accompany every man throughout his life (*Timaeus*, 90a, *Republic*, 619-20, *Phaedo*, 107d; cf. Heraclitus, Fr. 119: "A man's character is his *daimon*"); the proof of the soul's immortality based on the interplay of opposites (*Phaedo*, 70c-72e; cf. Heraclitus, Frs. 10, 60, 67, and, especially, 88) and on the soul's invisibility (*Phaedo*, 79c; cf. Frs. 54 and 123); and Socrates' determination to "direct my inquiries . . . to myself" (*Phaedrus*, 229e-230a; cf. Fr. 101: "I searched myself")— but to Plato, Heraclitus primarily signified one of "the wise" who assure us "that one of these processes must always be going on in us, since all things are always flowing up and down" (*Philebus*, 43a; trans. Hackforth). For Plato, there was no denying the epistemological and ontological dilemma posed by Heraclitus, and from the dilemma there was no escape save through a theory of Forms and an

---

9. The phrase from the *Timaeus* is translated by Cornford, *Plato's Cosmology* (London: Kegan Paul, Trench, Trubner & Co., 1937), p. 140. The echo of Heraclitus is perhaps more precise in the Greek—*Timaeus*, 41d: τὸ δὲ λοιπὸν ὑμεῖς, ἀθανάτῳ θνητὸν προσυφαίνοντες, ἀπεργάζεσθε ζῷα καὶ γεννᾶτε . . . ; Heraclitus, Fr. 62: ἀθάνατοι θνητοί, θνητοὶ ἀθάνατοι, ζῶντες τὸν ἐκείνων θάνατον τὸν δὲ ἐκείνων βίον τεθνεῶτες. A. E. Taylor, in his *Commentary on Plato's "Timaeus"* (Oxford: Clarendon Press, 1928), pp. 253-54, compares the two passages in a relevant way and refers as well to the Pythagorean "opposites."

accompanying, very elaborate, metaphysical system. Reordering the four roots of Plato's philosophy in a new pattern of relationships, one could say that Heraclitus and Empedocles were the scientists of unstable and interchanging elements in the sensible world and that Pythagoras and Parmenides were the theoreticians of a stable world of form beyond this one. Plato's physics and his metaphysics demanded not less than all four.

All pluralists—whether dualists like Heraclitus, or dualists and quaternists like Empedocles, or dualists, triadists, and quaternists like Pythagoras—all are at heart monists. The monistic yearning at the heart of pluralistic thought is unmistakable in Heraclitus, in Empedocles, and in Pythagoras, whose various philosophies can be interpreted as an attempt to discover and to assert an eventual unity somewhere or somehow beyond all the sensible pluralities. But if pluralists are monists at heart and in their emotions, all monists are pluralists in mind, in thought, and in observation—all, that is, excepting the extreme case like Parmenides, who denies outright and entirely the pluralistic evidence of the senses. Such extremity, which the rest of us cannot sustain, nevertheless behooves the archetypal thinker.

Of all the Pre-Socratic philosophers, Parmenides is the one who most demands to be understood in his relation to others and as an influence on them—as an element, that is, in a developing story and in an evolving tradition; if he is not so understood there is every likelihood that his thought will have no meaning or appeal at all. While Parmenides' poem is an extraordinarily difficult document to interpret alone, however, what Plato makes of him in his system-building is quite clear. Heraclitus and Parmenides are in Plato the two arch antagonists, representative spokesmen respectively for the many and the One, neither sufficient in himself and impossible to bring to peaceful terms, yet the loving-hating parents of a philosophic infant bearing some features of both, but at the same time differing from both, and going under the name neither of the father nor of the mother but of the midwife—Plato—who attended the birth. "Things taken together," Heraclitus says in Fr. 10, "are whole and not whole, something which is being brought together and brought apart, which is in tune and out of tune: out of all things can be made a unity, and out of a unity, all things" (trans. Kirk). In asserting the *necessary* coexistence and tension of opposites and their simultaneous mutual attraction and repulsion, Heraclitus was insisting on precisely that which Parmenides, in the series of questions and answers of Fr. 8, refused ever to admit to the philosophical dialogue. There are only two "ways," according to Parmenides, and of these, one is the Way of Truth and of Being, the other the Way of Appearance and Non-being. Between the two, Parmenides allows no third way nor does he permit compromise: something "is" or it "is not," and if it is not, it flatly does not exist, and therefore it can be neither spoken nor thought. With his denial of the entire world of plurality and appearance and his refusal to speak or think of the Heraclitean universe of connected opposites and perpetual process, Parmenides goes not only against common sense but against all the other senses as well. "That which can be spoken and thought needs must be; for it is possible for it, but not for nothing, to be. . . . For never shall this be proved, that things that are not are; but do thou hold back thy thought from this way of enquiry, nor let custom, born of much experience, force thee to let wander along this road thy aimless eye, thy echoing ear or thy tongue; but do thou judge by reason the strife-encompassed proof that I have spoken" (Frs. 6 and 7; trans. Raven). So, for Parmenides, it is hence with vain deluding senses—with "aimless eye," "echoing ear," and "tongue"—and hail to divinest, most clear-conceiving thought.

Parmenides may or may not have had Pythagoras and Heraclitus in mind when, in Fr. 8, he asserted of his reality, simply and atemporally, that "It is"; but in any case, with that assertion and all the consequences he draws therefrom, Parmenides denies both Pythagorean cosmogony and Heraclitean flux: within the One Being nothing evolves, because *"it is"*—hence there is no cosmogony—and within it there is perfect homogeneity of being—hence there is no flux or interchange of opposites. There is only Itself. "One way alone is yet left to tell of, namely that 'It is'. On this way are marks in plenty that since it exists it is unborn and imperishable, whole, unique, immovable and without end. It *was* not in the past, nor yet *shall* it be, since it now *is*, all together, one and continuous" (Fr. 8; trans. Guthrie). If we cast out the senses and consider the question solely with the mind, and if we do not, as Plato was later to do, postulate two different modes of being and two (or more) degrees of reality, then of course we must agree that Parmenides is right, as he goes on to demonstrate in his series of ironical questions and logical objections to every attempt to squirm free. "For what birth of it wilt thou seek? How and from what did it grow? I shall not allow thee to say or think 'from what is not', for it is not to be said or thought that 'it is not'. And what need would have prompted it to grow later or sooner, beginning from nothing? Thus it must either fully be or else not be. . . . The verdict on this lies here: It is or it is not. . . . How could what is afterwards perish? And how could it come into being? For if it came into being, it *is* not, nor yet if it is going to be at some future time. Thus becoming is extinguished, and perishing not to be heard of" (trans. Guthrie). Thus also process does not exist, nor does the world of the senses, nor does the *kosmos* that Heraclitus declared was composed of interlocked and interflowing opposites and that he claimed "always was and is and shall be: an everliving fire, kindling in measures and going out in measures" (Fr. 30). Except for the One Being, which is non-evolved, unfluctuating, whole, perfect, homogeneous, with neither history nor future, all else, according to Parmenides, is merely names "which mortals have laid down believing them to be true: coming into being and perishing, being and not being, change of place and alteration of bright colour" (Fr. 8, ll.38-41).

"How are we to deal with all of these combatants?" Socrates asks in the *Theaetetus*, referring to two philosophic camps very like the Heracliteans and the Parmenideans. "For, little by little, our advance has brought us, without our knowing it, between the two lines; and unless we can somehow fend them off and slip through, we shall suffer for it" (180e-181a; trans. Cornford). And in the *Sophist* we find the Eleatic Stranger following Socrates' advice so as to make agreement, for his own doctrine, from the Parmenideans and the Heracliteans—giving some substance to what he calls the Friends of Forms and some formal stability to what we may call the unceasing Fluxionists. "From this, however, it follows," the Stranger says, "first, that, if all things are unchangeable no intelligence can really exist anywhere in anything with regard to any object"—which must be the epistemologist's objection to Parmenides. "And, on the other hand, if we allow that all things are moving and changing, on that view equally we shall be excluding intelligence from the class of real things"—which must be the ontologist's objection to Heraclitus. "On these grounds, then," he concludes, "it seems that only one course is open to the philosopher who values knowledge and the rest above all else. He must refuse to accept from the champions either of the One or of the many Forms the doctrine that all Reality is changeless; and he must turn a deaf ear to the other party who represent Reality as everywhere changing. Like a child begging for 'both', he must declare that Reality or the sum of things is both at once—all that is unchangeable and all that is in change" (249b-d; trans. Cornford). This is the stroke that Greek philosophy had been looking for, the stroke that both Pythagoras and Heraclitus had anticipated, though neither had quite accomplished it; nor was Parmenides more successful, for having distinguished an intelligible world from a physical world, he then went on to deny, as his premises required him to do, the reality of the latter. It was left for Plato to separate the two worlds—corporeal and incorporeal, changing and changeless, many and one, sensible and intelligible—and declare that each had a kind of reality appropriate to it, then proceed to define the cosmogonical, epistemological, and ontological relationship existing between the two realms.

The paradox of Parmenides' "Way of Truth" is that, having denied any reality to a physical, sensory world, he goes on to describe his one reality, in notably sensory phrasing, as "complete on every side, like the mass of a well-rounded ball [εὐκύκλου σφαίρης], equal every way from the centre; for it may not be at all greater or smaller in this direction or in that . . . ; for equal on all sides to itself, it meets its limits uniformly" (Fr. 8; trans. Guthrie). In the *Timaeus*, Plato takes over this well-rounded sphere from Parmenides, but not until he has first purified it and placed it within a system that can account for its physicality and yet see that there is more to it than its physical makeup. "We must," Timaeus declares, "begin by distinguishing between that which always is and never becomes from that which is always becoming but never is." Now the universe or cosmos, Timaeus says, "has come into being; for it is visible, tangible, and corporeal, and therefore perceptible by the senses, and, as we saw, sensible things are objects of opinion and sensation and therefore change and come into being." Plato's cosmos, then, though Timaeus will soon describe it precisely in terms of Parmenides' well-rounded sphere, is obviously a place of Heraclitean flux; Plato's answer, which allows him, like the child, to have it both ways, is that the cosmos has been "constructed on the pattern of what is apprehensible by reason and understanding and eternally unchanging" and "is a likeness of something else." That something else is "the highest and most completely perfect of intelligible things"—the Forms as a single, unique whole, the Archetype, the Paradigm after which the Demiurge creates—and if we judge by the visible universe, as we may do because the Demiurge is the consummate craftsman in following his model, then the Forms are the perfect and transcendent Sphere, but, unlike the universe, without body or color or motion or change. The Sphere, as Jung says repeatedly of his archetypes, is a Parmenidean Form without content. The universe, on the other hand, by its Heraclitean coming-to-be, draws this Form down into a tangle of matter, gives content to it, and clothes it in the variegated garments of the natural and the psychic world. "Therefore he turned it into a rounded spherical shape, with the extremes equidistant in all directions from the centre, a figure that has the greatest degree of completeness and uniformity. . . . So he established a single spherical universe in circular motion. . . . His creation, then, for all these reasons, was a blessed god" (*Timaeus*, 27d–34b; trans. Lee).

"Fools—for they have no far-reaching thoughts, who suppose that what formerly was not can come into being or that anything can die and perish wholly. For there is no means whereby anything could come to be out of what in no way is, and it cannot be brought about or heard of that what is should perish" (Fr. 11). Laying about him, here as elsewhere, on behalf of Parmenidean doctrine, Empedocles characteristically batters philosophical fools (among them Pythagoras, whom he otherwise approves) with greater glee and gusto than Parmenides himself displays in snapping at the "hordes without judgment" or than Heraclitus shows in sneering at *hoi polloi*. Like Plato, Empedocles accepted Parmenides' rebuke to Pythagorean cosmogony, but he could hardly go on with Parmenides to deny all this pluralistic world and its inhabitants, since, as he says, he had himself earlier been "a boy and a girl, a bush and a bird and a dumb fish of the sea," and he now ruefully contemplates himself fallen into a world of Yahoos: "Of these I too am now one, an exile from the gods and a wanderer. . . ." (Fr. 115). In addition to its special virtues as poetry—a remarkable verbal energy, a bright mythic splendor, a pervasive strength of imagery, humor, and personality—Empedocles' work represents a halfway house—a summary and a projection—on the way to Platonism.

Though he was equal to name-calling with the best of them, Empedocles, departing from the practice of his doctrinal father Parmenides, drew positively from all his philosophic forerunners. For his belief in the immortality of the soul, its reincarnation and possible transmigration; for his adherence to the Orphic mysteries; for his faith that the activity of philosophy will purify and deify the soul of the philosopher and so release it from the wheel of reincarnations —for all these, Empedocles was indebted to Pythagoras, and he shared the faith of the Pythagoreans in the number four as a root— or *the* root—of nature and "of all things." The Pythagorean oath "by him that gave to our generation the tetractys, the fount and root of eternal nature," anticipated, and perhaps influenced, Empedocles' discovery of the *rhizōmata*, the four roots of all things.[10] For his account of universal creation in the *Timaeus*, Plato borrowed the four elements from Empedocles, placing under them a geometrical structure and over them a mathematical harmony drawn from Pythagoras.

While he respected Parmenidean logic as much as he admired Pythagorean religion, Empedocles was no more willing than Plato to join Parmenides in severing contact with sensory phenomena or to agree with the Eleatic master in his absolute denial of Heraclitean flux and motion. To satisfy a yearning toward Parmenidean monism without denying the reality of Heraclitean change is a delicate and difficult affair, and as from Plato it required a theory of Forms, so from Empedocles it called forth a theory of elements and of alternating cycles. Like Socrates' child, Empedocles succeeded in having it both ways by adopting the major insights of Parmenides and Heraclitus but with a radical variation on both: he replaced Parmenides' one changeless Being with four changeless elements; and he argued that movement from One to many and many to One is not, as Heraclitus would have it, simultaneous and paradoxical but alternating and cyclical—first the indivisible One, then separation into four, then reunion as the One, then separation. . . . According to Empedocles' cosmological vision, which is a corollary of his religious vision, a state of unmoving, stable, homogeneous unity,

10. The Pythagorean oath and the Empedoclean declaration shared language as well as imagery: the word translated "root" in the oath is the same as Empedocles' ῥιζώματα, but in the singular (ἀενάου φύσεως ῥίζωμά)—"mass of roots" or "element" is the definition in Liddell-Scott, citing both the Empedoclean passage and the Pythagorean oath.

symbolized in Empedocles as in Parmenides by the Sphere, obtained in a golden age of the past and will obtain again in the future, but not now when everything is in motion and change, ruled by the conflict of opposites. Now the universe is Heraclitean; in another time it was and will be Parmenidean. Time, which goes back and forth rather than forward, is essential to Empedocles' system but not to Heraclitus' (where the same Logos-fire has always burned and always will burn) nor to Parmenides' (where past and future are denied along with the denial of change). By declaring for alternating cycles, Empedocles manages to reconcile the eternal duration of Heraclitus' Fr. 30 with the denial of that duration in Parmenides' Fr. 8. Furthermore, by making his cycles perpetual, Empedocles gets rid of the Parmenidean objection to Pythagoras (why does it begin "later or sooner, beginning from nothing"?) since, as in a circle, the process has neither beginning nor end.

Besides the four elements—the ultimate, irreducible *archai*, the roots of the sensible world—there are two motive forces, called by Empedocles Love and Strife, ruling over the alternating movements toward unity and toward plurality. Love brings the elements into oneness—the blessed state of the Sphere; Strife separates them into four. Between those extremes the phenomenal world of appearance, motion, and change—the world, that is, as we know it, for there is no human existence at either extreme—perpetually comes into being, first in one direction, then in the other. "A double tale will I tell: at one time it grew to be one only from many, at another it divided again to be many from one. There is a double coming into being of mortal things and a double passing away. One is brought about, and again destroyed, by the coming together of all things, the other grows up and is scattered as things are again divided. And these things never cease from continual shifting, at one time all coming together, through Love, into one, at another each borne apart from the others through Strife" (Fr. 17; trans. Raven). Though they are themselves always the same, the four elements, coming to perfect rest under the rule of Love and to frantic motion under the rule of Strife, combine and recombine in such a way as to make up the ever shifting world of appearances. What the eye sees, therefore (and likewise with the other senses), is no more than a continual shifting of the appearances which rise out of and obscure the underlying elemental quaternity; but if the observer succeeds in seeing appearances with the eye yet understanding the four elements with the mind, he will have grasped the real reality of things, both the Heraclitean flux and the Parmenidean stasis. For Heraclitus, the basic reality *is* change, and the ultimate truth is a Cusanean *coincidentia oppositorum*. For Parmenides, on the other hand, there can be no coincidence of opposites because there are no opposites. Here again, Empedocles successfully begs for both: his four unchanging elements are the conflicting and cooperating opposites of the world of becoming; his Sphere symbolizes the world of being where the four cannot conflict because, under the beneficent rule of Love, they are harmoniously, indivisibly one: "equal to himself from every side and quite without end, he stays fast in the close covering of Harmony, a rounded sphere rejoicing in his circular solitude" (Frs. 27 and 28; trans. Raven).

The step from Empedocles to Plato is very small but very important, being a question, once again, of the definitive separation of the two realms of existence: in Plato the separation is modal, in Empedocles it is temporal. Empedocles' Sphere, when the rule of Love is complete (the σφαῖρος, which, according to Aristotle, Empedocles considered to be εὐδαιμονέστατος Θεός, "a most blessed god") corresponds to Plato's transcendent, nontemporal realm of Forms, a world separated from this one not in time but in mode of being and degree of reality. All else in Empedocles, except for this time when Love dominates entirely—the time of increasing Love, the time of increasing Strife, the moment of total Strife—has to do with the world of becoming (not with the world of being), with Heraclitean flux (not with Parmenidean stasis), with Plato's cave existence (not with the direct sun).

Drawing both broad outlines and specific details from this twofold Empedoclean tale of cosmogony and zoogony, Plato produced various myths about the human condition, about the fallen state in which our divine spirit is forced to live, and about the restorative powers of philosophy. The androgynous being of Aristophanes' brilliant and witty tale in the *Symposium* (189d) is none other than Empedocles' "whole-natured form"; the "double tale" of reversed half cycles that mirror one another, narrated by the Stranger of the *Politicus* (270a), is the same tale Empedocles tells in both his poem "On Nature" and in "Purifications"; and the *daimones* of the *Phaedo*, the *Symposium*, the *Republic*, the *Phaedrus*, and the *Timaeus* are, *mutatis mutandis*, the *daimones* of Empedocles' Fr. 115, demigods exiled from heaven, destined to walk the earth a spell ("thrice ten thousand seasons" in both Empedocles and Plato) until sufficiently purified by the divinifying effects of philosophy. Empedocles, like Pythagoras, normally occurs in a context of myth in Plato, for they were the two who taught him (in contrast to and conjunction with the lessons of epistemology and ontology learned from Heraclitus and Parmenides) about such things as the soul's immortality, reincarnation, purification, and possible escape from the wheel; for such truths as these, not the language of logic but only the language of myth will suffice.

And now the *telos*, the end and justification of this ancient Greek tale. It is the special genius of Plato and the most distinctive feature of his philosophy to embrace and reconcile virtually all imaginable contraries. He is, as it were, the narrator of Greek philosophy, presenting its chief characters—protagonists and antagonists—in thematic pattern, drawing them together and apart as figures in a dance. So doing, he makes his own philosophy the reason for the dance, its climax and its conclusion, for in that philosophy he takes up, opposes, correlates, and conjoins not only the characters but also the ideas, doctrines, and systems represented by the primal forerunners. The system that Plato constructed has very much the nature of a *complexio oppositorum*. It is both monistic and pluralistic (and succeeds in being both of them simultaneously rather than alternately); it combines formal and material explanations of the origin of the sensible world (merging the mathematical proportions and geometrical forms of Pythagoras with the four elements of Empedocles); it joins rational discourse to mythical narrative, completes prose statement with poetic enactment, and marries the dialectical language of consciousness to the symbolic language of the unconscious; it conceives of a world of sensible things participating in supersensible Forms with mathematical objects, *daimones*, Jungian archetypal images, and Yeatsian symbols serving as the point of participation between physical things on the one hand and intelligible Forms, the gods, disembodied archetypes, and pure meaning on the other hand; it comprehends different, contrasting degrees of reality in the physical and in the intelligible worlds; it posits both a microcosm and a macrocosm, the former being not a mere fragment of the latter but a compressed epitome, a full analogue, and a point-by-point imitation of it; it sees time as a reflection of eternity and eternity as an ideal encircling of time. Like a Jungian mandala or a squared circle, like Yeatsian gyres enclosed in a sphere, the Platonic system unites opposites in such a way as to be greater than any of them individually, greater even than all of them in sum.

Plato's predecessors (excepting Parmenides) addressed themselves to one major question: How did this universe come to be what it is? Implicit in that question and preliminary to it was another one that forced itself on Pythagoras, Heraclitus, and Empedocles: Out of what did the universe come? Where, why, and how did it have its start? Pythagoras was tripped up when he tried to pass from the formal to the material, when he tried to go directly from numbers to things. Making a blind leap from forms to things, Pythagoras tumbled into the gap (and was zestfully helped into it by Parmenides) that he had himself opened up but never really noticed. Heraclitus was much cagier than Pythagoras (or much "darker"—to a latter-day reader these qualities are much the same), hedging his bets on immanence and transcendence by never making it clear whether his Logos-fire is an immaterial principle or a material element. Is his fire an *archē* in the sense of a first principle, or an *archē* in the sense of an original substance? Heraclitus is too wily to commit himself—or at least the fragments to which we attach the name "Heraclitus" refuse to be committed. Heraclitus did not posit two different modes of existence; hence, there being no nearer side and no farther side, there was no Pythagorean gap for Heraclitus to fall into. Or, to adopt Heraclitus' own imagery: there are no river banks, there is only the river; and mortals do not fall into the river, they themselves *are* rivers always, like everything around them, flowing and streaming and wasting away. Empedocles tried a new way of accounting for this phenomenal universe: not content with a single archaic element, he declared for the full quaternity—air, earth, fire, and water—which, he said, combine and recombine, join and separate to compose the continually changing face of a totally physical universe. But the question remains: How and why did the process of the universe start? Empedocles had a twofold dodge by way of answer. First, he relieved himself of the burden of seeking a beginning by maintaining that his universe was a closed system comprising two half-cycles in perpetual alternation, constantly shuttling back and forth without beginning or end. Second, he introduced into his universe two causes of joining and separating which he named Love and Strife, and he tried to ally them as formal *archai* to the four elements as physical archai. Empedocles, in other words, smuggled Love and Strife into his closed system under the guise of formal principles and causes when it is perfectly clear that they are by nature as material as the four elements themselves: Love is a *physical* attraction of the elements, and Strife a *physical* repulsion; both come from within the physical system, not from outside it. Empedocles did not, like Heraclitus, refuse to commit himself; on the contrary, with characteristic *brio* he overcommitted himself, thereby showing a certain disregard for philosophical niceties. For Empedocles there was a nearer side but no farther side, and his leap into the abyss was rather like Gloucester's leap at Dover—either a jump from dizzying heights into nothingness or else a jump from this level ground to that precisely similar level ground half a foot away.

In contrast to Heraclitus, with much greater clarity than Pythagoras, and without the corporeal-noncorporeal confusion of Empedocles, Plato committed himself not to a philosophy of either/or but to a philosophy of both—both separate and different, both together and interdependent. He established a nearer and a farther side, and, like Pythagoras but with clearer and more conscious intent, he separated the two sides; having done so, however, he did not allow himself to be tumbled into the void. Plato closed the gap—that *chōrismos* of his own making—not by drawing together the sides but by filling the space between with such powerful beings and figures as Eros and other spirits, *daimones*, mythic characters, mathematical objects, archetypal images, symbols. Thus, as Socrates says is true of a spirit that "bridges the gap between" mortal and immortal, Plato "prevents the universe from falling into two separate halves" (*Symposium*, 202e). Adopting and extending the imagery of Heraclitus, Plato would say that the soul comes at birth from the near back of eternity, enters into that river of time which is both body and world, and issues on the far bank of eternity, leaving behind the body, the world, and the river as the residue of time, its witness and its hostage. The important thing is that both banks were there for Plato, as they were not for Heraclitus; so too was the river, as it was not for Parmenides.

The four elements of the *Timaeus* are perhaps the best illustration of Plato's genius in reconciling opposites: by nature they are half formal and half material; in origin they have been borrowed somewhat from Empedocles, somewhat from Pythagoras, and somewhat from Heraclitus, with Parmenides never far away, restraining Plato, by his logical objections, from drowning himself in a flood of mere phenomena. The *Timaeus* elements are Empedoclean in that they combine and recombine in different proportions to form different compounds, different appearances, different living shapes; but those elements are non-Empedoclean in that they are not themselves ultimate or immutable. Empedocles' four elements cannot be broken down any further—his air, earth, fire, and water are irreducible roots—but Plato's elements can be because, laying Pythagorean formalism over Empedoclean materialism, Plato assigns a geometrical form and a mathematical figure to each of the elements. Ultimately, Plato's *archai* are formal though they appear to us as material elements, and his individual elements are capable of interchanging being because their geometrical forms merge and interpenetrate and so forever become new elemental forms. This of course is not possible in Empedocles: air and water can combine to present a certain appearance, but air does not become water, nor water air; in fact, this continual interchange of natures is borrowed from Heraclitus, Plato's other scientist of physical process, who told how the elements perpetually lived each other's death.

The geometrical forms underlying and implicated in sensible reality in Plato have also their models to imitate—models that are more perfect and more purely formal than themselves. The shape of fire, for example, is only an imperfect imitation of the ideal, matter-free, pyramidal form which exists in a different, supersensible realm and in another way from fire. In the Platonic hierarchy everything "participates" in a formal reality superior to itself—so that fire participates in the pyramid as a mathematical object which in turn participates in the ideal pyramid, that being a real object of thought but not of experience. Going downward in the hierarchy (Forms → mathematical objects → physical things), everything "images," at a lower degree or intensity of reality, that which is above it: as above perfectly, so below imperfectly. Hence Plato's ultimate *archai* are not physical or sensible at all but are moral, metaphysical, and psychological; they are the Ideas or Forms—the Form of the Good, the Form of the Beautiful, etc.—on which the Demiurge modelled his universal creation. In the *Symposium* (210e–211b), Diotima describes to Socrates what might be called the philosopher's progress —a movement that exactly reverses the Demiurge's creation, going from the Heraclitean flux and pluralism of this world, where beauty, caught in the sensual music of human bodies, comes into being and passes away, to the Parmenidean stability of a transcendent world, where Beauty, freed of the sensual, is "absolute, existing alone with itself, unique, eternal."

In the *Timaeus*, Plato propounds a temporal metaphor, rather than a spatial metaphor, for this same longing of the philosophic spirit. Time, in the most pregnant, mythical, and symbolic passage in all of Plato (*Timaeus*, 37d), is an almost-sphere, circles upon circles yearning towards spherical perfection, a myriad revolutions throughout the universe participating in, imitating, and forever becoming, but never quite being, the closed and complete, glorious sphere of eternity. As Blake declared, eternity is in love with the productions of time, because, while it is the ideal model for those productions of time, eternity produces nothing itself. Time, on the other hand, while it produces Grecian urns and golden birds, longs after eternity and aspires forever to return to the sphere that first gave time its shape. Intermediate between the two, like *daimones*, geometrical figures, and archetypal images, are the heavenly spheres which in their endless turning imitate the One Sphere while also determining the process of time.

"No," Empedocles says of his virtually divine and unquestionably archetypal elements, his τέσσαρα πάντων ῥιζώματα, his ultimate, quaternal reality, "No, there are just these, but running through one another they become now some things and now others and yet ever and always the same" (Fr. 17). So too it could be said of the archetypal figures of Greek philosophy, of Pythagoras and Heraclitus, Parmenides and Empedocles, "No, there are just these, but running through one another they become now some things and now others"—now Platonic philosophy and Neoplatonic elaboration, now Plotinian mysticism and Augustinian theology, now Swedenborgian vision and Blakean symbolism, now Jungian pleromatic psychology and Yeatsian mummy-wheat poetics, "and yet ever and always the same": the four *rhizōmata* subtly interwoven and changed into something rich and strange, transformed to become the undying, invisible rhizome of Platonism both as a system and as a tradition. Its flowers are of a day, blossoming and fading in a man's lifetime, but the rhizome itself is as ancient as thought, as deep as psyche, whose limits, as Heraclitus says, "you would not find even by travelling along every path: so deep a *logos* does it have" (Fr. 45). From deep, deep down, where it is untouched by the frosts of time, merely strengthened by increase of age, the perennial rhizome still, even in our day, nourishes its bright, beautiful, brief flowers.

CHAPTER II

Numbers, Harmony, and Metempsychosis

Writing in 1930 to "Michael's Schoolmaster" (in inverted commas because that gentleman inhabited an imaginary and ideal world more than any real one), Yeats commanded that his son be taught "mathematics as thoroughly as his capacity permits" (*Ex.*, p. 321). This seems innocuous enough: the natural concern of any father that his son have the learning necessary to get on in a world where science lords it over all merely because it has at its command a whole array of mathematical symbols, geometrical figures, and intricate formulae that ordinary humanity—the poet and the common man —can never hope to understand. In fact, however, Yeats had another reason, more specific and at once both humorous and serious, for his injunction: "Teach him mathematics as thoroughly as his capacity permits. I know that Bertrand Russell must, seeing that he is such a featherhead, be wrong about everything, but as I have no mathematics I cannot prove it." Over and beyond the neat disposition of Bertrand Russell, there is an interesting assumption here: that without mathematics Yeats could not "prove," refute, or demonstrate anything in philosophy but that, conversely, *with*

54

mathematics he might expect to prove certain points "about everything"—which is without a doubt a large and important subject; it is also a typically Yeatsian one. Yeats's ignorance of mathematics is very much like his lamentable loss of Greek: with his "Greek gone," Yeats says, he could gather no more than "the broken bread of old philosophers" (*Ex.*, p. 60); with his mathematics nonexistent, he had no measuring stick that he might use to beat the head of Bertrand Russell and his philosophy. They are, Yeats implies, a symbiotic pair: philosophy, a love and search for the truth; and mathematics, a means to prove that truth when found. His lack of mathematics was therefore as serious to Yeats as his forgetting of the language that would have made not only Homer and the poets but also ancient philosophy accessible to him (Greek, fittingly, was the other subject Yeats wanted his son taught). Regrettable as his ignorance of mathematics no doubt was, however, Yeats's predicament was nothing like as dire as Jung's, for Yeats implies that, had he been taught, he could have learned some mathematics even though he might never have mastered all its complexities. It seems that Jung, on the other hand, was simply unteachable, thoroughly incapable, beyond both help and hope. According to his longtime friend Albert Oeri, Jung "was, frankly, an idiot in mathematics" (*Spring* 1970, p. 183). And yet, their mathematical frailty notwithstanding—a frailty amounting in the one case to mere idiocy[1]—both Yeats and Jung based a very large part of their thought on the formalizing patterns that the human mind discovers, apparently simultaneously, both within itself and outside itself in the universe and which it then formulates as the ordering principles, everywhere valid and immutable, of geometry and mathematics. Yeats and Jung were Pythagoreans through and through, it would be fair to say, in tendency and temperament, if not in learning or ability.

It may well be, of course, that the sense of awe and mystery with which Yeats and Jung regarded numbers was on the one hand exaggerated and on the other hand a direct consequence of their shared mathematical weakness (why should they not consider that a mystery which was so mysterious to them?); but however we explain it,

1. Or, as Jung himself puts it, with somewhat more of delicacy and compassion for his failure, "I am not gifted in mathematics . . ." (*Analytical Psychology*, p. 75). In a letter Jung referred to his "notoriously helpless state concerning higher mathematics" (*Letters*, II, 215), but as I shall suggest later, he thought himself pretty much a master of lower mathematics.

and deny it as they might, there is more than a hint of Pythagorean mysticism in what Yeats and Jung had to say on the subject. "Am I a mystic?" Yeats rhetorically asked Ethel Mannin in a letter written little more than a month before his death: "Am I a mystic?—no, I am a practical man. I have seen the raising of Lazarus and the loaves and fishes and have made the usual measurements, plummet line, spirit-level and have taken the temperature by pure mathematic" (*Letters*, p. 921). In the rhythms of his poetry and in the geometric designs of *A Vision*, Yeats "made the usual measurements" and came to conclude that "for the first time I understand human life" (*Letters*, p. 644) and that the true arcanum finally lies in "pure mathematic." If, in cosmic terms, numbers are, as Pythagoras maintained, the ultimate reality available to our minds, then they are also the ultimate mystery, deserving of all our awe and reverence. Thus the paradox in what Yeats says: numbers themselves are more mysterious and more powerfully affective—more *mystical*—even than the miracles of the resurrected body and the multiplied loaves and fishes that the numbers were put to confirm. Were it not for the numbers that make man one with the cosmos and with the perpetual rebirth of that cosmos, there would be no resurrected body, no multiplication of loaves and fishes. Yeats's disavowal of mysticism here is not very strenuous, nor is it at all defensive or peevish—"mystic," after all, so far as he was concerned, was not a horrid name—but Jung was unquestionably sincere when he angrily rejected, again and again, the name of mystic. Nevertheless, even when he is concluding a tetchy defense of himself and his favorite number ("I am . . . [not] responsible for the number four. . . . My critics seem to have the funny idea that I have a special liking for the number four and therefore find it everywhere"), Jung eventually succumbs to the alluring quaternity with this remark: "I will only mention in passing that . . . the number four possesses special mathematical properties" (*CW*, XIII, pars. 329-30). In light of the fact that Jung was "not gifted in mathematics" it may be just as well that he only mentions this in passing; moreover, one suspects that the "special mathematical properties" of the number four are not far remote from special mystical properties and that had Jung gone into too much detail he might have convicted himself out of his own mouth. All his statements to the contrary notwithstanding, Jung did have a great fondness for the number four and for what he would call its numinous qualities—a fondness which Pythagoreans and Neophythagoreans (who specially reverenced, among other numbers, the four and the ten) would well understand. Yeats had no special emotional attachment to any one particular number (though he cannot be said to have been altogether immune to the charms of two, three, and four); indeed, Yeats's view of matters mathematical was probably more genuinely Pythagorean and generally Greek than Jung's. Order and beauty, according to Yeats's notion, are to be found not in one number or another but in the rhythms established by proportionate relationship. Be that as it may, however, Jung's archetypes and his mandalas, like Yeats's symbols and his rhythms, were possessed of a numerical-mathematical structure that was somehow responsible for their affective power and that put Yeats and Jung in line with the best Pythagorean tradition.

"With respect to Hippasus," Iamblichus tells us in his *Life of Pythagoras*, "they assert that he was one of the Pythagoreans, but that in consequence of having divulged and described the method of forming a sphere from twelve pentagons, he perished in the sea, as an impious person, but retained the renown of having made the discovery. In reality, however, this as well as everything else pertaining to geometry, was the invention of *that man*; for thus without mentioning his name, they denominate Pythagoras."[2] The striking fact about this cautionary tale is that nowhere is it suggested that Hippasus impiously revealed what would ordinarily be deemed a religious mystery; always it is a question of a geometrical, mathematical, or intellectual mystery. As if someone were now to discover how to square the circle and were to publish that mystery for the initiate and the profane alike: death would be the only answer. "The knowledge of reality"—how to form a sphere from twelve pentagons, for example, or how to square the circle—"is always in some measure a secret knowledge" (*Auto.*, p. 482), according to the great Irish sometime mystic, sometime non-mystic; and then, concluding a section so that it is neither possible nor necessary for him to elaborate and explain the remark, he says, with just the right Yeatsian mix of meaning and madness, designed to tease the reader out of thought: "It is a kind of death." The knowledge of reality meant a kind of death for Hippasus, of course, but this is not what Yeats has in

2. Iamblichus, *Life of Pythagoras* . . . etc., trans. Thomas Taylor (London: John M. Watkins, 1965; reprinted from edition of 1818), pp. 47-48.

mind. He suggests, rather, that "knowledge of reality" transcends the human realm and human consciousness, or, as he says elsewhere, "wisdom is the property of the dead, / A something incompatible with life." Having discovered that it is number, numinous, ubiquitous, and immutable, that connects the human and the divine worlds and that simple numerical ratios determine the same order in human music and in the heavens, Pythagoras proceeded to assert a universal *harmonia*, a correspondence of above and below, a kinship among all living things, a pattern of cyclical recurrence in human experience, and a doctrine of reincarnation or metempsychosis. Or perhaps it was all the other way about: maybe he began with reincarnation, cyclical regeneration, and universal kinship and concluded with correspondence and *harmonia* and numbers as the basis of reality. In either case, the Pythagorean doctrines were so cunningly interwoven that to adopt one would lead initiates inevitably on to acceptance of all the others—as, indeed, Yeats and Jung accepted all the Pythagorean doctrines with only a few qualifications and explanations offered on the subject of reincarnation.

Yeats, enjoying one of his obstreperous and oracular moods, wrote in one of his last essays that "Man has made mathematics, but God reality" (*Ex.*, p. 435). But—it can be objected to Yeats—if reality itself be mathematical, what then? For man can be said to have drawn circles and squares and to have used numbers to trammel, contain, express, and order reality in the images of his own mind; but this does not mean that reality is not a squared circle or a *harmonia* of simple-number ratios. That is precisely what it is—in two more or less adequate symbols—as well as many other things besides; and the mind, even as it projects and receives images of order, is itself an important element, and deeply implicated, in the total reality. It might have been salutary if Yeats could have tried explaining his aphorism to Nicholas of Cusa, whom Yeats much admired and who was a good many steps ahead of him not only in time but in mathematical abilities as well. What Cusanus had to say on the matter—and acting the part of a good Pythagorean he traces the idea right back to "*that man*"—makes numbers to be the formal *archai* behind creation and the ordering principle of all reality, visible and invisible, created and uncreated. "Whether I be a Pythagorean or no, I know not. . . . But I thinke the Pythagoreans, which, as thou sayest, do Philosophize all things by numbers, very grave and witty men." This is the Idiot speaking, in Cusanus' book of the same title, and what he goes on to say would have had from Yeats, had he ever encountered the passage, entire agreement; nor should any suggestion of irreverence be read into this collocation of Yeats and the Idiot, since the Idiot is a mask for Nicholas in the same way as the wild old wicked man was for Yeats. The Idiot continues thus: "Nor do I believe that they meant our mathematicall number, which proceeds from our mind, for it is manifest, that cannot be the beginning of anything; they speak symbolically and rationally, of the number which proceeds from the Divine minde, of which mathematicall number is but the image. For as our mind is in relation to that eternall infinite mind; so the number of our mind, to the number of that mind."[3] Before ever that Number, "of which mathematicall number is but the image," was contaminated with space, with time, with creation, it existed in purity and perfection, being the "essential exemplar" to Nicholas and providing the formal principle for the "paradigm" and model of Timaeus, the Forms and Ideas of Plato, the archetypes of Jung, and the symbols of Yeats; "for I think," the latter says in *A Vision*, "as did Swedenborg in his mystical writings, that the forms of geometry can have but a symbolic relation to spaceless reality, *Mundus Intelligibilis*" (pp. 69-70). Of course this is true, and it is perfectly Cusanesque as well as being Jungian, Plotinian, Platonic, and Pythagorean: the realm intermediate between sensibles and universals, between the ceaseless flux and spaceless reality is the province of geometric figures, of "mathematicall numbers," of symbols—in each case, those discovered (not invented) powers which the mind can avail itself of to order chaos, to return for the eternal moment from the disjunct many to the Monad that they were in the beginning. Thus Yeats says, in our time, the same thing of geometry and mathematics as was said by Swedenborg in the eighteenth century, by the Idiot in the fifteenth century, by Saint Augustine in the fifth century, by Plotinus in the third century of our era, and before them by Plato in the fourth century B.C.; it is also the same thing implied, if not definitely stated, by Pythagoras (he first of all) in the sixth century B.C. When, back in the twentieth century, we hear Jung (plumping, as usual, for his favorite number) declare in his essay on "Mandala Symbolism"

3. *The Idiot* . . . etc., Book III, chapter 6; anon. trans. (London: William Leake, 1650), pp. 91-92.

that "the *tetraktys* . . . underlies all existence,"[4] we may be momentarily stunned by the daring, the absoluteness and exclusivity, of his numerology: *all* existence? *only* the *tetraktys*? This carries more than a hint of those mysterious "special mathematical properties" said (by Jung) to reside in the number four; but a moment's reflection will reveal to us that Jung's mathematics are not so very different from those of the Idiot (though this is not, of course, what Albert Oeri meant in his comment about his friend's abilities), and that they are both, Jung and the Idiot alike, displaying a very basic, archaic, and primitive mode of mental functioning in their mathematical reduction of "all existence." Moreover, as Jung was well aware, he had behind him the authority of "*that man*" in his exaltation of the *tetraktys*: "Ten is the very nature of number," Aetius tells us in his discussion of Pythagorean numbers. "All Greeks and all barbarians alike count up to ten, and having reached ten revert again to the unit. And again, Pythagoras maintains, the power of the number ten lies in the number four, the tetrad. . . . And so the Pythagoreans used to invoke the tetrad as their most binding oath: 'Nay, by him that gave to our generation the tetraktys, which contains the fount and root of eternal nature'" (DK 58B15; trans. Raven). This is an oath I doubt not Jung would have taken, for as Pythagoras to his generation, so Jung himself has given "to our generation the tetraktys."

Robert Benchley once remarked, with a certain reflexive logic, that people can be divided into two groups—those who divide people into two groups and those who don't. Pythagoras was undoubtedly the founder, and Pythagoreans of all times have been charter members, of the divider group: everything under the moon (though not beyond it) provides grist for their dualistic dividing mill. The Pythagorean Table of Opposites—putting (among other things) good, light, unity, straight, and male on one side as against bad, dark, plurality, crooked, and female on the other side—represents the most basic gesture of the creature that Jung calls "archaic man" (*CW*, VI, par. 963) in his effort "to bring order into the chaos of appearance" (*CW*, VIII, par. 870). Unity—which in one way of

---

4. *CW*, IX, pt. 1, par. 641. Jung's most thorough reading of number symbolism, commencing (naturally) with Pythagoras and centering (equally naturally) on the *Timaeus*, is to be found in "A Psychological Approach to the Trinity," *CW*, XI, pars. 179–93.

looking at it is pure order, but in another way of regarding it is mere chaos—must first be divided into two, that is, into opposites; and two, logically, must then be divided into four—which explains, incidentally, why Jung has little more than good-natured scorn for the number three or the triad: because, in his eyes (and in his phrase), it is nothing but a "mutilated," "disturbed," "defective" quaternity (*CW*, IX, part 1, par. 430; IX, part 1, par. 646; IX, part 2, par. 351). It is from precisely this Pythagorean passion for order that Jung, in his *Psychological Types*, first divides all humanity into "extraverted" and "introverted" and then redivides all humanity, according to another scheme, into four types, corresponding to the four functions—feeling and thinking, sensation and intuition. At roughly the same time that Jung was dividing all men into two groups and then into four, Yeats was being informed by his Instructors that the whole of human history should be divided into primary and antithetical cones and that, according to another scheme, the psychological types of humanity are all determined by the operation of four—as Jung always insisted, and Yeats agreed, not three or five, but precisely four—faculties: will and mask, body of fate and creative mind. For his primal division Jung took no personal credit (nor did Yeats for his, seeing that it was delivered to him through his wife's automatic writing). "It was the work of the old Pythagoreans," Jung says (*CW*, VI, par. 963), giving the very best and longest of philosophic pedigrees to that natural tendency discovered in his own mind and in the mind of any man who sets about making order out of confusion. This new Pythagorean also (though going under the old name of Basilides) commences his sermons to the clamoring dead by making the first, necessary division which will eventually lead to order and to the intellectual and emotional satisfaction of the congregation of the dead: "We must, therefore, distinguish the qualities of the pleroma," Jung/Basilides says. "The qualities are PAIRS OF OPPOSITES . . ." (*VII Sermones*, p. 11). There follows a Table of Opposites—including Good, Light, and The One on one side, as against Evil, Darkness, and the Many on the other side—which is entirely Pythagorean in composition and intention with, for variety, the odd echo from Heraclitus ("Living and Dead"), from Plato ("Difference and Sameness"), and—though Jung would not have known this—from Yeats ("Time and Space"). "So far as I myself can pass judgment on my own point of view,"

Jung declared, contrasting his approach with what he thought to be the monism of Freud and Adler, "it is not monistic but, if anything, dualistic, being based on the principle of opposites . . ." (*CW*, IV, par. 758). According to Jung's vision, the basic, primal act of the mind—and, in this sense, one of the archetypal acts of the mind (another, or *the* other, archetypal mental act being the reverse of this one: a return from plurality, through opposites, to unity)—is to divide in two and in four and so on until division runs its course and is transformed into its opposite to seek once again a state of undivided wholeness. This inherent intellectual-emotional urge to division and separation is to be accounted for, Jung says, as "a vague instinct for order" which, to achieve its desired goal, employs "the most primitive of all devices, namely counting" (*CW*, X, par. 743).

Whichever way we choose to regard number—whether as that which was in the beginning and that on which the created universe is modelled, or as the means which the mind possesses to give order to the swarm of things it encounters; whether, that is, we think of number as descending from above down to creation or as ascending from below up to a realm of order—in either case it supplies the invisible link (and ultimately the only link, since the connection must be formal and the essence of form is in number: without number there is no form) between above and below and between mind and phenomena. Numbers may be taken metaphysically as *archai* (formal *archai*, however, not material), or they may be taken psychologically as capacities of the mind. Both views bear the Pythagorean imprimatur, and both are granted equal possibility in Jung's statement that number "is the predestined instrument for creating order, or for apprehending an already existing, but still unknown, regular arrangement or 'orderedness'" (*CW*, VIII, par. 870). When Jung goes on to "define number psychologically," giving emphasis to his definition with italics, as "an *archetype of order* which has become conscious," he is doing no more than translating some very ancient ideas into the modern language of analytical psychology, for the Jungian archetype—like a Yeatsian symbol, like a Platonic mathematical figure, like Pythagorean numbers—is a powerful mediator, a great *daimon*, that connects two materially different but formally related *kosmoi*.

The first of the ten pairs of opposites in the original Pythagorean

Table of Opposites consists of Limit and Unlimited (πέρας καὶ ἄπειρον), and the second of Odd and Even (περιττὸν καὶ ἄρτιον), and as Aristotle, who is responsible for preserving the Table for us, suggests, it is from the joining of these two pairs of opposites that number comes and hence that the Pythagorean cosmogony commences: "these thinkers," he says, in a passage that immediately precedes the Table of Opposites, "also consider that number is the principle [ἀρχὴν—the etymological root of Jung's "archetype"] both as matter for things and as forming their modifications and their permanent states, and hold that the elements of number are the even and the odd, and of these the former is unlimited, and the latter limited; and the 1 proceeds from both of these (for it is both even and odd), and number from the 1; and the whole heaven, as has been said, is numbers" (*Metaphysics* A5, 986a15; trans. Ross, in Kirk-Raven, pp. 237-38). The Pythagoreans were without doubt indiscreet in saying that "number is the principle . . . as matter for things," and they suffered sufficiently for their indiscretion at the hands of Aristotle himself; but when they proceed to put "Good" on the same side as "Limit" and "Bad" on the opposite side along with "Unlimited," then they imply a moral and aesthetic judgment that was preeminently Greek and that Aristotle gladly concurred in: "For evil belongs to the unlimited, as the Pythagoreans conjectured, and good to the limited."[5] Greek thinkers generally, and Pythagoreans specifically, maintained that the limitless is evil and that only when quantitative limitation and measure are imposed on the unlimited to give it form is there anything good, ethical, or beautiful there. Hence it is that the Greek spirit of order, of limitation, of form subdues and transforms "All Asiatic vague immensities" in Yeats's poem "The Statues." The triumph, as the first line of the poem makes plain, was a Pythagorean one. In his copy of Burnet's *Early Greek Philosophy* Yeats marked a passage about Pythagorean doctrine that explains what was responsible for the power of the Greek statues in Yeats's poem. "The One or unit," according to Burnet's analysis of Pythagorean numbers, "is the Unlimited once limited; and, as the Unlimited is space, we see that the Pythagoreans, when they spoke of the One, meant a *point*. In the same

---

5. *Nicomachean Ethics*, B5, 1106b29: trans. J. E. Raven, Kirk-Raven, p. 240.

way, the number two means a *line*, three a plane, four and all higher numbers, the series of regular polyhedra."[6] From Limit and Unlimited and from Odd and Even comes the One, from the One comes the series of whole numbers, and from that series of numbers comes the principle of order and proportion which is the essence of form and beauty. Behind an object like a statue of Callimachus (which would be of the order of "four and all higher numbers") was this same progression and regression of Pythagorean numbers, and at the very beginning of that progression was the subjection of the Unlimited to Limit: from the solid statue to the plane figure to the line to the point—from four to three to two to one—and there at the beginning or the end, where the solid statue dissolves into abstraction and pure potential, is the form that was before images, the Idiot's Number that was before "mathematicall" numbers.

> Pythagoras planned it. Why did the people stare?
> His numbers, though they moved or seemed to move
> In marble or in bronze, lacked character.

Numbers do in themselves, being more formal than forms, more archaic than *archai*, lack character: like Jung's archetypes, but even more so, numbers are empty and unfilled, pre-experiential forms and patterns, of quite another order from our confused and painful emotions. In the lines that follow, however, "boys and girls, pale from the imagined love / Of solitary beds," understood the numbers and what they were; understood

> That passion could bring character enough,
> And pressed at midnight in some public place
> Live lips upon a plummet-measured face.

What Pythagoras planned and what the youth, educated by their instincts and their emotions, understand has to do with the necessary joining of form and passion, or Limit and Unlimited. Jung liked to describe an archetype as the self-portrait of an instinct, and that is precisely what the youth find in the archetypal image which is the number-formed statue: a portrait—as it seems a self-portrait—of sexual passion. That passion discovers its necessary

---

6. Burnet, *Early Greek Philosophy*, 1st ed. (London: Adam & Charles Black, 1892), p. 312. What Burnet says here corresponds to the cosmogonic system outlined by the Pythagorean Timaeus in Plato's dialogue.

form in the archetypal image, but ultimately in number. In a passage from *On the Boiler*, much quoted when "The Statues" is in question, Yeats said, "There are moments when I am certain that art must once again accept those Greek proportions which carry into plastic art the Pythagorean numbers, *those faces which are divine because all there is empty and measured*" (*Ex.*, p. 451). Though the italics are mine, the logic is typically Yeatsian and important to remark: *because* of emptiness and measurement, *therefore* the faces are divine. This is divine numerology with a vengeance. If the faces displayed "character," the result not of measurement but of experience, they would be human rather than divine; as it is, coming as near to the formal essence and the abstract proportion as it is possible to come in matter, they show none of the marks of experience or the corruptions of flesh. "But when the Doric studios," Yeats goes on, "sent out those broad-backed marble statues against the multiform, vague, expressive Asiatic sea, they gave to the sexual instinct of Europe its goal, its fixed type." What is that "goal" but a Platonic ideal form in which our passion may find its needful expression? What is the "fixed type" but a realized archetype? In those "empty and measured" faces, the "sexual instinct of Europe," the passion of "boys and girls," has found its own self-portrait and even today continues to imitate that ideal image created by Greek genius so long ago: "In the warm sea of the French and Italian Riviera I can still see it," Yeats remarks.

The living individual need not—or more likely *can*not—be conscious of the relation of instinct to image, for Yeats maintains that it is some greater mathematical mind—the mind of a Scopas or the mind of centuries—that measures the instinct out into its predestined typical mold. Though Maud Gonne's face, Yeats says, "like the face of some Greek statue, showed little thought, her whole body seemed a master-work of long labouring thought, as though a Scopas had measured and calculated, consorted with Egyptian sages, and mathematicians out of Babylon . . ." (*Auto.*, pp. 364-65). This mathematically calculated image, coming from far beyond Maud Gonne's conscious mind—coming, indeed, against her conscious desires, according to Yeats ("she hated her own beauty")—is essentially of that other, supermundane realm of numbers where nothing ever changes, because all is formal and empty, where the idea in its perfection suffers no deterioration though its enfleshed realization must inevitably, as witness Maud Gonne's "whole body," deteriorate in the most gruesome way. In séances, Yeats declares, these unembodied, essential forms—the Idea of Maud Gonne, as it were, quite apart from the physical fact of her—some of which have gone through countless incarnations in the effort to return to their own beauty while others have never suffered embodiment at all, can occasionally be called into images; and when the bodiless forms are thus momentarily evoked, we can know the latter —those never historically embodied—by their inhuman, mathematical regularity: "Sometimes, indeed, there is a strange regularity of feature and we suspect the presence of an image that may never have lived, artificial beauty that may have shown itself in the Greek mysteries" (*Ex.*, p. 53). It is as if one were staring on numbers themselves, staring on the miracle of Pythagorean proportions and harmonies so pure that they have never been struck on the lyre (or on the psaltery, for all of Yeats's experiments), so exact that they have never descended into a statue or a human body. This is the same miracle of numbers, only slightly tainted by being realized (which taint, however, is necessary to make the miracle accessible to us), that "the sexual instinct of Europe" found in Doric statues and that passion-driven boys and girls divined in "a plummet-measured face." When Yeats speaks elsewhere of "statues full of an august formality that implies traditional measurements, a philosophic defence" (*E. & I.*, p. 225), we can observe in the grammatical and logical apposition—"traditional measurements, a philosophic defence"—the belief that where one finds the first, one can be assured of the second, and vice versa. Thus, in "Under Ben Bulben," Yeats declares the philosophic/mathematic source of the artist's strength—"Measurement began our might"—which goes on to accomplish most complex effects, but out of what began?— Limit and Unlimited, Odd and Even, the first four numbers, the *tetraktys* itself, and the decad. Moreover, there is a teleology implicit in the artist's work which forces him to an end that is identical with the source of his strength: the artist's goal is to return the image of mankind, through plummet measurement, rhythmic calculation, harmonic mensuration, to the precarnate perfection of numbers— to return it, that is, to its first principle and its last and to beauty itself. The purpose set before the artist's "secret working mind," Yeats describes as nothing less than "Profane perfection of mankind." An archetype of wholeness or perfection concludes the human quest as also it initiates it.

Sounding Jungian by reason of his use of Jungian terminology (though this is no argument for a knowledge of Jung, since Yeats was independently using the same terms before the turn of the century), Yeats says of the "timeless individuality" or the essential form that determines the single life, "We may fail to express an archetype or alter it by reason, but all done from nature is its unfolding into time" (*Ex.*, p. 368). When he goes on to quote Plotinus to the effect that this form—essence, archetype, or timeless individuality—has "nothing to do with number or part," Yeats momentarily obscures the fact that the several ideas he is bringing together ultimately have their source in Pythagorean teaching; but he obscures only that he may the next instant clarify: "yet it seems that it can at will re-enter number and part and thereby make itself apparent to our minds." There are no mathematical figures in heaven: Yeats was in agreement with Plotinus, with Plato, and with Jung on that. Nonetheless, the point where the divine touches the human is in numbers, in geometric/mathematic form, and so long as spirit has not entered numbers, so long as beauty has not clothed itself in a rhythmic body, we are incapable of perceiving it. Woman's beauty perfects itself in eternity but realizes itself in time, and only the harmony of mathematical figures, joining time to eternity, makes the transit possible.

> A woman's beauty is like a white
> Frail bird, like a white sea-bird alone
> At daybreak after stormy night
> Between two furrows upon the ploughed land:
> A sudden storm, and it was thrown
> Between dark furrows upon the ploughed land.

The sudden storm that throws beauty onto the earth—out of a realm of numbers and into a world of things—represents, of course, incarnation which the Neoplatonists in particular, deriving their vision from the Orphic mysteries by way of Pythagoras and Plato, considered to be a catastrophic and most stormy night for the soul, that frail bird, "a white sea-bird alone." Whence came that beauty and how was it achieved? Yeats asks the question (*Poems*, p. 784) and answers it by the very terms of his asking.

> How many centuries spent
> The sedentary soul
> In toils of measurement
> Beyond eagle or mole,
> Beyond hearing or seeing,
> Or Archimedes' guess,
> To raise into being
> That loveliness?

Beyond Archimedes, no doubt, but not, I think Yeats would agree, "beyond hearing or seeing" of Pythagoras, whose ear was fine enough to pick up the infinitely pure rhythms of the Music of the Spheres, nor beyond Plato and Plotinus, the two mathematicians of the soul who followed most closely after the man-god who, like another Prometheus, gave mortals the gift of numbers. While the measurement and rhythms guessed by Pythagoras are unhumanly pure, beyond our hearing and seeing, yet they determine those rhythms that we can observe and experience: the measurement, the rhythms, of a woman's beauty, of Pythagorean statuary, of the poetry that presents them both.

To readers who may be puzzled or offended by the "arbitrary, harsh, difficult symbolism" of *A Vision*, Yeats offers an accounting that is half apology, half defense. The "hard symbolic bones" of the book deserve all those names and more, he says, and yet, the strange fact is that "such has almost always accompanied expression that unites the sleeping and waking mind" (*Vision*, p. 23). Poetry is one such expression, of course; dreams and visions are another. "One remembers," in this regard, Yeats goes on, "the Pythagorean numbers" as well as all sorts of subsequent systems based on numerological symbolism. Why geometry and mathematics should determine the imagery and the language of this revelatory mental state, where sleeping and waking touch and unite, where consciousness merges with the unconscious and individual mind with a collective mind, Yeats does not offer to explain; he merely points out that it almost always is so. And likewise Jung, who claimed to record the fact while shrugging the metaphysics. Jung could call the *tetraktys* "the basic number" (*CW*, XIII, par. 31) and could declare that four has "special mathematical properties"; and I should imagine that he might have been willing to encourage a little *sub rosa* reverence for the quaternity under the excitement of the therapeutic encounter—but in the *Collected Works* it is only occasionally that Pythagorean metaphysics and number mysticism are allowed to compromise the scientist's decorum. Yet, for all his attempt to be circumspect and proper "in the best modern way" and in keeping with the demands of his science, Jung cannot for long resist the statement that will reveal to the reader his belief in the Pythagorean doctrine that numbers were what was in the beginning—that numbers are the *archai* even of archetypes. Having accepted the mystery of the Pythagorean *tetraktys* as fervently as Christians accept the mystery of the Trinity, Jung never faltered in his adherence. Indeed, what really, deeply vexed Jung about Christian dogma was its numerological unfairness and its arbitrary opting for one mathematical paradox to the exclusion of any other—especially arbitrary when there was a superior paradox available: "Dogma," Jung complained bitterly, "insists that three are one, while denying that four are one" (*CW*, XII, par. 25). How could Christian dogma fail to agree with the axiom Jung quoted so often from his beloved Maria Prophetissa? "One becomes two, two becomes three, and out of the third comes the One as the fourth."[7] That, to the Pythagorean Jung, seemed so obvious, not to say so lovely, that it ought to have been undeniable, yet Christian dogma obstinately denied it for centuries. Jung had a momentary access of affection for the Catholic Church late in his life when the Church defined the dogma of the *assumptio Mariae* and thereby put together a quaternity of its own—Father, Son, Holy Ghost, and Virgin, "the One as the fourth"—which might have been expected to call wandering children such as Jung home from pagan fields. However, though he many times expressed his satisfaction with this new (for which read "old"—i.e., pre-Christian) dogma, and thought it more than long enough in coming, Jung had long since found a sufficient object for his faith.

The quaternity (and in this it is like other numbers, only in Jung's view more so) is a great force conducing to order, and at

---

7. Jung quotes this axiom many times; the present instance occurs at *CW*, IX, pt. 2, par. 237. That Maria Prophetissa was being Pythagorean in her axiom is perhaps obvious, but for extra confirmation cf. Vincent Hopper's remark in *Medieval Number Symbolism* (New York: Columbia University Press, 1938), p. 61: "It is a dominant cabalistic idea, directly Pythagorean in origin, that unity expands to trinity, which is always completed by the quaternary, which ideally returns to the decad or unity again."

times of psychic disorientation, Jung claims, it rises out of the unconscious of mankind into individual consciousness, where it "arranges the material of consciousness into definite patterns" (*CW*, XI, par. 222). While this setting in order occurs in human consciousness, however, it should be observed that the principle of order —the quaternio, the pattern, the mandala, the symbolic expression "that unites the sleeping and waking mind"—comes not from conscious mind but ("unbidden" as Jung always liked to maintain) from somewhere beneath, beyond, outside consciousness: it is a power that is not (at least not ordinarily) at the individual's command but apparently comes, to judge by what Yeats and Jung had to say of it, from Nature herself, from "objective psyche" in Jung's phrase, or from the *Daimon* as Yeats would have it. In the final analysis, order is order whether it manifests itself in the individual or the universe, and it is this formal identity—joining individual soul with world soul, *anima hominis* with *Anima Mundi*—that makes it possible (and since possible therefore necessary) for the smallest unit to comprehend and imitate the largest. The soul, being a number (as the Pythagoreans declared), is capable of understanding, through sympathetic intuition, something of the number-ordered cosmos in which it finds itself. It may have been Pythagoras himself—Aetius says it was, but historians still dispute the matter—who first used this word "cosmos" to signify the world or the universe as a whole. Until Pythagoras, or someone near him in spirit and in time, extended the meaning of the word to include, within the single whole concept, everything in the heavens and beneath them, κόσμος simply meant "order." As Aetius implies, it was on this original linguistic ground, and because he perceived a heretofore unknown, unimagined orderedness in the universe, that Pythagoras gave a new, very important, and lasting significance to the word: "Pythagoras first called the world [τὴν τῶν ὅλων περιοχὴν: the full contents of the whole; the sum of everything] by the name kosmos because of the orderliness of it." Already, before this great stroke of genius, *kosmos* applied to order in all sorts of human affairs: there was considered to be a *kosmos* appropriate to personal conduct, to community ritual, and to the practice of government, for example. So Pythagoras (or whoever) adopted a word and a concept already richly meaningful in the human sphere and projected it (but of course without depriving the word of its original application as well) into a superhuman sphere. Nor was he content to say merely that there was a *kosmos* about the universe: he called it by the *name kosmos* and so identified the universe, taken as a whole, as order, *the* order. Henceforth in Greek philosophy, simply by adopting this linguistic usage, simply by referring to the universe as "order" or "the order," Heraclitus, Empedocles, Plato, or any other thinker implies that he subscribes to the Pythagorean vision of a dominant principle of form and order that everywhere sets the pattern for all affairs human, natural, and divine. In the end (by the time of Plato and later) it is of little consequence whether Pythagoras himself first called the universe by the name *kosmos*: the idea is certainly consonant with everything we know to be Pythagorean. What, however, is more important in the context of the present discussion is to see that the linguistic, philosophic, and scientific idea world-*kosmos* is an archetypal idea—an idea that is the exclusive property of no one because it was not contrived by any one man. It was an accomplishment of Greek philosophy, and it continues to be an achievement of human thought and imagination.

In a manuscript version of stanza VI of "Among School Children," Yeats invoked the principle of *kosmos* in every meaning of the word from its earliest to its latest occurrence in Greek philosophy, and he did so not only on the authority of Pythagoras but in his very name:

> Caesar Augustus that made all the laws
> And the ordering of everything
> Plato that learned geometry and was
> The foremost man at the soul's meaning
> { That golden thighed far famed Pythagoras
> { World Famous, golden thighed Pythagoras
> Who taught the stars of heaven what to sing
> And the musicians how to measure cords . . .

Thomas Parkinson, who preserved this manuscript version, remarks that "the stanza exhibits a reasoned rhetorical order, from the individual soul as seen by Plato to the state as organized by Augustus, to the universe as directed by Pythagoras, a widening circle of meanings."[8] The meanings all commence at the center-point of *kosmos*

---

8. W. B. Yeats, *The Later Poetry* (Berkeley and Los Angeles: University of California Press, 1971), p. 101.

and expand outward to the various spheres—individual, communal, universal—that are ruled and formed by the one principle of *kosmos*. The stanza presents a series of corresponding *kosmoi*, different in scope but identical in form: *kosmos* of soul, *kosmos* of government ("government" is one dictionary meaning of κόσμος), *kosmos* of universe. It is on the assumption of just such corresponding *kosmoi* that Jung, after remarking that "the anima and life itself are meaningless in so far as they offer no interpretation," goes on to say: "Yet they have a nature that can be interpreted, for in all chaos there is a cosmos, in all disorder a secret order, in all caprice a fixed law . . ." (*CW*, IX, part 1, par. 66). The interpretation which "life itself" does not offer depends on the individual and his ability to discover the cosmos *because he participates in it*. According to Pythagorean-Platonic doctrine, which Jung here adapts to psychological use, like understands like, cosmos comprehends cosmos. "Our psyche," Jung says in his autobiography, "is set up in accord with the structure of the universe, and what happens in the macrocosm likewise happens in the infinitesimal and most subjective reaches of the psyche" (*Memories*, p. 335/309). In the history of Greek philosophy, κόσμος was drawn from the human realm, projected onto the heavens, then returned to the human realm again but now with all the overtones of universality and divinity clinging to it. The history of the word is like the alchemical transit of Mercurius—from below to above and back to below so that the power of the above may be joined to the below "that the miracle of the one thing may be accomplished."[9] It is very much "as above so below," macrocosm and microcosm. When Yeats says (in the 1925 edition of *A Vision*, p. 154) that Virgil's prophecy of the birth of a Messiah in his Fourth Eclogue was not "an act of individual genius" but was instead "united to something more profound and mysterious, to an apprehension of a mathematical world order," he is declaring his faith that one microcosm at least—Virgil—because he participated in the "mathematical world order" (which is as precise a translation of Pythagorean *kosmos* as one could wish), was capable of discovering the cosmos behind chaos. Virgil's prophecy was not a miracle, or it

---

9. Cf. Jung, *CW*, XIV, par. 288: ". . . the purpose of the ascent and descent is to unite the powers of Above and Below . . . in the opus there is an ascent followed by a descent . . ."; and again, *CW*, XII, par. 175: "This is in keeping with the axiom from 'Tabula smaragdina': 'What is below is like what is above that the miracle of the one thing may be accomplished.'"

was a miracle only in the sense that the universe and its order are miraculous, for miracle is to be defined as an occurrence outside the natural order, and Virgil, rather than going outside that order, put himself to read it correctly from within.

Even in discussing something as remote from miracle as the Swiss character, Jung returned to the anciently proclaimed truth, thanking Hermes Trismegistus for it, who could have thanked Plato, who certainly did thank Pythagoras: "Above and below have always been brothers, as we learn from the wise saying in the *Tabula smaragdina*: 'Heaven above, heaven below'" (*CW*, X, par. 912). Yeats quoted the Hermetic tag almost as often as Jung (not quite as often, but only because he wrote far fewer words), and it was on the assurance that things above are as things below that he wrote in his Journal, "Every symbol is an invocation which produces its equivalent expression in all worlds" (*Memoirs*, p. 166). If "all worlds" are *kosmoi*, then the symbol, once uttered, will set each of them vibrating at the same frequency which is its own specific frequency, because the symbol shares being with all the hierarchic worlds and is ordered by the same *kosmos* as they are. Jung, writing of "an enigmatic higher world and the ordinary human world" makes the same point and in so doing emphasizes the mathematical basis of *kosmos* and the *kosmoi*. Numbers, he declares, "do not only count and measure, and are not merely quantitative; they also make qualitative statements and are therefore a mysterious something midway between myth and reality. . . . [T]he opposition between the human world and the higher world is not absolute. . . . Between them stands the great mediator, Number, whose reality is valid in both worlds, as an archetype in its very essence. . . . Number . . . belongs to both worlds, the real and the imaginary; it is visible as well as invisible, quantitative as well as qualitative" (*CW*, X, pars. 777-78). I am not certain that I understand what Jung means in saying that numbers "make qualitative statements"; but neither am I certain what Pythagoreans meant when they said that the number of justice was 4 (or, according to others, 3, 5, 8, or 9); the number of marriage, 5 (or 3 or 10); the number of opportunity, 7; and the number of man, 250. That they meant much the same thing, however, of this I am confident.

It was probably because his mathematics shared the same state of non-being with his Greek that Yeats did not offer to reveal the mathematical formula that could express the movement of mind. The mere fact that he hadn't the mathematics necessary to write out the formula, however, in no way diminished Yeats's belief that there was such a formula—on the contrary, it very likely increased his belief. "The mind," he wrote in a note to *Michael Robartes and the Dancer*, "whether expressed in history or in the individual life, has a precise movement, which can be quickened or slackened but cannot be fundamentally altered, and this movement can be expressed by a mathematical form" (*Poems*, p. 823). Had he desired to set about translating his "mathematical form" into an equation, Yeats might well have availed himself of the very helpful discovery of the Pythagoreans that, as the number of justice is 4 and of man 250, so the number of mind is 1. Hence, however complex the left-hand side of his equation might be, the right-hand side could be put down as unity—M (for mind), νοῦς, a curve most subtle and complex but (Yeats thought) mathematically formulable, capable of being plotted and traced on a graph. If we can taken the right-hand side for Parmenidean monism, then the left-hand side must still accommodate and comprehend such diverse movements as the simultaneous opposites and continuous circular flow of Heraclitus, the alternating temporal reversals and quaternal separation/unification of Empedocles, the memories of past lives, present spiritual yearnings, and promises of future divinity of Pythagoras—all summing up to 1. Yeats, as I say, never attempted the formula (except in *A Vision*, where, though the verbal expression is complicated enough, the mathematical formulae are vastly simplified from any reality), nor have other men, better mathematicians than Yeats, such as Nicholas of Cusa, who would nevertheless have been sympathetic to the idea of a Heraclitean dualism resolved by mathematic equality in a Parmenidean monism. If a formula were ever worked out, then it would become binding for that particular mind because it would be the precise expression of that mind's essence. "All living mind," Yeats continues, after a few remarks on the Judwalis and their mathematical cunning, "has likewise a fundamental mathematical movement, . . . and when you have found this movement and calculated its relations, you can foretell the entire future of that mind." This would be no less than to determine and to state the *kosmos* of the mind, "whether expressed in history or in the individual life," and I would repeat that Yeats's failure to do so is less important than his faith in the possibility. Nor was Yeats the only man of his time to retain faith in the formulaic possibility: Jung's *Collected Works* represent the attempt to spell out psychological terms and to plot a generalized curve for all the various, number-based, archetypal movements of the human psyche—"Pairs of Opposites," *enantiodromia, complexio oppositorum*, quaternities, circular *uroboroi*; and on the other side of the equation, the *unio mystica* of the self.

It was just such an ideal as this one—manifold complexity balanced, across the equal sign, with oneness; simultaneous and alternating antinomies and quarrelling quaternal faculties contained and expressed as a single being—that Yeats pursued his life long under the name "Unity of Being." He sought, as it were, the formula or the equation that should represent the Pythagorean harmony of his own self. It requires a small effort of the imagination to realize that the Yeats who wrote in 1921 of the mathematical movement of all living mind and of the mathematical form harmonizing all life was the same Yeats who, fifteen years earlier, had written, "Art bids us touch and taste and hear and see the world, and shrinks from what Blake calls mathematic form, from every abstract thing, from all that is not a fountain jetting from the entire hopes, memories, and sensations of the body" (*E. & I.*, pp. 292-93). Yeats, however, answered his own objections to "mathematic form" with his doctrine of Unity of Being, which he says he found in Dante (though no one else has been able to find it there), who, according to Yeats, used that term "when he compared beauty in the *Convito* to a perfectly proportioned human body" (*Auto.*, p. 190). The body itself, when perfectly proportioned (the traditional belief that Christ was the perfect height, exactly six feet tall, no more, no less, appealed greatly to Yeats's imagination), with its "entire hopes, memories, and sensations" forming a unity, must be supposed to have been modelled on "mathematic form." That Unity of Being is more nearly a Pythagorean than a Dantean doctrine is more clearly revealed in the metaphor chosen by J. B. Yeats than in the one adopted by his son: "My father, from whom I had learned the term, preferred a comparison to a musical instrument so strung that if we touch a string all the strings murmur faintly" (ibid.). This is perfect correspondence, sympathy, Pythagorean *harmonia*. Yeats *fils* makes the philosophic provenance of the idea yet more obvious when he says, in *A Vision*, that "the human norm, discovered from the measurement of ancient statues, was God's first handiwork, that 'perfectly proportioned human body' which had seemed to Dante Unity of Being symbolised" (p. 291). The syntax here is as carefully considered, as adroit and as teasing, as the notion Yeats puts it to express. The perfectly proportioned human body, which was God's first handiwork, is the human norm, a symbol of the human ideal. But where do we now discover that norm, that representation of the Idea—in the human body? Not at all, for the human bodies around us are not God's first handiwork and are in general far from perfectly proportioned. We discover the norm rather in the measurement of ancient statues, where all is empty, purely formal, nothing but moving numbers and mathematic form. "Pythagoras planned it." Of course he did, and the statue, like J. B. Yeats's perfectly attuned musical instrument, is at least one stage nearer the formal purity of numbers than is the human body with its "complexities of mire or blood." Little wonder that Yeats, in an early version of "The Statues," concluded the poem with an imploring cry: "Come back with all your Pythagorean numbers."

With the considerable assistance of Florence Farr and Arnold Dolmetsch, as he tells us in "Speaking to the Psaltery," Yeats sought to avail himself, for the effective performance of his poetry, of those same rhythmic properties—intervals, proportions, ratios— discovered by Pythagoras as he fingered upon a fiddlestick or strings and thereafter transposed from the scale of the microcosm to the scale of the macrocosm. Human music is an imitation of divine music, because both are determined by the same *harmonia*, and the human soul is itself an *harmonia*—a numerical/musical attunement —in the same way as the world soul is. According to Pythagorean doctrine, "the essence of harmony lies, not in the sound, but in the numerical proportions";[10] hence the Pythagorean numbers, whose return Yeats so ardently desired, were responsible for the *harmonia*

10. F. M. Cornford, "The Harmony of the Spheres," in *The Unwritten Philosophy and Other Essays* (Cambridge, England: Cambridge University Press, 1967), p. 21. Elsewhere (*Plato's Cosmology*, p. 158), Cornford writes, "'Ἁρμονία is not the 'harmony' of simultaneous concordant sounds (συμφωνία), but strictly the adjustment of notes in the concordant ratios of the scale." Alister Cameron makes the same point about the intimate relation of number and harmony in an interesting passage in *The Pythagorean Background of the Theory of Recollection* (p. 26): "Perhaps the two most significant words in Pythagorean vocabulary were ἀριθμός [number] and ἁρμονία [harmony]. . . . Now the fact that the two words appears to be descended from a single root αρ (seen also in ἀραρίσκω [to join, fasten, fit together]) seems to me to indicate that somewhere in the unrecorded past, the Number religion, which dealt in concepts of harmony or attunement, made itself felt in Greek lands."

that was the soul's health and the world's *kosmos*. When Diogenes Laertius gives us the twofold information that Pythagoras "also discovered the numerical relation of sounds on a single string: he also studied medicine," he suggests by his grammatical-cum-logical correlation between sounds on a single string and the study of medicine what was indeed the case: that Pythagoras practised a double medicine, physical and spiritual. He was a physician both of the body and of the soul, employing drugs and simples to effect the one cure, music and poetry to effect the other. "It is also said," according to Iamblichus, "that of the sciences which the Pythagoreans honored, music, medicine and divination, were not among the least" (*Life*, p. 87). Indeed they were not among the least but among the greatest and were not three disparate, unrelated sciences thrown together in the illogic of a Thomas Taylor-translated Iamblichean sentence but essentially the one same art-science displaying three faces but set to reading identical cosmic harmonies. Behind the physiotherapy and psychotherapy of Pythagoras there lay a single belief which is shared by all animists, all homeopathists, and probably by all doctors (certainly by Jung) for whom the practise of medicine involves theory as well as technique: the belief that the universe is in all its parts a living being composed, as in the human instance, of physical body and subtly interwoven soul. The goal of either variety of medicine is to establish, in body or in soul, a *harmonia*, a proportionate relationship: the physiotherapist harmonizes elements appropriate to body (i.e., physical, chemical elements); the psychotherapist harmonizes elements appropriate to soul (i.e., numbers). Music—or poetry or philosophy—because its harmonies are numeric and nonphysical, is the obvious instrument for the psychotherapist. Laurens van der Post reports Jung as saying, "I should have been a mathematician and a physician and God knows what else besides, perhaps even a musician, to do my task properly."[11] And Yeats, though he did not himself attempt physical cures, never doubted the powers of poetry to introduce into the soul the same *kosmos* that Pythagorean music represented and produced as it drew its rhythms from microcosm and macrocosm. In the Esoteric Section of the Golden Dawn, Yeats says he learned that "every organ of the body had its correspondence in the heavens, and the seven principles which made the human soul and body correspond to the seven colours and the planets

---

11. *Jung and the Story of Our Time* (New York: Pantheon, 1975), pp. 244–45.

and the notes of the musical scale" (*Memoirs*, p. 23). The last item mentioned by Yeats as corresponding to the principles of soul and body—"notes of the musical scale"—reveals beyond question the source for this teaching. Adherence to the doctrine did not make a medical practitioner of Yeats, but it did make him want to check out the stars and the disposition of the heavenly order before he had his tonsils out (*Letters*, pp. 663-64), and it was undoubtedly some such belief that caused him to submit to the Steinach operation and to consider it a great success. It is the same essentially Pythagorean doctrine of correspondence that Jung has in mind when he refers to "the classical idea of the *sympathy of all things*" (*CW*, VIII, par. 924; Jung's italics) and when he goes on to quote from the great ancestor of medicine, Hippocrates: ' "There is one common flow, one common breathing, all things are in sympathy. The whole organism and each one of its parts are working in conjunction for the same purpose . . . the great principle extends to the extremest part, and from the extremest part it returns to the great principle, to the one nature, being and not being." As Jung goes on to comment of this doctrine of analogy, correspondence, and imitative harmony: "The universal principle is found even in the smallest particle, which therefore corresponds to the whole" (*CW*, VIII, par. 924). Believing as he did that the principle of *kosmos* obtained all up and down the hierarchy of creation, Pythagoras could scarcely fail to affirm the kinship of all living things—an idea in which Yeats and Jung enthusiastically acquiesced. By both of them we are told of all sorts of creatures—horses, dogs, martins, weaverbirds, "all warm-blooded animals who have souls like ourselves"[12]—living in closer proximity than man does to the instinctive bases of life but with whom he nevertheless shares those same life instincts. Plants also, Jung thought, are a part of the kinship, and "trees in particular were mysterious and seemed to me direct embodiments of the incomprehensible meaning of life" (*Memories*, pp. 67-68/75). It is hardly necessary to point out Yeats's feeling about trees—the trees in the

12. Jung, *Memories*, p. 67/74. Cf. *CW*, VII, par. 109: "There is nothing to prevent us from assuming that certain archetypes exist even in animals, that they are grounded in the peculiarities of the living organism itself and are therefore direct expressions of life whose nature cannot be further explained." Yeats believed this about martins—that they build their elaborate nests guided by archetypes ("Anima Mundi," p. 359)—and Jung maintained exactly the same of weaverbirds (see, e.g., *Letters*, I, 525-26 and *CW*, VIII, par. 435; also Chapter 8 below).

Seven Woods, for example—that they were great living presences; but it is perhaps less well known that he agreed with Jung about warm-blooded animals and about (Yeats's expression of a very common Jungian idea) "men who live primitive lives where instinct does the work of reason" (*Ex.*, p. 17) and about men who, through consciousness and civilization, have partly lost touch with the instinctive life-ties that bind all of nature in a whole: they all seemed, to Yeats as to Jung, bound in a universal kinship, different embodiments of the same divine energy. I would not say that this idea is uniquely Pythagorean. Of course it is not: it is the heart of animistic belief wherever and whenever that is found. What I would say, however, is that the Pythagoreans (whether founder or followers makes little difference) gave classic expression to an archetypal idea, and—distinguishing themselves from some others who adhere to animism—they offered a philosophic, scientific rationale for it. In a passage that, were it not so typically Jungian, could be called Pythagorean, Jung says, "This is our immortality, the link through which man feels inextinguishably one with the continuity of all life. The life of the psyche is the life of mankind. Welling up from the depths of the unconscious, its springs gush forth from the root of the whole human race, since the individual is, biologically speaking, only a twig broken off from the mother and transplanted" (*CW*, V, par. 296). There is no evidence that Jung took this notion of the kinship of all living things directly from the Pythagoreans—on the contrary, there is plenty of evidence that he did not. But the idea as we find it in Pythagoras is simpler, clearer, and neater than in Jung—and more primitive but more persuasive also, since it comes at just that point in the evolution of human thought (experienced by each of us individually as well) where religion takes on the added dimension of philosophy and animism acquires a scientific *logos*.

Neither could it be said that the periodic recurrence of events was an idea belonging only to Pythagoreans or that they were solely responsible for working it out; but their expression of the idea was as clear and as sharp as any—and a good deal more striking and more extreme than most, which is just what we want in the statement of a primal idea. "If one were to believe the Pythagoreans," according to Eudemus, "that the same individual things will recur, then I shall be talking to you again sitting as you are now, with this pointer in my hand, and everything else will be just as it is now, and it is reasonable to suppose that the time then is the same as now" (trans. Raven). Neither Yeats nor Jung was averse to the striking presentation of an idea; neither of them backed off from an idea merely because it was extreme; and both of them held firmly to the belief that history moves in recurrent cycles; but neither of them ever went quite so far as the Pythagoreans or captured the imagination with quite such a bold image as this one adopted by Eudemus from the Pythagoreans. Yeats flirted a good deal with exact recurrence (the notion of the Great Year, which so fascinated him, carries some overtones of exact recurrence)—but he ordinarily did so only to acknowledge the next moment that no one, not even himself with the Instructors' assistance, could see indisputably precise outlines in the fabulous, formless darkness of the future. Yeats preferred to speak in the language of Virgil's Fourth Eclogue ("A second Tiphys shall then arise, and a second Argo to carry chosen heroes; a second warfare, too, shall there be, and again shall a great Achilles be sent to Troy") which, though it seems to envision precise repetition, Yeats interpreted—and no doubt accurately—in a more general and symbolic manner. Every individual lives out the general pattern of humankind—but he does not live detail for detail the same life he once lived before.

> Another Troy must rise and set,
> Another lineage feed the crow,
> Another Argo's painted prow
> Drive to a flashier bauble yet.
>
> *(Poems, p. 437)*

It is another Troy, another lineage, another Argo, not the same ones, and if the bauble is to be flashier than before, it must, though fashioned to the same pattern, be different from the earlier one. Jung said (and so often that many readers tire of hearing it) that we tread the same paths, in the same direction and in the same manner, as our ancestors did, but he never maintained that any man is literally his own ancestor. It would have meant more determination than Yeats or Jung could ever be comfortable with to subscribe to the Pythagorean doctrine *au pied de la lettre.*

Much the same must be said of the archetypal, universal notion of metempsychosis, which was for the Pythagoreans a literal and assured fact—not a plausible explanation, as Yeats once called it, nor an hypothesis, as Jung preferred to consider it, but a literal and unquestioned, unquestionable fact of life. How, after all, could it be otherwise than literal and assured when the Master himself remembered the details of a quaternity of previous lives? For archaic man —a religious not a philosophical creature, untroubled by any overlay of complexly developed thought but therefore the more firmly possessed of the first and basic, as it were instinctual, beliefs of the human spirit—for him reincarnation was an obvious truth and one universally believed. Or at least so Yeats declared, and Jung agreed: "All ancient nations believed in the re-birth of the soul," Yeats says, then adds the enigmatic rider, "and had probably empirical evidence. . ." (*Ex.*, p. 396). Empirical evidence or not (Pythagoras' memory, which was more than sufficient for his own people, might not convince everyone), a belief in reincarnation, as Yeats says, was virtually universal, yet of independent and spontaneous occurrence, among ancient peoples. Yeats and Jung, however, in spite of the fact that their thoughts were quickened by the buried presence in them of archaic man, were not, in the full complexity of their thought and their being, archaic men. Hence Yeats adopts a walking-on-eggs language whenever he approaches the subject of reincarnation: he tends to lapse into the subjunctive, for example, and he wraps the frailty of his belief in protective "if" clauses or attributes it (as above) to other men in other times and other lands. Jung was about equally adroit with the same sort of language on this same subject. They believed alright—but not altogether nor all the time; and the language they use so skillfully (or evasively) suggests that for Yeats and Jung reincarnation was more a metaphoric and symbolic truth than a literal truth, more a psychological phenomenon than a metaphysical one.

The Yeats of the prose, and the man of daily life expressed in the prose (excepting *A Vision*, which is hardly your ordinary prose document), is noticeably more cautious about declaring for reincarnation than the Yeats of the poems and plays, who is a man of the ages and the depths rather than of the passing day. The mind of the prose is closer to the surface and ruled by the scientific scepticism of consciousness; the mind of the poetry, on the other hand, goes deeper, chooses to affirm rather than question, and in its deeper descent comes across that Pythagoras who, it may be, remains in the shadowy darkness at the bottom of every man's mind as he is also at the bottom and the beginning of the philosophic mind of mankind. Reincarnation is a doctrine that was believed everywhere in former times; and perhaps every man still keeps a private little corner of his mind where he can—or where he must—entertain the notion though he would not swear to it absolutely in an experimental laboratory nor bring it out often into the brutal light of dogmatic controversy. In the darkness where archetypal images fresh images beget, there he stays, the individual's own private Pythagoras. From the surface, however, the best we can get, so many centuries after Pythagoras, is hypothesis. "*If* men are born many times . . ." —that is not nearly strong enough for a genuine Pythagorean, not even when Yeats goes on to give it his fainthearted support by adding, "as I think" (*Ex.*, p. 306). Neither was the purely hypothetical language addressed to his father (*Letters*, p. 653) anything like adequate: "If you accept metempsychosis. . . ." "If . . . if"—the Orphic, Eleusinian, Pythagorean mysteries would hardly be revealed to a man of such tepid faith as that. But

> Many times man lives and dies
> Between his two eternities,
> That of race and that of soul,
> And ancient Ireland knew it all.
>
> (*Poems*, p. 637)

This, for a Pythagorean, is more like it: the deep mind speaking without any of the hesitations, qualifications, and scepticism of ephemeral consciousness. Ancient Ireland knew it all because she was Druid-educated; and were not the Druids, according to one tradition, initiated into the mysteries by Pythagoras himself? "We Irish," as Yeats says in "The Statues," were "born into that ancient sect" of Pythagoreanism and so believed in the soul's immortality and its reincarnation and believed that *anima hominis* and *Anima Mundi* are but the temporal and the eternal reflections one of the other.

> Though grave-diggers' toil is long,
> Sharp their spades, their muscles strong,
> They but thrust their buried men
> Back in the human mind again.

This is the great Pythagoras rising out of the unconscious—heroic, stark, statuesque, as masterful as the Christ in Piero della Francesca's "Resurrection"—to address the Irish through the lips of a latter-day Druid.

It was the other, the prose Yeats who recorded a watery, sceptical, and scientific attitude in the draft of his autobiography apropos of George Russell's comforting words to Maud Gonne about reincarnation: "I could see that Maud Gonne was deeply impressed, and I quieted my more sceptical intelligence, as I have so often done in her presence. I remember a pang of conscience. Ought I not to say, 'The whole doctrine of the reincarnation of the soul is hypothetical. It is the most plausible of the explanations of the world, but can we say more than that?' or some like sentence?" (*Memoirs*, p. 48). This is very much the attitude one ordinarily finds in Jung: that reincarnation is a hypothetical, unprovable (therefore untenable by the scientist) explanation for ascertainable psychic facts—specifically, an explanation for the autochthonous occurrence of archetypal images throughout the history of the psyche both individual and cultural; those facts, Jung would argue, as does Yeats, do not depend on the explanation, and though this may seem to one observer the "most plausible," it remains an hypothesis. "The contents of the unconscious," Jung wrote to a correspondent in 1936, "could be explained by reincarnation if we knew that there is reincarnation" (*Letters*, I, 209). However, as he goes on to say, "These hypotheses are at present articles of faith," and so the scientist (*qua* scientist) must leave them to the poet. One of the ascertainable psychic facts for which reincarnation is a plausible explanation is that men have believed, do believe, and will persist in believing in reincarnation, openly or secretly, and with just that degree of intensity and literalness permitted by the sophistication and nonpoetic spirit of their minds. That is to say, the idea of reincarnation is archetypal. Thus we are put in the odd and confusing, not to say circular, situation of explaining—in a hypothetical manner, to be sure—the existence of archetypes by the hypothesis of an archetype: reincarnation, an archetypal idea, could account for the existence of archetypal ideas. Archetypes, Jung declared, keeping up with the game and explaining the explanation by an archetype to account for the archetypes, "evidently live and function in the deeper layers of the unconscious, especially in that phylogenetic substratum which I have called the collective unconscious. This localization explains a good deal of their strangeness: they bring into our ephemeral consciousness an unknown psychic life belonging to a remote past. It is the mind of our unknown ancestors, their way of thinking and feeling, their way of experiencing life and the world, gods and men. The existence of these archaic strata is presumably the source of man's belief in reincarnations and in memories of 'previous existences' " (*CW*, IX, part 1, par. 518). Though Yeats, in a prose mood and a sceptical moment, would have understood this and perhaps agreed with it (he says much the same sort of thing in *Per Amica Silentia Lunae*), Jung's notion is too complex, too sophisticated, and too clever by half for any true Pythagorean. Nor is it very kind of Jung to put inverted commas around previous existences: that is no more than to add insult where injury has already been done. Pythagoras, however, can always take care of himself, and in old age Jung was forced to relent in his sophistication and let the Old Pythagoras in him (of whom, significantly, Jung had caught a glimpse in a dream) have a look out and say a word or two to the public. "The idea of rebirth is inseparable from that of karma," Jung says in his autobiography. "The crucial question is whether a man's karma is personal or not" (*Memories*, p. 317/293). In the psychologizing passage quoted earlier, Jung assumed, of course, that a man's karma is not personal; in the autobiography he shows himself much less certain. "Recently . . . I observed in myself a series of dreams which would seem to describe the process of reincarnation in a deceased person of my acquaintance. . . . I must confess . . . that after this experience I view the problem of reincarnation with somewhat different eyes . . ." (ibid., p. 319/295). In a passage that is strikingly Yeatsian in thought, Jung says, "I could well imagine that I might have lived in former centuries and there encountered questions I was not yet able to answer; that I had to be born again because I had not fulfilled the task that was given to me. When I die, my deeds will follow along with me—that is how I imagine it" (ibid., p. 318/294). The only thing that prevents Jung from being an out and out Pythagorean here—as the Pythagoreans themselves might argue—is the weakness of his memory: if he had a strong enough memory (the gift of the gods to Pythagoras) and could recall his "previous existences" as Æthalides, Hermotimus, Pythagoras, and any others (Paracelsus and Goethe perhaps?), then he would believe in reincarnation as fervently as he always believed in the numinous quaternity.

Heraclitus' witty gibe at Pythagoras and others ("The learning of many things does not teach intelligence; if so it would have taught

Hesiod and Pythagoras, and again Xenophanes and Hecataeus" [Fr. 40]) tells us most about Heraclitus himself and about what he took to be intelligence and the proper study of mankind; but it also tells us something about Pythagoras—that he was not a thinker of finicky restrictiveness or dry-as-dust nicety about where the limits of human enquiry ought to be set. Indeed, Pythagoras went in one direction back to the very archaic foundations of the universe and of human knowledge, and in the other direction he stormed heaven itself with the power of number. His glorious discovery—the same lesson in the beginning and in the end, at the bottom and at the top—was that as God moves in numbers his wonders to perform, so all our return—our song, our dance, our progress on the Great Wheel—will be, must be, in number also. Pythagoras alone in his time, according to Iamblichus, could hear the music of the spheres and yet not have his hearing utterly burned out by the superhuman purity of the music. Consequently he set about teaching other men, who were incapable of looking on "the first and genuine archetypes of things," in images and tunes their senses could bear: "Just, indeed, as to those who are incapable of looking intently at the sun, through the transcendent splendor of his rays, we contrive to exhibit the eclipses of that luminary, either in the profundity of still water, or through melted pitch, or through some darkly-splendid mirror; sparing the imbecility of their eyes, and devising a method of representing a certain repercussive light, though less intense than its archetype, to those who are delighted with a thing of this kind" (*Life*, pp. 34–35). Jung and Yeats also offered themselves to the weak-eyed and incapable as darkly-splendid mirrors of the same "first and genuine archetypes of things," the same harmonies, the same *kosmoi*, the same mathematics as Pythagoras. If they were "less intense than [their] archetype"—less intense than Pythagoras himself—they were so only because a different age produces and demands a different image, else it will not understand. Of necessity they were more complex, less archaic, less intense than the primal Pythagoras, but the mysteries they communicated were nonetheless Pythagorean in their essence.

CHAPTER III

Logos and the Sensible Flux

Heraclitus died without philosophic issue. "Unfortunately," G. S. Kirk tells us in a rather melancholy note at the end of his study of the cosmic fragments, "Heraclitus had no direct followers of note."[1] It would doubtless be less than consoling to the childless and discipleless but supremely proud Ephesian Master to know the extent to which, on the other hand, his *in*direct progeny have proliferated, for his indirect followers, from Plato to the present moment, are hardly inferior in number to *hoi polloi*, "the many" whom Heraclitus so cordially despised. For the most part, however, those secondary and tertiary disciples have followed at a considerable distance, refusing Heraclitus' absoluteness and his intransigence, and offering to their great ancestor an allegiance very much less than complete. "Subsequent thinkers," Kirk says, "were diverted by the Parmenidean fallacy (the ultimate solution of which was, however, of the utmost importance for the progress of philosophy) . . ."; such offspring as

1. *Heraclitus: The Cosmic Fragments* (Cambridge: Cambridge University Press, 1970), p. 404.

these—men of little faith, diverted by fallacy and blind to the already-proclaimed truth—would perhaps not have surprised Heraclitus (had he not already declared that "men always prove to be uncomprehending of the Logos which is as I describe it"?), but neither would they have particularly pleased him. If his philosophic paternity had to be by way of Parmenides, with a Socratic-Platonic midwife attending, then Heraclitus would likely have been reluctant to acknowledge any responsibility for the child—or any culpability in "the progress of philosophy." Like Pythagoras, Heraclitus stated four or five great primal, archetypal, and one-sided truths—truths which were intertwined and interwoven into a single and comprehensive if extreme vision, that vision that we call Heraclitean—and it was only thinkers of a later time, of a more sophisticated awareness, and of a more subdued temperament who found it necessary to smooth out Heraclitus' archaic angularity, to tone down his passionate utterance, and to dim his primal brilliance by joining Heraclitus' truths to other, equally one-sided truths and by explaining his "Sibylline frenzy" in rationalistic language.

Not everyone, however. Although Plato had to sauce Heraclitus with Parmenides before he could swallow either, and although Plato's solution has commended itself to the vast majority of philosophers since his time, there is yet one thinker (albeit not always honored with the name of "philosopher") who shows no fear of Heraclitus' extreme position—indeed he seems rather to favor it *because* it is extreme—and who displays a distinct affinity for the dark manner as well as the paradoxical matter of Heraclitus. It is, of course, W. B. Yeats who is strong enough thus to take his Heraclitus neat. In particular, Yeats never (and this is the greatest service he, as a disciple, could render to Heraclitus as his master) translates or inflates the poetry of Heraclitus' cryptic brevity into the prose of philosophic discourse. If anything, Yeats deepens the poetry and makes it yet more itself by concentrating the mystery and intensifying the Sibylline frenzy. G. S. Kirk, having noted Heraclitus' lack of direct followers, says that "doubtless this was partly due to his cryptic style of utterance," and he may be right; but for a follower of a much later age, it is precisely this cryptic manner that keeps the fragments alive and ever new to the inquiring mind: in twenty-five centuries their meaning has not been exhausted, or even dimmed really, by the exercise of analytical and discursive reasoning, nor will it be exhausted in twenty-five more centuries. Human intelligence has been put to the test to understand Heraclitus—stretching itself, expanding into new reaches and discovering unknown strengths of its own: understanding him, it has understood itself. Human intelligence does this, however—and Yeats is our best example—not by bringing Heraclitus to the rational surface but by descending with him into the paradoxical, a-rational, and inexhaustible depths. Consider this "prose" passage—pure Heraclitus in style as in thought—from *On the Boiler*: ". . . and this something else must be the other side of the penny—for Heraclitus was right. Opposites are everywhere face to face, dying each other's life, living each other's death. When a man loves a girl it should be because her face and character offer what he lacks, the more profound his nature the more should he realise his lack and the greater be the difference. It is as though he wanted to take his own death into his arms and beget a stronger life upon that death" (*On the Boiler*, p. 22; *Ex.*, p. 430). I say that this last sentence of Yeats's is as beautifully cryptic as anything in Heraclitus—it captures the style perfectly, almost as if Yeats had discovered a hitherto lost fragment—and it can tease us out of thought as effectively as any of the attested fragments of the Master. Though Heraclitus had no direct followers in his own time, I imagine that he would not have been displeased with his latter-day Irish descendant.

About Jung I am not so sure. I suspect that there might have been just a bit too much of the Swiss burgher about him to agree with Heraclitus' aristocratic tastes, and I am sure that Jung's tendency to psychologize at such inordinate length—his practice of explaining the inexplicable in five hundred more or less turgid pages and untangling the paradoxical in another five hundred—not to mention his polymath perversity (e.g., the footnotes and appendix to the *Mysterium Coniunctionis*), would have met with cool disdain from the man who first brought to perfection an expression that was poetic, paradoxical, brief, and brilliant and who assaulted Hesiod and Pythagoras, Xenophanes and Hecataeus for just this Jungian variety of misguided polymathy. Be that as it may, however, Jung's *Collected Works* are shot through with ideas for which Heraclitus is the primitive and archetypal spokesman, their first begetter (so far as we can see), and their stoutest champion. Jung may psychologize

Heraclitus' insights, he may occasionally misconstrue them, he may once or twice credit Heraclitus with the ideas of others and fail to credit him with his own—but that the real Heraclitus—real in the history of thought, much more real in the functioning of the human psyche—is a powerful and pervasive presence in Jung is undeniable. Of all the Pre-Socratics, there is no question, I think, but that Heraclitus was the favorite of both Yeats and Jung.[2]

Because he was speaking from the deepest reaches of the human mind, Heraclitus' fragments have about them (as commentators such as Cornford and Guthrie—and also Nietzsche—have noted[3]) a quality of inspired utterance, of prophetic revelation, of poetry and of religion. Jung, a psychologist and not a poet, saw these things fitfully and in part; Yeats, a great poet if only an amateur psychologist, saw them steadily and saw them whole—as we can observe in the cry of the Greek in *The Resurrection* when he realizes that a heart beats in the breast of the Christ whom he had supposed but a phantom: "O Athens, Alexandria, Rome, something has come to destroy you. The heart of a phantom is beating. Man has begun to die. Your words are clear at last, O Heraclitus. God and man die each other's life, live each other's death." The fragment of Heraclitus here half-quoted, half-paraphrased prophesies to all nations and to all ages—more perhaps to Yeats than to anyone else—because it is a message, shrouded in appropriate mystery, from the unconscious to the conscious mind of those nations and ages, offering itself for differing interpretation according to the differing consciousness of nation and age. Yeats's entire play, which culminates in the Greek's ecstatic cry, is virtually designed as a dramatic interpretation of the meaning of Heraclitus' fragment to the consciousness of the twentieth century by way of dramatization of events from the first century.

2. In his copy of Hermann Diels's *Fragmente der Vorsokratiker*, Jung made very frequent marginal marks against the fragments of Heraclitus—but against nothing else: the two volumes are unmarked except for the section on Heraclitus, but there frequently against both the Greek and the German. Yeats was not quite so exclusive, but he did mark passages of Heraclitus more often than any other Pre-Socratic in his copy of John Burnet's *Early Greek Philosophy*. (The copy of Burnet in Yeats's library, incidentally, is the first edition of 1892, which differs markedly from later editions. When one wants to measure Yeats's knowledge of the Pre-Socratics, one must be specific about the text—and the edition—he was using.)

3. See Guthrie, *Hist. of Gr. Phil.*, I, 413-15; Cornford, *Principium Sapientiae*, pp. 112-17 (chapter entitled "The Philosopher as Successor of the Seer-poet"); and Nietzsche, *Philosophy in the Tragic Age of the Greeks*, sections 5 through 8.

The fragment for which *The Resurrection* serves as a dramatized interpretation (Fr. 62 in Diels-Kranz; Fr. 67 in Bywater & Burnet; Fr. 242 in Kirk-Raven; Fr. 66 in Philip Wheelwright; and a fragment given a characteristically bad translation—which Yeats probably knew—by Thomas Taylor in his *Dissertation on the Eleusinian and Bacchic Mysteries*) might properly be translated thus: "Immortal mortals, mortal immortals, living the others' death, and dying the others' life." No other thought, it seems to me, and no other image seized on Yeats's imagination or teased and fascinated his mind so much as this one. The fragment is everywhere in Yeats—in poems, plays, essays, and letters—whether as allusion, as paraphrase, as quotation and misquotation, or as creative adaptation and interpretation. But while no other fragment found quite the same place in Yeats's affections as this one, he nevertheless recurs very frequently to other ideas of Heraclitus whether explicitly or implicitly, and whether the Heraclitus of reference be the Heraclitus of ancient Greece or the Heraclitus of the psychic substratum. The same goes for Jung: "Immortal mortals" had not the same luminous and numinous preeminence in his regard as in Yeats's (though Jung does quote the fragment in *Psychological Types*); rather Jung most often produces "old Heraclitus," as he familiarly calls him, to stand authority for the notion of *enantiodromia* (in spite of the fact that the word does not occur in Heraclitus as Jung incorrectly supposed). There was much more to Jung's Heraclitus than only *enantiodromia*, however, just as there was much more to Yeats's Heraclitus than "Immortal mortals, mortal immortals, living the others' death, and dying the others' life."

Yeats's Heraclitus, Jung's Heraclitus, and the Heraclitus of Yeats and Jung together made such darkly brilliant and brilliantly dark, primal statements as the following:[4]

---

[4]. I have chosen the specific fragments that follow because (1) Yeats either marked them in his copy of Burnet, or he quoted or alluded to them in his writings; or (2) Jung either marked them in his copy of Diels, or he quoted or alluded to them in his writings; or (3) both Yeats and Jung marked or quoted them. To be specific, Jung quoted (frequently) the second fragment (not a direct quotation from Heraclitus), and he alone is authority for (in the order quoted) DK 36, DK 10, DK 60, DK 101, and DK 45; Yeats alone is responsible for DK 76, DK 21, DK 80, the Homer passage (not in DK), and DK 30. This means that both men marked or quoted *Cratylus* 402a, DK 62, DK 111, DK 88, DK 8, DK 53, DK 51, DK 119, DK 20, and DK 63. (Yeats marked the *Cratylus* passage, not in Burnet but in Walter Pater's *Plato and Platonism*, where Pater says of Heraclitus, ". . . he cries out—his

Heraclitus somewhere says that all things are in process and nothing stays still, and likening existing things to the stream of a river he says that you would not step twice into the same river.
>   Plato, *Cratylus* 402a (WBY; CGJ)

πάντα ῥεῖ: all things are flowing [not a direct quotation but a compressed summary accepted by tradition as the essence of Heraclitus' teaching on natural process]
>   (CGJ)

Fire lives the death of earth, and air lives the death of fire; water lives the death of air, earth that of water.
>   DK 76 (WBY)

For souls it is death to become water, for water it is death to become earth; from earth water comes-to-be, and from water, soul.
>   DK 36 (CGJ)

What we see when awake is death, what we see asleep is sleep.
>   DK 21 (WBY)

Immortal mortals, mortal immortals, living the others' death, dying the others' life.
>   DK 62 (WBY; CGJ)

It is disease that makes health pleasant and good, hunger satiety, weariness rest.
>   DK 111 (WBY; CGJ)

Things taken together are whole and not whole, something which is being brought together and brought apart, which is in tune and out of tune; out of all things there comes a

---

philosophy was no matter of formal treatise or system, but of harsh, protesting cries —Πάντα χωρεῖ καὶ οὐδὲν μένει. All things give way: nothing remaineth.") I have indicated by initials after each passage the party or parties responsible. I have not tried to give all the fragments possible: Yeats and Jung marked a good many more fragments in Burnet and Diels than I have reproduced.

The translations I have chosen are by Burnet, Guthrie, Kirk (in *Presocratic Philosophers* and in *The Cosmic Fragments*), and Wheelwright—or, more often, are free adaptations from all these sources and retranslations of my own determined by the nature of the discussion.

unity, and out of a unity all things (ἐκ πάντων ἓν καὶ ἐξ ἑνὸς πάντα).
DK 10 (CGJ)

Living and dead, and the waking and the sleeping, and young and old are the same; for these by sudden reversal are those, and those again by sudden reversal are these.
DK 88 (WBY; CGJ)

It is opposition that brings things together. [This is the version WBY marked in Burnet.] What is opposed is helpful. [Guthrie's more accurate translation.]
DK 8 (WBY; CGJ)

The way up and the way down are one and the same.
DK 60 (CGJ)

One must know that war is common, and justice strife, and that all things come about by way of strife and necessity.
DK 80 (WBY)

War is the father of all and the king of all; and some he has made gods and some men, some bond and some free.
DK 53 (WBY; CGJ)

Homer was wrong in saying: "Would that strife might perish from among gods and men!" He did not see that he was praying for the destruction of the universe; for, if his prayer were heard, all things would pass away.
Bywater-Burnet 43 (WBY)

They do not understand how in being drawn apart it is drawn together [or: how by being at variance it agrees with itself]—an attunement of opposite tensions [or: backward-turning adjustment] as in a bow or a lyre.
DK 51 (WBY; CGJ)

This world-order [*kosmos*], the same for all, no one of gods or of men has made, but it was always and is and shall be—an ever-living fire, kindling in measures and going out in measures.
DK 30 (WBY)

I searched myself.

DK 101 (CGJ)

You would not discover the limits of *psychē* even by travelling every path: so deep a *logos* does it have.

DK 45 (CGJ)

ἦθος ἀνθρώπῳ δαίμων: A man's individuality is his *daimon*.

DK 119 (WBY; CGJ)

When they are born they wish to live and to meet with their dooms, and then they leave children behind to become dooms in turn.

DK 20 (WBY; CGJ)

They rise up and become wakeful guardians of the living and the dead.

DK 63 (WBY; CGJ)

Before going on to argue the coherence of these fragments and before demonstrating their relevance in a reading of Yeats or of Jung as well as their pertinence in understanding the vast implications in the similarities between Yeats and Jung, I might remark that Yeats was being Heraclitean in style and in content—deliberately so I think—when he had Michael Robartes pronounce the following "fragments" in *A Vision* (pp. 52–53):

> Every action of man declares the soul's ultimate, particular freedom, and the soul's disappearance in God; declares that reality is a congeries of beings and a single being; nor is this antinomy an appearance imposed upon us by the form of thought but life itself which turns, now here, now there, a whirling and a bitterness.
> After an age of necessity, truth, goodness, mechanism, science, democracy, abstraction, peace, comes an age of freedom, fiction, evil, kindred, art, aristocracy, particularity, war.
> Death cannot solve the antinomy; death and life are its expression.
> The marriage bed is the symbol of the solved antinomy, and were more than symbol could a man there lose and

keep his identity, but he falls asleep. That sleep is the same as the sleep of death.

Dear predatory birds, prepare for war, prepare your children and all that you can reach. . . . Love war because of its horror, that belief may be changed, civilisation renewed. . . . Belief is renewed continually in the ordeal of death.

There can be little question, in the face of these "fragments," that Michael Robartes, one of the masks of Yeats, had put himself to school to "crowing, mob-reviling, riddling Heraclitus" (as Timon of Phlius called him) as much as to Giraldus Cambrensis, and had learned more from the genuine fragments of that dark, daimonic Greek than he ever did from the desert-dancing Judwalis.

Heraclitus declared for the following truths: Everything in nature is in perpetual flux, and flux is reality; all things (including men and their consciousness) are always flowing, and the elements are in a state of continual change, of inter-transformation and exchange of characteristics; reality, both physical and psychological, is composed of endless opposites, and without these conflicting opposites the universe would collapse, yet these opposites are somehow, in a deeper sense, identical, opposed halves of a circular whole or reversed mirror images of one another; there is everywhere and always an enmity between the watery and the fiery elements, an enmity which in other guises would be between feminine and masculine, between physical generation and spiritual creation, between the many and the one; war and strife are the natural and necessary state of things, and from their operation comes the tension, the energy from pole to pole, that maintains all existence and is the *sine qua non* of life itself; behind the perpetual processes of nature and in the very chaos of their becoming, there is an invariable law or formula or balanced measure that is the virtually divine *Logos*; and this *Logos* that burns throughout nature burns also through the life of every man—it is his individuality, his *daimon*, the formula of his *psychē*. Yeats and Jung—with their opposites and quaternities, their *mysterium coniunctionis* and resolution of antinomies, their *uroboroi* and spheres, their masks and shadows, their *enantiodromia* and reversal of gyres, their individuation and Unity of Being—declared, in their own language, and declared again, for every one of these archaic doctrines first promulgated by the proud and—in his generation—

isolated Heraclitus of Ephesus. He is, however, isolated no longer, for he mingles now with the other great dead in the mind and works of Yeats and Jung, or more simply in that objective, collective, impersonal mind of humanity where Yeats and Jung also have now taken their place.

"In the phenomenal world," Jung says in the *Mysterium Coniunctionis*, the volume that he himself took to be his *magnum opus*, "the Heraclitean law of everlasting change, πάντα ῥεῖ, prevails; and it seems that all the true things must change and that only that which changes remains true" (*CW*, XIV, par. 503). It is important to remember the qualification with which Jung begins his comment— "In the phenomenal world"—for he would no doubt have agreed with J. H. Newman's brilliant (and platonizing) remark on this Heraclitean subject of change: "In a higher world it is otherwise, but here below to live is to change, and to be perfect is to have changed often."[5] There is more than a little of Heraclitus in Newman's observation; and in Jung's observation—because it is concerned solely with the "phenomenal world" or "here below"— there is nothing *but* Heraclitus. "Likening existing things to the stream of a river," Heraclitus too declared that "here below to live is to change," and conversely that to be at rest and at peace, unmoving and unchanging, is to be dead:

> Hearts with one purpose alone
> Through summer and winter seem
> Enchanted to a stone
> To trouble the living stream.

The stream alone, and not the stone that troubles it, is possessed of life in Yeats's poem. "Easter 1916" is, among other things, a profound examination—not precisely a confirmation but an exploration—of the Heraclitean doctrine that all things human and natural are in a state of flux, interchange, and transformation and then a questioning of whether, given this fact of human existence and apprehension, stability is possible or even desirable.

> The horse that comes from the road,
> The rider, the birds that range
> From cloud to tumbling cloud,

---

5. *Essay on the Development of Christian Doctrine* (London: Longman, Green, & Co., 1909), p. 40.

> Minute by minute they change;
> A shadow of cloud on the stream
> Changes minute by minute;
> A horse-hoof slides on the brim,
> And a horse plashes within it.

This is very much the Heraclitean stream that no man can enter twice, and there is no tribute more precisely attuned or more moving that this one of Yeats's to the perpetual change, the incessant flow, the ever fresh and new face that mere life insists upon or that life *is*. The poem enacts what Yeats elsewhere calls "that delight in what is unforeseen, and in the mere spectacle of the world, the mere drifting hither and thither that must come before all true thought and emotion" (*E. & I.*, p. 314). Undoubtedly Yeats's vision of perpetual change, and his feeling for that change, was influenced, if not entirely caused, by the incredibly swift changes in the weather and the climate of Ireland ("as uncertain as a child's bottom" in Simon Dedalus' simile) and the consequent changes in the appearance of the landscape: to anyone who looks, let us say, at Ben Bulben for any period of time, it is obvious that existing things are like the stream of a river where πάντα ῥεῖ, and that the stream itself, like the shadow of cloud reflected in it, "Changes minute by minute."

Not only is the stream Heraclitean but it is also, especially in the clouds streaming overhead and reflected on the surface of the stream, the procession of images of created objects reflected on the wall of Plato's Cave in the *Republic*: a third remove from reality and stability, from changelessness and knowledge. Far removed as it is from changeless reality, however—from the fire of the sun that is perfect reality—the stream is life all the same and not death.

> The long-legged moor-hens dive,
> And hens to moor-cocks call;
> Minute by minute they live;
> The stone's in the midst of all.

The question that the poem asks about change and stasis comes down to a question about life and death, for to achieve changelessness is to be no longer alive, whether one remains in the midst of life (like Constance Markievicz) or is violently removed therefrom (like the executed revolutionaries). For Heraclitus—and for Yeats in "Easter 1916"—rest and stasis are death, so that Parmenides was wrong to exalt his changeless and unmoving sphere, and so was Pythagoras wrong in imagining that harmony and cosmos have anything to do with peace and stability. Not at all, according to Heraclitus, who uses both these Pythagorean words—both *harmonia* and *kosmos*—but sees them as coming only from the heightened energy and vital tension produced by incessant change and conflict. "Every process," Jung says—and Heraclitus is the great fountainhead of process philosophy—"is a phenomenon of energy, and . . . all energy can proceed only from the tension of opposites" (*CW*, VII, par. 34), just as in the "backward-turning adjustment" or "harmony of opposite tentions" [παλίντροπος ἁρμονίη] of a bow or lyre—the image *par excellence* of Heraclitean/Yeatsian/Jungian energistic and vitalistic harmony.

Of course it is possible to take a contrary view of the matter, as Yeats does often, especially in his early poetry, and to yearn for the peacefulness and quiet of Pythagoras' kind of harmony as against the agitation and strife of Heraclitus' harmony. Michael Robartes speaks in "The Phases of the Moon" of the possibility, devoutly to be wished, of escaping from the wheel, of getting "Out of the up and down" and particularly of getting "Out of that raving tide"—both of them good Heraclitean images but with an emotional shading to them that hints at Parmenidean and Pythagorean desires. Likewise in an altered mood, Jung maintains that the psychotherapist should not give all his love and attention to the "raving tide" and the imbroglio that is the unconscious but "should also consider it just as important a task to defend the standpoint of consciousness, clarity, 'reason,' and an acknowledged and proven good against the raging torrent that flows for all eternity in the darkness of the psyche—a πάντα ῥεῖ that leaves nothing unaltered and ceaselessly creates a past that can never be retrieved" (*CW*, XIV, par. 125). It is ironic, since Jung has been accused of being excessively and indiscriminately in love with the "raging torrent" of the unconscious, that his principle objection to Joyce's *Ulysses* should have been on precisely this ground: that the novel merely presents a Heraclitean universe of flux without the focussing, staying effect of any consciousness from within that universe. "The presentation is consistent and flowing, everything is in motion and nothing is fixed" (*CW*, XV, par. 173).

If the Heraclitean doctrine that all things are always flowing is not on every occasion emotionally satisfying, and if the vision of nature and the unconscious as a raving tide and a raging torrent fails to appease man's universal monistic yearning, there is by way of compensation another doctrine intimately associated with the name of Heraclitus that is commended by Yeats and Jung in all seasons and that does precisely answer to the monistic demands of the human spirit. This is Heraclitus' teaching not about streaming and the watery element but about *logos* and the fiery element: "an ever-living fire, kindling in measures and going out in measures" (Fr. 30). It is the genius of Heraclitus, expressed in the most profound of paradoxes, to argue that the flowing stream and the bright flame are opposites, and ever at war, yet are the same; they are antinomies, yet are identical. Fire and water are in perpetual enmity, yet in their opposed, balanced, and backward-turning tension they compose a universe in which, the one above, the other below, they reflect one another—a single law that can be abstracted from the elements as perfect measure and pure fire, or that can be realized in the elements as incessant process and streaming water. "Since the time of Heraclitus," Jung says in *Psychology and Religion*, "life has been conceived as a πῦρ ἀεὶ ζῶν, an ever-living fire" (*CW*, XI, par. 60). This is true; but it is equally true that, since the time of Heraclitus, life has been conceived as an ever-flowing stream, and somehow the two, while opposed, are also the same. Jung himself gives us the clue to their identity-in-opposition when, in "Archetypes of the Collective Unconscious," he says, "in all chaos there is a cosmos, in all disorder a secret order, in all caprice a fixed law, for everything that works is grounded on its opposite" (*CW*, IX, part 1, par. 66). In the stream, we might continue, there is a fire, and in πάντα ῥεῖ there is λόγος.

There is a passage in "Anima Mundi" addressed to exactly these same questions that is of crucial importance but of extraordinary difficulty—it is difficult, that is, until we recall what Heraclitus had to say of the elements in process and of the fiery *logos* and what, after him, Plato had to say, in the *Timaeus* and the *Republic*, of intertransformative elements and of degrees of reality and knowledge. Yeats, after describing some group efforts in evocation wherein he and his fellow adepti had conjured up certain images that seemed to draw together all their minds and to join them in a Great Mind with minds of the past, goes on to speak of the images held in common and of the minds through which they moved. "The minds that swayed these seemingly fluid images had doubtless form"—mind, corresponding to *logos*, has form while the images, seeming to be fluid, stream on like everything in the phenomenal world—"and those images themselves seemed, as it were, mirrored in a living substance whose change is but form." Behind all change is a constant law, a secret order behind chaos, λόγος in πάντα ῥεῖ. The fiery *logos* descends to airy images which are reflected in a watery stream that is the movement of earthly matter. The order of descent is precisely the same as the arrangement of the elements in the *Timaeus* (55d–56a) from the most mobile to the most immobile, and it corresponds to the degrees of reality and knowledge in the *Republic*—from the sun of pure being, to the mathematical images of *aither*, to images reflected in water (flickering, reflected images on the cave wall), to the earth which is virtually inanimate and unreal. Or looking to Heraclitus' ordering, where the arrangement is hierarchical but is also circular ("The way up and the way down are one and the same"), we still see Yeats's scheme but more clearly and as it were diagrammatically: "Fire lives the death of earth . . . : etc.:

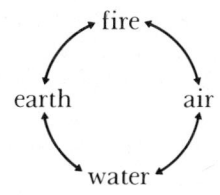

```
           fire
         ↗      ↘
     earth      air
         ↖      ↙
          water
```

"On a circle," as Heraclitus says, "the beginning and the end are common," and there is an identity in opposition determined by the very form—closed and perfect—of that circle. "From tradition and perception," Yeats continues, "one thought of one's own life as symbolised by earth, the place of heterogeneous things, the images as mirrored in water, and the images themselves one could divine but as air; and beyond it all there were, I felt confident, certain aims and governing loves, the fire that makes all simple" (*Myth.*, p. 346). From the heterogeneity and multiplicity of earth, by way of flowing images reflected in water and the vaporous images themselves of air, to the simplicity and unity of fire—such is the way up for Yeats as for Heraclitus; and the way down is one and the same. Fire—in a very slight paraphrase of Heraclitus and in a merger of a couple of fragments both beloved of Yeats—lives the death of earth and dies the life of air; air lives the death of fire and dies the life of water; water lives the death of air and dies the life of earth; earth lives the death of water and dies the life of fire; fire . . . —but in a circle, beginning and end are common.

"The maternal significance of water," Jung tells us in *Symbols of Transformation* (and tells us again in "Archetypes of the Collective Unconscious," and again in *Psychology and Alchemy*, and again in "The Meaning of Psychology for Modern Man," and again in "Child Development and Education," and again in *Mysterium Coniunctionis*, and again . . .) "is one of the clearest interpretations of symbols in the whole field of mythology, so that even the ancient Greeks could say that 'the sea is the symbol of generation'" (*CW*, V, par. 319). In keeping with the Heraclitean way up and down and his circle around, the sea is also a symbol of death—"Those dying generations . . . the mackerel-crowded seas . . . Whatever is begotten, born, and dies"—and, in contrast to fire which is masculine, it is a symbol of the eternal feminine, of mother, lover, and crone. Such a paradoxical and multivalent symbol the sea was for the ancient Greeks—for Heraclitus perhaps more than any other—and such also for Yeats and for Jung. I think Yeats was making an honest mistake (he was prone to honest mistakes of just this sort) rather than trying to cover his tracks or obscure his indebtedness when, late in his life, he wrote that "a German psycho-analyst has traced the 'mother complex' back to our mother the sea" (*Ex.*, p. 378). In any case, I am sure that for "German" we can safely read "Swiss," and to the authority of Gemisthus Plethon, whom Yeats shortly thereafter cites, we can confidently add the authority of C. G. Jung—who had it not only from dreams and suchlike but also from "the ancient Greeks." When Yeats, in "Coole Park and Ballylee, 1931," asks brightly and rhetorically, "What's water but the generated soul?" he is, as Norman Jeffares points out (with the relevant quotation from Porphyry's *De Antro Nympharum*), alluding to a typically Neoplatonic notion; but the Neoplatonists, as was their habit, were only taking over a seminal idea discovered in an earlier source—Heraclitus in this case (whom Porphyry indeed quotes in his fanciful interpretation of the significance of the nymph's cave in the thirteenth book of *The Odyssey*)—and decking it out in the gaudy, obscurantist terminology of a much later stage of thought.

Heraclitus identifies soul with fire; moisture therefore signifies death, since it extinguishes the fire that is the principle of individual life and is the balanced *logos* sustaining the cosmos as well. Yet—and this is altogether characteristic of one sort of Heraclitean paradox—the fiery soul is born out of its watery opposite, and in the end it returns to that opposite; moreover, between its beginning in moisture and its end in the same, the soul reverts frequently—rather too frequently according to Heraclitus—to a watery state by way of drunkenness and (probably) by way of that quasi-death which is sleep. As with fire, "It is death for souls to become water"; but conversely, and paradoxically, "soul comes into existence from water" (DK 36). Though "a dry soul is wisest and best" (DK 118)—obviously, just as it is wisest and best, not to say necessary and inevitable, for a fire to be dry—nevertheless, "Souls are exhaled from moist things" (DK 12), and, as is perhaps natural, they yearn to return again to that state of peace and of freedom from the tension of opposites that they previously knew and to enjoy once more a condition of liquid unconsciousness and soul drunkenness (where often, unfortunately, πάντα ῥεῖ rather too much): "To souls it is pleasure (or death)[6] to become moist" (DK 77); and "A man when he is drunk is led by a beardless youth, stumbling and not knowing where he goes, having his soul moist" (DK 117). Even in a gay and largely frivolous poem like "A Drunken Man's Praise of Sobriety," one can, if one wishes, discover Heraclitean imagery on the subject of drink, for it is apparently because of the pervasive moistness—water, water everywhere when he has a drop taken—that the speaker finally opts for a mermaid, who can stay on top of the waves, rather than for a punk, who would be all too likely to go under:

> No ups and downs, my pretty,
> A mermaid, not a punk;
> A drunkard is a dead man,
> And all dead men are drunk.

6. Most texts omit the parenthetical phrase, though Diels-Kranz includes it. G. S. Kirk, on the other hand, if he were to consider this a genuine fragment, would drop "pleasure" and retain "death" (*Cosmic Fragments*, p. 253), but in fact he prefers to take the whole thing as little more than a Neoplatonic gloss on Heraclitean doctrine (ibid., p. 340; ironically, the passage comes to us from Porphyry's *De Antro Nympharum*).

Absolutely right, so far as imagery goes, according to Heraclitus.

Water, as the maternal element, is both generative and destructive, Jung insisted, and he insisted even more frequently that "the sea is the symbol of the collective unconscious" (*CW*, XII, par. 57). Translating Heraclitus' language of elemental imagery into the metaphors of analytical psychology, Jung devoted a dozen volumes of the *Collected Works* and the greater part of his career to describing how the individual spark of consciousness—its own tiny *logos* fire—rises out of the sea of the unconscious to reach its zenith, like the sun, at mid-day/mid-life, and then slowly descends, desiring its own death, back into that same sea in the evening. In a passage (*CW*, XIV, par. 117) that can be taken as representative of twenty similar passages, Jung writes: "Just as the day-star rises out of the nocturnal sea, so ontogenetically and phylogenetically, consciousness is born out of unconsciousness and sinks back every night to this primal condition. This duality of our psychic life is the prototype and archetype of the Sol-Luna symbolism." Yeats does not lay his fire-water imagery out in quite this same pattern, but water always figures in his poetry as on the one hand generative, on the other hand destructive, and fire as the expression of creative, heroic spirit (*On Baile's Strand*, for example, is a dramatization of elemental conflict—Conchubar, earthy and watery, versus Cuchulain, airy and fiery—and the fire of Cuchulain's spirit is literally extinguished by water in his fight with the waves at the end). In the early poetry there is what Yeats later came to think of as a sentimental desire to submerge himself in the easeful waters of obliteration—"the waves of sentiment," as Yeats says in a letter to Æ, that would "rust the terrible mirror" of the blade of the will. "I fled that water" (*Letters*, p. 435), Yeats adds, and indeed he did, but not until he had written the poem about an enchanted lake isle (in photographs, incidentally, Innisfree clearly reveals a feminine aspect to it—a sort of *mons veneris* in appearance—not unlike the hair tent Yeats dreamed early on of closing over him), an island where "peace comes dropping slow" to soothe the weary soul but to moisten and drown it as well. Jung dreamed of an enchanted island also—"the enchanted island in the Upper Lake, where the wild ducks, plovers, and crested grebes nest in the reeds" (*Letters*, I, 37)—and originally, just as Yeats wanted to establish a Castle of the Heroes on an island in Lough Key, Jung intended to build his tower, which in the beginning he thought of as a gesture to maternal sources, on that enchanted island. If it can be pleasure to the soul to become moist, it can also mean death, and this we discover everywhere in Yeats: in the early poems the psyche is submerged in the moist that the world and all its conflicts may be obliterated; in the poems of Yeats's maturity, water and its destructive allies—the "blood-dimmed tide," the storm "bred on the Atlantic," the "sea-wind" that screams upon the tower, "the flooded stream," all of them erupting "Out of the murderous innocence of the sea"—are seen as the enemy that would destroy the vulnerable creations of psyche. In either case, the watery element signifies death to the psyche, as Heraclitus said and as Jung too always recognized when he spoke in psychological metaphor of the raging waters of the unconscious overwhelming and extinguishing the brave but fragile light of consciousness.

There are those students of Pre-Socratic thought who feel that Anaxagoras, because he introduced *Nous* (mind or intelligence) as the motive force and the controlling principle in the universe, should be accorded a grand and prominent position among those who collaborated in the construction of a world system. Yeats, however, was not among the Anaxagorists. In his copy of Burnet, Yeats marked a passage (p. 293 in the first edition) in which Burnet comments on Anaxagoras' substitution of "Nous . . . for the Love and Strife of Empedokles," and in the margin Yeats wrote, "Change to Primary conception," thus incidentally demonstrating that even the Pre-Socratics could be reduced to little more than a preparing of the way for the complete system of *A Vision* as that was revealed to Yeats by his Instructors. And having refashioned it into a more Heraclitean image, Yeats put this observation from Burnet right into *A Vision*, where Anaxagoras is seen more as a villain than as a hero of Greek philosophy because "he declared that thought and not the warring opposites created the world" (*Vision* [1937], p. 273). Not only was this a pernicious doctrine cosmogonically speaking (as Heraclitus knew) and psychologically speaking (as Jung knew), but it had the effect (as Yeats knew) of robbing the artist of the greatest subject his imagination had ever conceived: "At that sentence the heroic life, passionate fragmentary man, all that had been imagined by great poets and sculptors began to pass away, and instead of seeking noble antagonists, imagination moved towards divine man and the ridiculous devil" (pp. 272-73). With Anaxagoras, Yeats implies, the focus shifted so that creativity and destructivity were no longer located in the human and natural realm, where paradox and conflict are the order of the day, but in realms above and below the human/natural, which was in effect to deprive the great antagonists of the richest ground for their warfare. After Anaxagoras (or so Yeats suggests), good was projected upward, evil downward, and the conflict of opposites was taken out of the natural world—which then, as Heraclitus had already declared, would collapse, there being no strife to maintain the energy of existence or to impel mankind to heroic and creative deeds. But "there must be some such tension of opposites," Jung argues, with something of the same sense of exasperation as Yeats, "otherwise no energy would be possible, for, as Heraclitus has said, 'war is the father of all things'" (*CW*, VIII, par. 99). This casting of God and the devil out of the human realm—or the attempt to cast them out, for it can never succeed—exercised Jung as much as it did Yeats, and it seemed as wrongheaded to him on psychological grounds as it did to Yeats on artistic grounds. Consider, for example, this passage in *Symbols of Transformation* (similar to a number of other passages scattered throughout *CW*) where Jung merges psychology and theology to come up with a critique of Christianity based on the same objection as Yeats's disapproval of Anaxagoras: "The self, as a symbol of wholeness, is a *coincidentia oppositorum*, and therefore contains light and darkness simultaneously. In the Christ-figure the opposites which are united in the archetype are polarized into the 'light' son of God on the one hand and the devil on the other" (*CW*, V. par. 576). In the "'light' son of God" we have Yeats's "divine man," and in "the devil," as conceived by Christianity, there is nothing but "ridiculous" and unworthy foolery. It was all so much better before Anaxagoras and Christianity; and, in fact, beyond the reach of those two separators, deep in the psyche of man and of the universe, it remains the same, for the primitive warfare of Heraclitean opposites has not ceased there nor can it ever cease. "The conscious mind is on top, the shadow underneath,[7] and just as high always longs for low and hot for cold, so all consciousness, perhaps without being aware of it, seeks its unconscious opposite, lacking which it is doomed to stagnation, congestion, and ossification. Life is born

---

7. Yeats: "Every influence has a shadow, as it were, an unbalanced—the unbalanced is the Kabalistic definition of evil—duplicate of itself"(*Letters*, p. 256).

only of the spark of opposites" (*CW*, VII, par. 78). If Yeats was correct in his understanding of Anaxagoras, then there was good reason to anathematize him for his glorification of *Nous* as the serene and all-powerful Creator, for to deprive cosmogony of the warring opposites is also to deprive the universe of life and it is to take from mankind at the same time any impetus to creativity. "Without this continual Discord," Yeats says in *A Vision* (p. 94), "there would be no conscience, no activity"; and therefore, in a late letter to Dorothy Wellesley, he writes, "I begin to see things double—doubled in history, world history, personal history" (*Letters*, p. 887). Although Yeats goes on to speak of a unity we can be sure that those doubles of his were incessantly, in the best Heraclitean way, at one another's throats, living the other's death, dying the other's life.

On the doctrine of contraries Yeats had Blake for authority ("Without contraries is no progression. Attraction and Repulsion, Reason and Energy, Love and Hate, are necessary to Human existence"); on the embrace of opposites Jung had Nicholas of Cusa ("Nicholas of Cusa defined God himself as a *complexio oppositorum*" [*CW*, VII, par. 406]); and on Eros as a great *daimon* midway between immortal mortals and mortal immortals, a spirit of union through whose agency the fragmented sexual opposites are joined, Plato, in *The Symposium*, had Diotima and Aristophanes. But in the end the ancestral authority for them all—for Blake, Cusanus, Plato, Aristophanes, Diotima, Yeats, and Jung—when they were about these teachings, was Heraclitus. "One must know," the Heraclitus in them announced to them all, "that war is common, and justice strife, and that all things come by way of strife and necessity" (DK 80); hence one ought not to pray for an end to strife, which (according to a compound gloss offered by Aristotle and Simplicius) would be nothing less than "praying for the destruction of the universe, for there would be no melody without high and low, nor living creatures without male and female, which are opposites; and if the prayer were heard, all things would pass away." Cusanus himself, who pronounced often and in a variety of ways on the union of opposites in God, never said it more clearly than Heraclitus, the great original: "God is day and night, winter and summer, war and peace, satiety and hunger" (DK 67)—and Hippolytus, to whom we are indebted for preservation of this fragment, goes on to provide the appropriate gloss: "all the opposites: that is the meaning." To all of these descendants, finally, Heraclitus addressed the fragment

(DK 62) in which there are no verbs (which might pin down the meaning and limit it too much) but only substantives, adjectival attributes, and continuing participial actions in endless grammatical and logical inter-transformation—a fragment that could be glossed forever but never improved. In *The Presocratic Philosophers*, G. S. Kirk translates in a manner intended to suggest the variety of possibilities offered by the fragment—but finally, seeing that the possibilities for grammatical and logical combinations are nearly infinite, throws up his hands in despair and surrenders with a concluding "etc.": "Immortal mortals, mortal immortals [or mortal immortals, immortal mortals; *or* immortals are mortal, mortals are immortal; *or* immortals are mortals, mortals are immortals, *etc.*], living their death and dying their life." This translation, as Kirk well knows and no doubt intends, does not begin to exhaust the possibilities of the fragment. When Philip Wheelwright, for example, supplies the verb "become" rather than "are," he in effect glosses the fragment and points it in the direction of a particular interpretation involving temporal, cyclical transformations between incarnate and discarnate states; but Jung (though without specific reference to this fragment) points it back in the direction of psychological simultaneity when he says, "[M]an does not change at death into his immortal part, but is mortal and immortal even in life, being both ego and self" (*CW*, V, p. 284, note 182). Little wonder that during the last year or so of his life, when Yeats was putting together the ultimate mishmash of essays, poems, plays, and teachings in eugenics that was to be proclaimed from *On the Boiler*, he could scarcely write a page without this fragment insinuating itself, in part or in whole, in rhythm, in imagery, and in thought, into his text. As he at one point in that publication puts it, and truly, "[W]e have been haunted by those faces dark with mystery, cast up by that other power that has ever more and more wrestled with ours, each living the other's death, dying the other's life" (*On the Boiler*, p. 25; *Ex.*, p. 434). For Yeats, with his vision of doubles everywhere, as also, arguably, for Heraclitus and perhaps even for Jung—though he hedged his bets much more cautiously than Yeats was inclined to do—this state in which mirror images duplicate and reverse one another, or in which an image is thrown perpetually back and forth between a concave mirror and a convex one, applies to the course and the stages of an individual life; it applies to cycles of history; most of all it applies to the backward-tension and harmony and the symbiotic relationship between incarnate and discarnate beings. "To me," Yeats wrote to Ethel Mannin some three months before he experienced that *enantiodromia*, that "sudden reversal" of direction, by which his life turned into its own opposite and into its identical, inverted twin, "all things are made of the conflict of two states of consciousness, beings or persons which die each other's life, live each other's death. That is true of life and death themselves. Two cones (or whirls), the apex of each in the other's base" (*Letters*, p. 918). Then Yeats drew for Ethel Mannin, as the Instructors had twenty years earlier drawn for him, that empty image of reversed, interpenetrating cones which Yeats saw as embracing the same unlimited, unglossed, comprehensive significance as Heraclitus' fragment 62. There is a legitimate and useful sense in which one could say that half the poems of Yeats's maturity—and especially those poems that represent considered public performances, with their special Yeatsian grandeur and formal dignity about them: "Sailing to Byzantium," "The Tower," "Among School Children," "All Souls' Night," "A Dialogue of Self and Soul," "Blood and the Moon," "Byzantium," "Vacillation," "Under Ben Bulben"—that all of these may be construed as so many glosses on the formal, empty image of interpenetrating cones and as so many interpretations of the fragment that says, "Immortal mortals, mortal immortals [*or* . . . ,] living the others' death, dying the others' life."

It was very likely his adherence to Heraclitus' doctrine of opposition and paradox—projected into a dictum of psychological theory holding that everything psychic is paradoxical and contradictory ("every psychic phenomenon is compensated by its opposite" [*CW*, X, par. 292])—that allowed Jung, or caused him, to be so often self-contradictory, describing himself now as a monist, then as a dualist, and again as a pluralist (e.g., *CW*, IV, par. 758; *CW*, IX, part 2, p. 61. n. 74; *CW*, XVI, par. 177). Jung was not, however, the first man to have contradicted himself, nor will he be the last to do so, in an attempt to reconcile the undeniable fact of pluralism with an irresistible urge to monism. To see *Logos* in the sensible flux and the sensible flux in *Logos* is not a simple matter, and it is both understandable and forgivable that one and the same man should now feel that there is only the *Logos* whereas yesterday he felt that there was only the sensible flux.

> For one throb of the artery,
> While on that old grey stone I sat
> Under the old wind-broken tree,
> I knew that One is animate,
> Mankind inanimate fantasy.

This occurs in the *Collected Poems* just ten pages after the convincing evocation of the living reality of the sensible flux in "Easter 1916" and just ten pages before this firm declaration of faith in "The Tower":

> I mock Plotinus' thought
> And cry in Plato's teeth,
> Death and life were not
> Till man made up the whole,
> Made lock, stock and barrel
> Out of his bitter soul,
> Aye, sun and moon and star, all. . . .

"Between extremities / Man runs his course," as Yeats says in the first lines of "Vacillation," and between extremities also the *Collected Poems* run their course; but it is only thus, by the conflict and cooperation of warring opposites and by a dialectical running between extremities, that a poem and the entire *Poems* will generate the energy that is the sole source of poetic (as also philosophical and psychological) life. Each of the poems in *Collected Poems*, as well as the volume as a whole, and the entire patchwork complex of essays and monographs that constitutes Jung's *Collected Works* could fairly be seen to fit the Heraclitean description that Jung gives to the psyche and to psychological theory: "A psychological theory," he says in *Two Essays on Analytical Psychology*, "must base itself on the principle of opposition; for without this it could only re-establish a neurotically unbalanced psyche. There is no balance, no system of self-regulation, without opposition. The psyche is just such a self-regulating system" (*CW*, VII, par. 92). No balance and no energy without the warring opposites, no *Logos* without the sensible flux. The balance, the formula, or the measure by which the psyche regulates itself—since psyche, according to Jung, is an enclosed, self-contained system composed of parts in opposition, in strife, and in perpetual flux—is analogous to, indeed is identical with, the balance, the *logos* by which the individual "individuates" himself, and is therefore identical with the instressed and inscaped *logos* that directs a single poem or a volume of poems, the *logos* that is the measure determining the shape of a complete body of work—that complete lifework being the externally realized form of the internal process of psychic life.[8]

Before we can think of *logos*, however, whether *logos* within an individual's life and poem or an all-encompassing *Logos* that shapes the flow of all things from beyond life and death, we must attend to that universal play of opposites which is responsible for the dynamism of the entire phenomenal world, both physical and psychological. The opposites, as Yeats says of the Great Year, are reconciled in paradox at every conceivable level, for one can always imagine a Greater if not a Greatest Year, or a Lesser if not a Least Year, that will be divided into the same antinomial halves as the Great Year itself. Whether the Great Year be 10,800 years long or 18,000 years or 36,000 years is of little consequence in this Heraclitean universe of warring opposites and paradoxical union: "Whatever its length, it divided, and so did every unit whose multiple it was, into waxing and waning, day and night, or summer and winter. There was everywhere a conflict like that of my play [*Resurrection*] between two principles or 'elemental forms of the mind', each 'living the other's life, dying the other's death.'"[9] Natural cycles are infinitely divisible, as is the Great Year, as are cultural cycles, and as is the pattern of every life, because the universe is a self-regulating system reflected in, and reflecting, the self-regulating system of the human

---

8. This notion of a lifework as a vastly exfoliated "metaphor of self," with both the lifework and the self being determined and shaped by the same individual *logos*, is developed in greater detail in *Metaphors of Self: The Meaning of Autobiography* (Princeton: Princeton University Press, 1972), especially Chapter One and Chapter Three (which argues the thesis in the specific case of Jung).

On psyche as an enclosed, self-regulating, "logistical" system where opposite embraces opposite and where balanced and equal conflict never ceases, cf. two passages in *Memories, Dreams, Reflections* (pp. 346/318–19 and 351/323): "Just as all energy proceeds from opposition, so the psyche too possesses its inner polarity, this being the indispensable prerequisite for its aliveness, as Heraclitus realized long ago. . . . Indeed, this is inevitable, for, as Heraclitus says, 'Everything is flux.' Thesis is followed by antithesis, and between the two is generated a third factor, a lysis which was not perceptible before. In this the psyche once again merely demonstrates its antithetical nature and at no point has really got outside itself."

9. *Ex.*, p. 396. I think the misquotation is unintentional here—it should, of course, be "living the other's death, dying the other's life"—but it serves to suggest that the opposites really were, in Yeats's unconscious mind, essentially identical and therefore interchangeable.

mind with its "two principles" or its "elemental forms." What Yeats says of man in the first lines of "Vacillation" is true also of civilizations, of nature herself, and of the universe at large:

> Between extremities
> Man runs his course;
> A brand, or flaming breath,
> Comes to destroy
> All those antinomies
> Of day and night;
> The body calls it death,
> The heart remorse.
> But if these be right
> What is joy?

How—Yeats implies the question—how can we call it either death or remorse when the extremity, painful or tragic though it may seem to the individual, is a personal extremity only and one of a pair, and is set within a larger pattern, not individually determined, wherein it is balanced by its opposite according to the necessities and the wisdom of the system in its self-regulation. Though the body calls it death, out of death, in a longer view, comes life, as out of life, death: dying each others' life, living each others' death. In the life of the individual, there is, as Jung puts it, "the enantiodromia of life into death" (*CW*, V, par. 681), and—though Jung was ordinarily too cautious to say so, Yeats was not—there is also the enantiodromia of death into life. Heraclitus had long since declared on all these antinomies which set the extremities between which the gyres of human life endlessly whirl (in their whirling and union making up that Sphere which, existing outside the extremities, forbids us to call this ultimate death or remorse)—"Living and dead, and the waking and the sleeping, and young and old are the same; for these by sudden reversal are those, and those again by sudden reversal are these" (Fr. 88). This describes the dialectical movement of the mind, as Yeats said—"elemental forms of the mind": an archetypal movement—as well as encompassing both an individual life and life at large. "Every psychological extreme," according to Jung, "secretly contains its own opposite or stands in some sort of intimate and essential relation to it." Jung could hardly be clearer and firmer in his adherence to Heraclitean doctrine than he is here; and he continues with more teaching from the same elemental source: "Indeed, it is from this tension that it derives its peculiar dynamism. . . . [T]he more extreme a position is"—and what more extreme than the extremities of Yeats's poem, or the extremities of Heraclitus' living and dead?—"the more easily may we expect an enantiodromia, a conversion of something into its opposite" (*CW*, V, par. 581). The two stanzas that make up the third section of "Vacillation" enact precisely Jung's enantiodromian division of life: a period of physical strength, of ambition, of conquest, of the gyre whirling outward and, balancing/reversing this first period, a period of spiritual refinement, of reflection, of circumambulation about a center, of the gyre whirling inward to a point. "Get all the gold and silver that you can, / Satisfy ambition," until that day comes when the line of life turns back on itself, that day when you are "No longer in Lethean foliage caught," and then, at that supreme climacteric, like the sun at noon and the year at the summer solstice, "Begin the preparation for your death / And from the fortieth winter by that thought / Test every work of intellect or faith." The single and only difference between Jung's enantiodromia and Yeats's is that Jung said the line of life turned back on itself at age 35 (because that is when it happened with him: circa 1910), while Yeats says it is at age 40 (because that is when it happened with him: circa 1905). Otherwise Jung might have been offering a comment on this poem—or on half a dozen others in *Collected Poems*—when he said, "Every more or less normal life runs this enantiodromian course" (*CW*, XVI, par. 212). "Vacillation," reflecting life's typical pattern and the Heraclitean process of psyche, is constructed on a very elaborate series of antinomies—antinomies within stanzas (e.g. I), between stanzas but within a section (e.g. III), and between sections. As an example of this final encounter and resolution of antinomies we have the joy of IV, which finds its antinomic opposite in the remorse of V, both to be resolved in the pattern of alternating emotions, of intertransforming cones, that is the principle of the entire poem; indeed, the joy of IV and the remorse of V are resolved and both dissolved into a stoic resignation before the all-embracing pattern, or the encompassing *logos*, of VI: "let all things"—flame and foliage, joy and remorse, life and death—"pass away." Cast a cold eye on life, on death: let them pass away and let them return; let them return and let them pass away.

The turning backward, or παλίντροπος, of Heraclitus, the identity that he always maintained to exist in opposition, and the circle-closing that brings extremes together all find expression in one of Jung's favorite images or symbols—or perhaps we should call it an archetypal figure, since we can discover it in Yeats at the same time as in Jung and can trace it as far back at least as Heraclitus, if not further, and as far down as the dreams that seem to recur in all men everywhere: "In the age-old image of the uroboros lies the thought of devouring oneself and turning oneself into a circulatory process" —which is just the sort of thing Yeats does—turns himself "into a circulatory process"—in a poem like "Under Ben Bulben" which moves gyrelike down from the superhuman regions of Ben Bulben, through cycles of Irish experiences and the poet's trade, finally to the central, circular point which is W. B. Yeats, and then out through the eye that joins the hourglass cones to issue in that sphere that embraces both of these cones of life and death. "There," as Yeats says in another poem describing the circulatory process contained in the uroboros image, "There all the serpent-tails are bit." On that same image, Jung continues in the passage previously quoted: "The uroboros is a dramatic symbol for the integration and assimilation of the opposite, i.e., of the shadow. This 'feed-back' process is at the same time a symbol of immortality, since it is said of the uroboros that he slays himself and brings himself to life, fertilizes himself and gives birth to himself. He symbolizes the One, who proceeds from the clash of opposites . . ." (*CW*, XIV, par. 513). A symbol for the integration and assimilation of the opposite, for immortality, for the One, and for that which creates itself out of the clash of opposites—quite a rich symbol is the uroboros and as high in Yeats's affections as in Jung's.

If Jung was just a little shy of lending his name publicly and scientifically to a Yeatsian belief in the symbiotic relationship of incarnate and discarnate spirits (his letters and other noncanonical writings—*Septem Sermones* and *Memories, Dreams, Reflections*, for example —suggest he was not so shy privately and personally), he was not at all hesitant to maintain that Heraclitean relationship of opposition and identicalness for consciousness and the unconscious. (In his autobiography, Jung equates the unconscious with the "land of the dead," so in the end it may come to the same thing anyway, in spite of his reluctance to commit himself on incarnate and discarnate spirits.) In a passage that is redolent of Heraclitus and Yeats, except that Jung employs psychological and epistemological rather than cosmological and metaphysical terms, Jung, in an essay on "The Role of the Unconscious" (1918), writes, "I like to visualize the unconscious as a world seen in a mirror: our consciousness presents to us a picture of the outer world, but also of the world within, this being a compensatory mirror-image of the outer world. We could also say that the outer world is a compensatory mirror-image of the inner world" (*CW*, X, par. 23). Why not say it? Heraclitus had said it to his colleagues twenty-five hundred years earlier; and Yeats was off in Ireland proclaiming it at precisely the same moment that Jung was writing. "Conscious unconsciousness, unconscious consciousness, outer inner world, inner outer world, living the other's death, dying the other's life."

It was a favorite observation of Jung's that that which is true and adequate logically is not necessarily true or adequate psychologically: logical principles and psychological principles, he frequently insisted, are not coextensive or coterminous. "An exclusively rational analysis," Jung says, "must necessarily stop short at the . . . antinomies, for in a total opposition there is no third—*tertium non datur*! Science comes to a stop at the frontiers of logic, but nature does not—she thrives on ground as yet untrodden by theory. *Venerabilis natura* does not halt at the opposites; she uses them to create, out of opposition, a new birth" (*CW*, XVI, par. 425). Like God, her father and sometime spouse, or like Heraclitus, one of her first and greatest spokesmen on this question, nature thrives on paradox, and so does psyche, since it is altogether at one with "venerabilis natura." But the new birth or the new creation—Jung was consistent and logical in his argument about that which goes beyond consistency and logic—must always be at a different level of existence from the opposites themselves. "As opposites never unite at their own level (*tertium non datur!*), a supraordinate 'third' is always required, in which the two parts can come together" (*CW*, IX, part 2, par. 280). This is the truth of Heraclitus, the truth of Nicholas of Cusa and of Wiliam Blake, the truth of W. B. Yeats and of C. G. Jung: that in this world there is a continual antinomic opposition that is not to be reconciled by human reason but is brought to peace only transcendently in the paradoxical marriage of reason and non-reason, in the *complexio oppositorum* that draws all antinomies into unity, or in what Cusanus, in his *Vision of God*, calls the *Coincidentia contradictoriorum*: "Thou hast inspired me, Lord . . . , and I have learnt that the place wherein Thou art found unveiled is girt round with the coincidence of contradictories, and this is the wall of Paradise wherein Thou dost abide. The door whereof is guarded by the most proud spirit of Reason, and, unless he be vanquished, the way in will not lie open. Thus 'tis beyond the coincidence of contradictories, that Thou mayest be seen, and nowhere this side thereof."[10] Jung shifts the terms only slightly, from metaphysics to depth psychology, from Paradise to the human psyche, and from God to the self, when he says, "The confrontation of the two positions generates a tension charged with energy and creates a living, third thing—not a logical stillbirth in accordance with the principle *tertium non datur* but a movement out of the suspension of opposites, a living birth that leads to a new level of being, a new situation. The transcendent function manifests itself as a quality of conjoined opposites" (*CW*, VIII, par. 189). The transcendent function in Jung points toward the self realized, as in Cusanus it carries us past Reason and into the circular, wall-girt and mandala-like Paradise "wherein Thou dost abide."

Yeats, when speaking as poet rather than as mystic, turns his gaze away from Cusanus' "wall of Paradise" and back to a world of flux and sheer opposition, for as Yeats says, "If it be true that God is a circle whose centre is everywhere, the saint goes to the centre, the poet and artist to the ring where everything comes round again" (*E. & I.*, p. 287). Within the walls and at the center, there is no division nor any creativity; outside the walls it is otherwise. "No mind can engender until divided into two," Yeats says in a discussion of the poetry of Keats, Shelley, and Synge (*Auto.*, p. 345); and elsewhere in the same volume, he declares, "All creation is from conflict, whether with our own mind or with that of others" (p. 576)—a remark which has much the same sense about it as Yeats's famous

---

10. *Vision of God*, chap. 9; trans. Emma Gurney Salter (London: J. M. Dent & Sons, 1928), pp. 43-44. On the subject of the contradictories and reason, the Latin original (1565 ed. of the *Opera*) reads thus: ". . . cinctum contradictoriorum coincidentia, et iste est murus Paradisi, in quo habitas, cuius portam, custodit spiritus altissimus rationis, qui nisi vincatur, non patebit ingressus. Ultra igitur coincidentiam contradictoriorum videri poteris, et nequaquam citra."

observation that "We make out of the quarrel with others, rhetoric, but of the quarrel with ourselves, poetry" (*Myth.*, p. 331). This is doubtless well said and, what is more, it is structured very much as a Heraclitean fragment should be; yet it seems to me that on the question of conflict and creativity, or the question of opposites and a transcendent third, Yeats was at once more subtle and more comprehensive when he wrote the following in his diary: "Man can only love Unity of Being and that is why such conflicts [as those urged on us by discarnate spirits] are conflicts of the whole soul. . . . All that our opponent expresses must be shown for a part of our greater expression, that he may become our thrall—be 'enthralled' as they say. Yet our whole is not his whole and he may break away and enthrall us in his turn, and there arise between us a struggle like that of the sexes. All life is such a struggle" (*Ex.*, p. 302). Yeats would not be likely to enroll himself a disciple of any psychologist by adopting such terminology as "the transcendent function"; yet he suggests a way to Unity of Being that is strikingly like Jung's movement into and "movement out of the suspension of opposites, a living birth that leads to a new level of being" when he declares that "A writer must die every day he lives, be reborn, as it is said in the Burial Service, an incorruptible self, that self opposite of all that he has named 'himself'" (*Auto.*, p. 457). That he may achieve Unity of Being in "an incorruptible self" renewed daily, the writer exercises a capacity and is driven by a necessity that differs in name only from the transcendent function of analytical psychology: he transforms what had been, or had seemed, an external opposite ("all that our opponent expresses") into a contrary part of the self ("a part of our greater expression"), and out of that quarrel—a quarrel previously with "others" but now with "ourselves"—he not only makes poetry but also brings to birth the Jungian "supraordinate third," which is the same being as the Yeatsian "incorruptible self, that self opposite of all that he has named 'himself.'" Though this third is born of conflicting opposites, and though it is incorruptible, it must be perpetually renewed by union with its own opposite to create a new being at a yet higher level. But this is the genius of what Jung calls the transcendent function or of what we might call the daimonic progression: a sort of Platonic ladder made up of resolutions, integrations, and creations at successively higher levels of reality, freedom, and perfection. "I think all happiness depends on having the energy to assume the mask of some other self, that all joyous or creative life is a rebirth as something not oneself, something created in a moment and perpetually renewed . . ." (*Memoirs*, p. 191; cf. *Auto.*, p. 503). Not only is the opponent whom the writer integrates the opposite of himself, but so also is the resultant creation, the self born of the union of warring opposites; hence there is ever the necessity for conflict and union, birth and rebirth, and always at a higher level.[11] Daimonic opposites join to produce a third, which third unites with its daimonic opposite to produce another third, which third . . . and so on to a symbolic resolution of all the antinomies in the symbolic Sphere (purely symbolic, as Yeats argued, since the endpoint is infinity and, as on a circle, is also the beginning). The universe, according to Michael Robartes, is "a great egg that turns inside-out perpetually without breaking its shell" (*Vision*, p. 33), and so is the writer in his attempt to transcend himself, to become a mystic marriage of creatively warring opposites, to discover an incorruptible self, and to achieve Unity of Being.

It was to Heraclitean duadic opposites of a relatively low level of resolution and creativity that Yeats addressed himself in an early version of the final lines of "Among School Children":

> O dancing couple, glance that mirrors glance
> How can we know the dancer from the dance?[12]

These are the Heraclitean antinomies of the human and phenomenal world, reflections one of another, which, if resolved as they are locked in the dance, may restore and yield up anew the monad and the living, moving pattern of Unity of Being. In the final version, on the other hand, this lower-level resolution and union of man and

---

11. In his copy of Angelo Crespi's *Contemporary Thought of Italy* (London: Williams & Norgate, 1926), Yeats marked a passage on p. 160 describing "the resolution of all distinctions into the concrete unity of Spirit as self-conscious activity, whose only law, inherent in the very idea of *Spirit as a process, is the Dialectical necessity, if there is to be a process, that each moment in preserving its predecessor within itself, yet should be its negation. . . .*" What Yeats underlined (as shown in the quotation) could stand as a very fair description of process in a Heraclitean world, and in a note at the foot of the page Yeats related it all to himself in an exact description of what I have called above the daimonic progression: "I (let us say) *negate* Swinburne, as part of an historical movement. . . . But as transcendental ego I recreate his world. The transcendent ego may not be dialectical, but only the empirical."

12. Quoted by Thomas Parkinson, *W. B. Yeats, The Later Poetry* (Berkeley and Los Angeles: University of California Press, 1971), p. 107.

woman, of the dancing couple, of self and anti-self, has already occured—"O body swayed to music, O brightening glance": the swaying body is singular; the glance brightens because the *daimon* has been brought to perfect union with its opposite and shines forth from the third created out of this union of antinomies; and the dancer now, at an advanced stage of the daimonic progression, weds himself to nothing less than the pattern of dance. Is it not this supreme symbolic union—dance as the perfect being of dancer; dancer as the imperfect becoming of dance—that Yeats describes in *A Vision*, where cones forever imitate the sphere and are ever becoming the sphere, but must be content to symbolize it only and never be it because they are of this world, the sphere of another world? "The *Thirteenth Cone* is a sphere because sufficient to itself; but as seen by Man it is a cone. It becomes even conscious of itself as so seen, like some great dancer, the perfect flower of modern culture, dancing some primitive dance and conscious of his or her own life and of the dance" (*Vision*, p. 230). It is this consciousness of "his or her own life and of the dance," like the consciousness of the *Thirteenth Cone* that it is seen by Man as a cone yet is all the same a sphere, that transports the dancer for an eternal moment into the symbolic sphere. The dancer enters into his own eternity, for as the composite Yeats/Villiers de l'Isle Adam/St. Thomas Aquinas says several times, "Eternity is the possession of one's self, as in a single moment" (*Ex.*, pp. 37, 449; *Vision*, p. 139). What the dancer has done, in a supreme reconciliation of opposites, is to wed the sensible flux of his own life to the *Logos* that, as Heraclitus declared, is forever. Putting it otherwise, as Jung might be inclined to put it, one could say that in his performance the dancer unites the unconscious of the primitive dance with consciousness of his life and of the dance. "In this way conscious and unconscious are united, just as a waterfall"—or a dancing dancer—"connects above and below" (*CW*, XIV, par. 706). The sensible flux runs through the life of every individual and through the life of the universe; the *Logos* is the choreography of the sensible flux—or, if one chooses to personify and to anthropomorphize, the *Logos* is the choreographer of the sensible flux.

That there is a *logos*-formula not only for nature and the universe but for the individual also is the last great truth—a truth that is rather complicated in its Yeatsian/Jungian elaboration but an archetypal truth all the same—for which Heraclitus is responsible in the syncretic evolution of *Anima Mundi*. Though Guthrie accurately declares that Fr. 119 (ἦθος ἀνθρώπῳ δαίμων) is "scarcely translateable," he has himself done as good a job of translating it as any man can do: "A man's individuality is his *daimon*." Besides being his *daimon*—his antinomic, conflicting opposite and his destiny—a man's individuality displays the operation in him of his *logos*. Heraclitus internalizes man's destiny, his *daimon*, in the same way Plato does in the Myth of Er at the end of the *Republic* and in the same way the Instructors do in coming to give Yeats metaphors for his poetry. "By fate and necessity," Yeats says of the Instructors' teachings in *A Vision*, "is understood that which comes from without, whereas the *Mask* is predestined, Destiny being that which comes to us from within" (p. 86). This is good Heraclitus, embracing both the doctrine of opposites and the doctrine of man's *daimon*, but when Yeats elsewhere remarks, with a characteristic insouciance about scholarly niceties, "I think it was Heraclitus who said: the Daimon is our destiny" (*Myth.*, p. 336), there is nothing but the *sprezzatura* of genius to justify his addition to Heraclitus' book. Burnet (on whom Yeats generally relies for his Heraclitus) translates the fragment, "Man's character is his fate," making the Greek δαίμων into English "fate"; but Yeats transforms Burnet's "fate," which according to the Instructors is an external thing, into "destiny," which is internally determined through choice of the Mask; and then he blithely disregards the fact that "fate-destiny" was Burnet's translation of δαίμων, not of ἦθος. Thus, man's character slips between the cracks and simply disappears—*except* for the crucial fact that for Yeats the *daimon* is both the opposite and the twin of a man's character, or of his individuality, or "of all that he has named 'himself.'" There is thus in the end a sufficient depth and intensity to Yeats's misquotation and reinterpretation of Heraclitus (this is far from a unique instance of that technique in Yeats) to persuade the reader that Yeats understood his great forerunner in dark paradox better than the linguistically precise scholar coughing in his ink. If the *Daimon* is a man's individuality and his *logos*—that peculiar and unique balance that is his character and no one else's—and if the *Daimon* is also (as Yeats believed it to be) a man's opposite and his loving antagonist, then it is no dishonor nor an impoverishment of his doctrine to ascribe to Heraclitus the remark that "the Daimon is our destiny"; on the contrary, it is as great an honor as one poet can render to another, and is Yeats's brilliant, if partial, contribution to the exfoliation, accomplished by the ages, of the great flower that is only darkly present and potentially there in the tight-furled bud of Heraclitus' teaching.

I should imagine it was largely Heraclitus that Yeats had in mind (or that his scholarly informant had in mind) when he wrote, "The Greeks, a certain scholar has told me, considered that myths are the activities of the Daimons, and that the Daimons shape our characters and our lives. I have often had the fancy that there is some one myth for every man, which, if we but knew it, would make us understand all he did and thought" (*E. & I.*, p. 107). This daimonic doctrine is Heraclitean in the first instance (a man's individuality equals his *logos* formula equals his *daimon*); after Heraclitus it is Platonic (in the *Timaeus* every soul is given a *daimon* that is its individualizing, divinifying, and immortalizing partner); after Plato it is Plotinian (with the notion that there may be a unique archetype for each human soul); and after Plotinus it is both Yeatsian and Jungian, for this final theorist and psychologist of daimonism (Jung) was fond of arguing that a man's individuality is born with him, demanding to be realized in the course of a life, and that each of us is directed by what Jung, in a phrase sharply reminiscent of Yeats's notion of myths and Daimons, calls in his autobiography his "personal myth." The living of this "personal myth" is the same thing, if Yeats was correct in his information, as the performance in one's own life of the dance pattern traced out for us in advance and laid down by the *daimones*; it is also nothing less than Jungian "individuation," nothing less than the achievement of Yeatsian Unity of Being.

Is it proper, however, when the doctrine of Heraclitus is in question, to speak of "Unity of Being" and to suggest that "individuation" can have anything to do with his teaching? Was not Heraclitus, according to Plato, the spokesman for pluralism, diversity, and becoming rather than the champion of monism, unity, and being? And did he not argue that reality and truth pertain to an objective, impersonal *Logos* rather than to any subjective, individual view of it? The answer to the two questions, of course, must be "Yes, he was" and "Yes, he did"; but here precisely, if paradoxically, in this juncture of the two doctrines—on the one hand a doctrine of pluralistic process, on the other hand a doctrine of monistic *Logos*—we find Heraclitean authority for Yeatsian "Unity of Being" and Jungian "individuation." According to both of these latter-day doctrines of individuated unity—psychological and poetic doctrines rich with cosmological and metaphysical implications—ours is a diverse universe, a world that is simultaneously both one and many, a perpetual, pluralistic process directed by an unchanging monistic *Logos*. But whom did Yeats and Jung have to thank for the original statement of the archetypal idea of unity-in-plurality? Heraclitus, G. S. Kirk writes, "was the first thinker, as far as we know, *explicitly to define* a connexion between the apparent plurality of the phenomenal world and an underlying unity . . ." (*Cosmic Fragments*, p. 70). And Harold Cherniss confirms Heraclitus' priority when he says that he was the one who "discovered . . . that the whole world is a process and nothing else, a process that had no beginning and will never end, but that all things are one because the process has an ineluctable order, the order being a fixed proportion of change. . . . [Heraclitus] for the first time in Western thought declared that reality is not the world that we perceive nor any part of it but a formula that is at once hidden and manifested by this perceptible process."[13] This was an enormously important "discovery" for the psychologist who maintained that psyche itself is a process that both hides and manifests its own formula; and equally important for the poet who wrote to his father that art is not primarily "imitation of something in the outer world" but is instead creation, expression, and manifestation of an inner and hidden formula which is the subjective pattern of the artist's personality: "The element of pattern in every art is, I think, the part that is not imitative, for in the last analysis there will always be somewhere an intensity of pattern that we have never seen with our eyes" (*Letters*, p. 607). For the psychologist and the poet, the pattern or the formula may be cosmic and objective, but it is certainly and first of all individual, microcosmic, and subjective. In *Aion*, Jung tells us that "individuation is a 'mysterium coniunctionis,' the self being experienced as a nuptial union of

13. "The Characteristics and Effects of Presocratic Philosophy," *Journal of the History of Ideas*, 12 (June 1951), p. 333.

opposite halves and depicted as a composite whole in mandalas that are drawn spontaneously by patients" (*CW*, IX, part 2, par. 117). But Jung always maintained that a mandala—i.e., a circular figure —though composed of conflicting parts and many of them, is itself nevertheless supremely unified: it is, in its essence, defined by its unity and circularity not by its diversity and opposition. Thus, in his essay on "Flying Saucers" (which incidentally has almost nothing to do with flying saucers), Jung says, "The symbols of the self coincide with the God-images, as, for instance, the *complexio oppositorum* of Cusanus with the dyad, or the definition of God as a 'circle whose centre is everywhere and the circumference nowhere' with Angelucci's sign of the hydrogen atom" (*CW*, X, par, 806). Just so, in the best Heraclitean way, Nicholas of Cusa may say that God is to be seen beyond the gate which is the "coincidence of contrarieties," but this does not mean that God is in any way complex or plural: "For with Thee," Nicholas says, "speech and sight are one, since in reality they are not different in Thee, who art Very Absolute Simplicity [*qui es ipsa simplicitas absoluta*]."[14] Life as we experience it, life in a human perspective, is composed of the unceasing conflict and interplay of opposites which are, nevertheless, regulated, ordered, or contained in a reality of a higher order: everything is process, but there is an order behind that process, above it, and in it as a whole. "Listening not to me," Heraclitus says in a fragment that manages to save the plurality of phenomena while insisting on the unity of the formula according to which they change and interchange, "Listening not to me but to the *Logos* it is wise to agree that all things are one" (Fr. 50).

Of the one *Logos* and of the many *logoi*—the *daimon*-directed formulae and destinies of individual men—Yeats wrote in his Diary in 1930: "If reality is timeless and spaceless this is a goal, an ultimate Good. But if I believe that it is also a congeries of autonomous selves I cannot believe in one ever-victorious Providence, though I may in Providences that preside over a man, a class, a city, a nation, a world—Providences that may be defeated, the tutelary spirits of Plotinus" (*Ex.*, pp. 309-10). These tutelary spirits, the Heraclitean *daimones* with whom we are locked in loving battle, may be defeated, and yet is not their defeat also their triumph? Must we not suppose that this is what they wanted since it is what is? Yeats pushed his

14. *The Vision of God*, chap. 10; trans. Salter, p. 45.

dialectical theory of daimonism a step further in *A Vision* in his distinction—yet not a distinction either but an identity—between the Parmenidean phaseless sphere and a series of Heraclitean antinomic pairs: "The ultimate reality because neither one nor many, concord nor discord, is symbolised as a phaseless sphere, but as all things fall into a series of antinomies in human experience it becomes, the moment it is thought of, what I shall presently describe as the thirteenth cone. All things are present as an eternal instant to our *Daimon* . . . but that instant is of necessity unintelligible to all bound to the antinomies" (*Vision*, p. 193). So long as we inhabit a Heraclitean universe, which is to say so long as we are living, we are, of course, "all bound to the antinomies," but that says nothing about ultimate reality or the phaseless sphere, nothing about the thirteenth cone or the eternal instant, nothing except that they remain—*it* remains—unintelligible to us. Yet even as he acknowledges his entanglement in the Heraclitean antinomies and his consequent inability to see from above or outside those antinomies, Yeats declares his certain conviction of that which, though it is unintelligible to him, is not entangled in any antinomies and enjoys an existence untroubled by contrast or conflict: he declares his belief, that is, in the phaseless Sphere of Parmenides which, like the ultimate in jealous gods, insists that its existence is the only reality and that the apparent existence of the antinomies is mere illusion. Yeats, like Jung, was a monist who would not—who *could* not—deny mundane pluralism: more by choice and on faith than by necessity and on observation, however, they were both of them at the same time Parmenidean monists; but bound as they were to the antinomies—and intellectual history hardly shows us any thinkers more closely bound to the antinomies than Yeats and Jung—they had to be, and they passionately were, Heraclitean antinomists.

    Having gone this far with Heraclitus, or having attempted, out of Yeats and Jung, to exfoliate thus fully the great flower closed up in his paradoxes and riddles, the time comes when we must turn back on ourselves, reverse our Yeatsian gyres, perform a Jungian *enantiodromia*, and submit ourselves to a Heraclitean *palintropos*; for the fact is that much of this that we have traced to Heraclitus and have boldly called Heraclitean doctrine goes far beyond anything Heraclitus ever said or perhaps could have said. It may well be that, living when he did, Heraclitus did not possess even the language (leaving out of question the desire) to speak of—for example—the individual or the self in the way we have suggested that he did speak. Yet we intend Heraclitus no discourtesy and we do him, I think, no violence—Yeats and Jung did him no violence and no wrong—in thus teasing a system and a universe out of the dark brilliance of his fragments. What we are doing, as Yeats and Jung were doing, as Nietzsche and many others have done, is to tease that whole construct, with all the assistance Heraclitus can give us, out of the shadows and tendencies of our own minds and out of the dark depths of the collective human mind. Heraclitus, like the *daimones*, like the archetypes, like psyche itself, speaks the literal and dramatic language of myth. When he says that it is death to souls to become moist, he means pretty much just that: it is death to souls to become moist. Heraclitus wrote, or spoke, at just that point when language was becoming conscious, as later it would become self-conscious; but it was to be another century in the evolution of Greek thought— a period of history corresponding to a certain period of intellectual, psychological development in the individual—before the concepts of philosophy replaced the stories of mythology and the mysteries of religion, or before the unconscious impulses of psychology had been fully transformed into the conscious formulations of philosophy. (And poetry is forever returning us to its sources in the unconscious, to the stories of mythology and the mysteries of religion—returning us, as it were, from Plato to Heraclitus and Pythagoras, to Hesiod and Homer, and even earlier.) "You can refute Hegel," Yeats observed in his last letter, "but not the Saint or the Song of Sixpence" (*Letters*, p. 922). Yet it was this same refutable Hegel who said (in his *Lectures on the History of Philosophy*), "There is no proposition of Heraclitus which I have not adopted in my Logic."[15] While Hegel, as Yeats says, is subject to refutation, his great progenitor of Ephesus (and I am sure Yeats would agree) was an invulnerable to the assaults of logic as any Saint or the Song of Sixpence. Where does one begin a refutation of "For souls it is death to become water"? On what ground can logic stand to overthrow "Immortal mortals, mortal immortals, living the others' death, dying the others' life"?

15. *Hegel's Lectures on the History of Philosophy*, 3 vols., trans. E. S. Haldane (New York: Humanities Press, 1955), I, 279; the passage occurs in vol. XVII (Vorlesungen über die Geschichte der Philosophie: erster band) of the *Sämtliche Werke*, ed. Hermann Glockner (Stuttgart, 1959), p. 344.

There is no way to deny a direct statement of the psyche, no way to confute myth. If Heraclitus lived before the advent of an abstract, fully conceptual philosophic language, he was nevertheless immensely resourceful and undeniably fortunate in the daimonic mode he chose and perfected: he continues to live today because of the mode he adopted then. And so Heraclitus has his paternity after all, being incontrovertible father to a mode of thinking and irrefutable ancestor to a part of the mind of mankind.

CHAPTER IV

The One Being

Ἔστιν: "Is: Exists."

Right there, having said so much, Parmenides ought to have stopped; and he would have done had he been as faithful to his own expressed principles as he insisted his philosophical antagonists be. An inquirer into the nature of "what is"—someone, that is, like Parmenides who asserts "Is" and then tries to go beyond "Is" to discover and to proclaim how and in what way "it is"; and whose first discovery and proclamation is that "It is one"—such an inquirer will run immediately into a blind, blank wall ("I am that I am") and will be reduced either to silence or to the mumbling of tautologies and empty nothingness. Or worse, if he makes the positive, substantive statement, then he runs up against, and either destroys or is destroyed by, his assertion that "It is" and "It is one." For exactly contrary but equally compelling reasons, Parmenides and Cratylus should both have abandoned speech. That Parmenides did not join Cratylus in silence tells us only that here, once at least, the logician is abrogating his own logic. If "what is" is one, and if, as Parmenides says, reality, thought, and language are exactly coequal and coterminous, then we can say nothing but what is tautological, and that Parmenides has already said: "What is, is." With the birth of Parmenides' "Way of Truth," the same lament that greeted another birth must have gone over the Greek world: "The great god Pan is dead"; for Parmenides slew Pan with abstractions and denied nature with a thought so pure that it bore no smudge of the senses, a thought so absolute and all-encompassing that it was completely empty. After the lament for Pan, a hush as it were fell momentarily on Greek philosophy. The philosopher was closed and imprisoned within the bounds of his logic and his speech; he was fettered in just the same way as "what is"—"for powerful Necessity holds it in the bonds of a chain that hems it in all round." The extreme monism of Parmenides' truth forbade him any consciousness of reality—or it should have done—for to be conscious is to be separated, and Parmenides himself allowed there to be no separation, no division, in "what is"; it also prevented him (logically) from speaking of "what is," since the act of speaking, like the act of consciousness, requires a separation of subject and object, and it means movement, change, heterogeneity, and multiplicity in "what is." Historians of Greek philosophy have puzzled over Parmenides' reasons for writing his "Way of Seeming" after he had thoroughly demolished the grounds for such a construct in his "Way of Being." They might well address themselves to another and, as it seems to me, prior question: After having said "Is," or after having asserted "Exists," how can Parmenides go on to speak of that Being which, if it is one, full, and everything, is also—and therefore—unreal, unknowable, and ineffable?

Parmenides, however, was nothing if not confident, even recklessly so. His intellectual hubris is most apparent when he proceeds not only to describe the nature of "what is"—this I imagine Parmenides did not see as illogical or impossible; it came to seem so only with the advances made by Plato—but when he goes much further to describe, very daringly, the nature of "what is not," which is a performance that Parmenides had himself bitterly condemned in others and had previously tried to stamp out as the very worst of sins against logic. Parmenides' superb confidence that the single and only truth had been revealed to him was as great as Heraclitus' self assurance, and it filled him with an arrogance nearly as absolute as that of Heraclitus himself. Indeed, in one sense Parmenides is even more secure in his confidence than Heraclitus: so secure that he can, from his superior position, give an exposition of the "Way of Appearance and Illusion" that will be better than any other, and can toy with his creation even while knowing that it is nothing but appearance and illusion, since he has just finished giving an exposition of *the only* True Way. It is as if Yeats were to preface his *Collected Poems*—that most delicate, most faithful following of the sinuous, quick-changing path of the serpent, as Yeats calls it in one place, and in another place, "hodos chameliontos," which is none other than Parmenides' *hodos doxōn*, the "Way of Seeming"—as if he were to preface that brave and magnificent effort with a chilly statement of the "Way of Truth," denying in advance any validity, reality, or force to what would follow; or as if Plato were to preface the account of creation in the *Timaeus* not by saying, as he does say, that it is a likely story rather than certain truth but by saying that it is an assured falsehood with no likelihood about it at all. Neither Plato nor Yeats was so extreme, so negative, so daring but destructive; nor was Jung, who, though he acknowledged the subjectivity of his psychology, nevertheless maintained, Plato-like, that it was a likely—in fact a *very* likely—story.

"I have thought much," Yeats says in "Anima Hominis," "of the difference between the winding movement of Nature and the straight line, which is . . . the mark of saint or sage. I think that we who are poets and artists, not being permitted to shoot beyond the tangible, must go from desire to weariness and so to desire again, and live but for the moment when vision comes to our weariness like terrible lightning, in the humility of the brutes. . . . Only when we are saint or sage, and renounce experience itself, can we, in the imagery of the Christian Cabbala, leave the sudden lightning and the path of the serpent and become the bowman who aims his arrow at the centre of the sun" (*Myth.*, p. 340). Saint or sage or antipoetic poet and logician like Parmenides—they alone have nothing to do with the "Way of Seeming," the "Path of the Chameleon," the circumference of the circle; they alone aim for the sensorily empty, void, and desert-poor center, suffering neither desire nor weariness, denying the reality of process and of "the tangible," paying no tribute whatsoever to "coming into being and perishing, change of place and alteration of bright colour" (Fr. 8, ll. 40-41). Though Yeats, according to his own lights, was neither saint nor sage, he nevertheless recognized and acknowledged that other way of saint or sage opposed to the artist's way, that *hodos alētheiēs* or *hodos sphairēs* as against the "hodos chameliontos"; Yeats seldom spoke of that other way, however, simply because he thought it beyond the powers of speech. With Parmenides he would say "Is," and would insist upon it, but he would not go on to try to describe the nature of "what is" with nothing to hand but the frail tools of human discourse; neither would Yeats deny, as Parmenides did, the reality or the significance of the reflection in the stream, the play of light and shade on Ben Bulben, the perpetual flow of appearances over the face of nature, for there, in the "Way of Seeming," for all its instability and delusiveness, he hoped to discover symbols that would provide access to the "Way of Truth" itself. Similarly, in the first of the *Sermons to the Dead*, we are told that in the PLEROMA—which is Parmenides' One Being under another name—"both thinking and being cease" and we are informed also that "It is quite fruitless to think about the pleroma"; but the man who called himself Basilides was, like Yeats, writing many centuries after Parmenides, and the intervening centuries had developed an answer to the Parmenidean dilemma that was not available to the logician who devised a trap for his philosophical opponents but then, like Daedalus, found himself confined in a prison house of his own making.

When Parmenides, quite against his stated premises, descends from the first, monistic part of his poem, "The Way of Truth," to the second, pluralistic part of it, "The Way of Seeming," his subject is transformed from the One Being into "Whatever is begotten, born, and dies." What Yeats says about *A Vision*—"all the symbolism of this book applies to begetting and birth, for all things are a single form which has divided and multiplied in time and space" (p. 212)—applies also to Parmenides' "Way of Seeming" (but not to his "Way of Truth," since he denies that a single form can be "divided and multiplied in time and space"), and it applies with yet greater force to Yeats's own poems in which there is a continual alternation between division and multiplication on the one hand and unification on the other hand. The relevant fact about Yeats's poetic theory and practise is that, unlike Parmenides, he envisions not only a descent from truth to seeming but an ascent from seeming to truth as well. For Yeats, the transcendent world of Oneness is a creation of art (no doubt of philosophy also if the created system holds against the pressure of experience and the demands of reality) which, in contrast to the world of process, change, and decay, is unmoving, single, equal in all directions from the center, as Parmenides, Empedocles, and Plato all joined in saying of the spherical One. The two antinomic worlds figure in "Sailing to Byzantium" as "that country" (where all is pluralistic: birds, generations, bodies, songs) and as Byzantium (where all is monistic: golden bird, eternity, soul, song). They figure also in "The Dolls," where the living (and therefore dying) child is felt as an incredible insult by the dolls who have seen "Generations of his sort," and felt also as a miserably poor performance by the doll-maker himself whose wife—the watery, maternal source of all this nonartistic death and woe—apologizes to him in these wretched accents:

> My dear, my dear, O dear,
> It was an accident.

As Yeats sees it (here humorously, elsewhere more seriously), there is a world of accident and a world of essence, one of becoming and one of being, a realm of Heraclitean process and seeming and a realm of Parmenidean stasis and truth, a procreation of life and a creation of art. As he says in the intended preface to a collected edition of his poems, the artist is not the bundle of accidents that sits down to breakfast; in fact, *qua* artist, he is not a living man at all but is the work he creates, golden bird, poem, or statue. The poet descends continually into the world of becoming that he may rescue therefrom that sad bundle of accidents that does sit down to breakfast, transform the bundle into the essence of his own personality, and with it reascend to the world of being. The necessity that the two worlds be joined, yet the stark contrast between them, is of course what produces the agony of human life, the misery of growing up, and "that most fecund ditch of all" that is unhappy love. Yet, as Yeats tries to suggest, and as philosophers of Plato's school have always maintained, this paradoxical state, which is the source of so much sorrow, is also the source of the "uncontrollable mystery on the bestial floor" and of the only possible way to the transcendence of sorrow. Hence, in "Dialogue of Self and Soul," Yeats proclaims himself "content to follow to its source / Every event in action or in thought," so that he might "cast out remorse" and thereby be "blest by everything." Parmenides, however, was pre-Platonic (and very much pre-Yeatsian), and so, seeing the world around him as a wretched place, he turned his back on it and on all experience save mental experience, the better to think the necessary thought and to create a web of language that should be the equivalent of that necessary thought and the equivalent, therefore, of being or reality.

If Heraclitus was a sort of half mythographer/half philosopher of natural process, Parmenides was a logician who abandoned all poetry and myth and who strained toward, but never quite achieved, a thoroughly abstract and conceptual expression. It is a very instructive exercise, in this regard, to notice the different meanings attached to the word *logos* in these two great antagonists in Greek philosophy and in the human mind. *Logos* for Heraclitus is a fact and a force of nature, it is the universal and endless principle directing the process of nature, and as such it is the virtual equivalent of a god—in fact, the chief of the gods—in one of the old mythologies, though Heraclitus does not personify his *Logos* as Hesiod would have done. For Parmenides, on the other hand, *logos*, as he uses the word in Fr. 7, signifies, very simply, "reason," and reason here, as everywhere in Parmenides, is set off against those senses that would betray us into believing in the reality of "hodos chameliontos" and the "Way of Seeming": "For never shall this be proved, that things that are not are; but do thou hold back thy thought (*noēma*) from this way of enquiry, nor let custom, born of much experience, force thee to let wander along this road thy aimless eye, thy echoing ear or thy tongue; but do thou judge by reason (*logō*) the strife-encompassed proof that I have spoken" (trans. Raven). Thought, in such a passage as this, is unquestionably self-aware, but if language had attained to self-awareness in Parmenides, then, because of his premises and logical conditions, it would have nullified itself and sunk into silence—which is virtually the conclusion of the *Parmenides* of Plato.[1] The alternative to silence would be a transformation of the

---

1. Burnet translates the *logos* of Parmenides as "argument" and comments on the word in a footnote: "This is the earliest instance of λόγος in the sense of (dialectical) argument which Sokrates made familiar. He got it, of course, from the Eleatics. The Herakleitean use is quite different" (*Early Greek Philosophy*, 4th ed., p. 173). It is not inappropriate to remark that the second half of the *Parmenides* is probably the most extensive example of dialectical argumentation in the dialogues and that the conclusion to this exercise in Eleatic philosophizing, as I have remarked above, is that nothing at all can be said of the Eleatic One.

ontological premises—Parmenides' statement on being and non-being and his absolute denial of the latter—which is of course what Plato accomplished with his theory of Forms after demonstrating, in the *Theaetetus*, the *Parmenides*, and the *Sophist*, that silence is the ultimate, unhappy consequence of Parmenides' exclusive, monistic premise. In *Plato's Theory of Ideas*, W. D. Ross suggests that "the more Plato's interest was drawn to Eleaticism and the more he recognized Parmenides' greatness as the protagonist of the intellect against the senses, the more he also saw the barrenness of his system and his failure to account for the facts of sense-perception."[2] It was only when language got outside itself in Plato that the barrenness of Parmenides' system became apparent, and though Parmenides was never abandoned—not by Plato in his time, nor by Yeats and Jung in their time—his monism had somehow to be wed to pluralism so that the phenomena might be saved and speech returned to the philosophic community. "Now it is true," Paul Friedländer says of what Plato accepted from Parmenides and what he rejected, "that, in place of the simple, immutable, spherical being that the intuitive fantasy of this first ontologist, this awkward yet great poet, had also 'perceived with his mind,' Plato knew an abundance of visions, which were increased and enlarged with every new perception and, even though they drove toward unity, never again achieved the lonely rigidity of Parmenides' being. However, despite this contrast, we can see a remarkable agreement down to the level of language. It is the very predicates of the Parmenidean being—whole, simple, immutable—that Plato transferred to his archetypes."[3] With this in mind, when we hear Jung preaching that his pleroma is "endless, eternal, and entire," that it is "nowhere divided," and that it is "everywhere whole and continuous," we shall have no trouble in recognizing the terms applied by the "first ontologist" to his One Being and transferred by the second ontologist "to his archetypes." Likewise, Yeats is subscribing to this same composite ontology begat by Plato upon Parmenides, and he is simultaneously constructing a theory of multiple symbols in the sensible realm

2. W. D. Ross, *Plato's Theory of Ideas* (Oxford: Oxford University Press, 1951), p. 80.
3. Paul Friedländer, *Plato: An Introduction*, 2d ed. (Princeton: Bollingen/Princeton University Press, 1969), pp. 23-24.

resolved into a single symbol providing access to the intelligible realm, when he says: "I only speak of the *Thirteenth Cone* as a sphere and yet I might say that the gyre or cone of the *Principles* is in reality a sphere, though to Man, bound to birth and death, it can never seem so, and that it is the antinomies that force us to find it a cone. Only one symbol exists, though the reflecting mirrors make many appear and all different" (*Vision*, p. 240). Archetypes, symbols, Ideas and Forms—they were all attempts to affirm the truth of Parmenides' "Way of Truth" while denying his denial of the "Way of Seeming": only one symbol exists, which is the symbol of Being, but many appear to compose the world of Seeming.

There are many signs, Parmenides says (and in the very saying he deviates from the true and only way, which is the logical path of "Is"), on the Way of Truth that teach us about the nature of Being, and what these signs teach us—or what the goddess taught Parmenides and he now passes it on to us—is that "what is" is intelligible; it is uncreated and imperishable; entire, immovable, and without end; eternal, one, and continuous; indivisible, homogeneous, and "all full of what is";[4] motionless, without beginning or end, yet limited and "bounded on every side, like the bulk of a well-rounded sphere, from the centre equally balanced in every direction." All these, Parmenides informs us, constitute the nature of Being; curiously enough, however, he fails to mention what is surely the most striking fact about his Being: "what is" is entirely, purely, perfectly unreal. As Nietzsche put it, with a good deal of malice prepense: "Once in his life Parmenides, probably at a fairly advanced age, had a moment of purest absolutely bloodless abstraction, unclouded by any reality."[5] It could well be considered a bitter irony for Parmenides to have been granted the intuitive vision and revelation that was his, yet to be the "first ontologist" living at a moment when language was still too close to the concrete, material, and sensory realities that had shaped it ever to bear the strain put upon it by Parmenides' efforts at abstraction and conceptualization. He has his primacy and originality, but the consequence is that in expression Parmenides is forced to be abstract about that which is sensuous (the

---

4. Fr. 8, 1. 24. "All full of what is," incidentally, is a good translation for "pleroma."

5. *Philosophy in the Tragic Age of the Greeks*, section 9; trans. Marianne Cowan (Chicago: Henry Regnery Co., 1962), p. 69.

"pleroma" contains all qualities, yet Parmenides can legitimately say nothing of it but "exists" or "is") and to be sensuous about that which is abstract (to show that "what is" is eternal but finite—thus abolishing both time and space as illusions—and is intelligible rather than sensible he describes it, as Burnet has said, in physical terms and by material analogies). Nietzsche's zestful description of the peculiar nature of Parmenidean Being and his further description of the astounding proposition put to Greek philosophy by Parmenides and Zeno is of all possible descriptions the least reverent and the best: "Thinking and that single uncreated perfect globe of existentiality were not to be comprehended as two different types of being, since of course there could be no dichotomy in being. Thus an incredibly bold notion became necessary, the notion of the identity of thinking and being. . . . Thinking and that bulbous-spherical being, wholly dead-inert and rigid-immobile must, according to Parmenides' imperative, coincide and be utterly the same thing. What a shock to human imagination! But let their identity contradict sensation! Just that fact guarantees better than anything else that this was a conception not derived from the senses" (*Philosophy in the Tragic Age of the Greeks*, section 12, pp. 87–88).

Perhaps one ought not let Nietzsche's mockery carry the day, however, for Parmenides' effort was an immensely brave one though the failure of that effort, coming when it did and on the subject it concerned, was as inevitable as it was glorious. Yeats and Jung had reason to be grateful to Parmenides, for there is much of his thought in the writing of both men. In *Per Amica Silentia Lunae* (and elsewhere), Yeats distinguishes what he calls "two realities," and in so doing he both confirms and violates Parmenidean doctrine: confirms it because one of the realities is the same as Parmenides' Being, simple, single, homogeneous, immutable, eternal; but violates it because there is only *one* reality, according to Parmenides, and then violates it again, and more grievously, because the other reality is the reality of Heraclitean process and conflicting, embracing opposites. "There are two realities, the terrestrial and the condition of fire. All power is from the terrestrial condition, for there all opposites meet and there only is the extreme of choice possible, full freedom. And there the heterogeneous is, and evil, for evil is the strain one upon another of opposites; but in the condition of fire is all music and all rest" (*Myth.*, pp. 356–57). The heterogeneous and evil may be of the terrestrial condition but so also is life and speech and poetry. Yeats is notably brief, not to say vague, when it comes to speech about the Parmenidean condition of fire—"all music and all rest"—but so it must be, for it is out of conflict that energy and power flow, and out of conflict also that speech and poetry come. The dialogue of Soul and Heart in section VII of "Vacillation" is a dialogue between aspirants to the two realities, the two conditions, with the slight falsification (for the sake of getting the poem written) of granting speech to Soul, since Soul speaks for a condition where there is no more giving in speech than there is giving in marriage:

> *The Soul.* Seek out reality, leave things that seem.
> *The Heart.* What, be a singer born and lack a theme?
> *The Soul.* Isaiah's coal, what more can man desire?
> *The Heart.* Struck dumb in the simplicity of fire!

And that is exactly what would happen in the simplicity of the condition of fire, which, being one, continuous, homogeneous, indivisible, etc., allows not even for the light of separated consciousness that could articulate the condition. Nor does the condition of fire speak out but, like Parmenides' One, just *is*; only the opposites produce dialectic, hence speech, hence poetry. "In the momentary present the conflict of opinions will always rage, for 'war is the father of all,'" Jung says, with an assist from Heraclitus. "Truth is not eternal, it is a programme to be fulfilled. The more 'eternal' a truth is, the more lifeless it is and worthless; it says nothing more to us because it is self-evident" (*CW*, VI, par. 87). The eternal truth is also, one might say, tautological, bound either to silence or to inanity by the indistinguishable unity of Being and by the identity of thought and of "what is."

It was Yeats's great desire, being "a singer born" but also a seeker of the reality proclaimed by Soul, to hold in delicate balance the equal, if opposite, realities of "the terrestrial and the condition of fire." He wanted to find out eternity but to do so by the erring way of time: being poet rather than saint or sage, Yeats could not shoot straight for the center but he might all the same, he thought, describe the whole circle and thereby he would succeed, like the child of the Eleatic Stranger, in having both—both Heraclitus and Parmenides. "And there is not, and never shall be, any time other than that which is present, since fate has chained it so as to be whole and immovable. Wherefore all these things are but the names which mortals have given, believing them to be true." Yeats marked this translation of Parmenides' Fr. 8, ll. 36-39 in his copy of Burnet's *Early Greek Philosophy*, and in the margin he wrote, "Time as illusion." It was this Parmenidean denial of the reality of time and process, and his affirmation of the related notion of the eternal present, that Yeats had in mind when he wrote the little poem called "A Meditation in Time of War," as we can see in a passage from *Per Amica* that echoes the poem: "When all sequence comes to an end, time comes to an end, and the soul puts on the rhythmic body and contemplates all the events of its memory and every possible impulse in an eternal possession of itself in a single moment. That condition is alone animate, all the rest is fantasy . . ." (*Myth.*, p. 357). But this is in a sense too easy. What is much more difficult, but as desirable and as necessary as it is difficult, is to see the two opposed parties—time and the eternal moment, "all the rest" and "that condition"—as somehow identical, or as inter-involved entities, or as reality and a symbol of reality. Yeats succeeded in this more difficult, more desirable venture when he wrote to Olivia Shakespear of a medium who had sent him blind to a book containing plates from Dante—to plate 84 ("Dante entering the Holy Fire") and to plate 48 ("The serpent attacking Vanni Fucci," which "symbolises 'the temporal Fire'")—and then, realizing that this merger of the temporal and the Holy fires was what he had just finished working out in "Sailing to Byzantium," went on to comment thus: "The medium is the most stupid I know and certainly the knowledge was not in my head. After this and all that has gone before I must capitulate if the dark mind lets me. Certainly we suck always at the eternal dugs. How well too it puts my own mood between spiritual excitement, and the sexual torture and the knowledge that they are somehow inseparable!" (*Letters*, p. 731). Just so: "somehow inseparable"—but *not* a seamlessly homogeneous One Being that would make "spiritual excitement" and "the sexual torture" to be mere names which, as Parmenides says, foolish and deluded "mortals have laid down believing them to be true" (Fr. 8, l. 39). Even though they were "somehow inseparable," there were two fires for Yeats as there were two fires for Dante: the one fire, the fire of Plate 48, the temporal fire, is the "terrestrial condition," the Heraclitean fire that burns forever and is the *Logos*, the balance, the proportion, the rule of change, the inter-transforming, elemental opposites of this world; the other fire, the fire of Plate 84, the eternal fire, is the "condition of fire," the Parmenidean fire that is timeless and unchanging and in which, because it is one and homogeneous, there is no balance, no proportion, no conflict, no opposites, no elements, no change: "all music and all rest." What Yeats establishes is a correspondence and a parallel, and he asserts a great likeness between the two fires, but while they are somehow inseparable they nevertheless remain two.

It is on this question of "likeness" that Yeats, following in Plato's footsteps and accompanied by Jung, must take leave of Parmenides, for though Parmenides describes his Being in simile and analogy ("like the mass of a well-rounded ball"), the truth is that in his universe there can *be* no such thing as simile or analogy because there is no possibility of "likeness." This is the point that Timaeus is at such great pains to explain as a preliminary to his description—his "likely or iconic story"—of this universe of ours and his exposition of its coming-to-be. "According to these premises," he says—the premise that what is visible and tangible and possessed of a body must have come into existence, and the premise that a visible-tangible-corporeal object such as our universe must have been created after some model (παράδειγμα: paradigm)—"According to these premises, it is altogether necessary that this cosmos is a likeness (*eikōn*) of something" (*Timaeus*, 29b). What Timaeus argues, of course, is that this changing cosmos is a likeness of an unchanging one, and that becoming is a likeness, an icon, an image, of Being. This, however, is what Parmenides denied absolutely because his premise, prior to the more complex and accommodating premises of Timaeus, was that "what is, is" and "what is not, is not"—being and eternity exist, becoming and time do not—and the moment that premise is accepted, the universe is shorn of fiction and poetry, it is divested of its bright garments of mythology and of all the stories that begin "Once upon a time. . . ." Timaeus' recreation restores "likeness" as a valid tool for the epistemologist and ontologist; it reestablishes time and process as realities of a kind rather than mere illusions; it returns correspondence, simile, and analogy to the universe; and it opens the way to myth and to the "likely story," to

Yeats's symbols and to Jung's archetypes. Timaeus' recreation also, which is perhaps its greatest achievement and its profoundest homage to Parmenides, keeps the One Being perfect, whole, immutable, eternal, and inviolate while, at the same time, giving us a way to separate ourselves from it but then to relate back to it, to think about it, to speak of it, and to approach it. This is to make philosophy possible again after the shock of Parmenides, as it also makes possible both poetry and psychology.

Timaeus 37d: "The Demiourgos determined to make a moving likeness of eternity, and so, as he set the heavens in order, he created of the eternity that abides in unity an everlasting likeness [*eikōn*] moving according to number, and this likeness is what we call time." It is to precisely this passage, and none other, that I should point were I to try to locate *the* central, *the* essential rationale of the symbolic mode in the Western tradition. Yeats, of course, was familiar with this passage and so was Jung, but it is not their familiarity with *Timaeus* 37d that I have in mind when I say that the symbolism that both men practised and that both of them exalted with such enthusiasm could never have been without the Timaean passage. A whole tradition, a way of thought, a mode of poetry, a psychological language find their origin and their justification in this single sentence. Alfred North Whitehead, in his little book on *Symbolism*, makes the point brilliantly—but without specific reference to the *Timaeus* passage—when he says, "The contrast between the comparative emptiness of Presentational Immediacy and the deep significance disclosed by Causal Efficacy [i.e., the contrast between πάντα ῥεῖ and time on the one hand, and between the One Being and denial of time on the other] is at the root of the pathos which haunts the world.

'Pereunt et imputantur'

is the inscription on old sundials in 'religious' houses:

'The hours perish and are laid to account.'

Here 'Pereunt' refers to the world disclosed in immediate presentation, gay with a thousand tints, passing, and intrinsically meaningless. 'Imputantur' refers to the world disclosed in its causal efficacy, where each event infects the ages to come, for good or for evil, with its own individuality. Almost all pathos includes a reference to lapse of time."[6] All the meaning that is possible to symbolism arises out of the contrast yet contact of these two senses of the world, but they must not be so absolutely sundered—the one exalted beyond reach, the other cast down into sheer ignominy—that the symbol cannot, in its own nature, in its Being-and-becoming, join them. As Whitehead puts it, "There cannot be symbolic reference between percepts derived from one mode and percepts from the other mode, unless in some way these percepts intersect. By this 'intersection' I mean that a pair of such percepts must have elements of structure in common, whereby they are marked out for the action of symbolic reference" (ibid., p. 49). It is the "likeness" of time to eternity, as first argued by Timaeus, that justifies the symbolism of Yeats and Jung. Neither of them could agree, then, that "Time as illusion" says everything. Taken in itself, time may be an illusion; taken in relation to eternity, time is something more than mere illusion.

It is necessary, all the same, that the One Being remain the One Being, else a symbol will be no more than a natural fact and an archetype nothing but a psychological fact. In the right time and the right place, therefore, Yeats and Jung were as capable of defending Parmenides' One Being—defining it, for their diverse purposes, quite differently of course—as vigorously as Plato ever did and as warmly as they themselves spoke out for the perpetual change of Heraclitus. Yeats begins Book III of *A Vision* ("The Soul in Judgment") with a comment on Valéry's *Cimetière marin* and on the question raised by that poem of the real reality—whether the flowing world or the motionless absolute. After expressing great admiration for the poem, Yeats nevertheless parts company with Valéry, specifically when Valéry denounces Zeno—that Zeno who would have given Parmenidean monism a leg up by demonstrating that change is only apparent, a delusion of the senses, and that there is but one reality, a continuous and motionless sphere. "This metropolitan," Yeats says of Valéry, "who has learnt as a part of good manners to deny

---

6. *Symbolism: Its Meaning and Effect* (New York: Capricorn, 1959), p. 47. I have quoted at length because Yeats found Whitehead so congenial; as Yeats put it in a letter to Sturge Moore (p. 89), what he admired in Whitehead was "intensity of thought—which is Beauty." Whitehead was favorite reading for Yeats—shuffled in among his detective stories and tales of the Wild West—in 1926, i.e., just after publication of the first version of *A Vision*.

what has no remedy, cries out 'Cruel Zénon! Zénon d'Elée!', condemning that problem of a tortoise and Achilles because it suggested that all things only seemed to pass; and in a passage of great eloquence rejoices that human life must pass. I was about to put his poem among my sacred books," Yeats concludes, "but cannot now, for I do not believe him" (*Vision*, p. 217). Yeats himself, as he implies, being no French metropolitan, is not so well mannered or so sophisticated that he can deny reality—here the Parmenidean and Zenonian reality—merely because it is without remedy. That reality, moreover, is not only (and blessedly) without remedy; it is also, Yeats would claim, the heart's desire of all things that pass—or that seem to pass—and the end toward which all fleeting things move. Against Valéry and with the "beautiful young girl singing at the edge of the sea in Normandy," Yeats would sing "of the civilisations that there had come and gone, ending every verse with the cry: 'O Lord, let something remain'" (ibid., p. 220). Yeats here displays what elsewhere, with Parmenidean imagery, he calls a "sense for what is permanent, as distinct from what is useful, for what antiquity called the sphere as distinct from the gyre . . ." (*E. & I.*, p. 401). Parmenides would deny the gyre and difference, but everything else he would insist upon, and he was the first to do so: "what is" is permanent, it is truth prevalent, and it is "complete on every side, equally poised from the centre in every direction, like the mass of a rounded sphere" (in Burnet's translation of Fr. 8, ll. 42-44, marked by Yeats in his copy of *Early Greek Philosophy*).

When the Parmenidean fit is upon him, it is only the sphere, the One Being, the eternal and motionless reality that is desirable in itself to Yeats; all the passing many are sought not for themselves but, on the contrary, if sought at all it is because in their very passing they demonstrate their yearning toward that which remains. The truth is, however, that Yeats seldom shows himself entirely subdued to the Parmenidean mood, and very few of his poems attempt anything like a description of the reality of Parmenides. Observing the same logic and the same strategy as his ghostly communicants, Yeats was for the most part silent about that which, though it may have provided the motive for all he wrote, nevertheless surpassed human capabilities both of knowledge and of speech. "My instructors, keeping as far as possible to the phenomenal world, have spent little time upon the sphere, which can be symbolised but cannot be known" (*Vision*, p. 193). Yeats, like his instructors, chose to be silent about the sphere (after affirming ἔστιν, "it is"—"I knew that One is animate, / Mankind inanimate fantasy") not because speech was undesirable but because it was impossible. "Parmenides represented reality as a motionless sphere," Yeats says in *A Vision* (p. 211, n. 1), and that sphere is itself a symbol for the condition to which Yeats, along with all other men of the spirit, aspires, "but even the sphere," as Yeats has already pointed out many pages earlier in the same volume, "is not the changeless eternity, . . . but offers us the image of that which is changeless" (pp. 67-68). The sphere too, then, is an icon, a likeness, a symbolic image representing that which can be symbolized but cannot be known. It was important for Yeats to establish that symbolism does not function within this world but between this world and another one that enjoys an entirely different mode of being. Thus the Platonist-symbolist's creed: nature is "but a spume that plays / Upon a ghostly paradigm of things"—it must be so, for the spirit finds, and has always found, the alternative to that belief too grim to contemplate: if there be no ghostly paradigm, no place wherein the One Being dwells, "all music and all rest," then this present world is the whole of reality and is nothing but spume, frothy and vain, signifying nothing. To put the belief of the symbolist another way: if this world we live in is not a dream—then it is a nightmare. "The whole system," Yeats says of the Parmenidean-Heraclitean and Platonic construct of *A Vision*, "is founded upon the belief that the ultimate reality, symbolised as the Sphere, falls in human consciousness . . . into a series of antinomies" (p. 187). So the symbol mediates between two worlds and the symbolist maintains his position, as Socrates puts it, between two opposed camps, subscribing partially to both but wholly to neither, driven to his ambivalent position by the certain knowledge that an extreme monistic denial of this present world would render the symbolic process impossible, but an extreme pluralistic denial of the One Being would render it nugatory.

It was precisely this symbolistic desire to maintain the delicate balance between an intelligible One and the visible many—on the one hand and on the other hand, here and There (in MacKenna's way of rendering the intelligible realm of Plotinus), balanced on the seesaw point of *analogia* (proportion or analogy)—that required Timaeus to describe a cosmogony, an anthropogony, and a zoogony in which this our universe, a Living Creature embracing all living creatures, comes into being as a single, unique, sensible, and corporeal cosmos, modelled on a paradigm that never came into being but that has been for eternity, single, unique, intelligible, and incorporeal. Between the two—the sensible on the one hand and the intelligible on the other—exists the relationship that we call analogy, iconology, similitude, or symbolism. Of one such symbol that draws all the many into a likeness of the One, Jung says, "The dragon is probably the oldest pictorial symbol in alchemy of which we have documentary evidence. It appears as the οὐροβόρος, the tail-eater, in the Codex Marcianus, which dates from the tenth or eleventh century, together with the legend: ἕν τὸ πᾶν (the One, the All). Time and again the alchemists reiterate that the *opus* proceeds from the one and leads back to the one, that it is a sort of circle like a dragon biting its own tail" (*CW*, XII, par. 404). The circular idea and form, if not the specific dragon symbol, can of course be found earlier than the documentary evidence yielded by alchemy: the *opus* performed by the Demiourgos proceeds also from the one, the eternal model, and leads back to it, yearning for its beginning and end, its source and consummation. Nor is the symbol anything like exhausted or out of date, for, as Yeats declared in fine and prophetic phrase, "the serpent's tooth [is] in his own tail again . . ." (*E. & I.*, p. 356). What is only a dragonish and serpentine symbolism in our universe here, however, is pure and perfect reality in the condition of fire which Yeats (following Plotinus) denominates "There" in the poem of that title, the fourth of his "Supernatural Songs":

> There all the barrel-hoops are knit,
> There all the serpent-tails are bit,
> There all the gyres converge in one,
> There all the planets drop in the Sun.

The multiplicity of creation—"all . . . all . . . all . . . all"—is resolved into its own source in the "one" of line three; "There" the points of the circumference are all drawn into the center, as "here" the center proliferates in circumferential points.

"The point is the symbol of a mysterious creative centre in nature," Jung says in his last major work (*CW*, XIV, par. 40); and in the next paragraph he continues, "The most perfect form is round, because it is modelled on the point. The sun is round and so is fire. . . . 'God is an intelligible sphere whose centre is everywhere and whose circumference is nowhere.' " What Jung here in the *Mysterium Coniunctionis* ascribes to St. Bonaventura and describes in cosmological and metaphysical terms, he turns to psychological account in *Aion*, where he describes it as the profoundly inner archetype that draws human inquirers on—or draws them back—to monism: "Finally the self, on account of its empirical peculiarities, proves to be the *eidos* behind all the supreme ideas of unity and totality that are inherent in all monotheistic and monistic systems" (*CW*, IX, pt. 2, par. 64). For the individual, Jung implies, the self is both center and circumference, both paradigm and universe, a subjective experience and an objective cosmos—and in all cases like the intelligible reality of Parmenides but with the sensible complement added thereto by Plato: a point, on the one hand, that is a potential circle; a circle, on the other hand, that is an extended point.

It seems at first slightly ironic that in developing this same image and notion of sphericity elsewhere, Jung should seize on a passage in Parmenides that comes not from the "Way of Truth" (Fr. 8 on the "well-rounded sphere" is obviously apropos) but from the "Way of Seeming"—i.e., from what Yeats calls "hodos chameliontos," which Parmenides himself declares is mere illusion and deception. On second thought, however, there may be a certain appropriateness in Jung's looking to the "Way of Seeming," for that is the realm in which the psychiatrist must function and is the only realm about which he can speak. "In ecclesiastical as in alchemical literature the saying is often quoted [probably nowhere as often as in Jung himself, however]: 'God is an infinite circle (or sphere) whose centre is everywhere and the circumference nowhere.' This idea can be found in full development as early as Parmenides" (*CW*, IX, pt. 1, par. 572). What the common reader of Parmenides would inevitably expect here would be a neat (and convincing) quotation from Fr. 8 in the "Way of Truth"; what he gets, however, is Fr. 12 from the "Way of Seeming," a passage devoted to mating and birth, genesis and becoming, plurality and process: " 'For the narrower rings were filled with unmixed Fire, and those next to them with Night, but between them rushes the portion of Flame. And in the centre of these is the goddess who guides everything; for throughout she rules over cruel Birth and mating, sending the female to mate with the male, and conversely again the male with the female.' "

Jung's choice of Parmenidean texts demonstrates, if nothing else, that becoming has the same circular/spherical form as Being, and therefore that possibilities of symbolism exist in psychology and poetry that would be inconceivable were there only the One Being: the circular many of Fr. 12 may be taken to symbolize the single well-rounded sphere of Fr. 8, which, in Yeats's phrase, is the only symbol, though many appear; and that well-rounded sphere may, in turn, be taken to symbolize something that is altogether ineffable.

"In knowing, soul or mind abandons its unity; it cannot remain a simplex: knowing is taking account of things; that accounting is multiple; the mind thus plunging into number and multiplicity departs from unity." This is Plotinus (*Enneads*, VI, 9, 4; trans. MacKenna), who greatly admired Parmenides as a major contributor to the Platonic system, yet saw clearly the error of his antique predecessor's ways. "So get you gone, Parmenides, though with blessings on your head," was very much Plotinus' attitude when it came to the One Being of his Eleatic ancestor or to his own One—for the distinction must be made: Plotinus exalted The One so mightily (indeed, so wisely) that he would not associate even Being with it, much less counting or knowing. Counting obviously involves plurality, and so does knowing, as Plotinus recognized; but beyond that he also recognized (in part from his reading of Plato's *Parmenides*) that being and knowledge are correlative, but that The One is above either being or knowledge: we can know being but not The One. Being, for Plotinus, is to a certain extent implicated in becoming, and so, although he talked much of The One, he always did so in negative terms or in similes, analogies, and symbols; and he never talked at all of the One Being. "Standing before all things, there must exist a Simplex," Plotinus says, and this Simplex "will debar all telling and knowing except that it may be described as transcending Being . . ." (*Enneads*, V, 4, 1). This Simplex, which is one among many names for The One, like the Good of Plato's *Republic* (at least this is Plotinus' interpretation of the *Republic*), "transcends the Intellectual-Principle and transcends Being . . ." (*Enneads*, V, 1, 8). Not only is there no giving in marriage in heaven —how could there be where unity prevails at all levels?—but beyond that, according to Plotinus, at the furthest reaches of heaven, where The One dwells in a Yeatsian condition of fire and in "rest unbroken," there is also no intellection or knowing and no being or existence, at least not in any sense that can be understood by our minds in their present frail and pathetic state or spoken of directly in a human language that deteriorates even as it comes into being.

Plotinus, as before him Plato and after him a succession of Neoplatonists, maintained hierarchies of being and of knowing, beyond both of which, according to Plotinus, was The One. "The unity, then, is not Intellectual-Principle," he said—and this became Platonic doctrine for centuries to come, whether it had been Platonic doctrine before Plotinus or not—"but something higher still: Intellectual-Principle is still a being but that First is no being but precedent to all Being: it cannot be a being, for a being has what we may call the shape of its reality, but The Unity is without shape, even shape Intellectual" (*Enneads*, VI, 9, 3). Plotinus did not, however, scorn shape altogether—"coming into being and perishing, being and not being, change of place and alteration of bright colour"—and, devalue the sensible world as he might in favor of the intelligible realm, Plotinus would all the same not absolutely reject the visible world. In a fine passage, obviously much indebted to the *Timaeus* and the *Symposium* (as well as other dialogues)—a passage that Jung marked in his German-language copy of the *Enneads* and that goes a long way toward establishing the logic of Jung's archetypes as well as Yeats's symbols—Plotinus writes: "Admiring the world of sense as we look out upon its vastness and beauty and the order of its eternal march, thinking of the gods within it, seen and hidden, and the celestial spirits and all the life of animal and plant, let us mount to its archetype, to the yet more authentic sphere. . . ."[7]

7. ἐπὶ τὸ ἀρχέτυπον αὐτοῦ καὶ τὸ ἀληθινώτερον ἀναβὰς. The archetype, both as a word and as a concept, occurs throughout Plotinus' text. Hans-Rudolf Schwyzer (who, with Paul Henry, is responsible for the standard edition of the *Enneads*), in a very interesting article on "The Intellect in Plotinus and the Archetypes of C. G. Jung" (published in *KEPHALION: Studies in Greek Philosophy offered to C. J. de Vogel*), says that Jung was unaware of Plotinus' contribution to the development of a theory of archetypes. That Jung marked this passage would suggest that he had some knowledge of Plotinus on the archetype (though the word as translated in the German marked by Jung is "Ideale"). Moreover, on the flyleaves of the first two volumes of the Henry-Schwyzer edition of *Plotini Opera*, someone (but perhaps not Jung himself) copied out with great care, first in pencil, then in ink, two passages that included reference to archetypes: εν τῳ αρχετυπῳ ην ζωη (VI, 2, 7, 14: "the 'Being' of sensible things is just such a shadow of True Being, an abstraction from that Being complete which *was life in the Archetype*," trans. MacKenna); ει ημεις αρχετυπα και ουσια και ειδη αμα εκρατησεν αν ανευ πονων η ημετερα δημιουργια (V, 8, 7, 29: "To me, moreover, it seems that *if we ourselves were Archetypes, Ideas, veritable Being*, and the Idea with which we construct here were our veritable Essence, then *our creative power, too would toillessly effect its purpose* . . . ," trans. MacKenna).

That archetypal world is the true Golden Age. . . . For here is contained all that is immortal: nothing here but is Divine Mind; all is God [as Yeats put it: "Where there is Nothing, there is God"]; this is the very place of every soul. Here is rest unbroken . . . for all belongs to it eternally and it holds the authentic Eternity imitated by Time which, circling round the Soul, makes towards the new thing and passes by the old" (*Enneads*, V, 1, 4). This, as I say, goes a long way toward rectifying the Parmenidean denial of the world and of time and a long way toward articulating the *logos* of the symbolizing process.

In a very interesting passage in which he alludes to Parmenides, Jung seems to feel that the original Monist performed the Platonic *chōrismos*, the separation of the intelligible and the sensible realms that, after Plato, Plotinus pushed even further and filled in more completely with *daimones*, gods, and various hierarchies—only, apparently, that Parmenides sundered the realms absolutely and saw no relationship whatever between them: sheer opposites, as entirely antagonistic as truth and falsehood. "In the philosophical sense, it [i.e., Hellenistic syncretism with its classification of men into *hylikoi*, *psychikoi*, and *pneumatikoi*] established gradations between the Parmenidean poles of light and darkness, of above and below" (*CW*, VI, par. 964). Whether or not Jung is right here in his reading of Parmenides (it appears to be based on the "Way of Seeming" and therefore questionable as an interpretation of Parmenides), his general point is well taken: without two realms that differ in mode of being, and without gradations or hierarchies between those realms, archetypes are insignificant and symbols are loose-ended and powerless. "Symbol" is derived etymologically from the Greek *symbolon*, "a sign or mark to infer a thing by, a signal, token"; in the plural it refers to "the two pieces of a coin, etc., which two contracting parties broke between them, each preserving one part" in recognition of their agreement and unity;[8] and it comes originally from the verb, *symballein*, "to throw or bring together, to dash together, to

---

8. Definitions, slightly modified, are from the abridged Liddell-Scott *Lexicon*. Aristophanes, in his tale of original human wholeness split in two by Zeus as punishment for men's arrogance, uses the word "symbol" to refer to the two disjoined halves that seek wholeness and unity once again (and he finds the perfect simile for what he is describing in the sole or flounder that, with its strangely opposed sides, seems to have been sliced in two): "Each of us, therefore, is a *symbol* [a broken half] of a man, since each of us has been cut in two—just like flat fish, two made from one. And each of us seeks always for the *symbol* [the other broken half] of himself" (191d).

unite." If there is but One Being, as Parmenides stoutly insisted, there is of course no bringing together, no rejoining of the coin broken for future recognition of past oneness, and no cause for Whitehead's "pathos"; or, on the other hand, if (as in Jung's reading of Parmenides) there is nothing between the opposed worlds but an irremediable and hopeless antagonism—never unified in the past, never to be unified in the future—then all energy seeps out of the verb *symballein*, and the symbolizing process becomes enervated and lifeless: as a verb and a process they are rendered powerless to make any meaning of things by establishing relationships. In a dialectical exchange with himself that is not unlike the sermons of Basilides and the responses of the dead in *Septem Sermones*, Plotinus goes a step further in establishing the bases for the symbolic mode in the Western tradition when he concludes that we can have no knowledge of "the Transcendent" and can speak of it only "in the light of its sequels; unable to state it, we may still possess it" (*Enneads*, V, 3, 13 and 14). The sphere, as Yeats said, "can be symbolised but cannot be known," and when he wanted to put all into a phrase—as he rather often did want to do—he said, "Man can embody truth but he cannot know it" (*Letters*, p. 922). The ascent to The One via the symbolic mode—this is true for Diotima in the *Symposium*, for Plotinus in the *Enneads*, for Yeats in his greatest poems, and for Jung in his private experience if not always (or consistently) in his public science—is a combination of reason and vision, of ratiocination and intuition, of dialectics and mysticism. The man who succeeds in embodying truth in fullness, which is to say the man who lives his symbol and ascends to his own archetype, has succeeded in wedding dialectics and mysticism.

The dead who came shouting and shoving around the courtyard and the door of #228 Seestrasse in Küsnacht one fateful Sunday afternoon in 1916 (as Jung tells the story in *Memories, Dreams, Reflections*) received a sermon from the Gnostic psychiatrist—Jung disguising himself as Basilides preaching in Alexandria—that is a very adroit exercise in the adoption, but also the adaptation, of Parmenides as a primitive philosophic source. In a rhetorical riposte that might well have been brought against Parmenides, the dead of Jung's book challenge the preacher for speaking of the unspeakable: "What use . . . to speak of it? Saidst thou not thyself, there is no profit in thinking upon the Pleroma?" There is no profit at all, the preacher acknowledges; and in fact it is not only profitless to think of the pleroma, it is also impossible—and since impossible to think of it, therefore equally impossible to speak positively of it. "That said I unto you," the preacher responds, "to free you from the delusion that we are able to think about the pleroma" (Sermon I). Jung, as he often acknowledges, is dealing, even when consciousness is in question and much more when the unconscious is his object, with that which is invisible, intangible, inaudible, indefinable, unfixable, unstable, ineffable, unknowable—with that, in fact, which in description is in every way negative except that it is "affective." In its "in-" and "un-" negativity, Jung's psyche has much in common with the chaos of *Paradise Lost*, and it will inevitably remind the reader of the negative theology descending from Parmenides, and from Plato on Parmenides, to Plotinus and the Neoplatonists, and to the "docta ignorantia" of Nicholas of Cusa. Like Plotinus on The One, Jung offers a whole host of similes and analogies—likenesses straining toward symbolism—for the experience of psyche, and he can claim to speak of it "in light of its sequels," but he can never say *what it is* except negatively—which of course does *not* say what it is. When Jung starts offering up analogies and similes for the collective unconscious or for the pleroma, it must be admitted that it turns out to be remarkably like everything, as well as remarkably like nothing —which two are, epistemologically and ontologically speaking—and therefore psychologically speaking—remarkably like each other.

The only way out of chaos and negativity, for Jung as for Plato or Plotinus, the only way to honor Parmenides while getting free of him, was via the symbol and the quasi-mystical union that the symbol effects. "The unconscious can be reached and expressed only by symbols. . . . The symbol is the primitive exponent of the unconscious, but at the same time an idea that corresponds to the highest intuitions of the conscious mind" (*CW*, XIII, par. 44); so Jung says of the pleroma or the collective unconscious, which, so far as the psychologist is concerned, "takes the place of the Platonic realm of eternal ideas" (*CW*, XIV, par. 101). The only road to that realm of the unconscious, the eternal ideas, and The One—if the seeker be not saint or sage but poet, psychologist, or philosopher—is the road of mythology, likeness, and symbolism. Plato was perfectly clear about this, as Paul Shorey indicates: "Except in purely mythical passages, Plato does not attempt to describe the ideas any more than Kant describes the *Ding-an-sich* or Spencer the 'Unknowable.' He does not tell us what they are, but that they are."[9] There—for the First Ontologist Parmenides, for the Second Ontologist Plato, for the Neo-Second Ontologist Plotinus, and for all twentieth-century children of that Ontological Tradition—there is the crux of the matter: not "what they are, but that they are"; or for Parmenides, not "what it is" but only "is." Thereafter, the discourse must be mythic, iconic, symbolic. It was only by reintroducing the mythic mode that Plato circumvented the tautological dead end of Parmenides' illogical logic and enabled himself and his descendants to say —mythically and with as-if truths—not precisely what the Forms are but what they are like. Trying to describe how the collective unconscious or the pleroma connects with consciousness, Jung says that "a waterfall arises between Above and Below, a dynamic something that is the symbol" (*Letters*, I, 61). In the Hermetic waterfall that connects Above and Below, joining undifferentiated pleroma and differentiated consciousness, we have Jung's favorite way of describing, indirectly, what a symbol is: the waterfall is, as it were, Jung's symbol for a symbol.

Parmenides' One Being, however, was so utterly this world or so utterly other world, so absolutely Above or so absolutely Below— and in either case unknowable, ineffable, unreal—that he destroyed the dialectical approach to the mystical leap and made an ascent to the One Being impossible: either we *are* it, indistinguishably, or it is unattainable. It is a paradox, but true, that while Parmenides rendered symbolism impossible, he also rendered it necessary and, in the course of time, inevitable. Symbolism is impossible, that is to say, so long as we stay closed within the absolute premises of the One Being and so long as we shut out from our hearing the Siren song of Heraclitean process, disregarding the irrefutable reality of coming-to-be and perishing. Once admit process, however, all the while holding to the (superior) reality of The One, and symbolism is readmitted to the poetic universe. The symbol in Yeats—but it can only be symbolic, as he emphasizes in *A Vision*—is that which joins and mediates between Heraclitean process and Parmenidean stasis: a creation of this world, taken from the realm of *doxa*, a symbol nevertheless derives its form (its archaic typicality) from the other

9. Shorey, *The Unity of Plato's Thought* (Chicago: University of Chicago Press, 1904), p. 28.

world, and hence its meaning relates to the realm of *alētheia*. The Heraclitean stream issues from a Parmenidean needle's eye, and, like a waterfall, it connects Below and Above, this world and that one, it returns us to our source, and it symbolizes that which we can neither know nor say.

> All the stream that's roaring by
> Came out of a needle's eye;
> Things unborn, things that are gone,
> From needle's eye still goad it on.[10]

Let us say that The One is a true point, the ideal needle's eye, without extension or dimension, unmoving and immutable, pure potential, without awareness, intangible, unknowable, and ineffable; but let us say also that all the real circles of this world imitate, however clumsily, however clogged with gross materiality they be, that point of perfection. In so saying we shall have Parmenides' ἔστιν and his One Being, but we shall have Heraclitus' πάντα ῥεῖ and his *Logos* also; we shall have Plotinus' One and a possible dialectical/mystical ascent to it as well; we shall have the Platonic relationship between, on the one hand, the "eternity that abides in unity" and, on the other hand, "an everlasting likeness [of that eternity] moving according to number." To put it simply, we shall have Yeats's symbols and Jung's archetypes: two worlds and an unfailing bond between them. The historical Parmenides would allow none of this; but he it is, a presence in us as in Greek philosophy, who makes us —philosopher, poet, or psychologist—demand it all.

10. Yeats first wrote this little poem (later to be called "A Needle's Eye," *Poems*, p. 562) on the endleaf of Swedenborg's *Principia*; opposite the scribbled poem, Yeats drew two versions of interlocking cones, crossed both out, chose one to remain and wrote "stet" beside it, and added the note "see page 555." On p. 555, Yeats marked a passage in which Swedenborg discusses spirals and cones and the point from which such chronological/spatial unwindings come; in the margin, Yeats drew a number of concentric circles, with the first and the last looking very much like the diagram on p. 74 of *A Vision*. "Things unborn, things that are gone"—these exist in the "point" of Swedenborg, in the needle's eye, in the discarnate state removed from time and space: the sphere contracted and disappearing into the point that is its own center.

CHAPTER V

Gyres and Cycles, the Quaternity and the Sphere

I have suggested earlier that of the four Platonic *rhizōmata*, Heraclitus was unquestionably preeminent in the affections and in the esteem of both Yeats and Jung. When the dead came to Jung for their sermons, however, what they were taught by their preacher, both in his first words and in his overall vision, had more to do with a Parmenidean pleroma and an undifferentiated collective unconscious than it had to do with a Heraclitean universe of perpetual, *Logos*-directed flux; and similarly, the system that Yeats's Instructors revealed to him, while rich in Heraclitean implications and overtones, was, at least in its basic configuration and its largest outline, an Empedoclean system of continually alternating half-cycles set in a time without beginning and without end. After the revelations of *A Vision* were in the proof stage, the redactor of all that fabulous truth says that he went to reading some of the philosophy that the Instructors had earlier forbade him, in the hope that he might "find somewhere something from which their symbolic geometry had been elaborated"; Yeats's conclusions, though meagre, pointed to no one but Empedocles: "I read all MacKenna's incomparable translation of Plotinus, some of it several times, and went from Plotinus to his predecessors and successors. . . . And for four years now I have read nothing else except now and then some story of theft and murder to clear my head at night. Although the more I read the better did I understand what I had been taught, I found neither the geometrical symbolism nor anything that could have inspired it except the vortex of Empedocles" (*Vision*, p. 20). The "symbolic geometry" of *A Vision*, which Yeats could find historically only in Empedocles, is a matter of a perpetual alternation between unity and multiplicity, multiplicity and unity. The curious result of this ceaseless shuttling to and fro over the same tracks—as we can discover in Empedocles, in Yeats, and in Jung—is that the tracks themselves are eventually obliterated as particular and unique vestiges of time, and history, consequently, which is at first essential to the Empedoclean vision, becomes in the end irrelevant because lacking altogether in the quality of the unique event. Or to put it another way: because time is both dominant and cyclical in Empedocles, history, while it may be interesting, is *per se* trivial and merely incidental, and it acquires significance only when referred beyond itself. Pythagoras, Empedocles, Plato, and no doubt Heraclitus—as also Yeats and Jung—conceived of time in circular/cyclical terms; but if time is circular, and if history, both cosmic and human, falls into a pattern of alternating and perpetually recurrent half-cycles, then history itself is no more than (but under the pressure of genius may be as much as) a symbolism pointing the way to a recurrent collective experience that is repeated infinitely many times in the lives of individuals.

It is this repetition of general experience in the particular life that accounts for the myth or the collective "memory"—not really a memory, Jung would say, but an archetype—of a Hesiodic golden race of men: a symbolic image that comes from springs so deep in the collective psyche that it seems to be remembered rather than imagined and that provides us individually with an ideal goal toward which we must aspire—a state of wholeness and completion, as in Empedocles' "whole-natured forms" and as in Platonic Man, both of which, Yeats would say, symbolize the condition of the Sphere but are not it. A doctrine of alternating, cyclical recurrence

—the effect of which is to wipe out the particularity of history and replace it with the universality of myth—was Empedocles' special contribution to the whole complex system eventually inherited, through the Platonic tradition and the evolved human psyche, by Yeats and Jung. In a beautiful fusion of Heraclitus and Empedocles, Yeats says of the double cones of his *Vision*, "The passage from Phase 1 to Phase 15 is always, whether we call it a month or six months or twelve months, or an individual life, set over against a passage from Phase 15 to Phase 1; and whether we consider the cone that of incarnate or that of discarnate life, the gyre of *Husk* or *Will* cuts the gyre of *Spirit* or *Creative Mind* with the same conflict of seasons, a being racing into the future passes a being racing into the past, two footprints perpetually obliterating one another, toe to heel, heel to toe" (*Vision*, pp. 209-10). It is their shared sense that time wipes away its own footprints through recurrence and simultaneous reversal—Empedocles wed to Heraclitus—that makes Yeats and Jung so vexatious to readers possessed of a stricter sense of history than either of them could claim, or perhaps wished to claim. Yeats, like Jung, according to historically minded readers, was all too eager to dissolve the sharp outlines of history in the elusive configurations of myth, and both were more than willing to abandon any effort to discover the historical transmission of ideas in favor of a belief in the "autochthonous revival" (Jung's term) of those ideas.

Although the doctrine of perpetually recurrent, alternate half-cycles is specific to Empedocles, and although the doctrine of simultaneously conflicting opposites is specific to Heraclitus, it seems to have been more than natural and easy for Yeats and Jung to conflate the two doctrines and then to ascribe the composite idea (usually) to Heraclitus alone. I have already discussed *enantiodromia* in the context of Heraclitus' thought—for the simple reason that Jung regularly credited Heraclitus as the primal enantiodromian; the truth is, however, that the concept is at least as Empedoclean as it is Heraclitean—and more Empedoclean than Heraclitean when Jung adds, to his definition of *enantiodromia* as a "running counter to," the rider that this reversal of direction occurs "in the course of events" or "in the course of time" (*CW*, VI, pars. 708 and 709). But Jung's error in historical ascription (if error it be) is nothing beside the mad confusion that Yeats produced in the first edition of *A Vision*, where he says that, having been drawn back to antiquity in search of parallels for his gyres, "I am attracted to a passage in Heraclitus which I can, I think, explain more clearly than his English commentators" (p. 129). I quote this passage of Yeatsian explanation at length for several reasons: because it shows the casual ease with which Yeats substituted "Heraclitus" for "Empedocles"; because it demonstrates that, prior to the 1925 *Vision*, he had pored over Birkett (*lege* Burnet) on the Platonic rhizōmata more intently than he later wished to acknowledge; because the passage hints at the excitement Yeats felt at the notion that, with this very new/very ancient knowledge imparted by the Instructors, he (and he alone in his time) was capable of interpreting correctly the oldest texts in the Western world; and because it shows Yeats's own system in a slightly inchoate state that makes it in some ways easier to grasp than in the finished state.

> If now we consider these opposing gyres or cones as expressing Man and *Daimon*—those two first portions of being that suffer vicissitude into which *Anima Hominis* and *Anima Mundi* resolve—we can explain much in Parmenides and Empedocles, but especially this in Heraclitus: "I shall retrace my steps over the paths of song that I had travelled before, drawing from my saying a new saying. When Strife was fallen to the lowest depth of the vortex." ("Not as might be supposed," Birkett explains, "the centre but the extreme bound.")[1] "and love has reached the centre of the

1. The footnote in Burnet (1st ed., p. 226) to which Yeats refers goes thus: "The 'lowest depth' is not, as might be supposed, the centre; but is the same thing as the 'extreme boundary' (v. 178)." At this point Yeats drew his great diagram—to be found scattered here and there in various books in his library as well as on p. 72 of the 1937 *Vision*—in the margin of his copy of Burnet:

This would seem to dispose of Yeats's later claim that it was only "When the proof sheets [of *A Vision*] came [that] I felt myself relieved from my promise not to read philosophy" (*Vision*, p. 19), and that he then discovered that the "vortex of Empedocles" was similar to his gyres. It may be that Yeats, like Shelley (in Yeats's own phrase), "had more philosophy that men thought when I was young" (*Vision*, p. 211n.)—even if Yeats was unable to keep straight the names of philosophers and historians of philosophy.

whirl, in it do all things come together so as to be one only; not all at once, but coming together gradually from different quarters; and as they came together Strife retired to the extreme boundary . . . but in proportion as it kept rushing out, a soft immortal stream of blameless love kept running in." So far all is plain, and it may be this very passage that suggested Flaubert's dreaming man whose life goes wrong as his dream comes right. "For of a truth they (Love and Strife) were afore time and shall be, nor ever can (?) boundless time be emptied of the pair, and they prevail in turn as the circle comes round, and pass away before one another and increase in their appointed time."

And had we more than a few fragments of Empedocles and his school it might not be hard to relate the four gyres of our symbol to heat and cold, light and dark, the pairs of opposites, whether in the moral or physical universe, which permeate his thought. The single cone whose extreme limits are described as *Anima Hominis*, *Anima Mundi*, is said in our documents to be formed by the whirling of a sphere which moves onward leaving an empty coil behind it; and the double cones by the separating of two whirling spheres that have been one, and it may be that we have here what suggested to Parmenides thoughts that seemed to forestall certain of our latest mathematical speculations. "Where then it has its furthest boundary it is complete on every side, equally poised from the centre in every direction like the mass of a rounded sphere, for it cannot be greater or smaller in one place than another. . . . and there is not, and never shall be any time, other than that which is present, since Fate has chained it so as to be whole and immoveable."[2]

2. *Vision* (1925), pp. 132-33. I have left the passage exactly as it appears in Yeats's book, though it differs in a good many places from the original in *Early Greek Philosophy*. In spite of Yeats's plea, at another point in the book, for understanding ("I am correcting these pages at Thoor Ballylee and there is not a reference book in the house"—p. 153n.), I assume the differences are due not to absence of reference books—the passage quoted (and misquoted) is after all quite a long one, and I doubt that Yeats carried it in his memory—but simply to Yeats's scholarly nonchalance in transcription. Yeats's notion of "correcting" his pages is an unusual one, for this very note of explanation is tacked on to a passage about Macrobius, who, Yeats says, "translated Cicero's Greek into Latin at the end of the fifth century."

I should think that some at least of the first readers of *A Vision* must have paused in momentary wonder when they came upon this unknown, chatty, explanatory, and expansive Heraclitus. The answer, of course, is that the fragment is from Empedocles, number 35 in the ordering of Diels-Kranz. Like Jung, Yeats slipped easily between Heraclitus and Empedocles; but in defense of his confusion Yeats, if not Jung (because the former had fewer pretensions to exact scholarship than the latter), might say that both doctrines—"Heraclitus' *simultaneous* unity and plurality of the cosmos and Empedocles' separate *periods* of Love and Strife" (Kirk-Raven, p. 202n.)—are unquestionably archetypal anyhow ("archetype" is a word that Yeats used, and more than once, both before and after Jung presumably gave it its currency), and therefore come from a collective region of the psyche. So why bother overmuch about accuracy of historical credits? Jung's scholarship, as I say, would probably keep him from embracing this explanation in public, but the a-historical or anti-historical idea behind it is distinctly Jungian all the same.

Of souls that have progressed through cycles of transmigration almost to the point of escaping from the wheel, Empedocles says, "At the end they become prophets, poets, physicians, and princes among men on earth" (Fr. 146). It is more than a coincidence, and no accident at all of course, that Empedocles was all these things, and was moreover on the brink of becoming a god as well. If, stretching a bit the sense of "princes among men on earth," we say that Jung was three of these things (but not a poet), and that Yeats was three of these things (but not a physician), we may see how near they came to being full Empedocleans and how close, therefore, they presumably came to apotheosis in their most recent incarnations. "At this time," W. K. C. Guthrie tells us, "medicine was not separated either from philosophy on the one hand or from religion and even magic on the other" (*Hist. of Gr. Phil.*, II, 132-33). Guthrie is speaking, of course, of fifth-century Greece, but observers, both partisans and opponents, have not been wanting who would be willing to say the same of the analytical psychology of our century: part medicine and natural science, it also comprises a bit of philosophy, quite a lot of religion, and more than a dash of magic. Jung's experience was undoubtedly the same as Empedocles': "Some come in search of oracles, others to hear the word of healing" (Fr. 111); and one has only to consider some of the illnesses that Jung cured, and the means he used to cure them, to realize that the treatment Jung offered was as "psychic" as the affliction and that a half-visionary, half-prophetic intuition was probably more responsible than anything else for the cures he effected. "Apollo and Asclepius," Guthrie continues, "had the title *Iatromantis,* a single compound word meaning 'physician-seer' "; and poets, as Socrates points out in the *Phaedrus,* are mantic seers as well, men possessed by a divine madness. Yeats and Jung were both excellent examples of a certain type (with no derogation intended)—a type that E. R. Dodds has labelled the "shaman." It is a type of which Empedocles himself was not precisely an example, for he, being a shaman in full definition—a sort of throwback in fifth-century Greece, according to Dodds—was more paradigm than example, more archetype than type.[3] Of Renan's remark that Empedocles was "un Newton doublé d'un Cagliostro," Guthrie writes: "It might be fairer to compare the religious side of Empedocles with Newton's own interest in alchemy and the prophecies of Daniel: he has been called 'the first modern scientist and the last of the mages'" (*Hist. of Gr. Phil.,* II, 123, n.1). Jung, for his profound interest in alchemy and his efforts at prophecy, has been called much harder names than that; and so would Yeats have been had he not so warmly (and so wisely) despised science whenever it divorces itself from a larger wisdom and from a loving search for that larger wisdom: "Science," Yeats said in an

---

3. Dodds, *The Greeks and the Irrational* (Berkeley: University of California Press, 1951), especially pp. 145-46. Dodds sees Empedocles more as the last of the Greek shamans than as an archetypal figure; yet to later ages—the time of Yeats and Jung, let us say—Empedocles is as far back as can be seen with certainty and thus appears not as an anachronistic survivor from previous times but as the great primal figure and progenitor for times to be.

"Be that as it may," Dodds writes, "the fragments of Empedocles are the one firsthand source from which we can still form some notion of what a Greek shaman was really like; he is the last belated example of a species which with his death became extinct in the Greek world, though it still flourishes elsewhere" (p. 145). I do not imagine that Dodds intended "elsewhere" to include Ireland or Switzerland, but on the next page, describing Empedocles' "type," he provides a neat characterization of Yeats and Jung in their various roles: "If I am right, Empedocles represents not a new but a very old type of personality, the shaman who combines the still undifferentiated functions of magician and naturalist, poet and philosopher, preacher, healer, and public counsellor. After him these functions fell apart; philosophers henceforth were to be neither poets nor magicians; indeed, such a man was already an anachronism in the fifth century." Is there any better description of Jung than "magician and naturalist, . . . preacher, healer, and public counsellor"? Or of Yeats than philosopher, poet, and magician?

epigram that deserves to be posted in every sort of school of science whether the science be physical, natural, political, social, medical, or whatever—"Science, separated from philosophy, is the opium of the suburbs" (*Ex.*, p. 340).

Only a very small proportion of Empedocles' writings are extant —some 450 lines from two poems that together are said to have amounted to four or five thousand lines—but even from this tenth of the whole we can be assured of one thing: that his system was a system. It was comprehensive, detailed, and universally applicable; it concerned itself first of all with the soul of man and the soul of nature, but also with the body of man and the body of nature; it included cosmology and psychology, physiology and medicine, theology and religion. And it was all founded, in all its branches, on that simple "symbolic geometry" that Yeats, looking back to antiquity for another vision like his *Vision*, could find in Empedocles but nowhere else. For Empedocles (and for Yeats from the time he received the drawing of interpenetrating cones), everything in the cosmos, whether microcosmic or macrocosmic, was referable to that simple scheme of alternating cyclical recurrence. It was this "wheel of birth and death," moving from dark of the moon to full and back to dark again, that Yeats would reproduce as the Great Wheel in his *Vision*, saying that it is another way of representing the same reality as that of the interlocked cones, and explaining at the same time that the "wheel is every completed movement of thought or life, twenty-eight incarnations, a single incarnation, a single judgment or act of thought" (*Vision*, p. 81).

Jung, when he was being *Iatromantis* rather than objective scientist, was as determined as Yeats, and the two together were as determined as Empedocles, to discover that geometric/temporal scheme that could account for, describe, and prophesy both the movement of the animated cosmos and the movement of the individual soul: the movement, in either case, for Empedocles, Yeats, and Jung, of *psychē*. The scheme that Empedocles came up with, and that Yeats and Jung adopted with qualifications and variations, hinged on a doctrine of palingenesis: perpetual rebirth of microcosm and macrocosm, of *daimon* and the universe, and a pattern of cyclical change that returns things again and again to the point where they began. I have quoted Jung earlier (Chapter 2) at his most positive on the question of palingenesis: "I could well imagine that I might have lived in former centuries and that I had to be born again because I had not fulfilled the task that was given to me" (*Memories*, p. 318/294). This is as far as Jung will go, but in going so far he is very much in line with Empedoclean doctrine. The cosmos, according to Empedocles, is set the task of reachieving the blessed state of the Sphere through the unifying power of Love (probably every 30,000 seasons), after it has been broken up and dispersed in elemental fragments by Strife; analogously, the individual cosmos or *daimon* has its particular task, which is to purify and perfect itself through reincarnations lasting for 30,000 seasons before it can escape the wheel to which it has been bound because it put its "trust in raving Strife" and before it can once again enjoy that condition—the Sphere—of which the wheel could be considered only a pathetic and miserable imitation. Yeats, commenting on the Great Year of the ancients (a subject of intense interest to him), says that it could be thought of as "a lunar year of 360 days, each day 100 years," and he goes on to consider how the day becomes a month, which becomes a year, which becomes a century, etc., like so many circles within a circle, each turning at its own proper speed, until finally all the circles return to their beginning to render up, in the symbolic moment, the sphere composed of wheels and of all the periods that, when completed, are at rest but that describe, so long as they move, all change both natural and psychic. "If I may think of those days or incarnations as periods wherein symbolic man grows old and young alternately, as he does in certain other Platonic periods, I have, but for a different length and enumeration, my Great Wheel of twelve cycles" (*Vision*, p. 212). The "other Platonic periods" Yeats has in mind are almost certainly to be found in the myth in the *Statesman*— a myth which is in turn indebted to Hesiod's description of a Golden Race and which finds its symbolic geometry in the system of alternating half-cycles of Empedocles.

I do not know whether Yeats was thinking specifically of Empedocles when he concluded the dedication of the 1925 *Vision* to "Vestigia" with the following lines, but certainly the rhythm of rising and falling through cycles of incarnations and reincarnations of nature and the individual *daimon* is deeply Empedoclean: "Yesterday when I saw the dry and leafless vineyards at the very edge of the motionless sea, or lifting their brown stems from almost inaccessible patches of earth high up on the cliff-side, or met at the turn of the path the orange and lemon trees in full fruit, or the crimson cactus flower, or felt the warm sunlight falling between blue and blue, I murmured, as I have countless times, 'I have been part of it always and there is maybe no escape, forgetting and returning life after life like an insect in the roots of the grass.' But murmured it without terror, in exultation almost" (p. xiii). There would be little point in thinking of Yeats as a nature poet in the way of (for example) G. M. Hopkins: it was a symbolic great-rooted blossomer that had all, or most, of Yeats's love and not those actual, "sweet especial" Binsey poplars whose felling so grieved Hopkins because the loss of their unique beauty, he felt, left "a grievous gap" in nature herself. One cannot imagine Yeats saying, as Hopkins says in his journal, "The ashtree growing in the corner of the garden was felled. It was lopped first: I heard the sound and looking out and seeing it maimed there came at that moment a great pang and I wished to die and not to see the inscapes of the world destroyed any more."[4] Yeats would not have said this; Empedocles would have found it either incomprehensible or laughable. But nature means different things to different people and yields herself in one way to one man, in quite another way to another man. And if Yeats was not a nature poet in the Hopkinsian manner, he was very much a nature poet in the way of Empedocles' "On Nature" and his "Purifications." For Yeats, like Empedocles—and especially after he had just received an Empedoclean vision from the Instructors—could claim to have "once been a boy and a girl, a bush and a bird and a dumb sea fish," "the crimson cactus flower, . . . the warm sunlight falling between blue and blue, . . . an insect in the roots of the grass." Or as Fergus says to his titular companion in "Fergus and the Druid":

> I have been many things—
> A green drop in the surge, a gleam of light
> Upon a sword, a fir-tree on a hill,
> An old slave grinding at a heavy quern,
> A king sitting upon a chair of gold.

With the immensely extended view afforded by their assumption of a perspective comprehending many incarnations—a long series of

---

4. Entry of April 8, 1873: *The Journals and Papers of Gerard Manley Hopkins*, ed. Humphrey House and Graham Storey (London: Oxford University Press, 1959), p. 230. "A grievous gap" is also from the *Journals*: December 6, 1868, p. 189.

cycles and half-cycles—neither Empedocles nor Yeats was prone to be captivated, as Hopkins was, by the particular and unique, nonrecurrent natural detail, or desolated by its loss; nor was either of them likely to miss the forest for the trees. "Of these I too am now one, a fugitive from the gods and a wanderer," Empedocles says; and being thus in exile from his true home and essential condition, "I wept and wailed when I saw the unfamiliar place" (Frs. 115 and 118). Yeats murmurs his intuition of palingenesis ("countless times" he says, but it may not have been quite so frequent as the rhythm and the sense of his sentence required him to claim) "without terror, in exultation almost"; Empedocles, on the other hand, murmured his vision—he wept and wailed it—without exultation, in terror almost. Otherwise, they said one and the same thing and said it in virtually the same language.

The most convenient and the best introduction to the entire visionary scheme of Empedocles, and to his comprehensive prophetic-poetic system embracing all of natural process and the experience of the human soul—especially as Yeats understood that scheme and system, and his understanding was much the same as Jung's—is to record certain passages that Yeats marked in his copy of Burnet. It may be that Yeats failed to retain names and dates and languages well in mind, but he was a shrewd reader, and an ambitious one, and when he marked passages in reading he nearly always discovered the heart of the matter, and when he annotated passages he usually illuminated both his own thought and the thought of the text he was reading. The passages of Empedocles that Yeats marked, as Burnet translated them, are these:[5]

> I shall tell thee a twofold tale. At one time things grew to be one only out of many; at another, that divided up to be many instead of one. There is a double becoming of perishable things and a double passing away. The coming together of things brings one generation into being and destroys it; the other grows up and is scattered as things become divided. And these things never cease, continually

---

5. In his first edition, Burnet took the text of Empedocles from E. Stein's *Empedoclis Agrigentini Fragmenta*; that text differs both in wording and in the order of reconstruction from the text of Diels that Burnet adopted in the fourth edition of *Early Greek Philosophy*. I have given line numbers as they appear in the Stein-Burnet ordering of the first edition and then, for convenience, have added the numbers of fragments (and lines when necessary) as they appear in Diels-Kranz.

changing places, at one time all uniting in one through
Love, at another each borne in different directions by the
repulsion of Strife. Thus, as far as it is their nature to grow
into one out of many, and to become many once more
when the one is parted asunder, so far they come into being
and their life abides not. But, inasmuch as they never cease
changing their places continually, so far they are immovably[6] as they go round the circle of existence. (lines 60-73;
DK Fr. 17, lines 1-13)

At one time things grew together to be one only out of
many, at another they parted asunder so as to be many
instead of one;—Fire and Water and Earth and the mighty
height of Air, dread Strife, too, apart from these and
balancing every one of them, and Love among them, their
equal in length and breadth. Her do thou contemplate with
thy mind, nor sit with dazed eyes. It is she that is deemed
to be implanted in the frame of mortals. It is she that makes
them have kindly thoughts and work the works of peace.
They call her by the names of Joy and Aphrodite. (lines
76-84; DK Fr. 17, lines 16-24)

For, of a truth, they (i.e. Love and Strife) were aforetime
and shall be; nor ever, methinks, will boundless time be
emptied of that pair. And they prevail in turn as the circle
comes round, and pass away before one another, and
increase in their appointed turn.

For these things are what they are; but, running through
one another, they become men and the other races of
mortal creatures. At one time they are brought together into
one order by Love; at another, again, they are carried each
in different directions by the repulsion of Strife, till once
more they grow into one and are wholly subdued. (lines
110-119; DK Fr. 26; N.B.: Burnet's first-edition text from
Stein differs greatly from his fourth-edition text from Diels)

In it [i.e., the Sphere] is distinguished neither the bright
form of the sun, no, nor the shaggy earth in its might, nor
the sea,—so fast was the god bound in the close covering of

---

6. "Immovably" is the reading in the first edition; in the fourth edition Burnet has "ever immovable."

Harmony, spherical and round, rejoicing in his circular rest. (lines 135–38; DK Fr. 27)

[But now I shall retrace my steps over the paths of song that] I have travelled before, drawing from my saying a new saying. When Strife was fallen to the lowest depth of the vortex, and Love had reached to the centre of the whirl, in it do all things come together so as to be one only; not all at once, but coming together gradually each from different quarters; and, as they came together, Strife retired to the extreme boundary. Yet many things remained unmixed, alternating with the things that were being mixed, namely, all that Strife not fallen yet retained; for it had not yet altogether retired perfectly to the outermost boundaries of the circle. Some of its members still remained within, and some had passed out. But in proportion as it kept rushing out, a soft, immortal stream of blameless Love kept running in, and straightway those things became mortal which had been immortal before, those things were mixed that had been unmixed, each changing its path. And, as they were mingled, countless tribes of mortal creatures were scattered abroad endowed with all manner of forms, a wonder to behold. (lines 170–186; DK Frs. 35 and 36)

. . . this marvelous mass of mortal limbs. At one time all the limbs that are the body's portion are brought together into one by Love, and flourish in the high season of life; and again, at another time they are severed by cruel Strife, and wander each in different directions by the breakers of the sea of life. It is the same with shrubs and the fish that make their homes in the waters, the beasts that make their lairs in the hills, and the birds that sail on wings. (lines 247–253; DK Fr. 20)

Many creatures with faces and breasts looking in different directions were born; some, offspring of oxen with faces of men, while others, again, arose as offspring of men with the heads of oxen, and creatures in whom the nature of women and men was mingled, furnished with sterile parts. (lines 256–260; DK Fr. 61)

Four elements and two contrary forces to keep those elements in motion; a perpetual movement back and forth from one to many and many to one, from the complete dominance of Love in the blessed Sphere where "is all music and all rest" to the complete dominance of Strife where all is divided, elemental hostility (with the world as we know it—i.e., a world possible to human life—existing at neither extreme: Phase 15 and Phase 1 of *A Vision*); and all this complex of air-earth-fire-water, Love-and-Strife, Sphere-and-chaos, operating as a self-enclosed, self-perpetuating system, spinning gyrelike now one way, now the other way, within a time that never had a beginning and will never have an end—this is what Empedocles, the great system-maker, represented for Yeats, who was himself a confessed system-lover and an inspired system-builder. What Yeats made of it all, and how the symbolic geometry of Empedocles was filled in with the events and personalities of twenty-five centuries to become a complete reading of history and human psychology in Yeats's *Vision* (with some personal politics thrown in occasionally to make up the measure), we shall see in a moment. But what could Empedocles mean to Jung, who proclaimed himself an empirical scientist, hostile, by temperament and profession, to system of any kind? The answer is that much more of Empedocles' system informed Jung's empirical observations, both clinical and personal, and his scientific deductions, than the shaman of Küsnacht was always willing to acknowledge. The psyche, that great subject and object of Jung's science and of everything he wrote, is itself precisely an Empedoclean system, binary and quaternal, self-balanced and self-regulating (when healthy), striving ever to restore itself to the condition of the monadic Sphere, which is its essence, Jung agreed, and its entelechy. Most of the poetry of Empedocles that chances to remain casts his system in cosmological terms, but it can all be transposed—and was transposed by the alchemists and by Jung—to the compressed scale of the individual psyche. When it is so transposed, then it becomes apparent that Empedocles was no mean psychologist, and that his psychology, both as an experience and as a science, is writ, in a very Jungian way, all across the face of his majestic cosmology, and vice versa.

One thing, but not the only thing, that attracted Jung to Empedocles was his (Empedocles') insistence that the *rhizōmata*, the "roots of all things," were exactly the same in number as the seductive quaternity, so immensely satisfying to Jung, underlying all nature psychic as well as physical. "The alchemists," Jung says, "described their four elements as *radices*," which is a terminology closely akin to the analytical psychologist's "four functions"—the roots or the elements of all psychic behavior. These *radices*, Jung continues, correspond "to the Empedoclean *rhizomata*, and in them they [the alchemists] saw the constituents of the most significant and central symbol of alchemy, the *lapis philosophorum*, which represents the goal of the individuation process" (*CW*, XIII, par. 242). In *Psychology and Religion*, the alchemists are transmuted to become "old philosophers" ("The idea of those old philosophers was that God manifested himself first in the creation of the four elements"—*CW*, XI, par. 97), the Gnostics replace the Hermetics as the penultimate authority (Empedocles himself is ultimate), and God, as one might expect in a monograph on *Psychology and Religion*, is frequently brought into the argument by name ("the quaternity is a more or less direct representation of the God who is manifest in his creation" —ibid., par. 101). But by whatever name and in whatever age, the alchemists, Gnostics, Hermetics, and analytical psychologists are about the same work of deifying the quaternity, discovering the holy four almost everywhere and projecting it where they fail to find it ("We have, at last, to admit that the quaternity is something psychic; and we do not know yet whether, in a more or less distant future, this too may not prove to be a projection"—ibid., par. 95). And in the end the mystical quaternity is brought back home to its beginning and returned to its source to complete the circle whereby the four roots are transformed into the Sphere: "The *quaternarium* or quaternity has a long history. It appears not only in Christian iconology and mystical speculation but plays perhaps a still greater role in Gnostic philosophy and from then on down through the Middle Ages until well into the eighteenth century" (ibid., par. 62). In a footnote on this passage, Jung plants the root where it belongs: "I am thinking of the mystical speculations about the four 'roots' (the rhizomata of Empedocles), i.e., the four elements or four qualities (wet, dry, warm, cold), peculiar to Hermetic or alchemical philosophy" (ibid., p. 38, n. 9). Jung was not always wont to be quite so modest as he is here, for usually he makes it plain that he (as well as others) continued the work for the quaternity well beyond the eighteenth century. In a more characteristic vein, Jung says in "A Study in the Process of Individuation," apropos of a patient's drawing, "In this picture we have the quaternity, the archetypal 4, which is capable of numerous interpretations, as history shows and as I have demonstrated elsewhere" (*CW*, IX, pt. 1, par. 565). Though it may be grandiose and rather breathtaking, Jung's apparent assumption that his own effort is coequal with history is more like it: more like Jung ordinarily and much more like Empedocles.

"Most mandalas," Jung says of attempts to depict what he calls "a psychocosmic system," "take the form of a flower, cross, or wheel, and show a distinct tendency towards a quaternary structure. . . ." Any reader who cares to leaf through Jung's *Collected Works* will find a storehouse, perhaps a surfeit, of such mandalas, numbering in the hundreds, some from ancient texts, some drawn or painted by Jung's patients, others produced by Jung himself. At least as revealing as any of these mandalas from Jung, however, is the woodcut of "The Great Wheel" on p. 66 of *A Vision*—just across the page, appropriately, from Yeats's discussion of Empedocles' vortex and his Concord that "fabricates all things into 'an homogeneous sphere.'"[7] These and all the other mandalas drawn, painted, danced, or composed in the Western world during the last twenty-five hundred years are unquestionably indebted to Empedocles, though at times the debt owes less, perhaps, to the historical Empedocles than to the archetypal one. Alchemists foolish enough to abandon the quaternity of that great ancestor in favor of the trinity of Christianity and Thrice-Greatest Hermes, according to Jung, got "into difficulties with the four elements and the four qualities," and though Jung had nothing but love for alchemy so long as it remained true to the number four, he was not above gloating over these difficulties of the trinitarians as he watched them "flounder about in . . . attempts to interpret the axiom of Maria" (*CW*, XIV, par. 68). But these ungracious remarks about his predecessors are nothing by comparison with the irritation, barely restrained within parentheses, shown by Jung toward a woman patient who wandered, artistically and therefore aimlessly, from the true "quaternary structure" into vain and idle pentadic and triadic figures: "The mandala is exceptional in that it has a pentadic structure.

7. *Vision*, p. 67. On p. 90 of his *Statesman* translation/commentary, J. B. Skemp reproduces a drawing that any reader of *A Vision* would naturally take to be a diagram from that book. What Skemp is concerned with, however, is not Yeats's *Vision* but Empedocles' system and the relationship of that system to the myth in *The Statesman*. The old symbolic geometry makes for a tight little schematic bundle across the centuries. Once one is aware of it, it is difficult not to see it everywhere—this is certainly true for Yeats, at any rate.

(The patient also produced triadic mandalas. She was fond of playing with forms irrespective of their meaning—a consequence of her artistic gift.)"[8] There is meaning in those geometric, archetypal forms, Jung implies, and it is therefore a well-deserved rebuke that he offers to anyone who would toy playfully with the archetypes and attempt to express wholeness in any other than a quaternary or circular figure.

In Jung's quaternalizing eyes, five is readjusted to become four (except in the mandala where the woman patient flaunted her pentadic structure), and even the *quinta essentia* is for him, by a paradox if not a downright contradiction, a quaternity and a mandala. Discussing a painting in which "the ground structure . . . is a quincunx," Jung says (and listening to his patter we hardly notice the sleight-of-hand by which quintus is transformed into quartus), "This is a symbol of the *quinta essentia*, which is identical with the Philosophers' Stone. It is the circle divided into four with the centre, or the divinity extended in four directions, or the four functions of consciousness with their unitary substrate, the self. Here the quaternity has a 3 + 1 structure" (*CW*, X, par. 738)—which, as every reader of Jung would immediately suspect, is the cue for the appearance of "Maria the Copt or Jewess"; it is hardly necessary for Jung to tell us, now that 3 + 1 Maria has appeared to make us forget all about the quincunx, the *quinta essentia*, and the number 5, that "The number 4 as the natural division of the circle is a symbol of wholeness . . ." (ibid.). Both Yeats and Jung were aware of the

---

8. *CW*, IX, pt. 1, p. 346, caption to Fig. 5. I take it that the description of the patient—"Aged 58, artistic and technically accomplished"—contains a hint of moral suspicion. Jung furiously resisted the notion that there was anything "artistic" about his own mandala paintings—they were, he felt, more "serious" than that. (Ironically, I understand that a New York gallery proposed a show of Jung's "paintings" six or seven years ago; Jung, I am sure, would not have been amused by the notion.) The "artistic and technically accomplished" patient may have been the same woman (Jung describes her as "a talented psychopath who had a strong transference to me") who, from his own unconscious, spoke to Jung as his "Anima" and enraged Jung by telling him that his mandalas and his descriptions of visions and fantasies were really very artistic. Jung wasn't having any, however: "Then came the next assault, and again the assertion: 'That is art.' This time I caught her and said, 'No, it is not art! On the contrary, it is nature . . .'" (*Memories*, p. 185/178). What reads as a rather droll affair was not that at all for Jung (he thought himself close to madness), and he emphatically rejected the artistic claims of his Anima because they would make his mandalas out to be "merely" art rather than products of the unconscious psyche striving to become conscious.

great importance of such systematic and schematic quaternal structures in Blake (on p. 257 of the first volume of *The Works of William Blake*, Yeats produced a diagram, representing Blake's system, that might have come from a dozen places in Jung's *Collected Works*; and at pp. 358-59 of the second volume of the Nonesuch *Writings of William Blake*, Jung placed a marker against a drawing that squares the circle and quaternalizes the sphere very thoroughly indeed); but both of them were also aware, at least fitfully, that the necessity to quaternalize went much further back in history than Blake and much deeper down in the psyche than could ever be conveyed by saying that Blake "influenced" Yeats or Jung to structure everything by quaternities and circles. Even Empedocles did not do that—unless by "Empedocles" we mean an inborn psychic structuring, an inherent tendency and necessity, that turned up as a purer and more insistent formative influence in Yeats and Jung (and in Blake) than in most men. "These symbols," which men have not stopped producing from Empedocles' time to our own, Jung says, "are usually quaternary and consist of two pairs of opposites crossing one another (e.g., left/right, above/below). The four points demarcate a circle, which, apart from the point itself, is the simplest symbol of wholeness and therefore the simplest God-image" (*CW*, XIII, par. 457). As sure as the 3 + 1 quaternity conjures up Maria Prophetissa in Jung, a circle as the God-image will entail this footnote: "God is a circle whose centre is everywhere and the circumference nowhere." Even this favorite tag of Jung's, which he could trace as far back as the *Corpus Hermeticum*, had been anticipated, if not definitively stated, by Empedocles, who, according to Aristotle, called his Sphere εὐδαιμονέστατος θεός, "the most blessed god" (as, in fact, Jung was quite aware: cf. *CW*, XII, par. 433).

The most damaging criticism of Empedocles was one brought by Aristotle (and implicitly affirmed by Plato in the *Timaeus*): that he locates his two motive forces, Love and Strife, not outside but within a closed universe and a self-contained system. It is true that by closing everything, the four elements and the two forces, within his system, Empedocles came up with an answer to Parmenides (*Parm.*: "How and when did process have a start?" *Emp.*: "Because process occurs within a closed, cyclical system, it never did have a start."); but to get that answer Empedocles found it necessary to reduce Love to the same level of existence as the elements, which was in effect to deprive both Love and the Sphere of their proclaimed divinity. Love, like the elements, is uncreated and immortal—but it is also just as much inside time as they are. To put the Aristotelian-Platonic objection in another way: even if the *daimon* should fulfill its Jungian task and should, through progressive purification, escape from the wheel; even if the cosmic *daimon* and the individual *daimon* should succeed in reestablishing a perfected state according to their respective *logoi* and so earn their escape—yet where would they escape to? Would they go to dwell with the gods?—But the elements are gods and the Sphere is the most blessed god, and they are all right here in this natural universe. The condition of the Sphere, as some commentators argue, might be of longer duration than any other single stage in the cycle; it nevertheless remains a stage in the cycle. Yeats, in his intuitive murmuring, may have been more right about Empedocles' system than Empedocles himself: "I have been part of it always and there is maybe no escape" (1925 *Vision*, p. xiii). Where shall the *daimon* escape to if there is, at best, only the Sphere of the all, at rest for a certain period and no doubt blessed, but not outside this world and certain to be shattered by Strife once again? But if Empedocles' system invites this sort of question (and I believe it does), so also does Jung's psychology.

Disclaim any desire to construct a system as he might, and disavow all philosophical intentions as he would, Jung could not for long remain content to be the psychiatrist without a vision that he sometimes announced he was; and when that vision would out, it more often than not bore striking similarities to the system of Empedocles. In his important essay "On Psychic Energy," Jung argues that all "the psychic forces (drives, affects, and other dynamic processes)" should best be understood as hypostatizations and differentiations of a single psychic energy which "is in my view aptly expressed by the term 'libido.'" And how shall we think of "libido?"? Think of it, Jung says, as "Schopenhauer's 'Will,' Aristotle's ὁρμή, Plato's Eros, Empedocles' 'love and hate of the elements,' or the *élan vital* of Bergson" (*CW*, VIII, par. 55). No matter that we may not know what to make of any of these different designations that Jung claims to be synonymous with his "libido," or that, if we do know what to make of them, we may not find them all that much alike; and no matter that Jung is trying, not so subtly, to deprive the Freudians of one of their favorite words by extending its definition out of all recognition; the point is that Jung is putting together his own psychological-philosophical system, closing it up as tightly as Empedocles' system ever was, and stamping it with his own name—but then, as a precautionary measure, should anyone object, as Plato and Aristotle objected to Empedocles, providing himself an escape by calling it not speculative thought or a systematic construction but empirical observation and natural description. Elsewhere, at a time (March 1913) when he was redefining Freudian libido theory in a way that led to his eventual, inevitable break with psychoanalysis, Jung enlists just such allies as Empedocles (and Plato) in his cause when he says, "by libido I mean very much what the ancients meant by the cosmogonic principle of Eros, or in modern language, 'psychic energy'" (*CW*, IV, par. 661). Jung takes another page from Empedocles' book and borrows another aspect of his system when he declares that it is "a very natural state of affairs for men to have irrational moods and women irrational opinions" because "this situation is grounded on instinct and must remain as it is to ensure that the Empedoclean game of the hate and love of the elements shall continue for all eternity" (*CW*, IX, pt. 2, par. 35). There Aristotle would jump on Jung as he jumped on Empedocles, since Jung gets movement into his psychological world by confining love and hate there, just as Empedocles maintained his cosmogony by making Eros (more exactly, *Philia* or *Philotēs*) into (in Jung's own term) a "cosmogonic principle" and yet reducing *Philotēs*, along with *Neikos* (Strife), to the level of the elements. What Jung does is to make his psychology a closed system of four elemental "functions" and two psychic "forces," closely resembling, in its schematic outlines, Empedocles' closed system of four elements moved about by Love and Strife; and both of these resemble Yeats's system of four "faculties" spinning perpetually in and out on the primary and antithetical gyres. Where the three occasionally differ is on the question of the relationship of the system to the Sphere: Empedocles says that the Sphere lies within the cyclical system; Yeats says that the Sphere lies outside the cyclical system; Jung says that . . . he would prefer not to say. It must be admitted, however, that Jung so often implies that there is something outside the system, all the while denying that he, a psychologist, should say what it is, that some readers have felt themselves teased and then cheated: as if they had been led to something that might very well be water, that is indeed hinted to be water, but then were not allowed even to find out if it really is water, much less given the opportunity to drink of it.

"The Concord of Empedocles fabricates all things into 'an homogeneous sphere,' and then Discord separates the elements and so makes the world we inhabit," Yeats says, in a paraphrase of Simplicius on Empedocles; and then he continues with his own commentary: "but even the sphere formed by Concord is not the changeless eternity, for Concord or Love but offers us the image of that which is changeless" (*Vision*, pp. 67-68). As Jung puts it, "In the history of symbols, quaternity is the unfolding of unity," and that which is true in the history of symbols is true also in Empedocles' cycle, where "quaternity is the unfolding of unity" and unity the folding together of quaternity, the one sphere broken into four elements and the four elements reformed into one sphere. The difference between the quaternity and the sphere, as Jung goes on to point out, is that the sphere (like Parmenides' sphere—though Parmenides claimed otherwise—like Yeats's sphere, and like Jung's own pleroma) cannot be known but the quaternity can: "The one universal Being cannot be known, because it is not differentiated from anything and cannot be compared with anything. By unfolding into four it acquires distinct characteristics and can therefore be known" (*CW*, X, par. 774). From the *Sphairos* to separated, hostile *rhizōmata* and from separated *rhizōmata* to the blessed *Sphairos*, half-cycle perpetually reversing and alternating with half-cycle—thus the process of psyche in Jung, thus the pattern of history in Yeats, thus the movement of "all things" in Empedocles. Or as Yeats put it in successive revisions of a line for "The Gyres"—

> For the great gyres have tumbled us about
> . . . .
> The ancient gyre has tumbled us about
> . . . .
> Empedocles has tumbled us about
> . . . .
> Empedocles has thrown all things about.

It is easy to see in Empedocles' *Sphairos* both a memory and an anticipation: a memory of Parmenides' well-rounded Sphere and an anticipation of Plato's spherical Living Creature in the *Timaeus*.

"But he was equal on every side and quite without end, spherical and round, rejoicing in his circular solitude," Empedocles says, in language that points back to Parmenides' "well-rounded sphere, from the centre equally balanced in every direction . . . for being equal to itself on every side, it rests uniformly within its limits," and forward to Plato's Living Creature, the world's body, "rounded and spherical, equidistant in every way from centre to extremity." Like those other spheres, Empedocles' most blessed god was without parts, fruitful or otherwise, and, but for the near proximity of Strife (which seems inevitably to go hand in hand with sex in this world), his Sphere would remain throughout eternity as unproductive as the One Being of Parmenides. "Two branches do not spring from his back, he has no feet, no swift knees, no fruitful parts; but he was spherical and equal on every side" (Frs. 28 and 29, trans. Burnet). Were Strife not lurking nearby to divide all this suffocating harmony, then Parmenides' One Being would be all, and there would be for us no cosmos, no consciousness, no existence at all. Though he erroneously coupled Empedocles and Heraclitus ("Empedocles and Heraclitus thought that the universe had first one form and then its opposite in perpetual alternation" [*Vision*, p. 246]), Yeats was nevertheless clear on the main issues: that Love and Discord are equally necessary in the creation of the cosmos; and that the sphere formed by Concord is but a symbol of the transcendent Sphere. "Love and Discord, Fire and Water, dominate in turn, Love making all things One, Discord separating all, but Love no more than Discord the changeless eternity. Here originated perhaps the symbol expounded in this book of a phaseless sphere that becomes phasal in our thought, Nicholas of Cusa's undivided reality which human experience divides into opposites, and here too . . . we discover for the first time the Platonic doctrine of imitation—the opposing states copy eternity" (*Vision*, p. 247). Jung shied away from any metaphysical statement about changeless eternity and the phaseless sphere, but within the confines of time and the world he was in precise agreement with Empedocles and Yeats that there is, in the individual psyche as in history and in the cosmos, "a dual process running its measured course through vast periods of time, a drama entirely re-enacted" (*CW*, VI, par. 708). This is the twin movement Yeats had in mind when he said that he could see "in the changes of the moon all the cycles: the soul realising its separate being in the full moon, then, as the moon seems to approach the sun and dwindle away, all but realising its absorption in God, only to whirl away once more: the mind of a man, separating itself from the common matrix, through childish imaginations, through struggle ... to roundness, completeness, and then externalising, intellectualising, systematising, until at last it lies dead" (*Ex.*, p. 403). Jung many times described the archetypal pattern of the psyche's ascent and descent, and the subject usually encouraged him to indulge the poetic strain in his makeup, but he never did it better than Yeats does here, nor did he ever, though much of Yeats's language could be Jung's own ("separating itself from the common matrix," for example, is pure Jung), succeed more brilliantly in making the imagery and poetry of Empedocles' vision a part of his own expression.

Those who came to Empedocles "seeking prophecies" and wondrous cures as he went about among the citizens of Acragas, "an immortal god, mortal no more, honoured as is my due and crowned with garlands and verdant wreaths" (Fr. 112), undoubtedly came away satisfied—or so the tone of "Purifications" implies—because the seer-physician possessed a comprehensive vision of the cyclical pattern of human/cosmic history and the cyclical pattern of daimonic incarnations that allowed him to foresee and to prophesy the future individually, historically, and cosmically. Armed with the same vision—with the certainty, as Yeats put it, that the predestined pattern of history and of the psyche is "never progress as we understand it, never the straight line" (*Ex.*, pp. 403-04), but always the self-reversing twofold cycle of Empedocles—Yeats and Jung presented themselves confidently as prophets and wonder-working physicians, as men who could read the future because they had long since discerned, as in a vision or a comprehensive system, the historical and physical pattern of the past. To the current myth of evolutionary progress, Yeats opposed his counter-myth of cyclical repetition; to the nineteenth-century myth of infinite psychic improvement, Jung opposed his vision of alternating, constructive-destructive and conscious-unconscious, psychic opposites. Moreover, those alternating opposites at work in the individual psyche and in the collective psyche were certain to come out in the spirit and the experience of the age, so that Jung was as well provided with the instruments of historical prophecy as Yeats was. "Each age unwinds the thread another age had wound," Yeats says, himself winding up the clew of history on a pair of reversed gyres, "and it amuses me to remember that before Phidias, and his westward-moving art, Persia fell, and that when full moon came round again, amid eastward-moving thought, and brought Byzantine glory, Rome fell; and that at the outset of our westward-moving Renaissance Byzantium fell" (*Vision*, pp. 270-71). And now again, Yeats's vision told him, "amid an eastward-moving thought" once more, London, Vienna, Alexandria, Athens, Jerusalem (if one may reverse the order of Eliot's collapsing cities) are all falling, and Dublin and Zurich are falling too,

> And what rough beast, its hour come round at last,
> Slouches towards Bethlehem to be born?

"What rough beast?"—Jung had no doubt about the answer (though critics and scoffers maintained that he was slow to perceive that answer, indeed that he came up with it not before the fact but only well after the beast had appeared, settled in, and destroyed a good part of the world): it was National Socialism, Jung said, an eruption of bestial violence from the Teutonic unconscious, a violence which was just exactly as extreme, because it was its counterbalancing opposite, as the excessive intellectuality of Teutonic consciousness.

Jung read the future, as did Yeats, out of the past, and the past presented a pattern that was nothing other than the pattern of psychic *enantiodromia* blown up to historic proportions—or that same Empedoclean pattern reduced from cosmic to historic proportions. "One thinks"—now it is Jung looking back to cyclical climaxes of the past, the better to project them into the future—"of the chiliastic expectations of the Augustan age at the beginning of the Christian era, or of the spiritual changes in the West which accompanied the end of the first millennium. Today, as the end of the second millennium draws near, we are again living in an age filled with apocalyptic images of universal destruction" (*CW*, X, par. 488). Yeats, like Jung, saw civilization moving in such cycles of two thousand years, each of those cycles being in reality two half-cycles, those half-cycles again being divisible into contrary halves, and so on, consciousness balanced forever and at all levels against the unconscious, one historic gyre set off against another, a vortex whirling into and out of a vortex, the opposite of the first and yet its twin. "In other words every month or phase when we take it as a whole is a double vortex moving from Phase 1 to Phase 28, or two periods, one solar and one lunar . . ." (*Vision*, p. 197).

Possessed of the same unerring guide to the future as Empedocles —i.e., an understanding of that symbolic geometry that described all cycles, individual, historic, and cosmic—why should Yeats and Jung doubt their prophetic abilities? Being heirs to his system, were they not also heirs to Empedocles' visionary and oracular insight? It seemed so to Yeats, and to Jung likewise: looking back on what he had written ten, fifteen, and twenty-five years earlier—just long enough for history to show its hand and to reveal that it was the prophesied hand—each of them perceived, and modestly remarked, how shrewd he had been in forecasting the future from universalizing patterns of the past. "We stand perplexed and stupefied before the phenomenon of Nazism and Bolshevism because we know nothing about man" (*Memories*, p. 331/305), Jung said, but his use of the first person plural is merely a matter of courtesy and rhetorical convention, for elsewhere Jung reveals that he, if not his contemporaries, understood Nazism and Bolshevism very well and all along. In a congratulatory little exchange with himself over the years, Jung developed and illustrated, out of the experience of a quarter of a century, a pattern of psychic *enantiodromia* and its historic consequences, demonstrating that he had been all the while prophesying *à la* Empedocles, albeit in a rather general way and to uncomprehending ears. *Enantiodromia* is "a running contrariwise," Jung wrote in 1917; "sooner or later everything runs into its opposite. . . . Thus the rational attitude of culture necessarily runs into its opposite, namely the irrational devastation of culture" (*CW*, VII, par. 111). When he came to revise *Two Essays* in 1925, Jung added a note to this passage on *enantiodromia*: "This sentence was written during the first World War. I have let it stand in its original form because it contains a truth which has been confirmed more than once in the course of history. (Written in 1925)." Jung concluded the dialogue with himself, twenty-five years after he had initiated it, with this remark: "As present events show, the confirmation did not have to wait very long. Who wants this blind destruction? But we all help the daemon to our last gasp. *O sancta simplicitas*! (Written in 1942)." Thus commenting before, during, and after events, Jung could claim—and in essays published in 1945 and 1946 did claim[9]—to have foreseen and to have predicted the outburst of the "blond beast" that devastated Europe in the second World War.

Nor was Yeats without claims to prophetic foresight, and what he had foreseen pointed in the same recurrent, cyclical direction—in the direction of "Communist, Fascist," and other political criminals (*Letters*, p. 851)—as that which Jung had foreseen. Writing to Ethel Mannin during the international political and cultural chaos of 1936, when Empedocles had "thrown all things about" with a terrible vengeance, Yeats adopted a mantic voice not unlike the voice of the ancient shaman of Sicily nor unlike the voice of the contemporary shaman of Switzerland: "I have not been silent," Yeats said, though his speech was not, perhaps, what Ethel Mannin might have anticipated; "I have used the only vehicle I possess—verse. If you have my poems by you, look up a poem called *The Second Coming*. It was written some sixteen or seventeen years ago and foretold what is happening." As Jung had only his psychology for prophetic vehicle (*CW*, X, pars. 444 and 458), Yeats had only his verse, but psychology in the one case and poetry in the other foretold the same events —or so the practitioners of the two believed when they looked back on their earlier writings. "I am not callous," Yeats concluded his letter to Ethel Mannin, "every nerve trembles with horror at what is happening in Europe, 'the ceremony of innocence is drowned.'" Thus, with his own words, the poet-prophet of 1919 was vindicated in the political events of 1936.[10] If we study the prophetic poem of 1919, moreover, we shall see very clearly that it was the Empedocles within him that afforded Yeats his clairvoyant prescience, for "the widening gyre" of "The Second Coming," the "ancient gyre" that tumbles all about, is none other than the gyre of increasing Strife

---

9. "After the Catastrophe" (1945), "The Fight with the Shadow" (1946), and "Epilogue to 'Essays on Contemporary Events'" (1946), all in *CW*, X. In notes on pp. 219 and 227, Jung refers the reader to a paragraph in "The Role of the Unconscious" (*CW*, X, par. 17), written in 1918, in which he discussed the "blond beast" lurking in the Germanic unconscious. In the "Epilogue to 'Essays on Contemporary Events,'" Jung lays out all the evidence demonstrating his foresight and his psychological prescience with regard to World War II.

10. Yeats, of course, like Jung, was writing of his prophetic foresight with all the knowledge of hindsight; when deprived of that knowledge, neither man was nearly so clear-sighted as both later became. Their flirtations with Fascism, like their latter-day claims to prophetic foresight of what was coming, represent one of the more ironic, less savory ties between Yeats and Jung.

from Empedocles' cosmic cycle; and the history of 1936, as previewed in 1919, is seen to be approaching the point of Strife's complete dominance:

> Things fall apart; the centre cannot hold;
> Mere anarchy is loosed upon the world—

that point in time when what was once a perfectly ordered sphere, held in blissful, motionless peace by its center—"bound in the close covering of Harmony, spherical and round, rejoicing in his circular rest"—is in complete disorder and elemental disarray, the four elements separated, isolated, and fiercely hostile toward one another. Whether it is the "blond beast" of Fascism or the red beast of Communism that rises from *"Spiritus Mundi"* and the collective unconscious to set out for Bethlehem at the end of the poem is comparatively insignificant, since, as I remarked earlier, the Greek view that all things are cyclical—a view endorsed in full by Yeats and Jung—would transform the particulars of history into the recurrences of time and would generalize the specific political tyranny and anarchy of Fascists and Communists as the cosmic force of Strife waxing to its climax. Whether blond or red, the beast was in any case foreseeable, according to Empedocles, Yeats, and Jung, not merely twenty-five years in advance but, by the truly clearminded and farsighted, a thousand and two thousand years before. "The gyres! the gyres!" as the poem of that title (written during the latter half of 1936) exclaims: these are the selfsame gyres as those which have thrown all things about before and as those which will throw all things about again when history, as will certainly happen in time, is brought to its period, all things moving ever more swiftly and violently under the increase of Strife, and the cycle, at one of its two great climacterics, turns history back on itself to become its own opposite, retracing it steps once more but now in reverse.

In a passage that preceded the 1925 *Vision* by several years and so provided the Instructors with the symbolic geometry they needed to construct a system and give it back to Yeats in return, Yeats declared his faith in the mathematical exactitude of the Empedoclean half-cycles: "I do not doubt those heaving circles, those winding arcs, whether in one man's life or in that of an age, are mathematical, and that some in the world, or beyond the world, have foreknown the event and pricked upon the calendar the life-span of a

Christ, a Buddha, a Napoleon: that every moment, in feeling or in thought, prepares in the dark by its own increasing clarity and confidence its own executioner" (*Myth.*, p. 340). So Love and Strife do—each inevitably, helplessly prepares "its own executioner"—and within a few years the Instructors, with their perspective from "beyond the world," came to teach a man and his wife still "in the world" the mathematics of "heaving circles" and "winding arcs" that his poetry might reenact the same cyclical vision as the poetry of Empedocles had originally enacted twenty-five hundred years before. Granted insight into the precise mathematics of recurrent circles and arcs—those formally identical *kosmoi* directing the life of the individual, the age, and the universe—Yeats was provided with a knowledge half-Pythagorean and half-Empedoclean, a sacred marriage of the two great, primal metempsychologists, that in his own estimation was responsible for the strength of his finest poetry: "And I put *The Tower* and *The Winding Stair* into evidence to show that my poetry has gained in self-possession and power" (*Vision*, p. 8).

In the cycle of the world and the soul as projected by Empedocles, there is no cosmos and no human existence at either extreme—neither when Strife is entirely dominant nor when Love has bound everything "fast in the close covering of Harmony, a rounded sphere rejoicing in his circular solitude." Just so, according to Yeats, who had the information from the Instructors: there is no cosmos, nor is there any human existence, at Phase 1 and at Phase 15 when the gyres of Discord and Concord dominate completely. "Phase 1 and Phase 15 are not human incarnations because human life is impossible without strife between the *tinctures*" (*Vision*, p. 79). Of the *tinctures* and the climatic points of the two gyres, Yeats, continuing to speak in the accents of Empedocles, says, "At Phase 15 and Phase 1 occurs what is called the *interchange of the tinctures*, those thoughts, emotions, energies, which were *primary* before Phase 15 or Phase 1 are *antithetical* after, those that were *antithetical* are *primary*" (p. 89). After Phase 15, which corresponds to that moment in Empedocles' cycle when Strife disrupts the Sphere and begins its separation, things begin to pull apart as before Phase 15 (and before the Sphere) they had been drawn together. According to the scheme of historical phases in Yeats, as also according to the myth in the *Statesman* and the world cycle in Empedocles, we live in a period of increasing

Strife—very near the end of that half-cycle in Yeats's vision. This means that we have to look about equally far back and far forward in history to see, or to imagine, the condition of the Sphere: we are removed from it in either direction by almost exactly one half-cycle. It is during this period of increasing Strife, however (post-Phase 15 in Yeats), that there occurs—and historically did occur, Yeats says —what Empedocles calls "whole-natured forms" (οὐλοφυεῖς τύποι) and what Yeats himself describes as "Unity of Being." Jung finds this same ideal, not with Empedocles in cosmogony and anthropogony, nor with Yeats in history and the poet's creation, but in the psychology of the individual—in the archetype of the self (a whole-natured *typos*, if ever there was one), in "individuation" and in realization of "the god within." For Jung, the opposed cones or gyres are not historical but psychological—gyres of consciousness and the unconscious—but his anti-historical and atemporal ideal is no more to be discovered at one extreme or the other than is the "whole-natured form" of Empedocles or the Unity of Being of Yeats. It should be specifically noted that the *human* ideal is not to be found—not for any of the three, except when they are speaking symbolically—in the condition of the Sphere, for that condition is psychologically unconscious, it is poetically dumb, and it is logically and cosmologically as sterile as the "Is" of Parmenides. Before man came to register the world with his consciousness, as Jung puts it, and "to speak the word that outweighed the whole of Creation" (*CW*, XIV, par. 129), God and his universe were simply inarticulate and entirely "unconscious" (*CW*, XI, par. 638), nothing more than a roiling, undifferentiated pleroma; likewise, before Strife intervened to break up Empedocles' Sphere, Love may have reigned unopposed, but it was not *human* love, nor, especially, did it have anything at all to do with sexual love. Sexual love is a consequence of the action of Strife, first in separating the indivisible and sexless Sphere to bring "whole-natured forms" into being, then in separating the androgynous "whole-natured forms" to bring men and women into being. It is thus thanks to Strife, and our continuing in it, that we have our existence.

"Come now and hear this," Empedocles says in Fr. 62: "it is no erring or ignorant tale. Whole-natured forms first sprang from the earth, having a portion of both water and heat" (trans. Guthrie). As with Yeats and Jung, so with Empedocles, water is the female element and fire the male element; hence the bisexual, whole-natured forms are a "perfection," a human ideal, being that stage intermediate between the Sphere, which heard nothing of sex, and ourselves, who hear of practically nothing else. In the very long run, moreover, there is much worse to come, since the impersonal operation of Strife in Empedocles has the same effect as the threatened action of Zeus in the tale of Aristophanes in the *Symposium*. Having divided the original double creatures in two, Zeus lets it be known that he will continue to divide and redivide the foolish creatures until they cease to offend by their arrogance. Strife, having broken up the Sphere and the whole-natured creatures, will also, inevitably —but acting as if by an impersonal law of nature rather than from the very personal anger that motivates Zeus—go on to separate human beings, first into disjoined limbs, then into isolated elements of air, earth, fire, and water. In the 1925 *Vision*, Yeats presents the Empedoclean half-cycle in which Strife is on the increase very clearly —more clearly, indeed, than in the 1937 *Vision*, where Empedocles has had to submit to refinements, additions, and qualifications resulting from Yeats's post-revelation readings in philosophy. "I see the Lunar and Solar cones first, before they start their whirling movement, as two worlds lying one within another—nothing exterior, nothing interior, Sun in Moon and Moon in Sun—a single being like man and woman in Plato's Myth, and then a separation and a whirling for countless ages, and I see man and woman as reflecting the greater movement, each with zodiac, precession, and separate measure of time, and all whirling perpetually. But this whirling, though creative, is not evil, for evil is from the disturbance of the harmony, so that those that should come in their season come all at once or struggle here and there, the gyres thrown together in confusion, and hatred takes possession of all" (1925 *Vision*, p. 149). The only commentary necessary on such a passage as this is "cf. Empedocles," for it is all there: the condition of the Sphere ("nothing exterior, nothing interior"), the whole-natured creatures ("a single being like man and woman"), "then a separation and a whirling for countless ages," man and woman and all *daimones* caught up in the same cycles within cycles, the "disturbance of harmony" which occurs later in the half-cycle and produces disordered beings (hunchbacks and fools, for example), and the end of the half-cycle when Empedocles throws "the gyres . . . together in confusion," and Strife or Discord reigns alone ("hatred takes possession of all").

It may be, as Empedocles' cyclic vision asserted, that the ideal of wholeness would never have existed were it not for the differentiating and divisive effects of strife (as Yeats says, this is creative, not evil—evil comes later, with the disintegration of harmonious creatures); nevertheless, it was Yeats's opinion that in our time (very late in the half-cycle) the greatest barrier to wholeness or to Unity of Being or to reachievement of our original whole-natured form lies in what he calls "hatred." We will succeed in reintegrating our fragmented, Strife-divided state and will attain to the blessedness of the whole-natured creatures who symbolize (but are not) the Sphere, Yeats thought, only when we free ourselves of hatred. "It may be an hour before the mood passes," Yeats says of the transcendent experience in time, "but latterly I seem to understand that I enter upon it the moment I cease to hate" (*Myth.*, p. 365). Hatred here could well be seen, in psychological terms, as the internalization of the cosmic force of Strife, so that it becomes not something affecting us impersonally and from without but forms the very principle and definition of our being; then it is unquestionably evil. It should be recalled that the *daimon* of Empedocles suffers exile from the gods, and sees its own symbolic sphericity and wholeness disintegrate, for a crime very like the hatred Yeats speaks of: "Of these I too am now one, an exile from the gods and a wanderer, having put my trust in raving Strife" (Fr. 115). Hatred, "raving Strife," discord at the very heart of the individual cosmos—these are evil according to Empedocles and Yeats. "I think the common condition of our life is hatred," Yeats goes on to say in the passage just quoted; and in "A Prayer for My Daughter" he counterposes to this self-destructive, Sphere-destructive "common condition" an ideal of wholeness which is close kin to Jung's "individuation" and seems a symbolic imitation—which, because we are human, is the best we can do: a symbolic imitation—of Empedocles' *Sphairos*:

> Considering that, all hatred driven hence,
> The soul recovers radical innocence
> And learns at last that it is self-delighting,
> Self-appeasing, self-affrighting,
> And that its own sweet will is Heaven's will.

Jung would have approved this "self . . . self . . . self" that draws the circumference tight around a center of individual being in Yeats's poem, for it is also a common presence in all Jung's own psychology, and he would have approved it especially because Yeats's lines echo (very resoundingly) Jung's frequent descriptions of "individuation" as well as descriptions of the goal of that Jungian process. "The self is the total, timeless man and as such corresponds to the original, spherical, bisexual being who stands for the mutual integration of conscious and unconscious" (*CW*, XVI, par. 531). This is what Jung elsewhere (and frequently) calls "the Anthropos idea that stands for man's wholeness, that is, the conception of a unitary being who existed before man and at the same time represents man's goal" (*CW*, XII, par. 210). The bisexual Anthropos (= Platonic Man), which finds its mythic origin in Empedocles and its finest elaboration in the *Symposium*, is a symbol for that condition of the Sphere from which we have been separated and a symbol also for that same condition of the Sphere to which we aspire to return in the cyclical course of time. In his concept of "individuation" Jung could be more faithful to Empedocles only by quoting him directly and crediting him by name—which he does do in *Psychology and Religion* when he refers to the "perfect living being of hermaphroditic nature corresponding to the Empedoclean σφαῖρος, the εὐδαιμονέστατος θεός and all-around bisexual being in Plato" (*CW*, XI, par. 93). Psychologically, this "perfect living being of hermaphroditic nature" symbolizes the self just as, cosmically, it symbolizes the otherwise unknowable Sphere; and the *daimon* of Empedocles (which E. R. Dodds, in a good Jungian/Yeatsian phrase, calls "the indestructible self"[11]), like the *daimones* of Yeats and Jung, forever yearns to enjoy once again the blessed, but nonhuman condition of the Sphere.

With "all hatred driven hence," Yeats says, "I am in the place where the Daimon is," and there then comes into being a whole-natured creature, self-created but a divine creation also, and "I am full of uncertainty, not knowing when I am the finger, when the clay. Once, twenty years ago, I seemed to awake from sleep to find my body rigid, and to hear a strange voice speaking these words through my lips as through lips of stone: 'We make an image of him who sleeps, and it is not he who sleeps, and we call it 'Emmanuel' "

11. Dodds, *The Greeks and the Irrational*, p. 153.

(*Myth.*, p. 366). Emmanuel—"God with us": it is a daring passage and would be perhaps hubristic were it not for the fact that the voice seemed to Yeats a "strange" one, not his own, that was merely borrowing his lips for utterance. The passage is not, however, more daring or more grandiose than the claim of the Grand Original, Empedocles: "I an immortal god, no longer a mortal." This is surely the *daimon* purified and liberated, or about to be liberated, ascending (as Yeats has it) into its own archetype, even if the ascension be—as in Yeats's case it was—only for the symbolic eternal moment. This is the liberation that the individual may occasionally experience (cf. section IV of "Vacillation"); it is the liberation that the artist habitually verges upon ("the artist lives in the presence of death and childhood, and the great affections and the orgiastic moment when life outleaps its limits"—*E. & I.*, p. 325); and it is the liberation that, all Strife driven hence to be replaced by the unifying power of "a soft, immortal stream of blameless Love," the *daimon* may hope to enjoy when its time comes round to describe, in effect, a sphere: "It is the cycle which may deliver us from the twelve cycles of time and space. The cone which intersects ours is a cone in so far as we think of it as the antithesis of our thesis, but if the time has come for our deliverance it is the phaseless sphere, sometimes called the Thirteenth Sphere.... Within it live all souls that have been set free and every *Daimon* and Ghostly Self..." (*Vision*, pp. 210-211). Within it must dwell, then, if one's understanding is correct, the *daimon* that the history of philosophy knows as Empedocles, and perhaps also within it now, if their time for deliverance did indeed come recently, the *daimones* once called Yeats and Jung. "Abstain wholly from laurel leaves," Empedocles enjoins the fallen *daimones* in Fr. 140; and more emphatically and excitedly in Fr. 141: "Wretches, utter wretches, keep your hands from beans!" The purifying abstentions and rituals of Yeats and Jung were undoubtedly quite different from these of Empedocles; nevertheless, through their "purifications," Yeats and Jung too sought that same apotheosis, that same recovery and perfection of "the indestructible self," that same return to the Sphere foreseen by Empedocles in Frs. 146 and 147: "But, at the last, they appear among mortal men as prophets, songwriters, physicians, and princes; and thence they rise up as gods exalted in honour, sharing the hearth of the other gods and the same table, free from human woes, safe from destiny, and incapable of hurt" (trans. Burnet).

Yet there is one question that remains: Empedocles, Yeats, and Jung may be within the Thirteenth Sphere, but where *is* that Sphere? Is it inside time or outside it? Is the Sphere a part of the natural cycle or is it something totally removed from it, an ideal and a perfection of an entirely different order from the cycle, a state of being imitated and symbolized by joined cycles but never contained within them? There is no doubt, I am afraid, about the answer for Empedocles: the Sphere is one stage in an endless and cyclical temporal process. Empedocles offers us no eternity that is not a prisoner of time; but in that paradox—the paradox that subjects eternity to time rather than vice versa—he destroys eternity itself and contradicts the sense of it. We can only suppose, then, melancholy as the supposition may be, that Empedocles found his Thirteenth Cone when he leapt into Mt. Aetna (as, according to one tradition, he did, wanting people to think he had been assumed into the heavens); that his Sphere, reversing Yeats's dictum, is in reality a cone or a cycle; and that Empedocles therefore remains bound to that wheel of time that he himself reintroduced to Greek philosophy after Parmenides had abolished it. So for Empedocles. The answers for Yeats and Jung—I say "answers" deliberately as they have not quite the same response to make—will more conveniently await a reading of the myths of Plato's philosophy and a consideration of the relationship of those myths to the myths of Yeats's poetry and the myths of Jung's psychology. However, that Yeats and Jung followed Empedocles, if not into Mt. Aetna, yet in detail after detail of that symbolic geometry that describes the cycles of time and of human experience—this much is already certain.

CHAPTER VI

Mythos, Eidos, and the Daimon

The question is one of time and eternity and of hierarchies of becoming-Being that may be imagined to extend between time and eternity and so, in a certain sense, to unite them. It is a question also of *mythos* and *logos*, of brightly colored tales and blindingly pure reason, and of *daimones*, those great mythic figures who arise from the collective unconscious or from *Anima Mundi* to offer themselves as mediators with the proclaimed power to transport us from the confines of time to the freedom of eternity, from a world of swarming, multiple images to a world which is "all music and all rest" and where we can contemplate the unique *eidos* in its absolute perfection. The history of Greek philosophy, in its consideration of these questions, unfolds itself in time as if it were a composite psyche living a life of tremendous intellectual and emotional vitality of some two hundred years' duration. The process has been described as a movement from religion to science and from *mythos* to *logos*, which is fair enough; yet, throughout those two hundred years, the psyche always needed its *mythos*, and in our day it continues to need a *mythos*, so that there could be no question then, and there can be none now, of simply abandoning myth in favor of reason or of dispelling all stories to replace them with pure dialectic.

Anyone who wishes to see the history of Greek philosophy (and similarly the progress of individual psyche in its advance from an unconscious state to consciousness) as a simple transformation of *mythos* into *logos* must be given pause by a work like the *Timaeus*, for that entire dialogue (after the preliminary maneuvering) is, as Timaeus makes perfectly clear by his continual, casual interchange of the two words, both *mythos* and *logos*; nor is there any way to decide which of the two—were they separated, as they are not —would provide the better explanation of "all things," since both are regularly coupled with the adjective meaning "likely, probable": it is all a "likely tale" and a "probable account" (in a single sentence, at 59c-d, we have both *eikotas mythous* and *eikotas logous* as descriptions of Timaeus' discourse). What we should say, perhaps, is that in the *Timaeus* (which in a sense is the climax of the dialogues and the climax of the history of Greek philosophy), *mythos* and *logos* are held in perfect balance, being exactly coordinated complements of one another, and are merged by Plato in a new kind of reasoning and vision—mythic logic or logistical myth. As to the history of Greek philosophy leading up to the *Timaeus*: Pythagoras was a scientist of sorts, but his science had more to do with myth (or a mystical mathematics) than with logic; Heraclitus adopted *logos* as the key to his reading of the universe, but he chose nevertheless to speak largely in those mythic accents that brook no refutation. Parmenides was the first (and last) to hang his entire argument on *logos*, meaning by that the faculty of reason (Fr. 7: κρῖναι δὲ λόγῳ . . . ἔλεγχον; "judge by reason . . . the proof"), and the first (and last) to scorn myth as the nonsense and empty words of deluded men. Empedocles, as I have argued, restored mythology and time, after Parmenides had abolished them in favor of logic and eternity; to effect that restoration, however, he unfortunately had to close up those interstices of time through which, as Yeats at least felt, mortal men might slip into eternity. Plato returned Greek philosophy to the ideal of Parmenidean logic and eternity, but he all the same never released his hold on myth or on time. Far, indeed, from abandoning myth, Greek philosophy, in its supreme moment, created a *mythos* out of the dialectical progress by which it had eventually arrived at its true *logos*. Plato, that is to say, wrote the life—the intellectual biography and the spiritual "autobiography"—of Socrates; he invested that life with mythic dimensions; he founded his own system in the life of a particular man—the man Socrates, Plato's familiar, his guardian spirit, his *daimon*—and he thereby transformed that man into nothing less than the Platonic Idea of Man. What Socrates seeks, in the virtually mythic quest he pursues in the dialogues, is—if one may adopt a Platonic and Plotinian (also Yeatsian and Jungian) terminology—the Idea that makes him a man and *this* man, the archetype (of the self) that was uniquely his, the *eidos* of his individual humanity. Yeats, as a poet—likewise Jung, as a psychologist—took his own life for the stuff of myth; Plato did differently, but only in that he projected the myth not on to his own life but on to the life of Socrates. What all three sought, however—Yeats in poetic myth, Jung in psychological myth, and Plato in philosophic myth—was one and the same thing though under different names: Unity of Being; individuation; perfect merger with the *daimon* which will transport one to the *eidos* of his being.

"A failure of nerve," some scandalized commentators have termed Plato's frequent reversion to myth, coming as it did after Parmenides' astringent appeal to proceed entirely by dialectical argument and to judge only by reason. The same charge has been laid at Jung's doorstep, not because he reverted often to myth (though he did, of course, and consciously) but because he rejected a myth—Freud's myth—in favor of what he thought a vastly superior myth—what, on the first page of his autobiography, he calls "my personal myth." While Jung claimed to find Freud's myth too narrow and his explanation of the aetiology of neuroses too exclusively sexual, his critics scoffed at the claim, maintaining that the real reason for Jung's aversion was simply that Freud's myth was too hard for him, and that it required more intellectual discipline than Jung was capable of exercising. Hence, as his critics have it, Jung's failure of nerve in face of the uncompromising starkness of the truth about human psychology caused him to opt for a rosier and a gentler—also, the critics say, a less scientific and less coherent—myth about humanity. In a foreword to the book that Jung himself saw as signalling his inevitable break with Freud (*Symbols of Transformation*, first published in 1912), Jung wrote in 1950, "Hardly had I finished the manuscript when it struck me what it means to live with a myth, and what it means to live without one. Myth, says a

Church Father, is 'what is believed always, everywhere, by everybody'; hence the man who thinks he can live without myth, or outside it, is an exception" (*CW*, V, p. xxiv). The logic of Jung's argument may seem to wear a bit thin when he first says that the man who lives without a myth "lives a life of his own, sunk in a subjective mania of his own devising, which he believes to be the newly discovered truth," and then proceeds to the observation that, after *Symbols of Transformation*, "in the most natural way, I took it upon myself to get to know 'my' myth, and . . . to know what unconscious or preconscious myth was forming me . . ." (pp. xxiv–xxv). While it might seem logically hazardous to pass from a negative observation about the subjectivity of mythless man to a positive valuation of "'my' myth," the view of myth that Jung expresses here finds a good deal of confirmation and justification not only in his own various writings but also in Yeats's remarks on myth and in Plato's regular adherence to myth, whether in the mythologizing of Socrates' life or in those myths, specifically acknowledged as such, that are spotted here and there throughout the dialogues.

The relationship between the Socrates of the dialogues and the Socrates of history has been a fruitful source of confusion and an even more fruitful source of controversy in the history of Greek philosophy. The focus of both the confusion and the controversy (though they are by no means limited to this passage) is at that point in the *Phaedo* when Socrates, as portrayed by Plato, has gone as far as he can go with dialectical argumentation in proving the immortality of the soul. Yet, though Socrates' interlocutors have been forced to agree to specific points all along the dialectical way, they are by no means convinced or unquestioningly assured of the main thing: that the soul is immortal. And what is Socrates' response (which, except for his actual death, is the climax and the conclusion of the dialogue) to this last hesitation before full conviction? He first narrates an intellectual "autobiography" that sounds like a generalized biography of philosophic man of fifth-century Greece; and having finished that personal/impersonal tale—"'my, myth," as it were—he proceeds to a myth, frankly acknowledged as such, of the afterlife. I trust it will not seem sophistical to suggest that the "autobiography" narrated by Socrates, which leads him to affirmation of the existence of those Forms on which Plato's system depends, has for *Plato* (not for Socrates) the same mythic valuation as the myth of the afterlife has for the dramatic character of Socrates. Socrates' life is to Plato as the *Phaedo* myth (like the other so-called eschatological myths) is to the Socrates of the dialogues: both are "likely stories," *logoi* in the dramatic, brighter, and more appealing dress of *mythoi*, created for the most serious moral purpose—to exhort men to examine their lives and seek the good life, to care for their souls and win for them a worthy immortality, to love wisdom and pursue it, i.e., to practise philosophy as Socrates practised it and as Plato dramatized (and systematized) it.

R. Hackforth, in his commentary on the *Phaedo*, remarks that in their reading of the "autobiography" some Platonic scholars seem to want to "have it both ways"; but "surely," Hackforth complains, "the passage cannot be intended as both personal and suprapersonal."[1] Leaving aside the question of intention, which is now impossible to determine, I maintain—with implied authority from Plato's practise and expressed authority from the ideas of myth that Yeats and Jung held in common—that this is precisely the effect and the very great reward of viewing a life as mythic: one *can* have it both ways, and the "autobiographical" passage not only can be, but insists on being, read "as both personal and supra-personal." When it is "'my' myth," then it is mine, subjective and personal, while being also and at the same time a tale of humanity, objective and impersonal. Paul Friedländer remarks of the autobiography of Plato's Socrates that "what looked like a chapter in the history of philosophy turns out to be connected with the very core of Socratic existence,"[2] and the converse is equally true: in "proving" the immortality of the soul by "a thorough inquiry into the general question of the causes of coming into being and perishing" and by an examination of his own mental progress until that progress gave birth to a theory of Forms, Plato's Socrates provides the outlines for a history of (Platonic) philosophy, and those outlines are seen to be the same as the outlines of Socrates' own intellectual progress, only bolder and on a larger, suprapersonal scale. The making of Socrates' mind, as Plato imagined and recreated it, is the making of the mind of ancient Greece and, one step further, is the making of the

---

1. R. Hackforth, *Plato's Phaedo, translated with an Introduction and Commentary* (Cambridge: Cambridge University Press, 1955), p. 130.
2. Paul Friedländer, *Plato, III: The Dialogues, Second and Third Periods* (Princeton: Bollingen/Princeton University Press, 1969), p. 55.

mind of mankind; and this personal/impersonal character of all myth does nothing, as Yeats and Jung maintained, to lessen either the truth, factual and more than factual, or the emotional appeal of myth. "Thought seems more true," Yeats said of national myths, nor would he have hesitated to make the same claims for those myths that he felt to be from *Anima Mundi*, the activities of the *daimones*—"Thought seems more true, emotion more deep, spoken by someone who touches my pride, who seems to claim me of his kindred, who seems to make me a part of some national mythology, nor is mythology mere ostentation, mere vanity if it draws me onward to the unknown; another turn of the gyre and myth is wisdom, pride, discipline" (*Ex.*, p. 345). Thus " 'my' myth" flows from the same springs as national mythology, and it requires but a turn of the gyre—subjective to objective—for the personal/national myth to become the story of mankind, offering to us, as the myth of Socrates' life does, and demanding from us, as that mythic life also does, "wisdom, pride, discipline."

"What is the use of a religion without a mythos," Jung asks (*CW*, XI, par. 647), in a passage that would have won Yeats's warm endorsement, "since religion means, if anything at all, precisely that function which links us back to the eternal myth?" The same question might equally well be addressed to philosophy, viewing that as the logistically, rationally developed counterpart of religion. What is *logos* without its *mythos*? What is Plato without Socrates? What would the dialogues—the *Phaedo*, the *Phaedrus*, the *Republic*, the *Symposium*, the *Gorgias*, or the *Statesman* and the *Timaeus* (even though Socrates is not the mythic narrator in these last two)—what would any of them be without their myths? Shorn of their myths, these dialogues would be deprived of a good half—or more—of their life. (The comparative absence of myth is one thing, though not the only thing, that makes the early dialogues relatively uninteresting and that, at least to a nonspecialist, makes some of the middle and late dialogues—say, the *Theaetetus*, the *Parmenides*, the *Sophist*, the *Philebus*, and the *Laws* —at times little better than boring.) Mythless, the dialogues previously mentioned—and I take them to be the greatest of the dialogues—would be much poorer and thinner (though the myths add up to a very slight proportion of the whole, except in the *Timaeus*); they would lack any religious resonance, and they would have nothing like the hold on men's minds and lives that they have had for over two thousand years. Of another *Logos*, whose life was lived as a *mythos*, Jung goes on to say that some people feel "that Christ was nothing but a myth, . . . no more than a fiction. But myth is not fiction," Jung maintains: "it consists of facts that are continually repeated and can be observed over and over again. It is something that happens to man, and men have mythical fates just as much as Greek heroes do. The fact that the life of Christ is largely myth does absolutely nothing to disprove its factual truth—quite the contrary. I would even go so far as to say that the mythical character of a life is just what expresses its universal human validity" (*CW*, XI, par. 648).

Myth, judging by the statements of Yeats and Jung and by the mythifying performance of Plato, like the love that Diotima explains to Socrates (by way of myth, be it noted), is like a great *daimon*, mediating between man and the Idea of Man, and is moreover, for Plato, like a great *daimon* mediating between the Idea of *a* man and the idea of the Ideas. For if Socrates, more completely than anyone else of his time, embodied the Idea of Philosophic Man (*Phaedo*, 118: "of all those of his time whom we have known, he was, we can fairly say, the best man, and in all ways the wisest and most righteous"), then those Ideas (e.g., Goodness, Wisdom, Righteousness), by participating in which men succeed in being more or less philosophers, must exist somewhere, Plato decided, and more perfectly than they do in any of their human realizations. Thus, while Socrates himself shied away from anything that could be called a system, the entirety of his individual being became the proving ground and the life-giving source of Plato's system: his entire existence, both act and meaning, was dramatically translated, by means of myth, poetry, and dialogical art, into a full-blown and inclusive system. Or, shifting the focus very slightly, we could say that Plato derived his epistemology and his ontology largely from his rhizomatic predecessors (cf. their presence in the intellectual "autobiography" of the *Phaedo* and in half a dozen other dialogues concerned with piecing together the same philosophic system), and in those four *rhizōmata* he discovered the *logos* of his system; but he planted that *logos*, and gave it dramatic appeal and vitality, in the *mythos* of Socrates' life. What Plato did was to invest such biographical details as he chose from the life of Socrates with the meaning that he himself perceived (a part of which meaning he certainly felt he had received from Socrates) in human—and more than human—existence; and this is also what Yeats and Jung did, except that they drew directly from their own lives, rather than the life of some other man however intimately connected, and so saw those lives, their own lives, as the stuff of myth. "That we may believe all men possess the supernatural faculties," Yeats says in the last sentence of the 1925 *Vision*, "I would restore to the philosopher his mythology."[3] One thing demonstrated by the life of Socrates, as Plato mythologizes that life for the purposes of his philosophy, is just exactly, as Yeats says, "that all men possess the supernatural faculties"—those resident *daimones*, of which there is a unique one proper to every individual, that we may choose to cultivate in the Socratic way or to neglect if we are so foolish, but which are with us, from birth, in either case. The mythology that *A Vision* is intended to restore to the philosopher (and how sadly it has been lacking to the philosopher in our time) Yeats came by partly through an attentive listening to the Instructors (among them Plato) but also, as any student of the book can recognize, partly through a close reading of his own mythic life.

In his introduction to *The Resurrection*, Yeats says of the mythology that haunted his entire life until it finally issued in the revelatory *Vision*: "For years I have been preoccupied with a certain myth that was itself a reply to a myth. I do not mean a fiction," he goes on to explain, in language that any reader of Jung, or of the *Phaedo* and the *Timaeus*, will recognize immediately, "but one of those statements our nature is compelled to make and employ as a truth though there cannot be sufficient evidence" (*Ex.*, p. 392). Substitute "psyche" for "our nature," and deck the sentence out in scientific dress by inserting the word "heuristic" somewhere along the way, and what Yeats says here might have come from any one of the eighteen volumes of Jung's *Collected Works*. Likewise, Yeats's description of myth sounds like a virtual paraphrase of Timaeus before he commences his long εἰκότα μῦθον, his "likely myth" (29d), or again a paraphrase of Socrates after he concludes the "*mython*" in the *Phaedo*

---

3. *Vision* (1925), p. 252. Cf. the happy coincidence of phrasing in Ludwig Edelstein, "The Function of the Myth in Plato's Philosophy," *Journal of the History of Ideas*, X (1949), 480: "His dialogues gave to the philosopher a new mythology, and in this sense they constituted a new poetry."

(114d), which he advises his hearers to "employ as a truth though there cannot be sufficient evidence." The contrary nineteenth-century myth that Yeats had in mind he goes on to sketch briefly: "When I was a boy everybody talked about progress, and rebellion against my elders took the form of aversion to that myth." In Yeats's myth, the straight line of progress was replaced by the opposed gyres of Empedocles and Heraclitus—"an elaborate metaphor of a breaking wave intended to prove that all life rose and fell" (*Ex.*, pp. 392-93)—and the cyclical pattern that he originally drew out of his own life, and that determined that "certain myth" of his, came to seem to Yeats a fair prophecy of what would happen in the history of the twentieth century: "Our civilisation was about to reverse itself," he imagined, "or some new civilisation was about to be born from all that our age had rejected . . ." (*Ex.*, p. 393). Finally, the hints and surmises and intuitions from his own experience burst forth into a system in the Platonic manner: "Then unexpectedly and under circumstances described in *A Packet for Ezra Pound* came a symbolic system [*A Vision*] displaying the conflict in all its forms" (*Ex.*, p. 394). Symbolic of course it was, just as the system of the *Timaeus* (which, like the system of *A Vision*, embraces the history of Pre-Socratic thought, including Heraclitus and Parmenides, Pythagoras and Empedocles) is symbolic, just as the myths of the *Phaedo*, the *Phaedrus*, and the *Republic* are symbolic.

Let no man say to Yeats (or to Plato or to Jung) that his myth was a fiction, however, or that his system, because symbolic, was therefore less exactly conformed to the highest reality; and let no one suppose either that Yeats did not understand, as well as Plato or Jung, what relationship obtains between reason and a necessary story or between *logos* and *mythos*. "Myth is not," as Yeats says of the "dark, mythical secrets" in his *Cat and the Moon*, "a rudimentary form superseded by reflection. Belief is the spring of all action; we assent to the conclusions of reflection but believe what myth presents" (*Ex.*, p. 400). In his grammar of assent and belief, as in his rejection of naturalistic interpretations of mythology, Yeats agrees point by point with his predecessor Plato and with his contemporary Jung; and when Yeats goes on to tie belief, love, and myth into a neat little bundle, we are reminded that for Plato, Socrates, by virtue of his being the most perfect exemplar of Philosophic Man, was also the greatest of lovers at every stage of love's ascension from the bottom of the Platonic ladder right up to his impassioned love of Wisdom itself at the top and to his union with the *eidos* that gave him his being. "Belief is love," in Yeats's expression, "and the concrete alone is loved; nor is it true that myth has no purpose but to bring round some discovery of a principle or a fact. The saint may touch through myth the utmost reach of human faculty and pass not to reflection but to unity with the source of his being" (*Ex.*, p. 400). There is little comment to be made on this except to say that this is what the *Phaedrus* is all about, and that in the myth of that dialogue, Socrates (in spite of the fact that he was no more a "saint" than Yeats was) presents us with a vision of the winged soul achieving "unity with the source of his being" in quite the same way that Plato, in his dramatization of the whole mythic life of Socrates, offers us a vision of Philosophic Man succeeding to "unity with the source of his being."

Not a fiction but a necessary statement of the psyche, compelling belief of the total being rather than mere assent of the rational faculty, a "probable story," where "there cannot be sufficient evidence," about matters too tremendous for human language, that frail tool that would "slip, slide, perish" and give way entirely under the burden of meaning—thus the nature of myth, which avails itself of reason and language but transcends both, in the dialogical art of Plato, in the poetics of Yeats, and in the psychology of Jung. It is "childish," Jung says (also, he argues, "unscientific" or psychologically naïve—thus giving as good as he gets and responding to the gibes of his critics in their own coin), "childish" to maintain a "prejudice against the role which mythological assumptions play in the life of the psyche. Since they are not 'true,' it is argued, they have no place in a scientific explanation. But mythologems *exist*, even though their statements do not coincide with our incommensurable idea of 'truth'" (*CW*, VIII, par. 192). Except for the obvious scorn and exasperation—to be felt most keenly in the inverted commas around "true" and "truth" and in the italicizing of "exist"—this is precisely what Yeats meant when he said that a myth is not a fiction but a statement with its own mode of truth. (Jung's exasperation, as against Yeats's relative serenity, is a consequence, I should think, of the fact that Jung conducted his argument in the scientific community whereas Yeats disdained that audience and so suffered none of the frustrations, leading to ill-temper, of trying to convince hostile judges who were precommitted to an alien concept of "truth.") "The collective unconscious," according to its sponsor in modern scientific circles, "appears to consist of mythological motifs or primordial images, for which reason the myths of all nations are its real exponents. In fact, the whole of mythology could be taken as a sort of projection of the collective unconscious" (*CW*, VIII, par. 325). And critics say these myths are not "true"? They might as well deny the "truth"—i.e., the existence, the reality —of the psyche and (here Jung slips in his own little changeling in the hope of gaining for it the same recognition as that accorded to the psyche) the "truth" of the collective unconscious.

It is in the nature of the philosophic quest and in the nature of *mythos* as opposed to *logos* that when the philosopher as logician is compelled to silence, the philosopher as mythologist and as poet takes up speech. "As to the soul's immortality then," Socrates says in the *Phaedrus*, after he has reached the end of his dialectical "proof" of that immortality, "we have said enough, but as to its nature there is this that must be said: what manner of thing it is would be a long tale to tell, and most assuredly a god alone could tell it; but what it resembles, that a man might tell in briefer compass: let this therefore be our manner of discourse. Let it be likened to the union of powers in a team of winged steeds and their winged charioteer" (246a; trans. Hackforth). Having abandoned, of necessity, discursive language and thought and having gone as far as he can with the dialectical mode, Socrates launches into his great, Orphico-Empedoclean myth of the soul and its nature, which serves as prelude to his description of what love really is—or, more accurately, to his description of what love really is *like*, for love will not, any more than the soul, yield itself to a dialectical definition or a purely rational explanation. What either of them really is, we have not "sufficient evidence" or adequate language to say, "and most assuredly a god alone could tell it"; of *Psyche* and *Eros*, those two great *daimones*, we can speak only in the mode of likeness, only with *mythoi*, probable tales that we must, nevertheless, believe in if we have any concern for our immortal souls. Notice, however, this one highly significant fact about the *Phaedrus* myth and Socrates' logistical preamble to it: that Socrates speaks the language of resemblance, similarity, and likeness *only* in the introduction; the myth itself speaks a direct, dramatic, literal language because—and this is the nature of myth—it is not an explanation but an imitation and an enactment. It is a dramatized story, not a rational account. "Myths are original revelations of the preconscious psyche, involuntary statements about unconscious psychic happenings, and anything but allegories of physical processes" (*CW*, IX, pt. 1, par. 261). Jung was no doubt thinking of more primitive, less self-conscious myths than those we find in the Platonic dialogues, yet his description holds true for the *Phaedrus* myth: it is a revelation and statement about the nature of the living creature that produces it—i.e., about the nature of psyche, produced by psyche.

One of the most important words in the *Timaeus* derives from the same etymological source as the words translated as "resembles" and "likened" in the foregoing *Phaedrus* passage: ἐοικέναι (in the *Phaedrus* passage) and εἰκέναι (in the *Timaeus*)—both meaning "to be like" or "to look like." Only a god could say *what it is*; the best mortals can hope for is a likeness to what is, an *eikōn* that resembles reality, an *eikota mython* that imitates the truth just as time is an image (*eikona*) everlastingly imitating eternity. The entire universe, according to the final sentence of the *Timaeus*, is a vast symbolic organism, a huge mythic being, the fit subject of likely stories and tales, a sensible living creature that is a likeness (*eikōn*) of the intelligible Living Creature that served as its paradigm ("a visible living creature, an image of the intelligible, a perceptible god, supreme in greatness and excellence, in beauty and perfection," 91c). In the Christian myth, too, as in the *Phaedrus* and *Timaeus* myths, as in Greek myth generally, as, indeed, in all myth, human speech is somehow, in some "likely" way, linked with divine speech: "The life of Christ is just what it had to be if it is the life of a god and a man at the same time. It is a *symbolum*, a bringing together of heterogeneous natures" (*CW*, XI, par. 648). Myth is a similistic, a metaphoric, a symbolic imitation of divine speech—no more than "likely," it is true, and no doubt highly imperfect, but immensely important and valuable all the same, and it is the best we can do about matters on which otherwise we should have no choice but to remain dumb. I think Jung meant something like this when he wrote (*CW*, VI, par. 428) that modern psychology only proposes new and different myths—more conceptual, more scientific—for those same realities as religion so copiously, and for its time adequately, mythologized in past ages. Or again, in the language of *The*

Archetypes and the Collective Unconscious, "Psychology . . . translates the archaic speech of myth into a modern mythologem—not yet, of course, recognized as such. . . . This seemingly hopeless undertaking is a *living and lived myth*" (*CW*, IX, pt. 1, par. 302; Jung's italics). "Only one symbol exists, though the reflecting mirrors make many appear and all different," Yeats declared, meaning by "one symbol" the same thing Jung meant by "a *living and lived myth*" (though Yeats was loathe to recognize modern psychology as an adequate "reflecting mirror") and pretty much the same thing as Timaeus meant by his living creature, this one universe that has given rise to all the *mythoi* that we, its children and microcosmic counterparts, tell about it and about ourselves to beguile the time and to imitate eternity.

Likeness between one thing and another, simile, metaphor, symbol, myth, a meaning and an understanding drawn out of the web of correspondences between unlike-and-like entities—from such tenuous, but tensile, connections of likeness come all advances in human knowledge and thought, all achievements of culture and civilization, and (especially) all increase and refinement in the understanding of ourselves. It is this power in the perception of likeness that Jung has in mind when, in trying to work out the titular thesis of his *Symbols of Transformation*—the thesis that the psyche produces symbols, founded in archetypes, that transform undifferentiated libido-energy into differentiated personality—he writes, "We are in thorough agreement with Steinthal when he says that a positively overwhelming importance attaches to the little word 'like' in the history of human thought. One can easily imagine that the canalization of libido into analogy-making was responsible for some of the most important discoveries ever made by primitive man" (*CW*, V, par. 203). The analogies observed by our primitive ancestors and recorded in the likely stories of their myths may seem to our more sophisticated minds to be hopelessly crude or fantastic, yet Jung's point (and it is a point well worth taking) is that nothing in our edifice of culture and learning—not even science itself, or perhaps *especially* not science—would be what it is without that foundation of myth (which is fortunately still there, sunk however deep it may be in the unconscious), that capacity for imagining likeness, from which the edifice has all been painfully built up. We use the word "is" all the time, but we should not do so, according to Timaeus, when we are speaking rationally of this world of change and becoming; as Timaeus says and as Jung implies, we would do much better, speaking as natural scientists, to say "is like," "is an image of," "is an analogy for." In myth, however (this is so of the Timaean *mythos* or any other), "is" *means* "is like," because myth is a direct statement of the psyche: it is a drama that imitates psychic life, an *eikōn* or a symbol of the transformation of libido-energy forever taking place in, and constituting the process of, psyche.

"Give ear, then, as they say, to a very fine story (μάλα καλοῦ λόγου, which will, I suppose, seem fiction (μῦθον) to you but is fact (λόγον) to me; what I am going to tell you I tell you as the truth." So, in *Gorgias* (523a), Socrates presents his hortatory tale of the hereafter in the mixed colors of *logos* and *mythos*; he takes as truth, and urges his hearers to do likewise, this necessary statement of the immortal psyche, because the psyche itself will be eternally benefitted if we take its statements about itself for truth: the truth of psyche. These are "statements," as Yeats says, that "our nature is compelled to make and employ as a truth," and they are true, as Jung insists—deeply and importantly true—in the sense that they "*exist.*" Yeats argues the symbolic truth of these likely stories, Jung argues their heuristic truth, and Socrates their moral, ethical truth. Plato, it seems to me, in his creation of Socrates as a mythic figure and in his deployment of myths throughout the dialogues, argues the symbolic, the heuristic, and the moral, ethical truth both of his mythified Socrates and of his various *ad hoc* myths.

For the Socrates who is an actor in the dialogues, philosophy is a method and a moral imperative—the imperative to know thyself and become as like as possible to the divine. For Plato, too, the maker of those dialogues, philosophy is a method and a moral imperative, and it is besides, which it never was for Socrates, a system embracing everything beneath the moon and beyond it, a complete (if only likely) account of the human world of time and the divine world of eternity, and an explanation (this, perhaps, the most important) of the manifold, cosmic, and paradigmatic ties between the two worlds. Socrates' art was the art of the midwife, bringing to birth, and helping to judge as viable or nonviable, just such infants as Plato's thought; Plato's art was the art, on the one hand, of the dramatist, on the other hand of the system-maker. He was a sort of composite of the Socratic man and of the demiourgos, recreating Socrates in his dialogues and, like the tail-biter, imitating that Demiourgos whom Plato had himself created. In the *Phaedrus*, Socrates is playing his mythic role to perfection when he says that he will not join certain "wise men" (or "men of science" in Hackforth's apropos phrasing) in seeking naturalistic or rationalistic explanations for traditional myths; those men, Socrates says in effect, want to turn the grand "is" of *mythos* and of the psyche into the careful "is like" of *logos* and of science. But Socrates has a yet more interesting reason for declining the scientific gambit, and that is that he has a much more important myth in hand, a myth that cannot be dealt with adequately by reason or by science, a myth that is not only Socratic but Delphic and Heraclitean: the myth of himself. "I myself have certainly no time for the business," he says to Phaedrus, "and I'll tell you why, my friend: I can't as yet 'know myself', as the inscription at Delphi enjoins; and so long as that ignorance remains it seems to me ridiculous to inquire into extraneous matters. Consequently I don't bother about such things, but accept the current beliefs about them, and direct my inquiries, as I have just said, rather to myself" (*Phaedrus*, 229e–230a; trans. Hackforth). For Socrates to know himself and to be himself in fullness, for Socrates to observe in himself a likeness to divinity and push that likeness to the point of near identity, would be to become, so far as it lay within his capacities to become, Philosophic Man. To live "'my' myth," in other words, is to attain to the *eidos*—the Idea, the Form —and to the ground of "my" being. I suggest that the mythic mode —call it the mode of symbolism if you like—is the paradigm of that relationship that Plato terms, in the *Phaedo*, "participation" (*methexis*) and, in the *Timaeus*, "imitation" (*mimesis*).[4] In the case of Plato's Socrates, the relationship is that one obtaining between an individual life on the one hand and the ideal Form more or less realized in that life on the other hand; simply put, the relationship is a mythic, a daimonic one.

4. For these and other words used by Plato "to express the relation between Forms and particulars," see the extraordinarily interesting list of terms, "divided into a group of words implying or suggesting the immanence of Forms, and a group implying or suggesting their transcendence," in W. D. Ross, *Plato's Theory of Ideas* (London: Oxford University Press, 1951), pp. 228–30.

Surely this is the whole point of the *Apology*, which is an "apology" in the Greek sense that it is a defense and in the sense that it is an *apologia pro vitâ suâ*, but in no other sense. It is both a recounting of his myth by Socrates and a present performance, an acting, of that myth. "*Mimesis*," W. K. C. Guthrie reminds us, "meant acting as much as imitation, *mimetes* was often and *mimos* always an actor. The relation between an actor and his part is not exactly imitation. He gets inside it, or rather, in the Greek view, it gets inside him, and shows forth through his words and gestures" (*Hist. of Gr. Phil.*, I, 230). In the *Apology*, as in a dozen other dialogues, Socrates, *mimos* and mythic being, performs the role assigned to him (not by the Athenian citizens however) and confirmed by him, the role of Socratic Man or Platonic Man, scripted in the *eidos* of Philosophic Man. "God appointed me," Socrates tells the Athenians, "to the duty of leading the philosophic life, examining myself and others" (*Apology*, 28e; trans. Tredennick); to abandon that role—or, in Yeats's phrase, to break up his lines to weep—would be the ultimate denial and blasphemy. "Gentlemen, I am your very grateful and devoted servant, but I owe a greater obedience to God than to you; and so long as I draw breath and have my faculties, I shall never stop practising philosophy and exhorting you and elucidating the truth for everyone that I meet" (*Apology*, 29d). It is interesting to observe that the Socrates of the *Apology*, as nearly all commentators agree, is closer to the historic Socrates than the figure we hear questioning and discoursing in any of the other Platonic dialogues; if this is so, and if the Socrates of the *Apology* is acting the part of Philosophic Man as consciously and conscientiously as I suppose him to be doing, then this means that the myth of Socrates came (at least in part) ready-made to the hand of Plato, and moreover that myth in general—as Yeats and Jung both consistently maintained—is something that comes upon us, not quite of our own choosing, something that we live or that lives through us, and something that we discover and grow into but never invent or cut to our pattern.

It was his assurance that he had embraced his own myth and was performing his role as well as he knew how to do, that led Socrates to tell his judges, in words that have echoed ever since as the finest *apologia* of Philosophic Man, that "the unexamined life is not worth living." Yeats's myth was the myth of the Poet, Jung's the myth of the Psychologist; and just as we have the *apologia* for Socrates' myth of the Philosopher in the *Apology* and a full-dress performance of the same myth in a volume of other dialogues, so we have Yeats's *apologia* in his *Autobiography* (and other prose works) and his performance in the *Collected Poems*, and we have Jung's *apologia* in his *Memories, Dreams, Reflections* and his performance in the *Collected Works*. What Socrates says to his judges in the serene conclusion of the *Apology*, after being condemned to death—"You too, gentlemen of the jury, must look forward to death with confidence, and fix your minds on this one belief, which is certain—that nothing can harm a good man either in life or after death, and his fortunes are not a matter of indifference to the gods" (41d)—Yeats echoed in a letter to Dorothy Wellesley, and his confidence, I should think, was on the Socratic ground of fidelity to his mythic role: "To me the supreme aim is an act of faith and reason to make us rejoice in the midst of tragedy. An impossible aim, yet I think it true that nothing can injure us" (*Letters*, p. 838). Socrates, Yeats, Jung—"All perform their tragic play," for to do less would be to deny and destroy their individual *mythoi*. Those myths, as Jung has it, are "symbolic expressions of the inner, unconscious drama of the psyche which becomes accessible to man's consciousness by way of projection" (*CW*, IX, pt. 1, par. 7)—the soul's drama enacted in the two hours' traffic of a stage both tragic and comic. "This drama is an 'Aurora consurgens'—the dawning of consciousness in mankind" (*CW*, XII, par. 556), Jung says of the play in which Socrates assumed a leading role. Yeats produced his tribute to this drama in "Lapis Lazuli," a poem dominated by the Jungian and Socratic-Platonic conception of life as a mythic drama, fitted out with a variety of archetypal roles, a drama that, if conceived in the Platonic manner and faithfully performed, is also an imitation of divine life while being an aspiration toward that life.

> All perform their tragic play,
> There struts Hamlet, there is Lear,
> That's Ophelia, that Cordelia;
> Yet they, should the last scene be there,
> The great stage curtain about to drop,
> If worthy their prominent part in the play,
> Do not break up their lines to weep.
> They know that Hamlet and Lear are gay;
> Gaiety transfiguring all that dread.

Or as Socrates, who retained his gaiety even in the hour of condemnation and death, puts it to his accusers and judges: "You would have liked to hear me weep and wail, doing and saying all sorts of things which I regard as unworthy of myself, but which you are used to hearing from other people" (*Apology*, 38e). Socrates, who is eminently worthy of his prominent part in the play, declines the role knocked together for him by hostile human dramatists because he is already playing the myth of the Philosopher in a human/divine drama—tragic in spots but overall gay as every essentially creative act is—entitled (in Jung's version) "Aurora Consurgens."

"We, who are believers, cannot see reality anywhere but in the soul itself," Yeats says in one of his essays on "The Irish Dramatic Movement" (*Ex.*, p. 170), and though he does not put a name to his belief, it is unquestionably that same faith in soul as the only real reality that Socrates displays in the myth of psyche that he recounts in the *Phaedrus* and in the myth of himself that he enacts in the *Apology*. Yeats, in a fine phrase, goes on to call the personality that emerges from an actor's performance "the soul's image" (*Ex.*, p. 170). Personality moves, changes, and becomes in the course of time, but soul—that paradigm of which personality is a likeness and an image—remains at one with itself, unmoving and unchanging, in eternity. In his mythic character, Socrates, or any other actor worthy of his profession—Yeats and Jung for example—lives a life drawn between time and eternity, between a world of becoming and one of being, between personality and soul, a life of chronologically successive events that are viewed, however, as in every one of Socrates' myths, *sub specie aeternitatis*. "What we are to our inward vision, and what man appears to be *sub specie aeternitatis*, can only be expressed by way of myth," Jung says in the prologue to his autobiography—the prologue, that is to say, to his myth and his *apologia*: "Thus it is that I have now undertaken, in my eighty-third year, to tell my personal myth. I can only make direct statements, only 'tell stories.' Whether or not the stories are 'true' is not the problem. The only question is whether what I tell is *my* fable, *my* truth" (*Memories*, p. 3/17). Not that this was the first time that Jung had undertaken to tell "'my' myth"—not at all: he did it in his thirty-seventh year (but called it *Symbols of Transformation*), in his fifty-second year (but called it "The Structure of the Psyche"), in his seventy-sixth year (but called it *Aion*), and in his eighty-first year (but called it *Mysterium Coniunctionis*). These various expressions of the myth, comfortably gathered together within the *Collected Works*, from which *Memories, Dreams, Reflections* was excluded, may not immediately be recognized as mythic, but Jung himself offers us the necessary clue when he says that "No science will ever replace myth, and a myth cannot be made out of science" (*Memories*, p. 340/313). The contrary, however, is not true, for "Myths are the earliest form of science" (ibid., p. 304/282), and Jung specifically says that the language of psychology is "a modern mythologem . . . which constitutes one element of the myth 'science'" (*CW*, IX, pt. 1, par. 302). Psychology can parade as a strictly rational and scientific *logos* all it cares to—so can physics, for that matter—but it is all, at bottom, a *mythos* anyway and, in a very important sense, is "my personal myth," whether that be the myth of the Philosopher, the Poet, the Psychologist, or the Physicist.

There is a nice irony in the fact that in the Platonic grammar, physical science, which we might suppose to abhor mythic language, is treated as a variety of discourse incapable of ever being anything more than myth; and there is an even nicer irony in the fact that modern atomic physics, while not flying any banner inscribed "mythology," has come to the same conclusions about the ultimate nature of physical reality as Timaeus, who freely acknowledged that his conclusions constituted at best a likely myth. What is more, physicists have adopted the *Timaeus* account of physical reality—which they derived, of course, not from the *Timaeus* but from their own observations and reasoning—for the same reason, as I see it, that Jung's psychology (which he always called a natural science) happily settled for a likely *mythos*: psychology, like ancient cosmogony and modern physics, is an account of a world of movement and change, a world coming into existence in time and bound to the wheel of time, a world in which we can speak of being or of eternity—of the real underlying structure of things, their ground and their cause—only symbolically, only by way of images and myths. In his *Apology*, Socrates disavowed any interest in physical science, but that way was not open to Plato, whose temperament required a system that should include the physical with the metaphysical, the ethical with the mystical/religious, and the temporal with the eternal. But Plato recognized the difference (and the relationship) between the two, and he knew the appropriate language for either: "an account is of the same order as the things which it sets forth—an account of that which is abiding and stable and discoverable by the aid of reason will itself be abiding and unchangeable," Timaeus tells his listeners,

> while an account of what is made in the image of that other, but is only a likeness [*eikona*], will itself be but likely [*eikotas*], standing to accounts of the former kind in a proportion: as reality is to becoming, so is truth to belief. If then, Socrates, in many respects concerning many things—the gods and the generation of the universe—we prove unable to render an account at all points entirely consistent with itself and exact, you must not be surprised. If we can furnish accounts no less likely [*eikotas*] than any other, we must be content, remembering that I who speak and you my judges are only human, and consequently it is fitting that we should, in these matters, accept the likely story [*ton eikota mython*] and look for nothing further. (*Timaeus*, 29b-d; trans. Cornford)

Jung, as his critics have been quick to point out, was not always and "at all points entirely consistent" in his account of the natural (as he took it to be) phenomenon of psyche; but his critics fail to recognize that, given the object of his science, neither he nor anyone else could expect to be "entirely consistent" in the *mythos* that he dressed up as a *logos*. Jung was being more astute than his critics, and he disarmed their objections to his natural science in advance, when (in the best Platonic way) he called all science "myth" and his own particular branch of science "a modern mythologem."

Jung has had more than his share of criticism (though, as I have implied, he always gave as liberally as he received), one reason for this being, I imagine, that we all know a little something about psyche and so, while we may not claim any extraordinary authority, we nevertheless feel ourselves capable of judging the validity or otherwise of psychological theories. Few people, on the other hand, feel sufficiently familiar with elementary particles or quantum mechanics or the unified field theory to hazard a critique of modern atomic physics; hence most of us must depend upon the physicists themselves to reveal what they are about and to say what the philosophical and epistemological status of their science might be. In a fascinating book that he calls *Physics and Beyond: Encounters and Conversations*, Werner Heisenberg—sounding like nothing so much as Timaeus redivivus, reasserting his Pythagorean vision as the most up-to-date and probable account available of the basic constitution of the physical universe—hints that atomic physicists have had recourse to *Timaeus*-like *mythoi* precisely because they have found themselves caught in the Platonic bind: they have proved "unable to render an account at all points entirely consistent with itself and exact." As Niels Bohr puts it, in one of Heisenberg's "encounters and conversations," critics have complained that "quantum theory is unsatisfactory because, thanks to its complementary [the critics would say "contradictory"] concepts of 'wave' and 'particle,' it prohibits all but dualistic descriptions of nature." But this, Bohr maintains, is a very mistaken view, and "all those who have truly understood quantum theory would never dream of calling it dualistic." His argument—his Socratic *apologia* for quantum theory and his *Timaeus*-like justification for mythic language—goes like this:

> [Quantum theory is] a unified description of atomic phenomena, even though it has to wear different faces when it is applied to experiment and so has to be translated into everyday language. Quantum theory thus provides us with a striking illustration of the fact that we can fully understand a connection though *we can only speak of it in images and parables*. In this case, the images and parables are by and large the classical concepts, i.e., "wave" and "corpuscle." *They do not fully describe the real world and are, moreover, complementary in part, and hence contradictory*. For all that, since we can only describe natural phenomena with our everyday language, *we can only hope to grasp the real facts by means of these images*.
>
> This is probably true of all general philosophical problems and particularly of metaphysics. *We are forced to speak in images and parables which do not express precisely what we mean. Nor can we avoid occasional contradictions; nevertheless, the images help us to draw nearer to the real facts*. Their existence no one should deny.[5]

5. Werner Heisenberg, *Physics and Beyond: Encounters and Conversations*, trans. Arnold J. Pomerans (New York: Harper & Row, 1972), pp. 209-10.

I have quoted this passage at length, and have taken the liberty besides of italicizing a few particularly pregnant clauses and sentences, so that it will be apparent that I have not exaggerated the thoroughly Platonic nature of the dilemma in which modern (like ancient) physics has found itself. And modern psychology suffers from—or delights in?—an entanglement in precisely this same dilemma.[6] To borrow Jung's phrasing, both physics and psychology are modern mythologems constituting two elements "of the myth 'science.'"

There is, as I have suggested, yet another irony in the world view offered to us by modern physics: not only has the physicist found it necessary to speak in "images and parables"—*eikones* and *mythoi* (Socrates calls the entire Cave allegory in the *Republic* an *eikona*: 517a)—and not only is his account "complementary in part, and hence contradictory" (i.e., not "at all points entirely consistent with itself and exact"), but in addition the likely story of modern atomic physics—at least the likely story as Heisenberg narrates it—is very much the likely story of the *Timaeus*. "So far we had always believed in the doctrine of Democritus," Heisenberg writes, "which can be summarized by: 'In the beginning was the particle.' We had assumed that visible matter was composed of smaller units, and that, if only we divided these long enough, we should arrive at the smallest units, which Democritus called 'atoms' and which modern physicists called 'elementary particles'" (p. 133). These are also what Empedocles called "elements," with the single difference that Empedocles' "smallest units" were precisely four in number while "elementary particles" and "atoms" are innumerable. Long before the advent of modern physics, however, Plato refused to accept either the innumerable atoms of Democritus or the four elements of Empedocles as the ultimate, indivisible, and irreducible "roots" of the physical universe. The primary bodies composing the universe

6. Here occurs a happy coincidence (or a synchronistic overlap). One of the chief dialoguists in Heisenberg's book is the theoretical physicist Wolfgang Pauli, who later lived in Zurich where he became friends with Jung; from him Jung acquired a certain knowledge of the concepts of nuclear physics—concepts that he felt bore a striking analogy to the ways of modern psychology. See *CW*, VIII, pp. 229-30, n. 130, where Jung quotes a comment from Pauli on the text in progress, and *Letters*, I, 174-76, a letter from Jung to Pauli which draws parallels between the observational problems in physics and in psychology; also *Letters*, II, 308 on the same. Jung and Pauli published a volume in common, *The Interpretation of Nature and the Psyche*, with one essay by each of them.

are indeed, Plato said (with Empedocles), four in number, but those four primary bodies—air, earth, fire, and water—are neither ultimate nor irreducible: beneath the four primary substances, Plato argued, lies a mathematical symmetry and geometric harmony, *à la* Pythagoras; moreover, *à la* Heraclitus, air, earth, fire, and water are more like qualities than things and are forever interchanging their qualitative being with one another. But to put the problem, and its solution, in the terms of the modern nuclear physicist: "Perhaps there was no such thing as an indivisible particle. Perhaps matter could be divided ever further, until finally it was no longer a real division of a particle but a change of energy into matter, and the parts were no longer smaller than the whole from which they had been separated. But what was there in the beginning? A physical law, mathematics, symmetry? In the beginning was symmetry!" This, as Heisenberg goes on to say, sounds "like Plato's *Timaeus*" (p. 133). Indeed it does—very like; and it all comes back to the point made by Timaeus in the dialectical preface to his myth: the state of nature is such that we cannot, no matter how quick, shrewd, or sophisticated we are, give, in human speech, an account of physical process that will be at all points consistent and exact. This physical universe is through and through Heraclitean in the unceasingness and rapidity of its flux, and no account can halt the change so as to be itself stable—or if, for its own sake, it does call a halt, then that account will be still more widely inconsistent, since the flux does not itself cease for a moment. Call the *archē*, the principle and the beginning of the physical universe, now a particle and now a wave, and your story, though double, complementary, and contradictory, will be more likely than any other story current. It is nature herself—both physical nature and human nature—that compels us to mythic speech, be we poets or philosophers, physicists or psychologists.

Timaeus and Werner Heisenberg, Socrates and Plato, Yeats and Jung, all in the end produced *mythoi* out of themselves about the twofold nature into which each of us is born; and we should be very naïve, Jung told a correspondent in 1929, were we to imagine that merely by calling ourselves scientists we thereby get outside our own nature and outside general nature and become capable of rendering godlike *logoi* in place of our human *mythoi*. "Can't you conceive of a physicist that thinks and speaks of atoms, yet is convinced that those are merely his own abstractions? That would be my case. I have not the faintest idea what 'psyche' is in itself," Jung wrote to J. Allen

Gilbert (*Letters*, I, 57); but though he had no idea what psyche is in itself ("most assuredly a god alone could tell it," as Socrates says), yet there is lavish evidence that psyche told her tales continuously to Jung and through him, and his psychological science is really nothing more than a translation of those tales into another language, related but foreign. "Science"—that other language—"is the art of creating suitable illusions which the fool believes or argues against, but the wise man enjoys their beauty or their ingenuity, without being blind to the fact that they are human veils and curtains concealing the abysmal darkness of the Unknowable" (ibid.). If nature is the vehicle in which the supernatural is realized, as *anima hominis* is the sole vehicle for *Anima Mundi*, then any purely natural science, like psychology, will be reduced—or exalted—to the ways of art and to a language of suitable illusions, beautiful symbolisms, and ingenious myths.

In a long and important passage in "The Role of the Unconscious," Jung distinguishes between "the personal unconscious," which he says speaks the language of experience, and "the suprapersonal or collective unconscious," which he claims speaks only the language of myth—a language that individual psyche understands not because of any previous experiences in this life but because of its participation in the psychic collectivity. The individual psyche, because it has its share in the collective unconscious, produces what Jung calls "mythological fantasies," that is, "elements which do not correspond to any events or experiences of personal life, but only to myths" (*CW*, XI, par. 11); and these fantasies, according to Jung, "come from the brain—indeed, precisely from the brain and not from personal memory-traces, but from the inherited brain-structure itself" (ibid., par. 12). This is a very important point for Jungian psychology: if his argument is successful here, then Jung's psychology becomes a science that paradoxically transcends science but does not abandon it, and his mythography lays a claim to being the sufficient and necessary tale of mankind itself. What Jung attempts, and this is the crux of that attempt, is to reach what one very positively disposed critic calls "a goal that Jung's work has made eventually certain, namely, the reconciliation of science and religion."[7] It is in a mythology of the self, determined, shaped, and projected by "the inherited brain-structure," that Jung would effect

---

7. Edward F. Edinger, *Ego and Archetype* (Baltimore: Penguin, 1973), p. xiii.

this reconciliation of science and religion, those two modes of seeing the world and oneself that were collaborators in the beginning of Western thought but that have been antagonists for so many centuries now. "The truly creative fantasy activity of the brain," Jung argues, "creates . . . out of the history of mankind," out of "that age-old natural history which has been transmitted in living form since the remotest times, namely, the history of the brain-structure. And this structure tells its own story, which is the story of mankind: the unending myth of death and rebirth, and of the multitudinous figures who weave in and out of this mystery" (ibid.). Possessed of that same brain-structure, and compelled by it, Socrates outlined such a myth of the human soul in the *Phaedo*, the *Phaedrus*, and the *Republic*; and in the person of Socrates himself—surely one of the preeminent "figures who weave in and out of this mystery," an archetypal actor in the vast drama of the psyche and a full-fledged *daimon*—Plato told the same story again. Nor could he tell any other, because, as Yeats said, there is really only one story, one symbol. In his "autobiography," as in the dialogues at large, Plato's Socrates lives and tells his tale, which is also, inevitably, the tale of the human mind and an unfolding of the in-built, inherited history of its development.

"This unconscious," Jung goes on to say in the paragraph immediately following the one quoted above,

> buried in the structure of the brain and disclosing its living presence only through the medium of creative fantasy, is the *suprapersonal unconscious*. It comes alive in the creative man, it reveals itself in the vision of the artist, in the inspiration of the thinker, in the inner experience of the mystic. The suprapersonal unconscious, being distributed throughout the brain-structure, is like an all-pervading, omnipresent spirit. It knows man as he always was, and not as he is at this moment; it knows him as myth. For this reason, also, the connection with the suprapersonal or *collective* unconscious means an extension of man beyond himself; it means death for his personal being and a rebirth in a new dimension, as was literally enacted in certain of the ancient mysteries. It is certainly true that without the sacrifice of man as he is, man as he was—and always will be—cannot be attained. And it is the artist who can tell us most about

this sacrifice of the personal man, if we are not satisfied with the message of the Gospels.

It should be remarked (but at this point only in passing) that in locating the myth-making faculty in the inherited brain-structure, thus within the history of the human mind and very much within the confines of time, Jung can claim that what he is about is a respectable scientific activity; but there are also, philosophically speaking, some important and much less desirable consequences of this location of the mythifying capacity that will require examining a bit later. For the moment, however, we can leave it at this: that Yeats would certainly have agreed with Jung that it is the artist who knows most about the sacrifice of the personal man ("A writer must die every day he lives, be reborn . . . an incorruptible self"—*Auto.*, p. 457), a sacrifice performed with the precise intention of transforming the mundane into the mythic and of raising his own life to the level of myth, archetype, and idea. The artist makes his "choice," as Yeats has it in the poem of that title:

> The intellect of man is forced to choose
> Perfection of the life, or of the work,
> And if it take the second must refuse
> A heavenly mansion, raging in the dark. . . .

In a letter to Kathleen Tynan of much earlier date (1888), Yeats tells of his own choice to sacrifice the personal man in favor of "rebirth in a new dimension": "My life has been in my poems. To make them I have broken my life in a mortar, as it were" (*Letters*, p. 84). The poet "is more type than man," Yeats says, "more passion than type" (*E. & I.*, p. 509), and yet even more than type and passion he is archetype and idea: "he has been reborn," Yeats declares of the artist who exists in the phantasmagoria he has himself created, "as an idea, something intended, complete" (ibid.). Acting as the demiourgos of his own universe, the artist sacrifices his personal being to recreate himself in the image of an ideal paradigm, his own form disappearing in the larger form of an archetype, an *eidos*, the Platonic Idea of Man. "Irish stories make us understand why the Greeks call myths the activities of the daemons," Yeats wrote in an essay of 1902. "The great virtues, the great joys, the great privations come in the myths, and, as it were, take mankind between their naked arms, and without putting off their divinity. Poets have taken their themes more often from stories that are all, or half, mythological, than from history or stories that give one the sensation of history . . ." (*Ex.*, p. 10). Acting much more like a Yeatsian, daimonizing poet than like a fact-bound, historically minded biographer, Plato invoked and elaborated a myth of Socrates so that the latter (and with him his mythifier), become more type than man and more archetype than type, might put on divinity not, however, as personal man but as Man.

In *The Trembling of the Veil*, leading up to another account of this same mingling of *mythos* and the *daimon*, Yeats tells how certain of his friends, who were evidently very Jungian in their notions of psychology, "believed that the dark portion of the mind—the subconscious—had an incalculable power, and even over events. To influence events or one's own mind, one had to draw the attention of that dark portion, to turn it, as it were, into a new direction." As for himself, Yeats says, he performed this feat of psychic redirection, this (in Jungian language) symbolic transformation of generalized libido energy, by repeating "certain names" and imagining "certain symbolic forms which had acquired a precise meaning, and not only to the dark portion of one's own mind, but to the mind of the race" (*Auto.*, p. 372). We may, if we like, find proof of Yeats's nonscientific bent in his choice of a Freudian word ("subconscious") for a concept that is anti-Freudian/pro-Jungian, and Yeats here as everywhere expresses himself in a commoner and more traditional language than Jung ordinarily chooses; nevertheless, in his reference to "the dark portion of one's own mind," Yeats unquestionably means what Jung meant by the "personal unconscious," and by "the mind of the race" Yeats intends the same thing as Jung intended by the "collective unconscious." The two were agreed, moreover, that the collective unconscious or the mind of the race, call it what one will, is the source of many of our dreams, the habitat of the *daimones*, and the creative matrix of all genuine myths. Yeats goes on to describe a certain image he evoked which was seen or imagined at more or less the same time by several other people in very different circumstances, and he concludes his account of shared fantasies, not as Jung might do with some confident scientific propositions, but, in a very characteristically Yeatsian manner, with a series of hesitant, suggestive, open-ended questions: "Had some great event taken place in some world where myth is reality and had we seen some portion of it? One of my fellow-students quoted a Greek saying, 'Myths are the activities of the Daimons', or had we but seen in the memory of the race something believed thousands of years ago, or had somebody—I myself perhaps—but dreamed a fantastic dream which had come to those others by transference of thought? I came to no conclusion, but I was sure there was some symbolic meaning could I but find it" (*Auto.*, pp. 373-74). Plato, I should think, would give the first answer, Jung the second, and J. B. Rhine the third. Yeats was Yeats, however, not Plato or Jung or Rhine, and his reluctance to decide one way or the other was both caused and justified by his conception of the Poet and by his vision of his own life as a dramatization of that grand mythic role. The man who adopts and enacts the role of Poet will find all these answers valid, for the Yeatsian poet acts as the memory of the race, recalling beliefs of thousands of years ago and revitalizing them; he tells tales that are myths here but reality "There," and he transfers his fantasies and his phantasmagoria to others—not, however, as fiction but as a higher and more intense truth. Most important of all, because his poem partakes of the cosmos of a superior reality and the cosmos of the mind of the race, the poet brings order into this world of chaos and flux, he embodies a symbolic meaning in his verse, and he thereby, like any *daimon*, unifies the universe.

Thus for the poet as Poet; but if physics, ancient and modern, and psychology, ancient and modern, have proved "unable to render an account at all points entirely consistent with itself and exact," their inconsistency and inexactness are nothing beside the eager confusion of the poet when he descends into prose and, with that mundane instrument of a sadly fallible reason, tries to deal with the higher psychic reality and its operation in a physical universe. Consider Yeats in the land and language of scientific evidence, dealing in physical nature and photographs, hesitating an assertion but then, as soon as he seems to have half-committed himself, craftily withdrawing from the consequences of any sort of assertion in that essentially alien mode: "If symbolic vision is then but thought completing itself, and if, as we must now think, its seat is but the physical nature, and if thought has indeed been photographed, is symbolic thought, as all thought, a reality in heaven or earth, moving when we do not see it as when we do, a mid-world between the two realities, a region of correspondences, the activities of the daimons?"

(*Memoirs*, pp. 268-69). Three "if" clauses—one parading as a conclusion ("then"), the other two as almost-conclusions ("as we must now think" and "has indeed been photographed")—piled one on top of another to issue in a question which itself comes out as a sort of half statement: there is no doubt a kind of mad logic in Yeats's rhetoric here, but while a virtuoso performance, it is also a trepidating and confusing one. Two steps forward, three back, and one to either side, all the steps to be taken simultaneously—it is not an easy dance to follow; but the clue to Yeats's wonderfully tangled expression lies, I think, in his last phrase, for, as he makes abundantly clear in the two previously quoted passages, "the activities of the daimons" is another way of saying "myths." Yeats's peculiar prose is the result of his attempting to translate *mythos* into *logos*—poetry into science—and of trying to adduce physical proofs for psychic events. His attempt is only half-hearted, however (Jung, in the same circumstances, would have been a good deal less hesitant and modest, a good deal more assertive—and perhaps more convincing—than Yeats), because Yeats knows full well, in spite of his errant excursion into physical science, that one cannot photograph myths and that while the *daimones* may have a powerful effect in physical nature they will not be caught or held there even by a camera lens. Was it for this, to offer snapshot evidence of "mid-world" activities, that the *daimones* escaped into the Thirteenth Sphere? Yeats really knew better than to think so, though he occasionally faltered when his medium was prose and when his intention was proof before an alien audience of materialists.[8]

"The Greeks . . . considered that myths are the activities of the Daimons, and that the Daimons shaped our characters and our lives. I have often had the fancy that there is some one myth for every

8. In séances, Yeats says in "Swedenborg, Mediums, and the Desolate Places," "we are the spectators of a phantasmagoria that affects the photographic plate or leaves its moulded image in a preparation of paraffin" (*Ex.*, p. 54). I have seen some peculiar photographs of disembodied spirits emanating from Yeats's head—in appearance something like the balloons that contain the captions in comic strips but with vaguely defined human features drawn in and looking as if they were rather sick to their nonexistent stomachs—that I should have thought someone of Yeats's ordinary discernment would find sufficiently foolish. (One of these photographs is reproduced in *Yeats and the Occult*.) It seems, however, that Yeats was quite interested in the photographs and thought them pretty convincing. Half the letters that Yeats wrote to Sturge Moore have to do with photographs of ectoplasm oozing from psychical heads.

man, which, if we but knew it, would make us understand all he did and thought" (*E. & I.*, p. 107). This passage (from Yeats's *Ideas of Good and Evil*) I have quoted previously in the context of a discussion of Heraclitus' teaching about the *daimon*, but it has perhaps even more point when we come to Plato and his fully exfoliated doctrine of *daimones*—a doctrine that was of the first importance for the organic coherence of Plato's completed system but that was also to prove fatally attractive to his Neoplatonic successors who littered the universe with so many Authentic Existants, Supernals, and Celestials, Hypostases, Hierarchies, and Henads that the mind is forced to an abject surrender, helpless before the profusion and confusion of it all. The tendency of the original Platonic doctrine, however, was not toward dispersion and proliferation but, on the contrary, toward unification and oneness. The Yeatsian rule of "One man, one myth," for which there is a sufficiency of authority in Heraclitus and Plato, might seem to have the undesirable Neoplatonizing effect of multiplying the varieties and kinds of mid-world spirits out of all reason and beyond any possibility of comprehension. I think, however, that this is not the effect of Yeats's rule any more than it is the effect of the doctrine of *daimones* to which Plato gives a careful mythological articulation in the *Phaedo*, the *Republic*, the *Symposium*, and the *Timaeus*—that same theory to which he gives dramatic expression in the person of the Socrates of the dialogues. The teachings of Diotima about Eros in the *Symposium*, being a nice mixture of the earthy and the mystical, are very much to the point here, and they are also the original source, whether direct or indirect, for Yeats's notion of mid-world spirits whose activities compose the myths by which we are compelled to live. After Diotima denies that Eros is a god (θεός), and convinces Socrates of the truth of what she says, Socrates reports this ensuing exchange:

> " 'What would Eros be then?' I said. 'A mortal?'
> 'Far from it.'
> 'But what then?'
> 'Like the things earlier,' she said; 'midway between mortal and immortal.'
> 'What is that, Diotima?'
> 'Δαίμων μέγας, a great *daimon*, Socrates; for everything daimonic is midway between divine and mortal.' "

To Socrates' question of what power resides in the daimonic, Diotima replies in a language that Yeats was to repeat many times, in both prose and verse, whether he was conscious that he was echoing this first great formulation of the idea or not. The *daimonion*, Diotima explains, mediates between gods and men, and "being mid-way between the two it fills up the space completely, so that the whole is bound together to itself in one."[9] Philosophy, which is to be defined very simply as "love of wisdom," is as daimonic in its nature and its effects as Eros himself, for it too mediates between gods and men, closing up the gap between them and filling mortal men with a desire for that which is immortal and immortalizing. Only the gods possess wisdom, but only man loves and pursues it. Between the two is the love that binds them together and that draws the outlines of the myth for the man to live.

The specific details of the myth will necessarily be different for different men, yet the myth itself is not many but one, and the archetype (to give it its Jungian name) that establishes the pattern by which *daimon*-possessed men live has the effect of binding the many together, Eros-like, in one single whole and the effect of drawing diverse actors together in a drama that includes them all and is the work of none of them. The activities of the *daimon* that we call Eros determine a single great myth that countless men—Yeats among them—have lived, are living now, and will continue to live so long as men are men, mortal but with something of the immortal about them.

> I am content to live it all again
> And yet again, if it be life to pitch
> Into the frog-spawn of a blind man's ditch,
> A blind man battering blind men;
> Or into that most fecund ditch of all,
> The folly that man does
> Or must suffer, if he woos
> A proud woman not kindred of his soul.

So Yeats says of his own myth. Call the proud woman Maud Gonne, or give her the more general and Jungian title of "Anima"; in either case, she, like Yeats, is an actor in a drama for which the

---

9. 202e: ἐν μέσῳ δὲ ὂν ἀμφοτέρων συμπληροῖ, ὥστε τὸ πᾶν αὐτὸ αὑτῷ συνδεδέσθαι. The "filling up completely" makes for the oneness of Jung's "pleroma."

daimones are responsible. It is supremely important to notice, however, that no matter how unhappy Yeats may have been, no matter how much folly he may have suffered, he had the very great consolation of realizing (and the realization gave him the stuff of a good number of poems) that the myth was *his* myth, not Maud Gonne's: the myth ("I do not mean a fiction") of the Unhappy Lover and the myth of the Poet. Like Socrates living his myth before the Athenian judges—they, too, actors in a drama not of their making—Yeats affirms his role, and in his affirmation, i.e., in his most intense living of a myth that is daimonic in origin, Yeats, again like Socrates, becomes virtually divine, such great gifts have the *daimones* to bestow on the men whom they choose and on the men who choose them:

> I am content to follow to its source
> Every event in action or in thought;
> Measure the lot; forgive myself the lot!
> When such as I cast out remorse
> So great a sweetness flows into the breast
> We must laugh and we must sing,
> We are blest by everything,
> Everything we look upon is blest.

To Sean O'Casey, Yeats wrote that "the ancient philosophers thought a poet or dramatist Daimon-possessed" (*Letters*, p. 741), and he had every reason to agree with them. The poet who embraces his *daimon*, and who is so fortunate as to have for his own a myth as grand as Yeats's, finds his *daimon* and his myth, as Yeats does here in the conclusion of "Dialogue of Self and Soul," to be forces that focus, unify, and complete his being, and that do so by taking possession of him rather than he possessing them.

"Of course, I did not invent the term Eros. I learnt it from Plato." Jung, fearing that his empirical discoveries might be tainted by contact with philosophical concepts, was not always so eager to pay his philosophic debts as he shows himself in this letter (I, 465); and, indeed, in the sentences that follow, he reasserts his empiricist claims even as he acknowledges Plato's priority, and he incidentally implies that Plato must himself have been something of an empiricist, else how could he have mastered this concept of Jungian psychology before Jung had formulated it? "But I never would have applied the term," Jung says, "if I hadn't observed facts that gave me a hint of how to use this Platonic notion. With Plato Eros is still a daimonion or daemonium in that characteristic twilight in which the gods began to change into philosophical concepts during the course of centuries." There, no doubt, is the answer: Plato could understand something of Jungian Eros because Plato himself had passed only halfway from the *mythos* of psyche to the *logos* of reason: he experienced the mythic powers and he conceptualized them in "that characteristic twilight" midway between psychology and philosophy. While Jung may thus appear rather to patronize Plato, he nevertheless put to good and frequent use Platonic concepts of *ta erotika*. In *Two Essays*, Jung quotes the prophetess from Mantinea— "'Eros is a mighty daemon,' as the wise Diotima said to Socrates" —and proceeds to draw the psychological lesson from the philosophical concept: "We shall never get the better of him, or only to our own hurt. He is not the whole of our inward nature, though he is at least one of its essential aspects" (*CW*, VII, par. 33). Jung returns to the question—and to the *Symposium*—in *Aion*, where he again joins a psychology of the unconscious to the highest reaches of philosophical consciousness; he also raises the instincts to the level of *daimones* and demonstrates the importance of myth in maintaining the good health of the psyche. "All in all, it is not only more beneficial but more 'correct' psychologically to explain as the 'will of God' the natural forces that appear in us as instincts. In this way we find ourselves living in harmony with the *habitus* of our ancestral psychic life; that is, we function as man has functioned at all times and in all places" (*CW*, IX, pt. 2, par. 50). Just as in Yeats, where "the activities of the Daimons" is an equivalent expression for "myth," so also in Jung, "living in harmony with the *habitus* of our ancestral life" and functioning "as man has functioned at all times and in all places" means the same thing as "living a myth."

To see the face of God in the instincts—or, more precisely, to see the faces of the lesser gods, the *daimones*, in the instincts, and behind those daimonic faces the "will of God"—is basic to Jungian psychology. As Jung goes on to explain in the paragraph following the one just quoted, however, the divine face that he discerns in the instincts is not the Christian God but a Greek one, for Christianity, like Neoplatonism, has been a major disaster so far as the doctrine of the *daimon* is concerned. "I should also like the term 'God' in the phrase 'the will of God' to be understood not so much in the Christian sense as in the sense intended by Diotima, when she said: 'Eros, dear Socrates, is a mighty daemon.' The Greek words *daimon* and *daimonion* express a determining power which comes upon man from outside, like providence or fate . . ." (ibid., par. 51). Being a loyal follower of Thrice-Greatest Hermes and his Emerald Tablet (being, in other words, a good Platonist in his psychology), Jung joins the Above and Below here, since the power that he describes comes from outside and above, "like providence or fate," but it also comes from inside and below, like "the natural forces that appear in us as instincts." It was confusing when the Neoplatonists multiplied the *daimones* so extravagantly and gave them those abstract names that deprived them of all personality; but it was worse than confusing, Jung would say—a grave insult and deadly mistake—when Christianity transformed the *daimones* into "demons" and busily set about exorcising them everywhere. The Christian God has no ties with the instincts, but that way lies folly in Jung's view of the matter. You will get the better of Eros, Jung says, only to your own hurt. Any one of us can, of course, if he is so foolish, refuse to live his myth—Socrates could have wept before his judges, Yeats could have regretted his life—but the man who refuses his myth and quarrels with his *daimon* may be assured of doing harm to his immortal psyche.

In the myth of the *Timaeus*, after the Demiourgos has created the universe and the lesser gods, he turns over to those lesser gods the task of creating mankind, explaining to them that they are, by his will, immortal, but that the universe, in order to be complete, must contain not only immortal creatures but mortal ones also, and yet those mortal creatures are to have in them a soul, which is to say, an immortal principle. Those mid-world spirits, acting the part of superior *daimones*, set about their task of "weaving mortal to immortal" (41d), creating *kosmoi* in exact imitation (*mimoumenoi*) of their Father's creation of the *Kosmos*, and in each created body they place three kinds of psyche or soul. "Concerning the most lordly kind of soul we must think in this manner," Timaeus says: "that heaven has given it to each of us as a *daimon*—that which dwells in the top of our body and raises us toward our kinship in heaven" (90a). The man who neglects his *daimon*, according to Timaeus, will become as mortal as it is possible for him to be, and will no doubt fall into psychic illness, as Jung might put it. But the man who loves wisdom and pursues it all his life will become as immortal as is possible for human nature—will enjoy a splendid psychic vitality—"and because he is forever caring for (θεραπεύοντα) the divine element (τὸ θεῖον) in himself and maintaining in best order the *daimon* (εὖ κεκοσμημένον τὸν δαίμονα) that dwells along with him, he will be supremely blessed (εὐδαίμονα)" (90c). Timaeus floats his argument on a series of puns—puns that are literally divine—playing lightly on different senses of words in order to render the most serious of meanings. "*Therapeuein*" (which, by a happy coincidence, is etymologically the source of Jungian "psycho-therapy") means both "to care for, to heal," and "to do service to the gods, to worship." It is only through *daimon*-therapy, according to Timaeus, only through concern and reverence for the divine, daimonic, psychic element within us, that we will, each of us individually, realize and strengthen our immortality. The way that Timaeus would have us perform our worship is by maintaining an orderedness (*kekosmēmenon*) in the psyche, a daimonic order—i.e., *kosmos*—that, in the best Pythagorean manner, imitates the *kosmos* of the universe and of the lesser gods, those heavenly bodies whose circling provides the model of movement about a still center that we should copy. The man who does all this and lives his *daimon*-created myth thus intensely, Timaeus promises, will be "*eudaimon*": he will have a good *daimon* and will be (this is the adjectival meaning of "*eudaimon*") "fortunate," "happy," "blessed." As Yeats says of himself when he has achieved this supreme condition, "I am in the place where the Daimon is" (*Myth.*, p. 365); and in his description of the same experience in "Vacillation," he echoes not only the passage from the *Timaeus* but his own language in "Dialogue of Self and Soul":

> While on the shop and street I gazed
> My body of a sudden blazed;
> And twenty minutes more or less
> It seemed, so great my happiness,
> That I was blessèd and could bless.

"Bless," "blessèd," "blest," and "blessedness"—they are important words in Yeats's poetry, as a glance at the *Concordance* of Parrish and Painter will demonstrate, but no more important than the notion of

"Daimonic Man," as Yeats calls the psychological type representative of what was no doubt the favored phase, and his own phase (Phase 17), on the Great Wheel. Daimonic Man, because of full and joyous participation in his own myth, would of necessity be *eudaimon* and blessèd, even *eudaimonestatos*, "most blessed," as Empedocles said of his Sphere-God.

Jung, again in keeping with the doctrine of *daimones* set forth in the *Symposium*, distinguished two sorts of mid-world spirits, or two activities of those spirits, in his Basilidean sermons to the dead: there are those that we might think of as spiritual guardians (not unlike the *daimon* of the *Timaeus*, or of the *Phaedo* and the *Republic*) and those that appear to us as instinctual drives. The Eros of the *Symposium*, of course, being love earthly and heavenly, combines both in his nature. As E. R. Dodds puts it, "Eros has a special importance in Plato's thought as being the one mode of experience which brings together the two natures of man, the divine self and the tethered beast" (*Greeks and the Irrational*, p. 218). Here is how Jung, posing as a Gnostic but preaching a thoroughly Platonic doctrine, presented the matter to his peculiarly constituted congregation: "The world of the gods is made manifest in spirituality and sexuality. The celestial ones appear in spirituality, the earthly in sexuality. Spirituality conceiveth and embraceth. It is woman-like and therefore we call it *MATER COELESTIS*, the Celestial mother. Sexuality engendereth and createth. It is man-like, and therefore we call it *PHALLOS*, the earthly father." In this erotic doctrine of Basilides of Alexandria (from Sermon Five) there is more than a little of the *Symposium* Aristophanes, with his great *mythos* of primally androgynous mankind split into two yearningly incomplete halves which only Eros, performing a blessed therapy for the psyche, can join together and make whole again. The lover, Aristophanes claims, feels a desire, for which he can offer no rational explanation, "to join with and melt into his beloved and thus make one being out of two." So Yeats:

> And when we talked of growing up
> Knew that we'd halved a soul
> And fell the one in t'other's arms
> That we might make it whole.
>
> (*Poems*, pp. 456-57)

The lover may have no explanation for his desire, but Aristophanes has one, a good one and the same as Yeats's explanation, but it is mythical rather than logical: man was originally whole, he says, lover and beloved in one, and "the desire and pursuit of that wholeness is what we call love" (*Symposium*, 193a). Eros is not only a kind of superior bawd and a divine being in the account of Aristophanes but also a physician and a psychotherapist, for he heals and cures and restores us to original psychic health: "Our race would become happy [*eudaimon*—of course] if we were to give love its fulfilment and so return to the primal condition. . . . It is Eros who, restoring us to our primal nature and healing[10] us, will make us blessed and happy [*eudaimonas*]" (*Symposium*, 193d). This is a state of "radical innocence," as Yeats calls it, before any fall into division, a restoration of wholeness, a return to the sphere, to the eternal moment when one is "blessèd" and can "bless":

> and it seemed that our two natures blent
> Into a sphere from youthful sympathy,
> Or else, to alter Plato's parable,
> Into the yolk and white of the one shell.

Jung, being not only a Gnostic and an alchemist but also an erotic and daimonic physician in a shamanistic and Empedoclean way, knew all about the blent natures, the sphere, and the egg of Yeats's poem. He was also aware that the archetype had its historical origin in Plato (though the elements of the archetype went further back historically—to Heraclitus, Parmenides, and Empedocles—and further down psychologically), nor was Jung loath to draw on the authority of his ancient predecessor in developing his modern ideas. What Yeats and Maud Gonne achieved—or seemed in Yeats's memory to have achieved—would be, "psychologically" speaking, a "movement in a circle around oneself," Jung says, and this he goes on to describe in terms of Platonic philosophy and analytical psychology: "A similar archetypal concept of a perfect being is that of the Platonic man, round on all sides and uniting within himself the two sexes" (*CW*, XIII, pars. 38 and 39). In *Psychology and Religion*,

---

10. "*iasamenos*": performing the healing services of a physician (*iatros*). Aristophanes earlier (191d) uses the same word in the same psychic context: love "redintegrates our primal nature and attempts to make one being from two and thereby heal (*iasasthai*) the human wound."

Jung cites the *Corpus Hermeticum*, but more anciently and more relevantly the *Symposium*, as authority for the remark that "from time immemorial, man in his myths has expressed the idea of a male and female coexisting in the same body. Such psychological intuitions were usually projected in the form of the divine syzygy, the divine pair, or in the idea of the hermaphroditic nature of the creator" (*CW*, XI, par. 47). Each of these, according to Jung, refers to the archetype of "the rotundum, the round, original form of the Anthropos," for which another "historical synonym" is "the philosophical egg" (*CW*, IX, pt. 1, par. 532). These different historical synonyms, made vital again in Yeats's experience and in his poetry, "all point to the *anima mundi*, Plato's Primordial Man, the Anthropos and mystic Adam, who is described as a sphere (= wholeness), consisting of four parts (uniting different aspects in itself), hermaphroditic (beyond division by sex), and damp (i.e., psychic). This paints a picture of the self, the indescribable totality of man" (*CW*, XIII, par. 173). It is a remarkable living creature, this one, displaying, in its composite but unified nature, a bit of Pythagoras, somewhat more of Heraclitus, Parmenides, and Empedocles, and a great deal of Plato. Each of Plato's predecessors was mythic in his own way and to a certain degree, but it remained for Plato to tell the total myth, the Myth of Man, which he founded in the life of Socrates but, through the daimonic effect of myth itself, raised to the all-inclusive level of *eidos*.

The truth that Plato most often sets myth to secure is the dual truth of the soul's immortality and its reincarnation in a series of bodies. Therefore, the point of view that Plato adopts whenever he turns his hand to *mythos* and considers man as a mythic being is a point of view outside of time: man as he is essentially and eternally rather than as he is accidentally and temporally. Of course Plato sees man moving in time, but he also holds a vision of the stillness of eternity, and he maintains that temporal movement is merely an imitation, more or less imperfect, of eternal stillness. Socrates, because his *daimonion* compelled him to live a largely mythic life of philosophic quest, came closer than any of his contemporaries to a full realization of his eternal *eidos*: the Socrates moving in time was hardly distinguishable from the Socrates at rest in eternity. All the Platonic myths, as J. A. Stewart has remarked, "view man's present life *sub specie aeternitatis*—in God; exhibit it as part of the great plan of Providence—as one term of a continuous progress to be reviewed at once *a parte ante* and *a parte post*" (*Myths of Plato*, p. 102). The myth of the soul in the *Phaedrus*, the myth of the afterlife in the *Phaedo*, and the myth of Er in the *Republic* raise the spectator above time and space and situate him where he may look down on human incarnations and reincarnations from a point of view that could be imagined as that of Yeats's Thirteenth Sphere. It is there that the individual comes face to face with his *daimon* and there that he either has assigned to him (as in the *Phaedo*) or chooses (as in the *Republic*) the guardian spirit that will accompany him and become his destiny in the upcoming incarnation. It is "pitiful, laughable, and strange," according to Er, to see how the discarnate souls choose their *daimones* (620a), but it is not the absurdity of the business that interests either Socrates as narrator or Plato as creator; what both of them want to establish, and they consider it the one point of ultimate importance, is that the psyche is immortal. "If we are persuaded by me," Socrates says, then we shall believe that "psyche is immortal and capable of enduring all evil and all good," we shall select our *daimones* in the light of that belief and with infinite care, and thus, both in this life and in those lives to come, "we shall"—in the final words of the *Republic*—"fare well." Everything hangs on our belief in the soul's immortality and a complementary belief in an eternal world set over against this temporal world, a world of εἴδη or Forms above and behind this world of images and phantasmata.

Marriage with his own *daimon*, ascent thereby to the *eidos* of his being and ascent to the realm of Forms in general, and in that realm a blissful, eternal, nuptial consummation—thus the whole desire of the philosopher as Socrates describes him in the *Republic* (and elsewhere). In addition, what Socrates says of the philosopher in the *Republic* is much the same as what he claimed to have learned about the lover from Diotima in the *Symposium*: both yearn for the beatific vision (the lover yearns to look on Beauty Itself, the Philosopher on Good Itself); both seek to become godlike and immortal ("So the philosopher, in constant companionship with the divine order of the world, will reproduce that order in his soul and . . . become godlike": *Rep.*, 500d); both would ascend from this world of movement, plurality, and time to that other world of stillness, unity, and eternity. "But certainly it is always to the Condition of Fire . . . that we would rise," Yeats says (*Myth.*, p. 364), and I have already said that by the Condition of Fire, Yeats means what, in *A Vision*, he calls "the ultimate reality," that is, the "phaseless sphere" of Parmenides, which, as Yeats says of something else in another context, is "all transcendence" (*Poems*, p. 826). In "Swedenborg, Mediums, and the Desolate Places," Yeats talks of a man's "ruling love"—an indwelling spiritual force intimately related to, perhaps identical with, his *daimon*—describing it as that center of his psychological/moral being to which all his other loves have reference, and he says further, "our surrender to that love, as to supreme good, is no new thought, for Villiers de l'Isle-Adam quotes Thomas Aquinas as having said, 'Eternity is the possession of one's self, as in a single moment'" (*Ex.*, p. 37). Is not Yeats's "supreme good" much the same as Socrates' "Good Itself," his surrender to daimonic love the same as the lover's progress in the *Symposium*, and his eternity the same as the eternity so eagerly sought by both the Socratic philosopher and the Socratic lover? In that single moment of ecstatic consummation, the philosophic lover and the erotic philosopher discover eternity and the greatest happiness, the greatest blessedness, the greatest *eudaimonia* available to mankind. Both Yeats and Plato—the one embodying the truth in his own life, the other embodying it in the life of Socrates—conceived of a system that embraced all things human but that also transcended all things human.

In one intensely compacted sentence of "Anima Mundi," where he is treating of the "passionate dead" who "live again those passionate moments, not knowing that they are dead," Yeats implies all the antinomic and hierarchical aspects of his system; moreover, at the same time that he provides an excellent gloss on Platonic epistemology and ontology, he contrives to include virtually everything in Jung's natural, psychic system but only as a small corner of the inclusive Yeatsian system, an incidental clause in the comprehensive sentence. "The inflowing from their mirrored life," Yeats says of the "passionate dead," "who themselves receive it from the Condition of Fire, falls upon the winding path called the Path of the Serpent, and that inflowing coming alike to men and to animals is called natural" (*Myth.*, p. 361). If I may schematize where Yeats verbalizes and introduce terminology from *A Vision* to assist in understanding the metaphysics of this earlier book, I might draw out the meaning of Yeats's sentence as in the accompanying diagram.

THE RHIZOME AND THE FLOWER

Totally Disembodied, Pure Being, All Transcendence, Nothingness

SPHERE

Condition of Fire ETERNITY

Thirteenth Cycle (both Sphere and cone)

Formerly embodied, Mixed being/becoming

Condition of Passionate Dead: *Daimones*, creators of myths EVERLASTINGNESS

Winding Paths of Living

Aristophanic *symbola* to one another

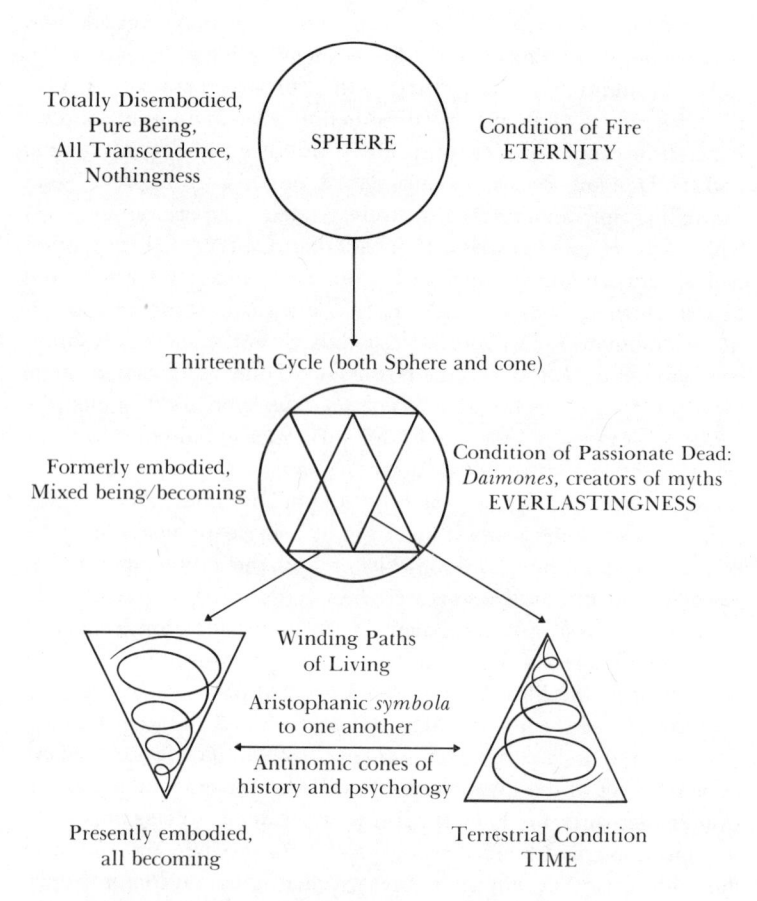

Antinomic cones of history and psychology

Presently embodied, all becoming

Terrestrial Condition TIME

The Parmenidean Condition of Fire (= the transcendent Sphere, "ultimate reality") inflows to the Thirteenth Cycle (which is both Sphere and cone) of the "passionate dead" (= *daimones*), which then inflows to the separated mirror opposites that the Thirteenth Cycle contains within itself as a composed unity, and these are on the one hand the natural instincts that determine animal and human life, and on the other hand the everlasting antinomies of this, our Heraclitean universe. Besides being Heraclitean antinomies, they are also Aristophanic *symbola*—broken halves of an original whole—which, when joined together, become a single *symbolon* (the marriage bed being a "symbol of the solved antinomy") pointing upward to the Thirteenth Cone, which on its other, transcendent side leads on to the Sphere. Yeats's three levels correspond to the three levels of Platonic ontology (pure being, mixed being-and-becoming, and pure becoming), epistemology (knowledge, true opinion, and ignorance), metaphysics (Ideas, mathematical figures, and phenomena), and theology (God, *daimones*, and mankind). To us who are on "the winding path called the Path of the Serpent"—Hodos Chameliontos—the inflowing, which was at first pure spiritual impulse, comes, Jung insisted endlessly, in the form of natural instinct. At the center of it all is *mythos*: the *eidē* inflow to the *daimones* whose activities compose those *mythoi* which inflow to determine human experience.

When, in "Among School Children," Yeats makes the exclamatory address that leads on to the great culmination of the poem:

> O Presences
> That passion, piety or affection knows
> And that all heavenly glory symbolise . . .

he is looking to beings of that same mid-world as in the sentence in "Anima Mundi." I shall not diagram either the "School Children" apostrophe or the "Anima Mundi" sentence but will content myself with the remark that the syntax and the metaphysics—the syntax being a neat structural analogue of the metaphysics—of the two are precisely the same and precisely Platonic. "All heavenly glory" inflows to the daimonic "Presences," which are the objects of knowledge for instinct-guided lovers, nuns, and mothers. The poem, like the prose passage, imagines ascending and descending levels of antinomic resolution and dissolution—from the antagonistic, strife-driven opposites of psychology and history to the joined opposites of an intermediate world of *daimones*, *eidola*, images and icons, to the mystic Sphere where there are not even joined opposites, and no images or icons, because "Where there is Nothing, there is God" (and vice versa). Yeats's "Presences," filling up the gap that would otherwise make this a "diverse" or a "multiverse" rather than a "universe," correspond very nicely to the Platonic *eidola* and *eikones* that have their own degree of reality, if not full reality, being likenesses of the perfectly intelligible Forms, and that can be imperfectly, intuitively, and mnemonically known by the lover (e.g., *Symposium* and *Phaedrus*), by the religious-philosopher (e.g., *Phaedo, Republic, Theaetetus, Phaedrus, Philebus, Laws, Epinomis*), and by the parent (for each of the first two is seeking, parentlike, an immortality in his offspring); and the *eidola* and *eikones* do specifically symbolize—they are, in another realm, likenesses of all heavenly glory, the eternal paradigm, the Forms that confer on them such reality as they possess. Eternity, through the mid-world of everlastingness, is the source of whatever we can call "meaning" in this lower world of time.

In one of the introductory passages to *A Vision*, the fictional John Aherne writes to Yeats this very shrewd remark, apropos of the "autochthonous" (as Jung would phrase it) occurrence of the same ideas in different places at various times: "That you should have found what was lost in the *Speculum* or survives in the inaccessible encampments of the Judwalis, interests me but does not astonish. I recall what Plato said of memory, and suggest that your automatic script, or whatever it was, may well have been but a process of remembering. I think that Plato symbolised by the word 'memory' a relation to the timeless . . ." (*Vision*, p. 54). What Plato said of memory (primarily in the *Phaedo*, the *Meno*, and the *Phaedrus*) is that it is the specific human faculty by which the soul, when in an incarnate state, is capable of recollecting knowledge that it acquired in a previous discarnate state. Psyche thus recalls in time what it knew out of time, and therefore, as Cebes says in the *Phaedo*, "learning is really recollection" (72e); or as Jung several times puts it (with the appropriate Platonic references), "Cognition is recognition." For Plato, memory—or, more exactly, anamnesis: recollection—gives support to a doctrine of metempsychosis, and it is regularly used by Plato's Socrates to prove the immortality of psyche; moreover, in conjunction with the account of universal creation in the *Timaeus*, it implies a doctrine of eternity and symbolizes, as Yeats/Aherne says, "a relation to the timeless." It is in securing just these truths—psyche's immortality, metempsychosis, and an eternal world of Forms—that Plato, as I have pointed out, most often resorts to myth. Hence, the myth of Aherne, Robartes, the Judwalis, and the *Speculum* (not to mention the Instructors) that Yeats wraps around his *Vision*, though he could scarcely be said to keep a *very* straight face in narrating it, has a kind of daimonic logic of its own, as do all the myths in Plato, and is neither trivial nor outrageous, as might at first seem to be the case.

The woman who speaks the poem called "Before the World was Made" (second of the series "A Woman Young and Old," *Poems*, pp. 531-32) has more than a fair portion of Platonic anamnesis in her psychic makeup—or if not she, then her creator has—as witness her remarks about her essential ideal face in the first stanza:

> If I make the lashes dark
> And the eyes more bright
> And the lips more scarlet,
> Or ask if all be right
> From mirror after mirror,
> No vanity's displayed:
> I'm looking for the face I had
> Before the world was made.

What was there "before the world was made"? The woman who speaks here and her creator seem to know the answer as well as Timaeus and his creator: indeed, the two latter-day Platonists may have learned it from Timaeus and his creator if they did not intuit the truth as a consequence of anamnesis. Before the world, and before time—which began when the world was made—there was eternity and in it the eternal paradigm, composed of *eidē*, the Forms on which the entire universe was modelled. So the woman's living face—a series of imperfect reflections and reflections of reflections in "mirror after mirror"—is a blurred, muddy, distorted likeness or an *eikon* of the *eidos* or pattern laid up in an eternity beyond the heavens. What the speaker of the poem goes on to require of her lover is that he see in her beauty the same transcendent beauty—i.e., Beauty Itself—that Diotima tells Socrates is the visionary goal of every lover: "I'd have him love the thing that was / Before the world was made." What was "before the world" remains now beyond the world, perfectly still and unmoving, altogether unaffected by changes occurring in time.

"My works," Jung informs us in *Memories, Dreams, Reflections*, when the question of life after death has come up, "are fundamentally nothing but attempts, ever renewed, to give an answer to the question of the interplay between the 'here' and the 'hereafter'" (p. 299/278). Jung seems to feel that this may be rather surprising—or scandalous—coming from an empiricist and natural scientist, so he hastens to add, "I have never written expressly about a life after death; for then I would have had to document my ideas, and I have no way of doing that." This is quite true, of course, but only for the natural scientist, not for the philosopher or the poet (though Yeats did, unwisely, pull out the odd snapshot now and again as documentary proof for his spiritualist intuitions). Jung goes on to say, in the very best Timaean and Socratic way, that even now, in a book that was to be denied a place in the *Collected Works*, "Even now I can do no more than tell stories—'mythologize'" (ibid.). The language is Timaean and Socratic—Yeatsian also—but it seems to me that there is nevertheless an important difference in the mythologizing and symbolizing mode as practised by Jung on the one hand and as practised by Plato, Timaeus, and Yeats on the other hand; and this returns us to the question left up in the air at the end of the previous chapter: what and where is that mythic and symbolic Thirteenth Sphere into which, we may suppose, Plato, Yeats, and Jung have been liberated? The question, essentially having to do with time, is not an easy one, but it is extremely important for an understanding of what Yeats means by the title "The Symbolism of Poetry," what Jung means by the title *Symbols of Transformation*, and what differences there are, as well as similarities, in the two varieties of symbolism. A doctrine of symbolism and the mythic mode, adequate to our present needs, can be outlined, and its varieties demonstrated, by examining Parmenides, Empedocles, and Plato on time and eternity.

Parmenides (in "The Way of Truth") affirms eternity for his One Being—i.e., for his Sphere—and therefore, since there is nothing but the Sphere or the One Being, he denies the world of time and all cycles of change. This, as I have previously argued, renders the symbolic mode impossible because, in denying the world of time and the senses, it denies the symbolic vehicle. Empedocles, with his "four roots of all things," reintroduces motion, change, and that "alteration of bright colour" to the universe that had been denied by his Eleatic predecessor; he reasserts time, and thus he reconstitutes the symbolic vehicle, but he also translates Parmenides' Sphere from its unmoving, changeless eternity to a bondage in time where, like everything else, it is subject to eventual change, disintegration, and destruction. Thus, while Empedocles provides us with the vehicle, there is no place for it to carry us except "round and round

... Like an old horse in a pound." Time never had a start and has never existed, according to Parmenides' "Way of Truth"; time never had a start but has always existed, according to Empedocles' "On Nature." The final refinement goes to Plato: time, according to the *Timaeus*, had a start, it exists now, and it will continue everlastingly. What this last myth tells us is that the Sphere of eternity was the model (παραδείγμα, "paradigm") on which time was created, and it is the unmoving, ideal Form that time, in its circular movement, imitates. Eternity is thus the archetype of time, and time, in turn, being the effect of the circular progress of the planetary lesser gods through the heavens, becomes the archetype of human motion: ascent and decline, rising and falling, all those periods and cycles which are figured—archetypally, so far as humans are concerned—in the mathematical, circular movement of time. This latter is very much the concept of time in Empedocles, where we find reference to "revolving time" and "circling time," and where human experience imitates this cyclical movement of time. On the other hand, however, time, in the Empedoclean scheme, imitates nothing. In Empedocles, time is the archetype for human movement, but for time itself there is no archetype. Plato, in effect, sets up an ontological hierarchy: cycles of human/natural experience imitating the everlasting revolutions of the heavens imitating the absolute and unmoving Sphere of eternity. The symbolic and mythic vehicle in Plato can thus transport us from the disordered world of the senses to its archetype, which is ordered revolving time, to time's Archetype, which is eternity.

But what about Yeats, and what about Jung? Are they with Plato, or are they with Empedocles? Yeats's answer is, I think, reasonably clear and was the consequence—or the cause, or both—of his being a symbolist poet in temperament, in theory, and in practise. The cycles imitate the Sphere, they symbolize it, and they yearn for it— but they never *are* the Sphere. Yeats unquestionably joins Plato in a Thirteenth Sphere that, viewed as it were from the other side, is eternal, unmoving, noncyclical, and nontemporal; and like the eternity he enjoys with Plato, Yeats offers to us who are still in time an example for symbolic imitation: he is now, like Plato, a "*Daimon* and *Ghostly Self.*" Jung, on the other hand, seems to me to refuse the Platonic challenge and so to remain locked in time with Empedocles, or, more often, pleading scientific discretion, he refuses to be committed. The question that must be addressed to Jung, if we would know the nature and locale of *his* Thirteenth Sphere, is this: Are the archetypes that he talks so much about—the archetypes that determine human psychology and conduct as the cyclical movement of time determines human movement—are those archetypes modelled on Archetypes that are outside the natural/human system? Though all is admittedly symbolic—symbols of transformation and symbols of individuation—Jung ordinarily declines to say where we are to locate that which is symbolized, whether inside or outside time. Nevertheless, it is pretty clear, I think, that Jung does psychologically the same thing Empedocles did cosmologically but which Yeats refused to do poetically, theurgically, or metaphysically: i.e., Jung locates the Sphere within the cycle, and for him, as for Empedocles, eternity remains a hostage to time.

It might seem that Jung is pointing in the other direction, away from Empedocles and toward Plato, when he describes certain visions in his autobiography and then offers this observation: "We shy away from the word 'eternal,' but I can describe the experience only as the ecstasy of a non-temporal state in which present, past, and future are one. Everything that happens in time had been brought together into a concrete whole. Nothing was distributed over time, nothing could be measured by temporal concepts" (*Memories*, pp. 295-96/275). In saying that "we shy away from the word 'eternal,'" Jung very properly speaks in the first person plural, for he does indeed, throughout the *Collected Works*, shy away from both the word and the concept (his shying away is often to be observed precisely in the use of inverted commas or in the paradoxical phrase "relative eternity"); but while "we" may be taken to include virtually all psychologists and psychiatrists, not to mention practitioners of such harder-headed sciences as physics, biology, and geology, it has nothing to do with a poet like Yeats, or a philosopher like Plato (who, in the *Timaeus*, is also a physicist, a biologist, a geologist—and something of a psychologist). Moreover, even here in the autobiography where he can speak more freely than in the *Collected Works*, when Jung switches from the first person plural to the singular to describe his experience as "the ecstasy of a non-temporal state in which present, past, and future are one," he chooses, or inadvertently falls into, a language that is clogged by temporality, and for all he may say to the contrary, he thereby implicates that visionary experience in time. Eternity knows nothing of present, past, and future. Is it not precisely the Empedoclean Sphere that Jung describes in the foregoing passage, rather than the Yeatsian/Platonic Thirteenth Sphere or Paradigm? To understand eternity properly, it is necessary to go back before the past (cf. the *Timaeus* and "Before the World was Made") and forward after the future (cf. the *Phaedrus* and *A Vision*), and then necessary also to free oneself even from the unavoidable linguistic, conceptual trap inherent in the use of the words "before" and "after" (cf. the *Republic* and the *Timaeus* discussions of being and becoming). But the eternity, or the "nontemporal state," that Jung describes here is dependent upon time and determined by it: it is first a vast expansion and then a drastic compression of time. Neither an expansion nor a compression of time leads to eternity, however, nor does a combination of the two. Time relates to eternity and not vice versa: eternity, though imitated by time, remains in itself, apart, untouched, unchanged, and unchanging.

For Empedocles, and also I think for Jung, time was never created, hence was not modelled on anything outside or beyond itself. Like the four elements and Love and Strife, time is a part of Empedocles' system and is wholly within that system with no reference outside it. The *Sphairos* comes to be in time, it is destroyed in time, and so, in a certain sense, it is a creation of time. So also with Jung's archetypes: so far as Jung is ever willing to say, the archetypes evolve in the course of time and are not modelled on anything existing "before the world was made" or on anything existing beyond the constructive and destructive reach of time. The archetypes are a product of human experience—"They are in a sense the deposits of all our ancestral experiences, but they are not the experiences themselves" (*CW*, VII, par. 300)—which has been ongoing for aeons, coming to be and perishing, like Empedocles' Sphere but unlike Parmenides' One Being. "I have often asked myself whether the term 'archetype' (primordial image) is a happy one," Jung wrote to a correspondent in 1946; and after some consideration he concluded, "I must leave it to the philosopher to hypostatize the archetype as the Platonic eidos. He wouldn't be so far from the truth anyway" (*Letters*, I, 418). Disregarding the fact that Jung did not always leave hypostatization of the archetype to the philosopher, one might question whether he is altogether right here, since the

Platonic *eidos* is not a consequence nor the "deposits" of experience but is the pre-existent paradigm of human experience.

> Plato thought nature but a spume that plays
> Upon a ghostly paradigm of things. . . .

Jung comes closer to the mark in "Instinct and the Unconscious" (which I would suggest is a very significant title for an essay that contains this observation), where he writes, "In Plato, however, an extraordinarily high value is set on the archetypes as metaphysical ideas, as 'paradigms' or models"; and after a review of theories of archetypes in medieval philosophy, he arrives at scholastic doctrine, which is much closer to his own: "But in scholasticism we find the notion that archetypes are natural images engraved on the human mind, helping it to form its judgments" (*CW*, VIII, par. 275). They are *natural* images, Jung says, and in so saying he allies the archetypes with nature, time, and the instincts as against supernature, eternity, and the Forms. Even when he declares in *Psychology and Alchemy* (*CW*, XII, par. 329) that "the archetype is, so to speak, an 'eternal' presence," he compromises the only real sense of eternity with the hesitant "so to speak" and then destroys it utterly with his inverted commas.

Memory—and here we should recall "Aherne's" acute observation that "Plato symbolised by the word 'memory' a relation to the timeless"—is as important in Jung's science as anamnesis is in Plato's theory of Forms. So far as his science is concerned, however, the memory in question is a racial memory rather than a Pythagorean, a transmigratory, or a daimonic memory. Discussing Platonic anamnesis, F. M. Cornford writes: "Obviously it is only knowledge of a certain kind that can be thus recovered. Historical knowledge in the widest sense—the facts and events of human or natural history—is not contained in the inner consciousness" (*Principium Sapientiæ*, p. 55). Ironically enough, Cornford arrives at this observation after drawing on two quotations from Jung having to do with a scientific discovery that Jung certainly, and Cornford presumably, would explain by way of archetypes: Robert Mayer's idea about the conservation of energy, they agreed, was an archetypal idea. But the truth is that Jung really cannot say how time-evolved archetypes are transmitted to or inherited by the individual, and this is why so many of Jung's readers have been exasperated, or worse, by his descriptions of the archetypes. Reincarnation explains the archetypes for Plato, and hypothetically for Yeats, but Jung, as a scientist, refuses the gambit. It may be that in saying, as he frequently does say, that ontogenesis repeats phylogenesis, Jung is trying to stretch time out until it encompasses eternity, but it will never work. Phylogeny, like ontogeny, is time-bound, as is the memory in Jung's science, whether it be personal or racial; but anamnesis in the Platonic sense is not confined in time, and neither are the Forms. In his introduction to the Penguin *Meno*, W. K. C. Guthrie says that what the Socratic experiment in that dialogue teaches "could be expressed as the difference between empirical and *a priori* knowledge, the one referring to the natural, changeable world in which we live, and the other to universal and timeless truths." The "empirical," the "natural," and the "changeable"—these are the terms of Jung's science, terms that he himself insists upon. They are also the terms of Yeats's poetry, but not the only ones. In his Thirteenth Sphere, as in the creation myth of the *Timaeus*—that Cone/Sphere between time and eternity where the *daimones* disport themselves as the will of God and exert their tremendous influence on the psychologies of men—Yeats now takes his place with Plato, while Jung, like Empedocles, remains bound to time and nature. The Platonic rhizome flowers in Jung's science, certainly, but it is a natural blossom, not a supernatural one, destined to pass and to return in time rather than to rest in eternity: his psychology is, as Jung often proclaimed it, a *natural* science. If this is a philosophical limitation, however, it may also be a methodological virtue—for what would we say of a psychology that presumed to analyze the Psyche of God rather than the psyches of men?

CHAPTER VII

The Poetics of Mummy Wheat

"I am finishing my belated pamphlet," Yeats wrote to Dorothy Wellesley in 1938, apropos of *On the Boiler*, "and will watch with amusement the emergence of the philosophy of my own poetry, the unconscious becoming conscious. It seems to me to increase the force of my poetry" (*Letters*, p. 904). Yeats was not always so kindly disposed toward philosophy as he shows himself here; on the contrary, "philosophy is a dangerous theme," he observed in the preface to *The King of the Great Clock Tower*, and he followed that observation with his "Prayer for Old Age" (*Poems*, p. 553), the first two stanzas of which pray in these accents:

> God guard me from those thoughts men think
> In the mind alone;
> He that sings a lasting song
> Thinks in a marrow-bone;
>
> From all that makes a wise old man
> That can be praised of all;

> O what am I that I should not seem
> For the song's sake a fool?

Yet it was not wisdom that Yeats shunned so much as the praise of *hoi polloi*: he would have been happy, I think, to be "a wise old man" after the pattern of Heraclitus, living in isolation and sustained by a gleeful bitterness, or the pattern of "Timon and Lear / Or that William Blake / Who beat upon the wall / Till Truth obeyed his call" (*Poems*, p. 576), or the pattern of Plato, perpetually unsatisfied and scornful of all comfortable accomplishment ("'What then?' sang Plato's ghost. 'What then?'")—but not "a wise old man" after the pattern of Wordsworth "withering into eighty years, honoured and empty-witted" (*Myth.*, p. 342).

When Yeats says that he "will watch with amusement the emergence of the philosophy of my own poetry," he speaks as one curiously detached, an onlooker like anyone else, taking pleasure in the appearance of thought for which he claims no personal credit or responsibility, as if that thought, though coming from his mouth and his pen to be sure, were the product of an impersonal mind— the Great Memory and Great Mind, as Yeats was eager to name it. It is to be remarked that the "philosophy" that Yeats speaks of is a *process* first of all, an ongoing transformation, *mythos* becoming *logos*, "the unconscious becoming conscious," a psychic drama ("Aurora Consurgens," Jung called it) that is nothing less than that coming to consciousness of mankind which occurred historically in ancient Greece to be repeated in the life of philosophic everyman and specifically to be repeated here in the poetry and prose—philosophy as *mythos* and philosophy as *logos*—of W. B. Yeats. In an intensely relevant passage in the pamphlet from which he was amused to watch his philosophy emerge, Yeats wrote of the way in which he thus imagined his own mind to be a sort of epitome of past minds. "I am philosophical, not scientific," Yeats says at the outset; few readers, I imagine, would be surprised to hear this, and fewer yet would disagree. This philosophical, nonscientific bent, Yeats goes on to explain,

> means that observed facts do not mean much until I can make them part of my experience. Now that I am old and live in the past I often think of those ancestors of whom I

have some detailed information. . . . Then, as my mood deepens, I discover all these men in my single mind, think that I myself have gone through the same vicissitudes, that I am going through them all at this very moment, and wonder if the balance has come right; then I go beyond those minds and my single mind and discover that I have been describing everybody's struggle, and the gyres turn in my thoughts. Vico was the first modern philosopher to discover in his own mind, and in the European past, all human destiny.

(*On the Boiler*, pp. 21-22; *Ex.*, p. 429)

The first "modern" perhaps, but surely not the first *ancient* nor the *last* modern to do so, for this discovery was made as long ago as the "autobiography" of Socrates and the systematic construct of Plato—encompassing the minds of Pythagoras, Heraclitus, Parmenides, and Empedocles and embracing "all human destiny"—and has been made again as recently as the twentieth century in the thought and work of (for example) Yeats himself. When he says that he lives in the past, Yeats means, among other things, as he makes sufficiently clear elsewhere, that he lives in the unconscious with those ancestors now dead but returned thereby to the human mind, and that that past in which he dwells, like the ancestors and the unconscious, is not merely a personal past, nor only a familial and national past, but a racial, collective, and universal past as well. From his "single mind," Yeats passes by way of the intermediate minds of family and nation—and certainly those intermediate minds were vastly important to Yeats: did he not try to make out that Blake was an Irish poet and one of the O'Neils?—to his eventual goal which is the Great Mind, focussed now, however, as the gyres turn back on themselves once more, in Yeats's own single mind. If we trace our ancestry and the family tree right down to the roots—beyond Blake, beyond Vico, beyond Swedenborg and Boehme, beyond Paracelsus and Plotinus—we shall eventually find the ancestors deep in the unconscious of mankind, far back in the history of Greek philosophy, the quaternal *rhizōmata*, archetypal tendencies and possibilities, the great progenitors of human thought in whom we recognize an ultimate, intellectual and spiritual ancestry rather than a proximate, blood and kin ancestry. Yeats wonders "if the balance has come right"; the answer to his question is to be sought in the emergent philosophy with its four balanced and counterpoised elements; in the fully articulated Platonic system that gave force to the poetry; and in that visionary poetry itself from which the philosophy emerges not as a theme but as a process ("the unconscious becoming conscious") imitated, dramatized, and embodied.

When he went about from cottage to cottage with Lady Gregory gathering stories from the Irish peasantry, or when he "climbed to the top storey of some house in Soho or Holloway" in search of "the wisdom of some fat old medium" (*Ex.*, p. 30), as also when he read Swedenborg's *Spiritual Diary*, Yeats, as he tells us, came again and again, in all these places, upon an "ancient system of belief"; or as he puts it, with reference to one of Jung's great ancestral figures, "like Paracelsus who claimed to have collected his knowledge from midwife and hangman, I was discovering a philosophy" (*Ex.*, p. 31). Where better to discover that ancient philosophy, as old as human thought—a philosophy having more to do with the unconscious and that other world of discarnate spirits than with consciousness and this world of incarnate life—than in the traditional mythology of country people, in the ghostly presences evoked by a medium in séance, and in the writings of the man who could describe, to Yeats's great satisfaction, what it is like when angels and the dead copulate? Where better, since Yeats thought of philosophy as a transition from a state of unconsciousness to consciousness, and mythic tales, séance spirits, and angels and the dead, like visions and dreams, all rise up from the unconscious, as ancient as the night, to startle, and to dismay or to delight, our ephemeral consciousness? Jung took the same view of the matter when, in *Psychology and Alchemy*, he remarked that "night after night our dreams practise philosophy on their own account" (*CW*, XII, par. 247), and again in *Psychology and Religion*, where he describes the provenance of all such psychic figures and expressions: "The unconscious is the matrix of all metaphysical statements, of all mythology, of all philosophy (so far as this is not merely critical), and of all expressions of life that are based on psychological premises" (*CW*, XI, par. 899). The unconscious, Jung always argued, and Yeats agreed, is everywhere and at all times pretty much the same and so serves to unite men in the darkness of night, while consciousness is everywhere different and divides men in the light of day. There is therefore, at least in origin, a coherence and unity about all mythology and philosophy that makes of them a single statement of the one unconscious—perhaps it should be the One Unconscious—no matter how consciousness may dress up its tales and thought in the most recent fashions to make them appear new and different. Yeats was passionately committed to the notion of a Perennial Philosophy, no doubt obscured in our time by the unnatural prevalence of "merely critical" philosophy; what this offered him as a poet was a symbolic expression of virtually timeless and universal validity.

The ubiquity, antiquity, and unity of Yeats's tradition—which, to give it its proper name, is Platonism, rooted, as we have seen, in the quaternity of Pre-Socratics and in the unifying unconscious—gave to the symbols of his poetry, as Yeats believed, a supernatural power and a universal significance. In a note to accompany *The Winding Stair and Other Poems*, Yeats could say of his symbols and their interpretation: "In this book and elsewhere I have used towers, and one tower in particular, as symbols and have compared their winding stairs to the philosophical gyres, but it is hardly necessary to interpret what comes from the main track of thought and expression" (*Poems*, p. 831). Of writers in "the main track" Yeats names Shelley, Swedenborg, and Aquinas, and he refers vaguely to "certain classical authors" whom we may take to include not only Plato but the four *rhizōmata* as well, for they are the fountainhead of Yeats's "main track of thought and expression," and if they did not in fact deal often in towers, they assuredly did deal in philosophical gyres, and they were responsible for first projecting those archetypal images of square and circle, or quaternity and sphere, to which the square tower of Yeats and the round tower of Jung later conformed. Winding stairs, tree, tower, and full moon, or, more basically and schematically, cones, triangle, square, and circle, or, yet more basically and numerically, two, three, four, and one—for this kind of symbolic projection, structuring, and ordering Yeats had the authority of ancient tradition and equally ancient psyche. And to the alternating progression and regression of numbers—unity to duality to trinity to quaternity and back to unity again—Maria Prophetissa would surely have given her Pythagorean blessing.

Looking at Yeats's library, in which a good number of volumes of philosophy bear annotations by Yeats designed to bring them in line with the terminology of *A Vision*, one has the distinct impression that

Yeats believed the entire history of Western philosophy was but prolegomena to the revelation vouchsafed him for *A Vision*, and he seems, at least at times, to have felt much the same sort of thing about all those who were closest to him—specifically his wife and children. Of course, the story of the genesis of *A Vision* is known to everyone: the story of how, on the fourth day, "in a hotel at Ashdown Forest," even she, Mrs. Yeats, began to write in automatic script. But the children also were evidently, as Yeats imagined, sent as part and parcel of the revelation, and he thought it good, as he told John Quinn in a letter, to hold his daughter and son responsible for "the completion of my philosophy" (*Letters*, p. 673)—that philosophy which had really got under way with his wife's automatic writing and had come to a full head of steam with *A Vision*. Not, so the notion goes, that *Yeats* gave this significance to his family but that they had it, as it were, objectively and by the determination of the daimonic Instructors: not Yeats's doing but the doing of a Mind working its will over the centuries. "Conjunctions" was written about Michael Yeats:

> If Jupiter and Saturn meet,
> What a crop of mummy wheat!

and about Anne Yeats:

> The sword's a cross; thereon He died:
> On breast of Mars the goddess sighed.

"I was told," Yeats wrote to Mrs. Shakespear, not only "that my two children would be Mars conjunctive Venus, Saturn conjunctive Jupiter respectively; and so they were—Anne the Mars-Venus personality," but also he was given the extraordinary assurance "that they would develop so that I could study in them the alternating dispensations, the Christian or objective, then the Antithetical or subjective" (*Letters*, pp. 827-28). And do you know, he goes on to tell his correspondent in a tone of wonderment, "it is very strange" but the Instructors have provided me with just exactly those edifying offspring they promised; or, as Yeats puts much the same point in the poem called "Gratitude to the Unknown Instructors":

> What they undertook to do
> They brought to pass;

> All things hang like a drop of dew
> Upon a blade of grass.

The perfect little globule-world and microcosm, hanging in mid-air on something so fragile that it is almost nothing: impossible, yet there it is real and existent. The curious reader will find just what the Instructors gave Yeats, and what Yeats made of it, in these Mars-Venus and Jupiter-Saturn conjunctions, by consulting pp. 207–08 of *A Vision*; and if one does look the passage up, he will discover also that these two "conjunction personalities" are remarkably like the types that Jung was describing in *Psychological Types*, at almost exactly the same moment as Yeats was writing *A Vision*, as "extraverted" and "introverted" attitude-types (Yeats: "These two conjunctions which express so many things are certainly, upon occasion, the outward-looking mind, love and its lure, contrasted with introspective knowledge of the mind's self-begotten unity, an intellectual excitement.")

Everything was grist for the mill, and was so intended by the all-providing, occasionally maleficent but usually beneficent spirits: "We have come to give you metaphors for poetry," and behold you shall name them Anne, "Mars conjunctive Venus," and Michael, "Saturn conjunctive Jupiter." At the end of the previously quoted letter to Olivia Shakespear, Yeats says, "I have written a lot of poetry of a personal metaphysical sort," and he includes in the letter a poem "on the soul" ("He and She"), after which he remarks, "It is of course my centric myth" (p. 829). This is a neat, if perhaps unintentional, response to those critics who find Yeats's myth eccentric: not at all—it is "centric" in every way, at the very heart and center of the ancient and universal tradition, the most recent statement of an antique and complex truth that is the "main track of thought and expression" in the Western world. Structurally also, Yeats's myth "that was itself a reply to a myth" (*Ex.*, p. 392) was, as he says, "centric," a nest of circles within circles, spheres within spheres; it was in addition, in keeping with the myths of the great Greek originals, cyclical, enantiodromian, palintropian, transmigrational, and repetitive, in contrast to the linear, nonrepetitive myth of progress that had been invented by shallow modernists in the nineteenth century in disregard of the great truths discovered, but never invented, by antiquity, truths that were to be rediscovered, but of course not invented, by Yeats in the twentieth century.

In the dedication of the 1925 *Vision* to "Vestigia," Yeats speaks of the group of "young men and women" who met in London and Paris ("nearly forty years ago") "to discuss mystical philosophy," and, whatever the motives of the others may have been (a search "for spiritual happiness or for some form of unknown power," perhaps), as for himself, Yeats says: "I wished for a system of thought that would leave my imagination free to create as it chose and yet make all that it created, or could create, part of the one history, and that the soul's. The Greeks certainly had such a system . . ." (p. xi). When, nearly forty years on from those youthful days, the system, unbidden and by way of revelation, suddenly fell into Yeats's lap, he realized of course that it was not new but old, as old as the Greeks ("What I have found indeed is nothing new"), or as old as human awareness of time itself, a truth from beyond consciousness, from beyond nature or the natural, and from beyond the grave; for those revelations came to him from that realm of the dead where the mediatorial *daimones* disport themselves as our unconscious, just as, in reverse perspective, we, during our brief lives, provide the *daimones* with a moment of consciousness.

Even Leo Africanus, Yeats's familiar and his own proper *daimon*, who later (it seems) became altogether too independent of and dominant over the conscious mind of his living counterpart, when questioned by Yeats about his ontological status, replied that "he was part of the unconscious, but also, most certainly Leo Africanus the geographer."[1] Likewise, with apparent puzzlement, Yeats says that the system of *A Vision* certainly came to him objectively and from outside the reach of his conscious mind; yet, "again and again" the Instructors "insisted that the whole system is the creation of my wife's Daimon and of mine, and that it is as startling to them as to us" (*Vision*, p. 22). If the spirits, however, *daimones* and Instructors alike, are elements of the unconscious, then they have as good a reason for being startled as Yeats and Mrs. Yeats: in the moment of transit, through the awareness of the living man and wife, the spirits, too, attain to consciousness of their own being and their meaning.

1. Virginia Moore records this exchange between Yeats and Leo Africanus in *The Unicorn* (New York: Macmillan, 1954), p. 236.

"Immortal mortals, mortal immortals, living the others' death and dying the others' life": it is a regular, if not altogether natural, intercourse between mortal and immortal, living and dead, fruitful to both parties but no doubt somewhat startling for them both as well. Or as Yeats explains the paradox of the unconscious becoming conscious in *A Vision*, "Those who taught me this system did so, not for my sake, but their own"; and in a footnote he hastens to explain his rather obscure explanation: "They say that only the words spoken in trance or written in the automatic script assist them. They belong to the 'unconscious' and what comes from them alone serves. My interpretations do not concern them. In the mediumistic conditions it sometimes seems as if dreams awoke and yet remained dreams" (*Vision*, p. 234).

"The Gift of Harun Al-Rashid," in which Yeats assumes the mask of Kusta-ben-Luka, a philosopher with a "thirst for . . . old crabbed mysteries," and gives Mrs. Yeats the role of the old philosopher's young bride, offers a hint of the origin and the nature of the recovered knowledge later set forth in *A Vision*. The poem poses as a letter from Kusta-ben-Luka/Yeats which, at his command, was hidden centuries ago, to be discovered much later, in a carefully chosen and appropriate hiding place: "Carry this letter" into the Caliph's library, Kusta-ben-Luka writes, "Pass books of learning from Byzantium," and finally,

> Pause at the Treatise of Parmenides
> And hide it there, for Caliphs to world's end
> Must keep that perfect . . . ,
> So great its fame.

And so it has been: the Treatise of Parmenides, which disallows all change and dissolution, has itself remained inviolate and has preserved the letter intact to our time. What that letter describes is the experience in revelation that Kusta-ben-Luka had so long ago and that Yeats had in the years after 1917, a revelation transmitted to the old philosophers through the sleep-talking and the automatic writing of the young brides. After his bride begins to speak in the night, Kusta-ben-Luka asks himself, "was it she that spoke or some great Djinn?" Now a Djinn is nothing but a *daimon* in a caftan, so that the answer that Kusta-ben-Luka returns to his own question—

"I say that a Djinn spoke"—is identical to Yeats's answer as delivered up in *A Vision*. Once started, the revelations flow from *daimones* dwelling in depths of the mind:

> Truths without father came, truths that no book
> Of all the uncounted books that I have read,
> Nor thought out of her mind or mine begot,
> Self-born, high-born, and solitary truths,
> Those terrible implacable straight lines
> Drawn through the wandering vegetative dream. . . .

What are these mathematic, geometric, and schematic skeletons of truth underlying the fleshed experience, the disordered chaos of life, and "the wandering vegetative dream"—what are they but the basic, primordial images, the inherent formal patterns, the numbers, the disembodied archetypes? For like Plato, Kusta-ben-Luka, as a result of his visionary experience, "thought nature but a spume that plays / Upon a ghostly paradigm of things." This is the "arbitrary, harsh, difficult symbolism" for which Yeats half apologized in *A Vision*, but as he says there, "We can (those hard symbolic bones under the skin) substitute for a treatise on logic the *Divine Comedy*, or some little song about a rose, or be content to live our thought" (p. 24).

For such a treatise as Parmenides (for example) produced on logic, Yeats himself later substituted a whole host of songs, and many of them about roses, but only after articulating the hard symbolic bones into the complete skeletal system of *A Vision*. Yet, some of the later lines of "The Gift of Harun-al-Rashid" seem to deny Parmenides' role in the truths spoken by the young bride in her sleep.

> All those abstractions that you fancied were
> From the great Treatise of Parmenides;
> All, all those gyres and cubes and midnight things
> Are but a new expression of her body
> Drunk with the bitter sweetness of her youth.

The truths, now, are seen as an expression of the young bride's love, abstractions underlying the rich, warm reality of her whole being: "A quality of wisdom [drawn] from her love's / Particular quality." But what of the actual content of the truths? Are not those truths, at least in part, Parmenidean truths? In a note to the poem, Yeats demonstrates clearly enough that what in one sense comes from the unconscious, from the totality of Mrs. Yeats's being, and from his and his wife's *daimon*, in another sense comes from the archetypal figures of ancient philosophy. Defending the presence of Parmenides' Treatise in the Caliph's library, Yeats says, "It does not seem impossible that a great philosophical work, of which we possess only fragments, may have found its way into an Arab library of the eighth century. Certainly there are passages of Parmenides, that for instance numbered 130 by Burkitt [*sic*] and still more in his immediate predecessors, which Kusta would have recognized as his own thought. This from Heraclitus for instance: 'Mortals are Immortals and Immortals are Mortals, the one living the others' death and dying the others' life'" (*Poems*, p. 829). Besides introducing yet another variation on the spelling of John Burnet's name,[2] this ingenious note, particularly in the coupling of the archetypal antagonists, Parmenides and Heraclitus, points up the analogy to be drawn between the operation and development of individual mind and the operation and development of the mind of humanity in early Greek philosophy. The Treatise of Parmenides and the fragments of Heraclitus, "Kusta would have recognized as his own thought," Yeats says; but how much more Kusta/Yeats would have recognized as his own the synthesis effected by Plato not only from Parmenides and Heraclitus but from Pythagoras and Empedocles as well—"all those gyres and cubes and midnight things."

Writing of the kind of learning displayed in *A Vision* and of the poetry that "gained in self-possession and power" as a result of that learning, Yeats distinguishes (in the poem entitled "On a Picture of a Black Centaur by Edmund Dulac") between the supernatural ("old mummy wheat") and the natural ("wholesome food") and maintains that, as a poet who has been granted a vision, he is and must be equally committed to both:

2. I have heard it suggested that Yeats was really not such a poor speller as everyone supposes but that his impossible handwriting merely makes his spelling seem so bad; of course it is of no consequence, but I think that that explanation simply will not wash in view of his Burnet-Birkett-Burkitt ditherings. In this same volume (*The Cat and the Moon*), with an Olympian disregard for nominal accuracy, Yeats refers to "that strange 'Waste Land' by Mr. T. C. Eliot. . . ."

> What wholesome sun has ripened is wholesome food to eat,
> And that alone; yet I, being driven half insane
> Because of some green wing, gathered old mummy wheat
> In the mad abstract dark and ground it grain by grain
> And after baked it slowly in an oven; but now
> I bring full-flavoured wine out of a barrel found
> Where seven Ephesian topers slept. . . .

Whether the "green wing" that drove the poet half insane is to be identified with the "horrible green parrots" of the second line of the poem, so that the gathering of mummy wheat becomes a reaction against those raucous birds; or whether the green wing is to be identified with the beetle of Yeats's remark to Cecil Salkeld when he was composing the poem ("Eternity is in the glitter on the beetle's wing"—Hone, p. 327), so that the gathering of mummy wheat is a sort of harvesting of eternity, is not clear. What is clear, however, is the contrast between natural fruition, which occurs in the course of time and in the light of day ("What wholesome sun has ripened"), and supernatural revelation, which comes from outside time and speaks to us of "gyres and cubes and midnight things" from "the mad abstract dark." It is all very well, the "full-flavoured wine" from sun-ripened grapes, but one ought not drink too much of it on an empty stomach; and what is wine anyway, Yeats implies, without bread, or bread without wine? What is the natural without the supernatural, what is time without eternity, and what is the consciousness of the incarnate state without the unconscious inhabited by discarnate spirits? The "old mummy wheat"—chthonic and forgotten truths, long-buried and long-neglected in the tomb—gathered, ground, and baked into bread, is the dark but necessary complement of the bright wine; or as Yeats has it in *A Vision*, the lyric poetry requires the hard symbolic bones of a system—the wine and the blood need the bread and the body—just as the hard symbolic bones (for Yeats was a poet after all) would be nothing without the lyric poetry.

In "All Souls' Night," which stands as epilogue to *A Vision*, Yeats returns to "the mad abstract dark" and to that tomb where the supernatural, living-dead, mortal-immortal mummy wheat awaits its destined discoverer, for, as he says:

> I have mummy truths to tell
> Whereat the living mock,

> Though not for sober ear,
> For maybe all that hear
> Should laugh and weep an hour upon the clock.

Maybe they should indeed, since the "mummy truths," as they have nothing at all to do with the clock, will seem eccentric and mad to the living and the sober; but seen *sub specie aeternitatis* they will be understood to be centric truths, a part of the ancient system of belief and knowledge, and the ground of all human comedy, all human tragedy. In the final stanza of the poem, being out of the natural world and enjoying the company of the damned and the blessed, we also find ourselves—where else?—deep-wound in the poet's mind where the spiritually potent dead continue their existence as elements of the collective psyche:

> Such thought—such thought have I that hold it tight
> Till meditation master all its parts,
> Nothing can stay my glance
> Until that glance run in the world's despite
> To where the damned have howled away their hearts,
> And where the blessed dance;
> Such thought, that in it bound
> I need no other thing,
> Wound in mind's wandering
> As mummies in the mummy-cloth are wound.

The vision is a profoundly cyclic and centric one, winding round and round itself to become self-sufficient by reason of both its vastness and its particularity, expanding now to the far bounds of *Anima Mundi*, contracting now to the tight focus of *anima hominis*, and finding the thought of the one, held "tight / Till meditation master all its parts," indistinguishable from the thought of the other: both are expressions of the ancient and universal tradition. Buried so long ago and ignored or forgotten by the multitude, the "mummy truths" here and the "mummy wheat" elsewhere, like the rhizome itself, flower again, as if miraculously, in the proper, the necessary, the destined intellect and soul. It was such mummy truths as these, available to him from the time of his marriage on, that Yeats felt gave to his poetry—which otherwise, he feared, risked being too much a private affair—its vastly increased significance and resonance.

In the meeting of mummy truths and personal emotion, a great poetry of the soul—of psyche—was engendered: "What a crop of mummy wheat!" What Yeats glimpsed in revelation were those evanescent figures visible or half-visible to the supernatural eye in the psychic state to which he gave a local habitation and a name, calling it "Byzantium":

> Before me floats an image, man or shade,
> Shade more than man, more image than a shade;
> For Hades' bobbin bound in mummy-cloth
> May unwind the winding path.

There is a double winding and unwinding of the mummy-cloth here, a two-way transit between life and death, incarnate and discarnate states, consciousness and the unconscious. The insubstantial figures that the speaker can half make out in that twilight state of the psyche that Yeats symbolizes in Byzantium are the same as those archetypal images that may pass before the closed eye in the instant between waking and sleeping, a state half-conscious and half-unconscious, analogous to the momentary condition that in the poem separates life and death and while separating them, by the very fact of separating, also joins them.

> I hail the superhuman;
> I call it death-in-life and life-in-death.

This is a ghost no doubt, but a Hermetic and Heraclitean ghost ("immortal mortals") and one after the manner of Leo Africanus, more an inhabitant of the unconscious than a dweller in heavenly mansions or in some far region of the hereafter.

A visionary given the opportunity to visit sixth-century Byzantium as Yeats imagines that city—a Byzantium altogether of the soul and not at all of history—would find "all about him . . . an incredible splendour like that which we see pass under our closed eyelids as we lie between sleep and waking, no representation of a living world but the dream of a somnambulist. . . . [C]an even a visionary of today wandering among the mosaics at Ravenne [sic] or in Sicily," Yeats asks rhetorically, "fail to recognize some one image seen under his closed eyelids?" (*Vision*, p. 280). As in Jung, the visionary—not far removed from the madman and the poet, the one overwhelmed and lost in the unconscious, the other glorying in its proferred images as he avails himself of their power—discovers historical parallels and mythological similitudes for what he may have supposed was only his private, perhaps half-deranged, vision or dream. When he discovers those parallels, those similitudes, what can the visionary suppose their source to be but some atemporal, objective, extrapersonal mind—some "general cistern of form," as Yeats calls it (*Myth.*, p. 351)—speaking to him in dreams as to history in its cyclical progress and to mythology in its recurrent motifs, providing him the same images and forms as it provided, and at large continues to provide, to history and mythology? Though he was at times, Yeats says, "overwhelmed by miracle as all men must be when in the midst of it" (*Vision*, p. 25), he was not in much danger of complete submersion or total failure of conscious control. As a man he was too conscious and self-conscious, as a poet too devoted to his craft, ever to abandon himself or his verse to the stream and flow of images from the unconscious. It was George Yeats, never W. B., who did automatic writing—and so much the better for the poetry, which gained great strength through the content of the automatic writing, yet never abandoned that strength by itself becoming a mere automatic record of unconscious doings. Others proclaimed that the ideal of poetry; Yeats never did.

Yeats had, as he felt, looked upon miracle, but he was not overwhelmed, or not for long anyway, and he was not utterly destroyed, as men have been by that experience, because he was able to retain consciousness of himself looking even as he looked. "I am awake and asleep, at my moment of revelation, self-possessed in self-surrender," Yeats tells us (*E. & I.*, p. 524), and the paradoxical, Heraclitean state of mind that he thus describes could well be taken to be the psychic *sine qua non* of Yeatsian visionary poetry. What came to him out of the Great Mind, through the agency of his own and his marital *daimon*, because it was the product of that symbolic moment when antinomic realms are joined, had the effect, Yeats believed, of transforming personal emotion into general truth and of making the mind of the poet, "self-possessed in self-surrender," one with the mind of mankind as it had developed, progressed, turned back on itself, and occasionally transcended its own nature through the ages. Anyone familiar with some of the photographs of Yeats in old age might be forgiven a certain confusion if he supposed that in the following quotation Yeats was describing his own appearance with the words "a look of some great bird staring at miracle," for it was, I believe, an effect that he deliberately sought. He had, after all, stared at miracle until it formed itself into a system; he was, as all agreed and as he desired, a rather strange bird; and the look that he describes as that of Byzantine statuary was one that he could fairly appropriate, since his own psychic state in *A Vision* was at one with the psychic state that he symbolized under the name of Byzantium. "Even the drilled pupil of the eye," at the historic moment of Byzantium and in the state of the psyche figured by that city, "undergoes a somnambulistic change, for its deep shadow among the faint lines of the tablet, its mechanical circle, where all else is rhythmical and flowing, give to Saint or Angel a look of some great bird staring at miracle" (*Vision*, p. 280). Relatively few people I should imagine have ever seen a great bird staring at miracle, or, if they have seen one, were aware of what they were seeing (though Attracta would seem to know what she is talking about in *The Herne's Egg* when she says, with ecstatic assurance, "There is no reality but the Great Herne"). For myself, I cannot claim to have seen any great bird, herne or other, staring at miracle (except, as I say, in those late photographs); yet I think I see what Yeats means, and while he disclaimed both sainthood and angeldom, preferring the name of artist ("we artists . . . are the servants not of any cause but of mere naked life, and above all of that life in its nobler forms, where joy and sorrow are one, Artificers of the Great Moment"—*E. & I.*, p. 260), what he describes here as the typical—I would say archetypical—spiritual artifact of Byzantium at its apogee, he elsewhere describes as his own state of mind, of soul, and of entire being in the transcendent experience which he calls "happiness" and "in those brief intense visions of sleep." Then, he says, in those supreme moments, when he looks upon miracle, upon archetypes, paradigms, and Forms, "I am in the place where the Daimon is," (*Myth.*, p. 365); he might have said also that he was in the holy city of Byzantium, where the "sages standing in God's holy fire" are—which again is not very different from being in Beulah, where (presumably) William Blake is.

According to Yeats (and Jung agreed), it is the function of rhythm, drawn out under the hand of sculptor, painter, musician, or poet, or put to other uses by theurgist, hypnotist, and therapist, to bring us to that place where the dead yet live and sleepers wake, to that place or state that we may call indifferently Byzantium or Beulah or the conscious unconscious. Rhythm, in Jung's terminology, effects an "*abaissement du niveau mental*," and it is in that state of lowered but not entirely obliterated consciousness—when, as Yeats has it, "we are lured to the threshold of sleep" (*E. & I.*, p. 160)—that we behold visions and fantasies, we stare at miracle, and we look on mummy truths. Here the psychiatrist invokes "active imagination" while the poet calls it "the one moment of creation." In either case, contents and powers of the unconscious become, more or less and momentarily, accessible to consciousness. "The purpose of rhythm," Yeats says in his essay on "The Symbolism of Poetry," "is to prolong the moment of contemplation, the moment when we are both asleep and awake, which is the one moment of creation . . ." (*E. & I.*, p. 159). The poet's creative life, like the life of a dancer dancing—"Dying into a dance, / An agony of trance"—is lived in a trancelike poise between the two, between the all-uniting unconscious and separating consciousness, between the universal and the personal, "Between his two eternities, / That of race and that of soul." In his one moment of creation, he beholds Byzantium in himself and surveys the land of the dead, being one of them and not one of them:

> Wound in mind's wandering
> As mummies in the mummy-cloth are wound.

Yeats's language, here and in any number of other poems, is intended, with its rhythmic effects, to reproduce in both poem and reader something of that same state of conscious unconsciousness as was the poet's in his moment of creation. The rhythms of "All Souls' Night" are hypnotic and ritualistic; indeed, the poem itself is a ritual, and like ritual of every sort it draws the individual and his consciousness into an infinitely larger ordering beyond himself or his consciousness: "the pattern more complicated of dead and living," to avail oneself of Eliot's phrasing in "East Coker."

What Jung called "the rhythmic tendency" is profoundly instinctive in nature, or at least so he came to feel. It manifests itself in the infant's instinct to suck and in the sexual instinct, but it is broader in its reach than either of these alone: "it is a peculiarity of emotional processes in general. Any kind of excitement . . . displays a tendency to rhythmic expression, perseveration, and repetition"

(*CW*, V, par. 219). Also, however, according to Jung's psychological observations, "Every emotional state produces an alteration of consciousness which Janet called *abaissement du niveau mental*. . . . The conscious then comes under the influence of unconscious instinctual impulses and contents. These are as a rule complexes whose ultimate basis is the archetype, the 'instinctual pattern'" (*CW*, VIII, par. 856). As Jung sees it, then, any particularly strong emotion brings with it a tendency to rhythmic expression, and at the same time it produces a state in which the unconscious is much closer than usual to consciousness so that archetypal contents of the unconscious approach the threshold of consciousness. The psychotherapist may induce such a state deliberately by "active imagination" ("You choose a dream, or some other fantasy-image, and concentrate on it by simply catching hold of it and looking at it. . . . A chain of fantasy ideas develops and gradually takes on a dramatic character. . . . In other words, you dream with open eyes"), or of course it can happen spontaneously to someone of an imaginative intensity. What goes on, in either case, is the same: "In this way conscious and unconscious are united, just as a waterfall connects above and below" (*CW*, XIV, par. 706). As Jung points out, this is virtually a description of σύμβολον, a symbol, which connects the unconscious with consciousness, transforms inchoate energies of the former into directed activities of the latter, and brings contents up from the dark of the unconscious into the light of consciousness. "If you suspend the critical faculty, I have discovered, either as the result of training, or, if you have the gift, by passing into a slight trance, images pass rapidly before you. . . . But the images pass before you linked by certain associations, and indeed in the first instance you have called them up by their association with traditional forms and sounds. You have discovered how, if you can but suspend will and intellect, to bring up from the 'subconscious' anything you already possess a fragment of." The word "subconscious" (as well as a few other tricks of expression) will betray to the astute reader that the foregoing is Yeats on "evocation" rather than Jung on "active imagination."[3] As to the content of what they say, however,

---

3. The Yeats passage is from *Myth.*, p. 344. In a footnote to "The Symbolism of Painting," Yeats describes the technique for freeing imagination that he and his fellow occultists had developed, and it is clear from his description that their technique corresponds to the "active imagination" of Jung: "I had learned, and my

and the way they suggest arriving at this state where emotion, the archetypes, instinct, and rhythmic expression all touch, there is not a particle of difference.

That the visions so beheld are (or at least may be, and sometimes are) archetypal and mythic is likewise a cardinal point in both Jung's psychology and Yeats's poetics. "Fantasy-products," the psychotherapist maintains, "arise in a state of reduced intensity of consciousness (in dreams, deliriums, reveries, visions, etc.). In all these states the check put upon unconscious contents by the concentration of the conscious mind ceases, so that hitherto unconscious material streams, as though from opened side sluices, into the field of consciousness" (*CW*, IX, pt. 1, par. 263). Having described the relationship into which consciousness and the unconscious are thus brought, Jung proceeds in the next paragraph to ally this state of mind to the psychological process that presented myths to consciousness in the past and that continues to present archetypal figures to consciousness in the present. "Reduced intensity of consciousness and absence of concentration and attention, Janet's *abaissement du niveau mental*, correspond pretty exactly to the primitive state of consciousness in which, we must suppose, myths were originally formed. It is therefore exceedingly probable that the mythological archetypes, too, made their appearance in much the same manner as the manifestations of archetypal structures among individuals today." To be quite frank, I think that a good part of a certain show is given away by Jung's language here: "pretty exactly," "we must suppose," and "exceedingly probable" are the phrases of a man who has not to hand that proof he often claimed to have, and who in fact recognizes that he can never have the proof that he and others might desire, since the subject hardly allows for empirical demonstration. Not everyone has found what Jung says here "exceedingly probable," and not everyone will feel the force of "we must suppose." Not everyone, no—but Yeats did (or he would have done if he had ever read Jung). Yeats even felt that he had the hard empirical proof—snapshots of myth-making spirits carrying on in and above his own cranium—that Jung no doubt desired but could never produce. And interestingly enough, Yeats too, like Jung, felt

---

fellow-students had learned . . . to set free imagination when we would, that it might follow its own law and impulse" (*E. & I.*, p. 151n.) The result was fantasies and visions (Yeats describes one of them) that had not quite the intensity "either of a dream or of those pictures that pass before us between sleep and waking."

that instincts were somehow at the bottom of it all (I shall, nevertheless, defer a full consideration of the relation between instincts and archetypes to the following chapter, where it more properly belongs). In the dark of the unconscious both Yeats and Jung discerned shadowy forms and vague outlines, and they were agreed that those forms were in some sort representations of the instincts; to the psychologist they were, in addition, "archetypes," and to the poet they were "myths," "wisdom," and traditional "subject-matter."

In a piece written late in his life and intended as an introduction to a never-published complete edition of his works, Yeats says that he condemns "all that is not tradition" and explains what he means by saying further that "there is a subject-matter which has descended like the 'deposit' certain philosophers speak of" (*E. & I.*, p. viii). He might have written "certain psychologists" here, for that, of course, is how Jung often described the archetypes—in *Two Essays*, for example, they are "deposits of the constantly repeated experiences of humanity" (*CW*, VII, par. 109). Whether it was to be defined by philosopher or psychologist, Yeats goes on to say that "this subject-matter is something I have received from the generations, part of that compact with my fellow men made in my name before I was born." While this "deposit" or "subject-matter" comes from tradition, from the past, and from those long dead, however, it also came to Yeats from within himself in certain moments of what he calls "super-normal experience": "I cannot break from" traditional subject-matter, Yeats says, "without breaking from some part of my own nature, and sometimes it has come to me in super-normal experience; I have met with ancient myths in my dreams, brightly lit; and I think it allied to the wisdom or instinct that guides a migratory bird" (*E. & I.*, p. viii). There, in very succinct form, is Jung's whole theory (not theory, however, but incontrovertible fact according to its discoverer and champion) of instincts, archetypes, and the collective unconscious and Yeats's whole theory of instincts, myth, and *Anima Mundi*. "Where got I that truth?" Yeats asks rhetorically in a poem that has to do with such mummy truths as these ("Fragments," *Poems*, p. 439); and having asked himself, he proceeds to answer himself:

> Where got I that truth?
> Out of a medium's mouth,

> Out of nothing it came,
> Out of the forest loam,
> Out of dark night where lay
> The crowns of Nineveh.

The first inkling of that complex truth about psyche that Jung spun out into more than seven thousand pages of *Collected Works* came to him out of a medium's mouth (cf. his dissertation, *On the Psychology and Pathology of So-Called Occult Phenomena*); and subsequently much more came to him out of nothing, the forest loam, and dark night, just as Yeats learned his mummy truths from "Swedenborg, Mediums, and the Desolate Places," from dreams, myths, and visions, from ghostly Instructors and the unsatisfied dead. These are all of them—mediums and the dead alike—intermediaries and means to the unconscious, for as Jung puts it in a startling formulation (startling, I mean, for a natural scientist, but it is true the phrase occurs in the autobiography rather than in the *Collected Works*), "the unconscious corresponds to the mythic land of the dead, the land of the ancestors" (*Memories*, p. 191/183). Moreover, as Jung goes on to say of the soul or the anima (that aspect of total psyche which "establishes the relationship to the unconscious"), "Like a medium, it gives the dead a chance to manifest themselves" (ibid.). One scarcely need ask Jung, "Where got you that truth?" The evidence is all there in the chapter of his autobiography that he calls "Confrontation with the Unconscious." That the Yeats who talked about a traditional subject-matter that was the deposit of generations, a compact with his fellow men, received by him in mythic dreams and allied to basic instincts, would have understood Jung very well here can hardly be questioned.

After quoting Blake on what are nothing other than the two worlds of Plato's metaphysics—"There exist in that eternal world the eternal realities of everything which we see reflected in the vegetable glass of Nature"—Yeats asks himself whether certain figures in a vision of his own are " 'the eternal realities' of which we are the reflection 'in the vegetable glass of Nature,' or a momentary dream? To answer is to take sides in the only controversy in which it is greatly worth taking sides, and in the only controversy which may never be decided" (*E. & I.*, p. 152). That this was "the only controversy" worth taking sides on did not, of course, prevent Yeats from engaging in a good many other, quite unrelated controversies; nevertheless, he was undoubtedly sincere when he implied that it was for him a matter of the greatest importance to determine what might be called the ontological relationship between himself, on the one hand, and visionary figures, spirits of the dead, and discarnate beings in general, on the other hand. Or to put it more simply, Yeats felt it a matter of great urgency to decide how this, our present world relates to that other, superhuman world in a "two-world metaphysics" derived from Plato, his predecessors and successors. Indeed, the question was so important to Yeats and he thought it so urgent that he choose that he sometimes chose, with the utmost assurance, one side and other times chose, with equal assurance, the other side. "No matter what I said," Yeats warns the reader of "Blood and the Moon," with apparent reference to what he has just said in "Dialogue of Self and Soul," the poem that immediately precedes "Blood and the Moon" in *Collected Poems*:

> No matter what I said,
> For wisdom is the property of the dead,
> A something incompatible with life.

This is fair warning, since Yeats had a moment before declared that a living man can attain to wisdom, can bless and be blest, can be *eudaimon*, precisely by the intensity of his living and the intensity with which he chooses that life that has been determined for him by the *daimon* that is his. "The Daimon . . . brings man again and again to the place of choice, heightening temptation that the choice may be as final as possible, imposing his own lucidity upon events . . ." (*Myth.*, p. 361). This activity of the *Daimon* offers us less certainty, perhaps, on the question raised in "Blood and the Moon" than it at first appears to do, for the *Daimon* is of that other world whose special property is wisdom, while the narrator of "Self and Soul" seems to have worked out his wisdom within the confines of life and the poem. To whom does the wisdom, in either poem, properly belong? Is it the property of the *daimon*, working through his "mediatorial shades," or is it the property of the living man, earned for him by his life and his affirmation of his myth? Who will offer to say where the *daimon* leaves off and the living man begins? But then, as Yeats said, this is "the only controversy which may never be decided." Actually, it is decided again and again in the *Collected Poems*, now this way, now that, but never ultimately except as the two antinomic decisions, held together as one in a state of antagonistic serenity, themselves form an ultimate decision, so that they become but opposite sides of the one reality.

Yeats was nothing less than brilliant in the ingenious variety of ways that he found for conducting this same internal/external dialogue in different places. Sometimes it is a dialogue between separate poems, as in the foregoing case of "Blood and the Moon" and "Dialogue of Self and Soul." But the same argument is also carried on within "Self and Soul," for "Soul" in that poem stands for the same truth as the speaker of "Blood and the Moon"—or as "The Soul" in "Vacillation." In "The Tower," on the other hand, the dialogue is between Yeats the boldly assertive poet and Yeats the scholarly footnote-writer: the former, with fine flourish and reckless daring, can "mock Plotinus' thought / And cry in Plato's teeth," and he can brandish in their faces his own faith that "Death and life were not / Till man made up the whole . . ." etc.; but in a chastened footnote the scholar takes it all back and exculpates the two great Masters by demonstrating that they too, as much as Yeats poet-and-scholar, were of two minds about transcendence and immanence—"When I wrote the lines about Plato and Plotinus I forgot that it is something in our own eyes that makes us see them as all transcendence. Has not Plotinus written . . ." etc. (*Poems*, p. 826). Whether or not a poor memory ("I forgot . . .") is sufficient excuse for maligning Plato and the "man in whom Plato lived again" I am not sure, but however that may be, it is clear that through the device of poem-and-note Yeats manages to continue, extend, and intensify the only controversy that it is worth taking (both) sides on.

It is in prose, however, that we find Yeats's consummate performance in surrounding the controversy by adopting at once all sides of it as his own. When he comes to try to sort out what I have called the ontological relationship between himself and certain visionary figures, Yeats employs a syntax that is extremely complex and adroit and that, by being simultaneously assertive and hesitant, contrives to say something and *at the same time* deny it; then, going further, Yeats implies—but still without going outside the syntactic strategy of the sentence, much less outside the essay—that he never said what he said, never denied what he had said, and is even now not denying either his statement or his denial. It is in his essay on

"Magic," when he talks of one of his many lower-case and Roman-type visions, that Yeats, as it seems to me, rises to his most brilliantly obscure and self-controverting heights. Of the particular vision, Yeats says, "It may be, as Blake said of one of his poems, that the author was in eternity." Thus, though he drops a "may be" into his sentence, Yeats begins clearly and boldly enough. From here on, however, for two terrifying sentences, it is every reader for himself, and Yeats, laying qualifications over hesitations until his mummy truth is bound and wound inside a dozen impenetrable phrases and clauses, shows the reader precious little mercy.

> In coming years I was to see and hear of many such visions, and though I was not to be convinced, though half-convinced once or twice, that they were old lives, in an ordinary sense of the word life, I was to learn that they have almost always some quite definite relation to dominant moods and moulding events in this life. They are, perhaps, in most cases, though the vision I have but just described was not, it seems, among the cases, symbolical histories of these moods and events, or rather symbolical shadows of the impulses that have made them, messages as it were out of the ancestral being of the questioner.
>
> (*E. & I.*, p. 36)

Very likely; but the reader who does not want to express an opinion one way or the other—or both ways—can surely be forgiven his reluctance. As to the manner of expression here, we will do best simply to applaud Yeats's performance, not try to analyze it: the syntax is peculiar, to say the least of it, but it no doubt functions as Yeats desires, so it had better be left at that. As to what the sentences say, I think I see what Yeats is getting at, particularly in the last two parenthetical phrases, and it is much the same as what he was to say some thirty-six years later about his traditional subject-matter, about "ancient myths in my dreams, brightly lit," and about the connection of both of these with the instinct of migratory birds. It is also much the same as what Jung meant when he declared (with a good deal more of certainty than Yeats was willing to hazard) that "the archetypes are simply the forms which the instincts assume" (*CW*, VIII, par. 339), for it is the old vexatious question of where and how archetypal figures are generated: are they from a spiritual mirror world, or from aeons of ancestral experience laid up in memory, or from pre-existent models (paradigms) suddenly recalled or revealed? Or are these all somehow one and the same explanation? Yeats sometimes seems to feel that they are, and because he was a poet he gets away with the game as he might not be able to do as a philosopher or a natural scientist. Here Yeats inclines to an answer that combines the first two possibilities, but even when thus inclined Yeats never abandoned the third possibility, and it is this fact which permits one to say that as Yeats's subject-matter was traditional (of the universal and ancient tradition), so the mode of his poetry, and particularly the mature poetry, was—I use the word in its Platonic sense—ideal.

"I am convinced that in two or three generations it will become generally known that the mechanical theory has no reality, that the natural and supernatural are knit together, that to escape a dangerous fanaticism we must study a new science . . ." (*E. & I.*, p. 518). While Yeats states his conviction that the natural and supernatural are knit together, he does not (as does Plato in the *Timaeus*) offer to describe the stitch responsible, but elsewhere he has some extraordinarily interesting and Platonizing things to say about it. In a passage in his journal, written in 1913, Yeats speculates about why messages from the supernatural that come through a medium are invariably shallow, corrupt, and "imperfect," and his conclusion is that these "objective messages" (as Yeats calls them to distinguish them from subjective messages that "come from the apparently free action of the mind") can never escape imperfection because they come through the senses. But Yeats, while he feels that "all objective messages, all that comes through hearing or sight—automatic script, for instance[4]—are without speculative power, or at any rate not equal to the mind's action at its best" (*Memoirs*, p. 267), nevertheless continued to believe that such revelations, though imperfect, remained all the same revelations of an existent supernatural world. "All that is objective," Yeats says of these imperfect revelations, "suggests a mirror life or at times a fragmentary consciousness as if

---

4. In *A Vision* there are descriptions both humorous and anguished of the problems caused by imperfect transmission of the message consequent upon its coming through the sensory medium of automatic script. This journal entry is dated July 1913, so Yeats had an explanation of the difficulties he was to encounter more than four years before he encountered them.

cast from a distance, or from a sphere which has no real likeness to this sphere." One explanation, then, of the supernatural thrusting into the natural world is the Heraclitean one of opposed and united, mortal/immortal mirror worlds with the one possessing strength where the other is weak—like consciousness and the unconscious—but being weak where the other is strong. As Yeats goes on to say of that mirror life, that other sphere, "The power of thought and expression is . . . sufficient for the practical, in which the spirits excel us often as they always do in knowledge of fact. It is only in speculation, wit, the highest choice of the mind, that they fail."[5] The vision which Yeats, in prose, treated to such an involuted description, as it arrived from the supernatural world through the highly imperfect sensory medium of MacGregor Mathers, his wife, and Yeats himself, must have carried with it much of the character of its mirror-life origins—which would no doubt account in part for the peculiarity we have noticed about Yeats's description of that vision: Yeats believed in a spiritual reality behind the vision, but he distrusted (as Plato would have done) the physical medium through which it came and therefore hesitated (especially as he was writing prose) to assert definitively what the nature of the spiritual reality might be.

There is also, Yeats implies of this same vision, in addition to the mirror-life aspect, an ancestral, instinctual origin for archetypal figures. In various places, both in prose and in poetry, Yeats broached the idea that memory (a collective memory, however, not an individual one) and instinct are somehow the same and that both of them enter into our dreams and visions in the guise of archetypal or mythic figures. That this idea is Jungian is obvious and will be dealt with later; that it occurs also in Plato—in the form of a myth, naturally—is perhaps less obvious. In the myth of the soul in the *Phaedrus*, memory is identified with Eros, who may occupy a place among the immortal gods but by mortal men is experienced as the most powerful of instincts: according to Socrates, memory of the Form of Beauty, contemplated in eternity, becomes the instinctual

---

5. *Memoirs*, p. 267. Kathleen Raine tells me that this is indeed true and that the "Daimones . . . must often feel the desperate frustration of trying to get any kind of sense or knowledge into this world." On the other hand, Miss Raine agrees with Yeats too when he says that the spirits are lacking in "wit," so that, as she puts it, "one does not expect anything better than rather silly practical jokes from the 'other world.'"

power that we know as Eros, impelling us to rise on the wings it nourishes to reattain the pure vision that we imperfectly recall when we see beauty in this world. When Yeats comes to this identification of memory with instinct, he for once sounds more like the psychologist than the philosopher—not like a behavioral psychologist, however, but an analytical psychologist, and the latter may not be so very different from the philosopher as Jung sometimes maintained (though the former certainly is). As Yeats saw the matter, what the race has achieved in a collective effort and left behind in the "memory of Nature" (*E. & I.*, p. 46) is inherited by each of us individually in the form of instinct. From one side it shows us the face of memory, from the other side the face of instinct. "I know now that revelation is from the self," Yeats begins one of his many statements of belief in these matters; but as one might guess, he does not, any more than Jung, equate the self with the ego, nor does he imagine that the self that is the source of revelation is something isolated and ephemeral. On the contrary, revelation, he says, is "from that age-long memoried self, that shapes the elaborate shell of the mollusc and the child in the womb,[6] that teaches the birds to make their nest; and . . . genius is a crisis that joins that buried self for certain moments to our trivial daily mind" (*Auto.*, p. 272). Here, with a Jungian fit upon him, Yeats diverges somewhat from Plato in that he would make anamnesis more a matter of family and race than of the individual; yet the divergence is not great, for, as Diotima tells Socrates, we seek immortality both through propagation of the family line and through individual creation or philosophizing. "This is the proposition on which I write," Yeats informed Dorothy Wellesley in a late letter: " 'There is now overwhelming evidence that man stands between two eternities, that of his family and that of his soul' " (*Letters*, pp. 910–11); or, widening the circle of memory and eternity from family to race, Yeats says in "Under Ben Bulben":

> Many times man lives and dies,
> Between his two eternities,
> That of race and that of soul. . . .

6. In Jung's terms, both psychologically and physiologically ontogeny recapitulates phylogeny.

Offered a choice between group immortality and individual immortality, between propagation and reincarnation, "between immortality in time (everlastingness) and eternal life,"[7] Yeats characteristically chooses . . . both.

In being so avid of immortality, however, Yeats brings himself back into line with the full teaching of Plato in the *Meno*, the *Phaedo*, the *Phaedrus* and the *Republic* (where the individual soul's immortality is bound up with a doctrine of reincarnation and anamnesis), the *Symposium* (where immortality is achieved through reproduction and continuation in time), and the *Timaeus* (where the distinction between eternal being—one kind of immortality—and temporal becoming—another kind of immortality—is set forth). It was not to Plato, however, but to William Blake (when Blake was in a very Platonic mood, nevertheless) that Yeats turned when he was concerned with the third possible explanation for the appearance of archetypal figures in visions. In his commentary on Blake's *Works*, Yeats quotes Blake—"Vision, or imagination, is a representation of what actually exists, really and unchangeably"—and then offers this bit of Platonizing paraphrase by way of explanation: "A vision is, that is to say, a perception of the eternal symbols, about which the world is formed . . ." (*Works of Blake*, I, 307). This is as much as to say that the figures glimpsed in vision are to be identified with the model or the paradigm—the intelligible Living Creature—after which the Demiourgos fashioned this visible universe in the *Timaeus*. What we perceive in vision, then, though it be as in a glass darkly, is nothing less than the Forms, and with this stroke Yeats demonstrates that for him, at least in certain moments, Jung's archetypes are the same creatures ("living creatures" in the *Timaeus* —*zōa*, which brings us back to Blake) as Plato's Forms.

It is particularly when he is contemplating the artist's role that Yeats insists on all possible explanations at once for his vision and creation. The artist works under the guidance of the *daimon*—thus the mirror-life of a spiritual world in his work; he creates out of the common passions of the "great forefathers"—thus the "age-long memoried self" in his work; and for his ultimate model he looks not to that which is passing but to the eternal Forms—thus the ideal and

---

7. Guthrie's phrase (*Hist. of Gr. Phil.*, IV, 388) in a brilliant and intensely relevant discussion of the *Symposium*.

"the eternal symbols" in his work. It is a delicate balancing act that the artist performs, poised between the natural and the supernatural, between all human experience as it comes down to him and the ideal image of man—the *eidos* of Man—that he would project in his poem or statue. He is poised at a point which is both end and beginning: in himself the human past concludes, but out of himself he creates a new, ideal image of humanity.

> Poet and sculptor, do the work,
> Nor let the modish painter shirk
> What his great forefathers did,
> Bring the soul of man to God,
> Make him fill the cradles right.

It may be that God creates man in his own image, but if so, Yeats suggests in these lines from "Under Ben Bulben," the artist, working out of the spiritual history of the race, first created that ideal image and presented it to God that he might see himself more clearly, know himself better, and so thereafter create more intensively. Yeats carries Romantic doctrine a step or two beyond Coleridge and makes the creative process—creation of poetry, of soul, and of world—virtually a circular affair: the poet's creation may be an imitation of God's, but God's creation must wait on the poet's for the cradles to be filled right. Which comes first it would be difficult to say—as difficult as saying what the soul is ("what manner of thing it is would be a long tale to tell, and most assuredly a god alone could tell it" [*Phaedrus*, 256b]), or as difficult as saying, once and for all, and with none of the "thoughs," "perhapses," "it seemses," and "as it weres" of Yeats's prose, what the origin of archetypal figures is. Nevertheless, it is clear that for Yeats creation is a human/divine and mortal/immortal affair that is both circular and continuous: if the first, then necessarily the second, and since both, then obviously Heraclitean, Platonic, and more generally ancient Greek, for among those people the circle and the sphere were known to be perfect and divine figures.

Yeats insists on the circularity of the creative process in the stanza that follows this one in "Ben Bulben," returning at first to antique sources and arriving at last at the artist's goal, to discover that they are, in essence, the same.

> Measurement began our might:
> Forms a stark Egyptian thought,
> Forms that gentler Phidias wrought.

These "Forms" of Egyptian thought and "Forms" of Phidian sculpture are of course not unrelated to the "Forms" of Platonic metaphysics, and the legend is that either Plato himself visited Egypt, and was there initiated into those mathematical mysteries that underlie his theory of Forms, or that he acquired the same learning from Pythagoreans whose Master, *that man*, had spent time with the Egyptians, picking up from them the divine mathematics and doctrines of the soul's immortality for which he became famous in Greece. In any case, Yeats imagined that every civilization, every work of art, every example of creative energy will find its origin in such prehistoric, preconscious, Eastern-Mideastern sources as these. "A famous philosopher," Yeats says, without revealing who that man might be, "believed that every civilisation began, no matter what its geographical origin, with Asia, certain men of science"—and these gentlemen Yeats names as little as he names the famous philosopher—believe "that all of us when still in the nursery were, if not African, exceedingly Asiatic." It is not altogether easy to know what Yeats has in mind with that marvellous phrase—"if not African, exceedingly Asiatic"—but I should imagine that the infant's Asiaticness was supposed to reside more in mental or psychic processes than in physical appearance. I am sure that Yeats was not thinking of Jung among his "men of science," but the notion he expresses here looks a little like Jungian ontogeny/phylogeny peeking out of humanity's youthful, almond-shaped, delicately slanted eyes. The ancient Irish, Yeats goes on to say—but now he posits an historic transmission rather than a psychic universality in phylogenetic development as the cause—were undoubtedly "if not African, exceedingly Asiatic": "Saint Patrick must have found in Ireland, for he was not its first missionary, men whose Christianity had come from Egypt, and retained characteristics of those older faiths that have become so important to our invention."[8]
What is interesting is that where Irish Christianity, every civilization,

---

8. *The King of the Great Clock Tower, Commentaries and Poems* (New York: Macmillan, 1935), pp. 45–46.

and all humanity find their beginning—in "Forms" and specifically in the *eidē* of their various natures—the artist finds his end, his goal, or his "purpose." Michelangelo, Yeats says, or any other artist capable of creating the human form divine, leaves proof:

> Proof that there's a purpose set
> Before the secret working mind:
> Profane perfection of mankind.

No wonder that in another poem Yeats calls for silence while Michelangelo works, for what he is creating, in "Long-legged Fly" as in "Ben Bulben," is nothing less than the model to which God will need to look so that he may get the cradles filled right: it is the *eidos* of humankind, an archetypal figure, Platonic Man, or, as Yeats calls him in "Long-legged Fly," "the first Adam." There is a subtle but very effective circularity about "Long-legged Fly," both in the movement of the poem and in the activities it describes. Each stanza comes around and back to the refrain:

> Like a long-legged fly upon the stream
> His (Her) mind moves upon silence.

This stream is certainly, in one sense, the Heraclitean stream where all flows, but here, in each case, it is likened to silence as the creative, contemplative mind circumscribes and surrounds the perpetual tumble and flow, stills it to silence, and draws it into a circle where beginning and end are one.

Moving between, on the one hand, Forms that are *a priori*, eternal, unchanging and, on the other hand, forms that are slowly developing, evolving, perfecting, forms that are created by the individual and by tradition, the Janus-faced artist of "Ben Bulben" illustrates a favorite notion of Yeats's: that "in the beginning of important things—in the beginning of love, in the beginning of the day, in the beginning of any work [also in the beginning of 'every civilisation': *E. & I*, p. 472]—there is a moment when we understand more perfectly than we understand again until all is finished" (*E. & I.*, p. 111). Yeats's concept, and it is a very important and useful one, is of a systemic unity realized (for example) in the process of a poem but existing before and beyond it: the *eidos* of the poem. It is as if the essence of the myth we are living were apparent to us only when purely potential or when purely realized, but not in between when we are living the realization or the myth. The perfect —and perfectly abstract—patterns of Being are clogged and confused by the events of their becoming, and are apparent again only in the end when becoming has been transformed into Being. The Demiourgos of the *Timaeus*, looking to a pre-existent, eternal paradigm, brings into existence a world that imitates, as intensely as it is capable of doing, its pre-existent model; but while that creation was more or less instantaneous, the psychological world in which we participate unfolds itself in time: the latter is the artist's immediate subject, the former his ultimate subject.

> Quattrocento put in paint
> On backgrounds for a God or Saint
> Gardens where a soul's at ease;
> Where everything that meets the eye,
> Flowers and grass and cloudless sky,
> Resemble forms that are or seem
> When sleepers wake and yet still dream,
> And when it's vanished still declare,
> With only bed and bedstead there,
> That heavens had opened.

Yeats is speaking Platonically, and in quasi-technical language, when he talks of "forms" glimpsed by the artist in vision and imitated by him in his work, just as nature imitates the paradigm on which the Demiourgos modelled his creation. The example of "bed and bedstead" is of course the one chosen by Plato (or Socrates) in the *Republic* to illustrate his notion of Forms and the unworthiness of the artist as the copier of a copy of a copy. Yeats's defense of the artist, directed against Plato but ironically derived from him—as if Yeats felt that Plato had nodded for a moment (596b) in the *Republic* —is that when the visionary and creative fit is upon him the artist can look to the Forms for his paradigm and model as much as ever the Demiourgos did.

Great artists, Yeats says (he offers Shakespeare, Dante, and Villon as examples), create out of their multiple, chaotic, and confused experience—or so the experience seems to the onlooker—something so intensely unified, something so far beyond all divisions and dichotomies of this life, that we can only think of them as being godlike creators of their own *mythoi*: "We gaze at such men in awe, because we gaze not at a work of art, but at the re-creation of the man through the art, the birth of a new species of man . . ." (*Auto.*, p. 273). I would suggest that there is no better definition and no clearer illustration of the Platonic *eidos*—here the Form of Man—and its relevance in artistic creation than this final phrase: "a new species of man." Beyond all the reincarnations of Pythagoras, beyond the flux of Heraclitus, beyond the cycles of Empedocles, there is, for the Yeatsian artist, always the Sphere of Parmenides, there is the archetype of what Yeats (like Jung) calls the self, there is the *eidos* of Artist and of Man—there is the *eidos* of *this* man if we allow Yeats to answer, as he wished to do, "yes" to Plotinus' question: "Is there an Ideal Archetype of Particular Beings?" I assume that the voice that once addressed the sleep-waking Yeats in the night also meant to say that there is an *eidos* of particular beings: "One night I heard a voice that said: 'The love of God for every human soul is infinite, for every human soul is unique; no other can satisfy the same need in God'" (*Myth.*, pp. 347-48). Going back in his late old age to his druidic St. Patrick and a Christ whom not all Christians would recognize (but I must say parenthetically that Jung, whether a Christian or not, would have recognized him as an old friend, for this is precisely what he had in mind when he spoke of a true *imitatio Christi*), Yeats writes: "I was born into this faith, have lived in it, and shall die in it; my Christ, a legitimate deduction from the Creed of St. Patrick as I think, is that Unity of Being Dante compared to a perfectly proportioned human body, Blake's 'Imagination,' what the Upanishads have named 'Self': nor is this unity distant and therefore intellectually understandable, but imminent, differing from man to man and age to age, taking upon itself pain and ugliness, 'eye of newt, and toe of frog'" (*E. & I.*, p. 518). I fear that Yeats's spelling, not for the first time, played him false here, for I am sure that what he meant to say of the self's unity was not that it is "imminent"—which is unfortunately a real word, and the error was therefore missed by editors, but it means nothing in this context—but that this unity is "immanent" (as opposed to "transcendent"). This unity, I think Yeats means, is not imminent, or about to happen soon, but is immanent, pervading the self's being: one element of the definition of self, and perhaps the most important element according to Yeats, is its unity. "Somebody has said that all sound philosophy is but biography," Yeats remarked (*Ex.*, p. 235), and whoever it was said that (if not Yeats himself, then perhaps Nietzsche) could have had the same effect by saying, "The self's unity is immanent," or by agreeing with Yeats when he agreed with Blake: "as Blake said, 'God only acts or is in existing beings or men'" (*Myth.*, p. 352). This is what Yeats's poetry is all about, both as statement and as enactment: it is about life's multiplicity, behind which, before and after which, there is, for the artist-as-Demiourgos, an "*eidotic*" unity on which he fixes his gaze and his desire. Thus one characteristic movement of Yeats's poems (admittedly not the only one), in imitation of the direction of his gaze, is from plurality to unity: behind many if not all of his poems is the monistic emotion and the vision of the idealist.

"Who can tell," Yeats asks himself in "A Bronze Head" as he contemplates a bust of the wasted Maud Gonne—"Human, superhuman, a bird's round eye, / Everything else withered and mummy-dead":

> who can tell
> Which of her forms has shown her substance right?

In spite of the fact that he rather juggles and transposes his Platonic terminology ("forms" and "substance"), Yeats's question is still the old one having to do with the self and its Form—perhaps in this specific case one should say the self, its Form, and its forms. That same nearly ideal beauty that was Maud Gonne's, Yeats imagines in "Broken Dreams," though tranformed and destroyed in the course of time, will after death be returned to its prenatal, its precarnate perfection:

> Vague memories, nothing but memories,
> But in the grave all, all, shall be renewed.

It is this supernatural beauty in natural body, the archetype realized, that Yeats says he meets in visionary moments of unconscious consciousness, those moments, as it were, when he enters the symbolic "holy city of Byzantium":

> always when I look death in the face,
> When I clamber to the heights of sleep,
> Or when I grow excited with wine,
> Suddenly I meet your face.

This, given the poet's visionary sleep-waking, dead-living state, must surely be the Face of all Maud Gonne's faces, the Form of her Beauty from which all the forms assumed by that Beauty in the course of time were no better than a falling away. It was Yeats's consolation—a consolation that he murmurs to himself in half a dozen poems—that though beauty be worn away and strength destroyed by the effects of time, yet both beauty and strength continue their existence, more perfect than ever they have been or could be in time, somewhere beyond the world, somewhere beyond time, in a "place beyond the heavens," as Socrates describes it in the *Phaedrus* (247c), that "none of our earthly poets has yet sung, and none shall sing worthily." It is only with Socrates' gratuitous slur on the poets that Yeats would disagree, not with his location of the Forms; or perhaps rather than disagreeing, Yeats would merely observe that there are poets and there are poets, and that it is only earthly poets who are incapable of the Beatific Vision, not poets like himself for whom vision is both the beginning and the end of the poetic act.

"All lives that has lived; / So much is certain," Yeats told himself in "Quarrel in Old Age," after a rancorous experience in which Maud Gonne's beauty had seemed, at least momentarily, to cease to exist; but as Yeats goes on to say, finding comfort in the saying, it only seemed so, for in reality her beauty continues to exist in a more perfect form, in another condition and place.

> Old sages were not deceived:
> Somewhere beyond the curtain
> Of distorting days
> Lives that lonely thing
> That shone before these eyes
> Targeted, trod like Spring.

The syntax of the last two lines is not particularly easy, but I think the following a reasonable paraphrase of the passage: somewhere beyond time there continues to exist, in an immutable state, that unique beauty which was Maud Gonne's and which, protected as by a shield[9] from injury, change, and corruption, the poet's eyes

---

9. Yeats to Maurice Wollman: "Your note on 'targetted' is quite correct" (*Letters*, p. 840). According to Hone, "Mr. Wollman had enquired whether 'targeted' ir Yeats' 'Quarrel in Old Age' meant 'protected as with a target, a round shield'" (p. 441n.).

looked upon (exactly as the souls look upon the Forms in the *Phaedrus*) before ever that beauty entered into a mortal body, into time, and into the cycles of nature. "All souls have a vehicle or body," Yeats remarked in "Anima Mundi," and he thereby escaped, as he hoped, "from the abstract schools"; and he continues a few lines later, "Beauty is indeed but bodily life in some ideal condition" (*Myth.*, p. 349). Beauty exists perfectly only beyond the world and only imperfectly within the world; but from beauties within the world one can ascend in creative imagination to the "ideal condition," to that Beauty that was before the world was made and that is now the natural-supernatural object of the visionary poet. "Heart's" retort to the speaker of "Young Man's Song" (who fears that his beloved will change into "a withered crone") is to precisely the same effect as Yeats's comforting words to himself about "that lonely thing" existing beyond time:

> Uplift those eyes and throw
> Those glances unafraid:
> She would as bravely show
> Did all the fabric fade;
> No withered crone I saw
> Before the world was made.

Again as in the *Phaedrus*, it is Eros that nourishes the soul's wings and delivers the lover now, as before the world was made, to his vision of the Form of Beauty itself. Presumably it was something like the *Timaeus* Demiourgos who, looking to that and other Forms, first brought beauty into the world and into time; but the perspective is reversed in "The Results of Thought," where it is the poet—acting, it is true, like a demiourgos to all those friends and acquaintances who have fallen away from their own *eidē* in time—who can restore them, in disregard of their pathetic present images, to pristine beauty and strength. It is a very considerable boast when the poet says of his power to restore what time has taken away:

> But I have straightened out
> Ruin, wreck and wrack;
> I toiled long years and at length
> Came to so deep a thought
> I can summon back
> All their wholesome strength.

A considerable boast, yet justified in the light of such poems as "In Memory of Major Robert Gregory," "A Prayer for My Daughter," and "Among School Children."

"Beauty," Yeats wrote to Æ, "is the end and law of poetry," (*Letters*, p. 343). It is his love of Beauty that draws the poet on and back, as it is love of Wisdom that draws the philosopher and love of the Good that draws any soul that has looked on the Good Itself and can summon up a memory of it, however thin and imperfect that memory be. Thus, Yeats declares that "literature should return to its old habit of describing desirable things" (*Ex.*, p. 92), and thirty-six years later he returned to the same point with renewed emphasis, for the literature produced in the intervening years was scarcely designed to please Yeats or to satisfy his ideal: "I still think that artists of all kinds should once again praise or represent great or happy people."[10] This Yeatsian ideal is hardly more fashionable now, three-fourths of the way through the twentieth century, than it was at the beginning of the century, or than it was halfway between the beginning and the present moment; but that in no way affects that ideal, which remains as far beyond this or any other century as beyond all faddish corruptions and fashionable changes. *If* beauty exists, Plato's Socrates argued, then it exists unchanged and unchanging forever; *if* beauty exists, Yeats argued, then poetry can have no other end and law but "to find the beauty in all things, philosophy, nature, passion . . ." (*Letters*, p. 343). Or, to adapt Newman's expression to a belief shared by Socrates, Plato, and Yeats alike, "*If* beauty exists, *since* beauty exists," it must be a Form in a world outside this world of becoming, and it must be the object, the end, and the very being of poetry. Yeats was still being Socratic/Platonic when he called this ideal of poetry "truth" ("I think with you," he wrote to his father, "that the poet seeks truth, not abstract truth, but a kind of vision of reality which satisfies the whole being" —*Letters*, p. 588), since Plato's Socrates, in his existence as in his

---

10. *Ex.*, p. 451. After reluctantly banishing all poets—specifically poets who imitate nature rather than the Forms—from his ideal commonwealth, Socrates says, "We can admit no poetry into our city save only hymns to the gods and the praises of good men" (607a). Yeats may not have been altogether consistent in his notion that poets should praise great men (the poem about "a man with a monkey and some sort of stringed instrument" that follows immediately upon his comment would almost certainly not have been admitted by Plato into his Republic), but then neither was Socrates altogether consistent: cf. the *Phaedrus*.

argument, maintained a unity of Forms. Yeats was also Socratic/Platonic when he changed the name of the ideal from beauty to truth to ecstasy, for "ecstasy," as he described it, "is from the contemplation of things vaster than the individual and imperfectly seen, perhaps, by all those that still live. . . . Yet is not ecstasy some fulfilment of the soul in itself, some slow or sudden expansion of it like an overflowing well? Is not this what is meant by beauty?" (*Auto.*, p. 471). This may never have been quite the sense of the word before, but we can hardly deny Yeats his meaning once he has so put it, in that way and with that intensity. "Beauty," "truth," "ecstasy," "the Good"—they are more or less interchangeable as words to describe the ultimate goal, since they are all examples of language stretched beyond its discursive limits, attempting to mediate between a mortal and an immortal realm, being the creation of this temporal world of change but with reference to an eternal world of Forms.

It should not be imagined, however, that Yeats's poetry is, in any pejorative sense, "ethereal," as if, having nothing to do with the contamination of this mortal world, it were floating, disembodied, in a thin spiritual air of Forms too meagre to sustain gross corporeal life. Had that been the case, Yeats would never have been so delighted by the extract of monkey glands[11] given him in the Steinach operation, nor would he have been so happy to think of himself as a "wild, old wicked man" with his ambiguous "stout stick under his hand" who could teach "all those warty lads" down by the seashore a few tricks of the dark if he were so inclined. Yeats, as I have said, because he was an artist and therefore chose to follow the path of the serpent, was neither saint nor sage, those men who "renounce experience itself" to follow "the straight line" and aim their "arrow at the centre of the sun" (*Myth.*, p. 340), and he had nothing about him of the Arnoldian Shelley, a "beautiful and ineffectual angel, beating in the void his luminous wings in vain."[12] One could fairly adapt to Yeats himself what he wrote about Donne (and Yeats no doubt intended such a personal application, since he wrote the

---

11. If that is what it was: there are various surgical procedures—ranging from implantation of foreign glands to injection of glandular extracts to simple ligature of the *vas deferens*—that go under the name of the "Steinach Operation."

12. From the final paragraph of the essay entitled "Byron," *Essays in Criticism*, Second Series.

passage not in an essay on the "Metaphysical Poets," or any other place like that, but in *The Trembling of the Veil*—i.e., one of his volumes of autobiography): "Donne could be as metaphysical as he pleased, and yet never seemed unhuman and hysterical as Shelley often does, because he could be as physical as he pleased . . ." (*Auto.*, p. 326). One cannot say how it is with angels, but there is unquestionably many a saint who seems hysterical and there is the occasional sage (of Parmenidean persuasion) who seems unhuman on exactly these ground. This, however, is the beauty and the paradox of the theory of Forms: it is a metaphysical system designed to rescue the physical world from the total contempt of the saint and the sage. The express intention of the research work and the theorizing of Plato's Academy was "to save the phenomena" (σῴζειν τὰ φαινόμενα) by developing hypotheses that could comprehend and account for them all. "There is," as W. K. C. Guthrie puts it, "historical truth in the dictum that the object of the doctrine of Forms was not to abolish the sensible world but to save it" (*Hist. of Gr. Phil.*, IV, 496, n. 4). Parmenides (and after him some of the Neoplatonists—who, however, had not his excuse as a great, primitive original) was all too ready to abandon the phenomena, all too happy to reject the world of the senses and to deny the body altogether with a perfectly "unhuman," if not hysterical, rigor. Not so Plato, and even more not so Yeats. Nevertheless, while their desire was to save the phenomena, what Plato discovered and Yeats rediscovered, was that the only way to secure the physical world was with a metaphysical doctrine: the only way to give reality and value to a world in time, where all "is begotten, born, and dies," is by postulating a world of eternity and of Forms where nothing is begotten, nothing is born, and nothing dies.

In the *Republic* (479-480), Socrates distinguishes between those he chooses to call *philodoxous*—"lovers of opinion" who admire all the beautiful colors and sounds of the natural world but are incapable of imagining the Form of Beauty itself—and those he calls *philosophous* —true "lovers of wisdom" who, at least at the beginning of their ascent, admire the world's beauties no less than do the *philodoxous*, but who also know that all "beautiful sounds, colors, and the like" are only beautiful because of their participation in, or imitation of, or relationship to the Form of Beauty itself. Yeats could hardly have been capable of such ingratitude or rudeness as to call Lady Gregory and Synge *philodoxous* while reserving for himself the name of *philosophos*, but that is what the distinction that he draws in "A People's Theatre" between his own art and their art comes to, all the same. In the drama of Lady Gregory and Synge, Yeats says, there is "much observation and a speech founded upon that of real life" (*Ex.*, p. 253), but as for himself, "I . . . have never observed anything, or listened with an attentive ear, but value all I have seen or heard because of the emotions they call up or because of something they remind me of that exists, as I believe, beyond the world" (*Ex.*, p. 254). Whether or not Socrates and Plato would have approved of Yeats's enthusiasm for calling up emotions (one reason Socrates banishes poets is his own admitted susceptibility to their emotional appeal), they would certainly have had to grant Yeats the name of *philosophos* for valuing sounds, colors, and the like of this world only "because of something they remind me of that exists . . . beyond the world." "Anamnesis" Plato called it. Yeats's drama and his poetry are ritual enactments of anamnesis, a rhythmic reminder of that which was before the world was made, a recall of the eternal from harmonic patterns observed in the temporal, a movement from multiplicity to unity and from chaos to cosmos. Yeats adopted a more Jungian terminology to make the same Platonic point when (in an essay dated 1901—i.e., eighteen years before Jung ever used the word "archetype" in writing) he quoted Goethe as saying, "Art is art, because it is not nature!" and then offered his own Platonic-Blakean-Jungian gloss on Goethe's *mot*: "It brings us near to the archetypal ideas themselves, and away from nature, which is but their looking-glass" (*E. & I.*, p. 101-02). Whether Yeats places more emphasis on the adjective "archetypal" than on the noun "idea" (thus orienting himself toward Jung's notion of a "deposit" left by centuries of psychic life) or places more emphasis on the noun "idea" than on the adjective "archetypal" (thus orienting himself toward Plato's paradigmatic Forms) is not easy to determine—nor is it terribly important to decide. Here, as so often, Yeats would no doubt prefer it both ways—as I think Blake would also—because of the poise that the artist as visionary and creator must maintain.

It is a very delicate balance that Yeats, under the banner of "symbolism," would strike—and in his best poems does strike—between a natural world of becoming and a supernatural world of Being, between archetypes as a deposit and archetypes as a paradigm. In "The Symbolism of Poetry," Yeats calls for "a casting out of descriptions of nature for the sake of nature" (*E. & I.*, p. 163), just as in the *Republic* and the *Laws* Plato insists that we ought not cultivate any art that imitates life or nature but only one "that bears a resemblance to its model, beauty" (*Laws*, 668b). The Yeatsian artist, instead of holding a looking-glass up to nature—which is foolishness redoubled, since nature is itself a looking-glass—"would seek out those wavering, meditative, organic rhythms, which are the embodiment of the imagination, that neither desires nor hates, because it has done with time, and only wishes to gaze upon some reality, some beauty" (*E. & I.*, p. 163). Yeats later abandoned the languorous, world-weary pose and periods of this early prose style ("The Symbolism of Poetry" is dated 1900), but he never turned away from the ideas of poetry that he expresses here; on the contrary, he deepened them, extended them, and set about sharpening their expression. In 1916, sounding like Socrates in the *Republic* or the Athenian Stranger in the *Laws*, Yeats wrote to his father that he thought the greatest art not imitative in a vulgar sense—i.e., it is not a mere imitation of nature or of the spectacle of life; but he was willing to allow that art to be imitative in a much subtler, more Pythagorean and Platonic way: it might be said to imitate (as time does eternity) "an intensity of pattern that we have never seen with our eyes" (*Letters*, p. 607)—or as Yeats would, I think, be willing to say, altering his expression to bring it into line with the *Phaedrus* doctrine of Forms, "an intensity of pattern that we have never seen with our eyes" in *this* life. It is through a formal meticulousness, Yeats insisted, that the artist must demonstrate his fidelity to the Forms, and the worst heresy would be for the artist "to deny the importance of form, in all its kinds, for although you can expound an opinion, or describe a thing, when your words are not quite well chosen, you cannot give a body to something that moves beyond the senses, unless your words are as subtle, as complex, as full of mysterious life, as the body of a flower or a woman" (*E. & I.*, pp. 163-64). Taking a step back from the creative process, we might say that the *poet* imitates nature, creating forms as full of mysterious life as those created by/in nature, but the *poem* must not. As Yeats says in another essay, the "little ritual" of verse resembles the "great ritual of Nature" in that both are "copied from the eternal model" (*E. & I.*, p. 202). Contemporary artists, however, are so stupid or so perverse (Yeats thought) that they cannot see these truths that define and justify their very existence as artists; and the worst of the modern lot—worse even than statesmen and journalists and the base-born *polloi*, which is to say they are very bad indeed, outrageously, unspeakably bad—are performing artists, actors who think their slovenly speaking of verse is more "natural" than the proper and beautiful verse-reading or verse-speaking of Homer, Yeats, and Florence Farr. Those actors may, of course, be right in a sense, but the naturalness or likeness to life of their performance is in Yeats's eyes no excuse, rather a self-condemnation, since all they do by imitating human nature and the drivel that passes for social conversation is to destroy the exact and delicate contours of the artist's carefully chosen language—"as full of mysterious life, as the body of a flower or a woman"—and mangle those rhythms that put him in touch not with the natural world but with a supernatural one, unearthly and esoteric, Orphic and Pythagorean.

> But actors lacking music
> Do most excite my spleen,
> They say it is more human
> To shuffle, grunt and groan,
> Not knowing what unearthly stuff
> Rounds a mighty scene.

This gleefully splenetic poem (I would say the glee rather outweighs the spleen) was written twenty years after Yeats had come to the conclusion that "the common condition of life is hatred" and had resolved to drive all hatred hence that he might recover radical innocence. Clearly, however, some things are unforgivable—the lies of the statesman and the journalist; the coupling of Folly and Elegance; most of all the actor's insolent and idiotic annihilation of beauty—and not to hate them would be more soul-destroying, more unfaithful to the *eidos* of Beauty, than hatred itself.

One might suppose that Yeats, feeling as he did about actors and the stage, would have agreed with Henry James's rueful comment after his own unhappy encounter with the theatre ("You can't make a sow's ear out of a silk-purse"), and like James would have given it up as a bad show ("The thing fills me with horror for the abysmal vulgarity and brutality of the theatre and its regular public"[13]) to turn back to his own proper art. But Yeats apparently felt that the

13. James's remarks are from a letter to his brother William dated Jan. 9th, 1895.

stakes were too high for him simply to turn away. He seems to have believed that if he could reduce the actors to immobility while introducing them to the correct way of speaking verse (that is, his own way of speaking verse in a high-pitched, incantational monotone: "eccentric" some have called it, but Yeats thought it "centric" and entirely traditional—just like Homer, he said[14])—if he could do all this, working with such recalcitrant and objectionable types as actors, then, on the principle that the greatness of a work is partly determined by and directly proportionate to the greatness of the difficulty overcome (like the Demiourgos outdoing himself because of the might of *Ananke*—Necessity—in the *Timaeus*), then he might expect to create something very, very great. The poet of tragic drama, as Yeats tells us in his essay on "The Tragic Theatre," is attempting the most and may therefore hope to accomplish the most, but his art must be supernatural rather than natural—or better yet, it should be a product of that spiritual state where the natural and the supernatural meet in conscious unconsciousness to reveal those mummy truths that consciousness alone could never perceive but that, in an unconscious state, would remain inchoate, without that necessary focus that only consciousness can bring. It is "in mainly tragic art," Yeats says, that "one distinguishes devices to exclude or lessen character, to diminish the power of that daily mood, to cheat or blind its too clear perception." This, as I have

---

14. The story in Hone (p. 321) is lovely; anyone who can read it and still not recognize that Yeats had great humor (as apparently some have done) is to be pitied: "On one occasion a woman, whom afterwards he discovered to be an expert in voice production, challenged his method of reciting verse. 'Will you kindly tell me, Mr. Yeats, why you read your poetry in that manner?' 'I read my poetry as all the great poets from Homer down have read their poetry,' was the reply. 'Will Mr. Yeats give me his authority for saying that Homer read his poetry in that manner?' 'The only authority I can give you is the authority that a Scotsman gave when he claimed Shakespeare for his own country, "The ability of the man justifies the assumption".'" On the same "authority" Yeats claimed Blake for Ireland.

Yeats may not, after all, have been far from the mark when he claimed that his verse-speaking was Homeric. W. B. Stanford, in a fascinating and beautiful book called *The Sound of Greek* (Berkeley: University of California Press, 1967), gives indications of how classical Greek sounded, and in a phonograph record accompanying the book he illustrates his ideas with readings from (among others) Homer. Except that Yeats was notoriously tone-deaf, while Stanford's reading is most distinctive for its variations in pitch and tone (somewhere between song and speech), there *is* an intriguing similarity between Stanford's rendition of Homer and Yeats's rendition of Yeats (as preserved on records). Stanford, incidentally, throws in the first line of "Innisfree" as a kind of lagniappe for Yeatsians.

already pointed out, is analogous to what Jung called "active imagination," a technique for diminishing the mundane clarity of consciousness[15]; tragic art, according to Yeats, has built-in "devices" for accomplishing the same end, for retaining the visionary glory that dies in the common light of day, and he goes on to suggest what some of those devices are: "If the real world is not altogether rejected, it is but touched here and there, and into the places we have left empty we summon rhythm, balance, pattern, images that remind us of vast passions, the vagueness of past times, all the chimeras that haunt the edge of trance; and if we are painters, we shall express personal emotion through ideal form, a symbolism handled by the generations, a mask from whose eyes the disembodied looks . . ." (*E. & I.*, p. 243). This is the mode and the effect not only of symbolic painting and tragic art but is the typical movement and manner of Yeats's finest poems as well. It is also akin to the philosophic progress and the movement of several of the greatest of Plato's dialogues: from the "real world" of bodies, flux, and multiple movement, by way of a dialectical ascent, to the "really real" world of the "disembodied," "ideal form," unity and stasis which is characteristically presented as *mythos*, a sort of "symbolism handled by the generations" (cf. the "eschatological" myths at the end of *Gorgias*, *Phaedo*, and *Republic*).

Sixty-one poems in *The Collected Poems of W. B. Yeats* begin with the word "I."[16] In another forty-one poems the same pronoun

---

15. "A great work of art is like a dream; for all its apparent obviousness it does not explain itself and is always ambiguous." So Jung says, adopting a simile that was one of Yeats's favorites (cf. "Circus Animals' Desertion"). The artist, Jung goes on, "has plunged into the healing and redeeming depths of the collective psyche, where man is not lost in the isolation of consciousness and its errors and sufferings, but where all men are caught in a common rhythm which allows the individual to communicate his feelings and strivings to mankind as a whole" (*CW*, XV, par. 161). In the last paragraph of the essay quoted above, Yeats says very much the same thing, though in his expression one feels the presence of the poet rather than the psychologist: "Tragic art, passionate art, the drowner of dykes, the confounder of understanding, moves us by setting us to reverie, by alluring us almost to the intensity of trance. The persons upon the stage, let us say, greaten till they are humanity itself. We feel our minds expand convulsively or spread out slowly like some moon-brightened image-crowded sea" (*E. & I.*, p. 245).

16. Or sixty-two (the American edition includes the first seventeen lines of "The Hero, the Girl, and the Fool," beginning "I rage at my own image in the glass"—in the English edition the poem is called "The Fool by the Roadside"), or sixty-five (the Allt/Alspach *Variorum Edition* includes, in addition to "The Hero, the Girl, and the

occurs in the first line, though not as the first word (e.g., "What shall I do with this absurdity," the first line of "The Tower").[17] In itself this fact is insignificant and unimportant, but it serves as an index to a pervasive mode in the poetry that is of the first importance: a mode that transforms the personal and "egoistic" into the impersonal, mythic, and "eidotic." The typical psychological and philosophical progress of Yeats's poems is from *ego* to *eidos*, proceeding (like Plato's dialogues and like the lover of *Phaedo* and *Phaedrus*) by way of *logos* and *mythos*, and passing from this temporal world about us to the eternal world of the work of art through exercise of memory and *anamnesis*. It is a very long way—but Yeats does not neglect or fail a single step—from "I have met them at close of day" to "A terrible beauty is born"; a long way (though circular) from "I sought a theme and sought for it in vain" to "In the foul rag-and-bone shop of the heart"; a long way from "I have heard that hysterical women say" to "Their ancient, glittering eyes, are gay"; a long way—perhaps the longest of all—from "I walk through the long schoolroom questioning" to "How can we know the dancer from the dance?"; and it is even a good distance (though the poem is only six lines long and otherwise quite different from the other four poems) from "I, the poet William Yeats" to "When all is ruin once again." All these poems (except the last) begin with the "real world" of agitation and divided aims, multiplicity, social trivia, and hysterical women; their language and rhythms are at the outset casual, conversational, with little sense of grandeur about them, "polite meaningless words." The context in which "I" goes about his activities is mundane and quotidian, and those activities are themselves bound

---

Fool," three poems beginning with "I" included in neither the American nor the British standard editions).

The Parrish/Painter *Concordance* omits "I" in its listing, but in his preface Parrish gives the number of occurrences of all words omitted: "I" occurs 2132 times (plus 132 times in contracted forms)—exceeded only by "the" (8436), "of" (3320), "a" (2841), and "that" (2357). I have access to no computer and so have no intention of trying to determine at what stage in each of the poems the 2132 "I's" occur. The assumption of the present argument is that "I" would occur much more frequently at the beginning than at the end of poems—especially poems of Yeats's maturity.

17. By way of contrast, in only ten poems does the final line begin with "I"; in only eight poems is the final word "me," "I," or "mine'; and in twenty-one poems "I'" occurs in the final line but neither as the first word nor as the last. Moreover, there is a noticeable decrease in the number of times "I" occurs in the last lines of Yeats's mature poetry, but "I" continues its presence as the first word or in first lines very regularly throughout the mature poetry.

to time by the verb tenses that describe them ("I have met," "I sought," "I have heard," "I walk"). The final lines of these same poems, on the other hand, state timeless truths (in the one instance by way of a rhetorical question) of quite another world than the shallow and ephemeral one in which they began. "A terrible beauty is born"—and shall not die now that the poet has commemorated it; "the foul rag-and-bone shop of the heart" is where *all* the ladders start *always*—in the future, now, and as long ago as the ascent Diotima describes in the *Symposium*; the "ancient, glittering eyes" of the Chinamen are not in the temporal world of the hysterical women but are instead of the timeless world of art, creations of the poet's imagination ("I delight to imagine them seated there") and therefore as much in a state of happy foreverness as the imagined melodies of Keats's urn; and questioning rather than stating the unity of dancer and dance merely emphasizes the condition of timeless presentness in which that Unity of Being or unity of the self is "immanent" (here the correct spelling is crucial, for the unity is specifically *not* to be conceived of as "imminent"). And the rhythms, from being casual and conversational at the outset, have become, very gradually and step by indiscernible step, ritualistic and incantational, demanding to be half-sung to the accompaniment of a psaltery or chanted, as it were in ectasy and rapture. Yeats's rhythms allure us, as readers, "almost to the intensity of trance," to that "moment when we are both asleep and awake, which is the one moment of creation," and there, "plunged into the healing and redeeming depths of the collective psyche" (as Jung puts it), "where all men are caught in a common rhythm," the reader joins the poet, both of them "self-possessed in self-surrender" (*E. & I.*, p. 524; cf. the quasi-mystical transport that reading his own poetry could occasionally induce in Yeats: *Myth.*, p. 364 and "Vacillation," section IV).

From "*ego*" to "*eidos*," from "I" to "terrible beauty": even a poem as entirely concerned with public political events as "Easter 1916" is given depth and resonance, and it acquires a significance far beyond local politics and Irish history, by the implicit presence of Yeats's philosophic thought and its progress up the Platonic ladder. What begins as "casual comedy" and informal verse movement (where repetition implies trivial pointlessness) opens out in the middle sections into a much richer verse movement, incantatory but still remarkably flexible (where repetition implies ritual mysteries—

"To murmur name upon name, / As a mother names her child / When sleep at last has come / On limbs that had run wild"), and finally to pure chant at the end, the whole poem comprising a speculation on the nature of ultimate reality and on the place that human action occupies in that reality. The poem offers no answers to the questions that it raises but instead is itself the answer: it speculates but does not call to action, it uses language to explore reality rather than language to incite to political gesture. The poem embraces contradictory responses, yet makes them in a sense a single response by presenting them simultaneously and in the same words. With a deliberately ambiguous and paradoxical phrasing, Yeats manages to have it both ways throughout the poem.

> We know their dream; enough
> To know they dreamed and are dead;
> And what if excess of love
> Bewildered them till they died?
> I write it out in a verse. . . .

There is a careful ambiguity about "enough," balanced syntactically alone at the end of the line, qualifying both our knowledge of "their dream" (we know all we need to know about that, foolish and/or heroic as it was) and our more certain knowledge of their death: "dead" at the end of the next line admits no enjambment—there is no running on, as there is with "enough," over the line or beyond death. Their death is a final reality, as their dream is not, and yet "A terrible beauty is born" out of that death: the paradox can be turned over and over but it will never be resolved. The following two lines likewise demand to be read in opposed senses: "what if . . ."—"*so what* if their great love brought them death? Is not death a small price to pay for everlasting glory? They may be dead but are heroes forever, and what finer fate could they desire?" *Or*, the lines could—must—be taken to mean, "And what if they were merely, foolishly bewildered and deluded into dying for nothing? What do we say then? Then the whole affair becomes too terrible to contemplate, and they are dead, irretrievably dead, in a death utterly futile and vain." Yeats sometimes worried that he was incapable of acting because he was too much given to analyzing the motives of action. In one such instance (an imbroglio involving Yeats, Edmund Gosse, Lady Gregory, and Robert Gregory in which Yeats felt himself honor-bound to write Gosse an indignant letter but reason-bound to analyze his motives and analyze his analysis—until, though at least three letters were written, none was ever sent), Yeats remarked to himself in his journal, "Then there is this difficulty, that words are with me a means of investigation, rather than a means of action" (*Memoirs*, p. 254). No better comment could be made on "Easter 1916." The real ingenuity of Yeats's investigation through words is that in exploring diverse motives for diverse actions, Yeats manages to embody all those actions, and to justify and celebrate their contradictory motives, yet manages also to make them a single, complex response by the unity of the poem. "Easter 1916" is as much ontological as it is political, and in a sense it even resolves those antinomies in the mysterious ritual of sound that concludes the poem.

Like "Easter 1916," "The Circus Animals' Desertion" begins with "I," but it concludes, after returning on itself and after affirming the commonest passions and the most vulgar emotions of mankind, not with "ego" but with the complexly composed personality of self—that same self, now fully realized in and as the poem, for which Yeats argued an immanent unity. The "I" of the poem "greatens," and very much by the "devices" of Yeats's tragic art, until, as Yeats says of "persons upon the stage," it is "humanity itself." When "I" lies down in the penultimate line of the poem, he is lying down with "humanity itself," having been in effect transformed into that symbolic living creature by the process of the poem and by the various myths explored along the poem's way. "Elaborate modern psychology sounds egotistical," Yeats writes in "The Trembling of the Veil," "when it speaks in the first person, but not those simple emotions which resemble the more, the more powerful they are, everybody's emotion, and I was soon to write many poems where an always personal emotion was woven into a general pattern of myth and symbol" (*Auto.*, p. 151). When Jung said that the archetypes are self-portraits of the instincts, he had in mind these same simple emotions that are so like "everybody's emotion" that they are, for the individual, inescapable and immensely powerful. Unquestionably the three "heart-mysteries" or passions transformed into serene art-dreams in the three central stanzas are emotions of that sort, instincts that force themselves on us as powerful emotions and that can be projected, in "a general pattern of myth and symbol," as archetypal figures in the work of art. "That sea-rider Oisin," the Countess Cathleen, the Fool, the Blind Man, and Cuchulain—they are all images of simple emotions, "emblems" signifying in the first instance common human passions, but transformed in the last instance into figures in a work of art, woven into the tapestry of a dream (*The Wanderings of Oisin, The Countess Cathleen, On Baile's Strand*) so successfully that "it was the dream itself enchanted me":

> Players and painted stage took all my love,
> And not those things that they were emblems of.

In the final stanza, professing to have a ladder no longer—claiming, that is, that he is no longer capable of transforming personal emotion into something emblematic, symbolic, mythic—the poet comes down off his stilts (the stilts of section I, the stilts of "High Talk," and the stilts of Yeats's introduction to the *Oxford Book of Modern Verse*[18]) to "lie down where all the ladders start, / In the foul rag-and-bone shop of the heart." In the course of proclaiming his ladder gone, however, Yeats puts together a new ladder that reaches higher than any of those whose loss he laments. Structurally, "The Circus Animals' Desertion" is triadic (three sections, three stages in the argument, three stanzas in the central section, three works recalled, three islands or "allegorical dreams," etc.); thematically, it is duadic (the antinomic relation between "heart-mysteries" and "the dream," between life and art, between the chaos of personal emotion and the cosmos of "those masterful images"); philosophically, however, and psychologically, the poem is monadic—all of a piece

---

18. "Then in 1900 everybody got down off his stilts; henceforth nobody drank absinthe with his black coffee; nobody went mad; nobody committed suicide; nobody joined the Catholic church; or if they did I have forgotten" (*Oxford Book of Modern Verse*, p. xi). Yeats's ability to forget things—from languages and names and the fact of immanence in Plato and Plotinus to instances of suicide, madness, and religious conversion—was more a strength than a weakness by virtue of the strategic uses to which he put it. His capacity for forgetting became almost a faculty in itself—the opposite counterpart, as it were, of the faculty of memory. Of the Heraclitean relationship that obtains up and down the hierarchy of beings, Yeats wrote to Joseph Hone, "What I do not see but may see or have seen, is perceived by another being. In other words is part of the fabric of another being. I remember what he forgets, he remembers what I forget" (*Letters*, p. 728). That puts rather a heavy burden of remembering on Yeats's twin-opposite; but Yeats's memory was no doubt more for timeless things—that is to say, it was *anamnesis*. I have expanded on this subject in "W. B. Yeats's Daimonic Memory," *Sewanee Review*, LXXXV (1977), 583-603.

and yearning for the monistic reality of Parmenides. The poem realizes a unity that is the unity of Beulah or Byzantium, the unity of heart and dream, of waking and sleeping, of consciousness and the unconscious—the unity of the self and of the artifact—and it makes that unity fully immanent.

"Lapis Lazuli," too, moves from the multiplicity and confusion of our hysterical world, through the archetypal, mythic figures of tragic art, to the unity of the poet's creative imagination at the end where "accomplished fingers" draw "mournful melodies" from the tragic scene below to bring delight to the ancient eyes of the three imagined Chinamen. Those Chinamen, as they exist in the last seven lines of the poem, as I have already remarked, are entirely imagined, for they are not even on the lapis lazuli carving that gives the poem its title. The poem, which is one of Yeats's supreme achievements, leaves little to be said about it. (The perfect finish of the poem—it is all *there* and achieved—leaves nothing for the critic to complete. This is comparable to the way the poem seems to have come to Yeats, more immediately and more fully finished in first draft than most of his poems: "the manuscript has the 'feel' of a poem that grew naturally and rapidly," according to Jon Stallworthy.[19]) What the poem desires, really, is the kind of reading that can follow faithfully from those hysterical women to the three Chinamen, from chatter to incantation, from the modern drawing room to "the little half-way house" where the poet's imagination creates with greatest intensity because freed of any necessity to copy nature. The contours of the final lines are supernatural, and the melodies picked out by Chinese fingers, existing only in this poem and Yeats's imagination, have much in common with the Music of the Spheres and with the notes that Pythagoras "fingered upon a fiddle-stick or strings," the same that "a star sang and careless Muses heard." "Lapis Lazuli" has a little to do with the modern world and a little with the cycles of civilization; it has rather more to do with Shakespeare's tragic drama, with Callimachus' statuary, and with the lapis lazuli carving; but it has most to do with itself, with a certain vision of art that it both states and embodies (though the stuff of art be tragic, art is itself always gay by reason of the energy that goes into creativity), and with the personality of the

---

19. *Vision and Revision in Yeats's "Last Poems"* (Oxford: Clarendon Press, 1969), p. 45.

artist, projected as myth in the course of the poem. When Yeats remarked (as quoted earlier) that "if we are painters, we shall express personal emotion through ideal form," he was thinking less of the practice of the generality of modern painters than of the ideal painter of his own conception. In painting such as that of Augustus John, according to the sometime subject of John's portraiture, "man is studied as an individual fact, and not as that energy which seems measureless. . . . It is a powerful but prosaic art, celebrating the 'fall into division' not the 'resurrection into unity' " (*Auto.*, p. 502). In Yeats's terminology, John painted character rather than personality. Whatever one may think of this as an estimate of John's painting (it seems to me really quite generous in view of some of John's portraits of Yeats), it is unquestionably most relevant, by way of inversion, as a description of Yeats's own art, which very often begins with the "individual fact" and the "fall into division" but dramatizes and so celebrates the "resurrection into unity." In "Lapis Lazuli" the seemingly measureless energy that Yeats extolls is present in a double sense, for while it accomplishes the "resurrection into unity" it is also the poem's subject: it exhibits the creative energy—and the gaiety of the artist—that it is about.

"I walk through the long schoolroom questioning": "Among School Children" commences, in the present tense, with the "individual fact," as Yeats calls it, presented in the slightly singsong rhythm of the children's activities, all performed "in the best modern way." Stanza II also begins with "ego," but there is already a greatening of the "I," not yet to the level of humanity, but to the level of an "ego" that includes both past and present in a dream of a mythic figure, real in the poet's past and real still, but in a different way, in his present consciousness: "I dream of a Ledaean body, bent / Above a sinking fire, a tale that she / Told. . . ." By the end of the stanza, the past, revivified in the speaker's consciousness, becomes an integral part of the present and confers upon the present, by the act of memory, a tremendous resonance of meaning that otherwise the present can never bear ("Plato symbolized by the word 'memory' a relation to the timeless"). In stanza III, the "I"—still poised between past and present, maintaining that precarious balance that we call "memory" (a balance that will eventually establish in the poem a relation to the timeless), and dreaming a dream of the unconscious but doing it while remaining conscious of the present—recedes to the second line, as if (in Jung's terminology) "ego" were gradually giving way, and ceding ontological and psychological priority to "self" as an entity superior to "ego." ("The ego is only the subject of my consciousness, while the self is the subject of my total psyche"—*CW*, VI, par. 706; by "self," Jung says, "I understand a psychic totality and at the same time a centre, neither of which coincides with the ego but includes it, just as a larger circle encloses a smaller one"—*CW*, IX, pt. 1, par. 248.) In stanza IV, as consciousness merges more fully with the unconscious to produce the higher third, the "I" is pushed back to the fifth line—and "I" never occurs again in the remaining four stanzas. It is in the sixth stanza, when "ego" has been abandoned for a stanza and a half in favor of a contemplative and "greatening" self—the poet as all men—that Yeats turns directly to some of the mummy truths that gave depth and coherence to his thought and poetry, and though for a moment he mocks those great discoveries of his predecessors and scorns their systems because their propounders withered, as men, into mere scarecrows, the truth is that the poetics of this very poem—indeed of this very stanza—are poetics garnered by Yeats from the mummy wheat of Pythagoras' metempsychosis and his doctrine of cosmic harmonies and from the mummy wheat of Plato's two-world metaphysics and his doctrine of Forms. Ironically, having interred the *men* in stanza VI, Yeats resurrects their composite *doctrine* in stanzas VII and VIII to turn his poem (as Thomas Parkinson has convincingly demonstrated) from an anticipated pessimistic conclusion to the actual conclusion which is exalted and ecstatic.

Through an intensity of memory, reverie, and mythifying imagination in the central stanzas, Yeats transforms the commonplace "real world" of the first stanza into the Platonic "really real" world of the final stanza. The egoistic focus of the first stanzas is soon left behind, and thereafter the eid*e*tic capacity of stanzas III and IV becomes (if I may again avail myself of a word created some pages back) an eid*o*tic vision in stanzas VII and VIII. That is, the speaker's ability (as the dictionary defines "eidetic") to produce at will "visual images having almost photographic accuracy":

> And thereupon my heart is driven wild:
> She stands before me as a living child.
>
> IV
>
> Her present image floats into the mind . . .

that ability is replaced in stanzas VII and VIII by a vision, no longer controlled by conscious will and altogether independent of memory, that is not a vision of the changing images and changing forms to which the living (and dying) Maud Gonne has been subjected but a vision of the Form of her forms and a supreme vision of the unity of the paradigm that holds, in oneness and at rest, all the multiplicity and flux of the created world. From egoistic present to eidetic past-in-present to eidotic timelessness, from present awareness to memory to *anamnesis*: the poem dramatizes the philosophic progress and could well be taken for a paradigm of the Yeatsian poetic process. While past and present are both time-bound, however, and the passage between them is therefore a natural one, eternity is essentially different, and no natural progress, but only a metaphysical leap, from the natural to the supernatural, a complete turn from sun-ripened grapes to mummy wheat, will bring us from time to eternity. For six and a half stanzas, the poem is a sort of dialectical ladder which, when climbed up, is discarded for the transcendent leap into the world of Forms of stanza VIII. Yet the leap too is a part of the same poem that began so naturally and serves to bring the entirely natural and the purely supernatural within the unity of the single poem.

Like mythic and archetypal figures, like *daimones*, like the poet himself, the "Presences" of stanza VII point in two directions and unify the universe of the poem as they also unify the universe of the Platonic system. In worshipping images (*eikones*), nuns and mothers, though they are not conscious of this, are really worshipping Forms (*eidē*) which those images, abstracted from a world of perpetual process, merely imitate. Performing an act of *anamnesis* of which they remain unconscious (else their mythic role would be that of philosopher rather than of nun and mother), nuns and mothers recall in this world of time, and very much as in a glass darkly, Forms they viewed in a world of eternity "before the world was made." This is Plato's familiar two-world metaphysics with an intermediate realm of spirits, "images," or "Presences" holding the two together: the living-dying child on the one hand, the Form that we might call the Human Form Divine on the other hand, and in between the abstract image of "childness." The mother worships "childness" as the lover worships physical beauty, but beyond "childness" is the Human Form Divine, and beyond physical beauty is absolute

Beauty; turning the matter around, "all heavenly glory" is symbolized in the images, which are informed by spiritual Presences, and those images, in turn, are accessible to lovers, nuns, and mothers. "Among School Children" progresses by way of a series of triads (Plato, Aristotle, Pythagoras; passion, piety, affection; etc.), but the controlling vision—the eventual goal toward which it moves and the emotion that determines that movement—is overwhelmingly monadic: the desire to discover and to assert that for all the multiform changes among pluralities there is somehow, somewhere a unity from which they proceed and to which they return. The failed unities of the first six stanzas of the poem are only stages on the way to the triadic and duadic unity of the final stanza, where Yeats asserts, in the form of rhetorical questions, first a natural, organic trinity (leaf, blossom, and bole all-in-one), then a natural/supernatural *complexio oppositorum* (dancer-and-dance). It is all self now, no ego left, and all Unity of Being: a self-circumscribed circle of pattern and performer, the *mythos* fully realized and the *eidos* perfectly immanent in the poem and as the poem.

Writing in 1902, Yeats declared that "literature dwindles to a mere chronicle of circumstance, or passionless fantasies, and passionless meditations, unless it is constantly flooded with the passions and beliefs of ancient times" (*E. & I.*, p. 185); and then, from a postrevelatory perspective (1924), he added the following footnote, which takes nothing back from the earlier statement but adds an important complement to it: "I should have added as an alternative that the supernatural may at any moment create new myths, but I was timid. 1924." Of course he had good reason—a very *timely* reason—for adding the note, since Yeats in 1924 was sorting out the exciting new myth that the supernatural had been creating before his very eyes over the previous seven years (and more). One might question whether that myth was new or old, but in the end it makes little difference, since it was composed of "the passions and beliefs of ancient times" renewed in a grand myth of our time—supernatural mummy wheat, buried beyond recall of memory and beneath the reach of conscious mind, but miraculously sprouting in a poetry of the twentieth century.

CHAPTER VIII

Psychology of the Pleroma

Jung, too, harvested a great crop of old mummy wheat, which he first formed into the visionary loaves of *Septem Sermones ad Mortuos* and then baked into the bread that he called "analytical psychology." The grain that he gathered had been planted centuries earlier in the obscurity of Gnostic, Hermetic, and alchemical texts, and there, where rational intellect could scarcely penetrate (as anyone who has brought mere rational intellect to Valentinus or Paracelsus can testify), the mummy truth long remained, neglected and forgotten, sunk out of sight in that portion of the human psyche that we are now accustomed to call the unconscious. Jung was harvesting his wheat at much the same time as Yeats, yet, working in that dark together, they remained unaware of one another. As Jung says, in a passage that not only describes well the two men at work in the fabulous darkness and that echoes, in phrase after phrase, Yeats's expression in *Per Amica Silentia Lunae*, but that could also stand almost as a comment on the final lines of "Among School Children":

> And so it is with the hand that guides the crayon or brush, the foot that executes the dance-step . . . : a dark impulse is

the ultimate arbiter of the pattern, an unconscious *a priori* precipitates itself into plastic form, and one has no inkling that another person's consciousness is being guided by these same principles at the very point where one feels utterly exposed to the boundless subjective vagaries of chance. Over the whole procedure there seems to reign a dim foreknowledge not only of the pattern but of its meaning. Image and meaning are identical; and as the first takes shape, so the latter becomes clear. Actually, the pattern needs no interpretation: it portrays its own meaning.

(*CW*, VIII, par. 402)

What Jung describes here and in countless other places is what his whole life and his entire work were about—i.e., the great drama, both individual and universal, of the unconscious becoming conscious. That drama played itself out phylogenetically in ancient Greece, to be repeated ontogenetically in the autobiography and *Collected Poems* of Yeats and in the autobiography and *Collected Works* of Jung. The drama in question can be endlessly repeated, studied, and admired, but it needs no more interpretation than the unified image of dancer and dance in "School Children." It is specifically an instinctive performance the dancer gives, moved by a "dark impulse" that determines a pattern that is its own meaning, "like some great dancer," in Yeats's phrase, "the perfect flower of modern culture, dancing some primitive dance and conscious of his or her own life and of the dance" (*Vision*, p. 240). But man is not the only dancing animal, according to Jung: certain bees also dance, and so do birds—at least in some of Yeats's poems and plays they do; and those creatures, we must assume, are guided entirely by "dark impulses," or by instinct, rather than by that variety of conscious awareness that, in the animal realm, is unique and specific to human beings.

In fact, Yeats and Jung knew more about the birds and the bees than most of us. They may sometimes have drawn rather different conclusions from their knowledge of all that natural show—Yeats being inclined to "save the phenomena" with a supernatural explanation, Jung being inclined to save them while remaining, if possible, within nature—but they were warmly agreed about the kinship of all nature; more specifically, they were in agreement about the instinctual legacy that determines identical patterns of behavior for all species of animal life, including the human species. As to birds, Yeats could declare:

> The Primum Mobile that fashioned us
> Has made the very owls in circles move.

And though the owls are an image of disintegration, ruin, and desolation in the poem, they pursue a very human—an all too human—pattern (the lines are from the fourth of the poems collectively titled "Meditations in Time of Civil War," written when Yeats's mood was one of great discouragement and desolation); and indeed the pattern is an archetypal one, for as Yeats says in *A Vision* (1925), where history and the story of the human soul are seen to be, like the movement of the attendant owls, profoundly circular, "All circles are but a single archetypal circle seen according to different measures of time."[1] The Primum Mobile is of course itself a sphere that encloses spheres—the heavenly bodies, the owls, and ourselves—and moves them after its own pattern, like the archetypal circle that determines all other circles in its own image.

Jung was familiar with this same tale of the birds and the bees, and he, like Yeats, read the lesson of their activities in human terms. Man is *not*, according to Jung (and the number of times that Jung insisted on the fact requires one to emphasize his negative), "He is not born as a *tabula rasa*, he is merely born unconscious" (*CW*, IV, par. 728). This beginning makes him one with the birds and bees and insures that he, like they, commences life outfitted with an elaborate, performed instinctual system that will determine the possibilities and necessities of his behavior as much as their inherited instincts determine patterns of behavior for birds and bees. Man "brings with him," as Jung explains the matter of psychological inheritance, "systems that are organized and ready to function in a specifically human way, and these he owes to millions of years of human development. Just as the migratory and nest-building instincts of birds were never learnt or acquired individually, man brings with him at birth the ground-plan of his nature, and not only of his individual nature but of his collective nature" (ibid.). When Jung goes on in the following paragraph to say, "I have called this congenital and pre-existent instinctual model, or pattern of behav-

---

1. P. 140. Plato says much the same thing in the Seventh Epistle (342–43), where, in a slightly different terminology, he treats of Yeats's "single archetypal circle."

ior, the *archetype*," he gives to his bullish scientific critics the signal to react as if he had waved a red rag in their faces. Yeats, on the other hand, would have remained very calm—or more likely would have been thoroughly delighted—upon receiving the Jungian formulation, for if he had known of it he could have joined Jung's authority as a natural scientist to that of Henry More as a supernatural scientist. "But what if Henry More was right," Yeats asked (and in spite of the vagaries of his syntax and the question-form in which he cast his sentences, there can be no doubt that Yeats believed More was right), "when he contended that men and animals drew not only universals but particulars from a supersensual source? May we not be compelled to change all our conceptions should it be proved that, in some crisis of life perhaps, we have access to the detailed circumstantial knowledge of other minds, or to the wisdom that has such knowledge for a foundation; or, as Henry More believed . . . that the bees and birds learn to make comb and nest from that *Anima Mundi* which contains the knowledge of all dead bees and birds?" (*E. & I.*, p. 414). Jung would probably have declined to go along with the notion of access to "particulars," and he might have been uneasy about Yeats's insistence that "knowledge of other minds" can be detailed and circumstantial, but otherwise, if he were allowed to call *Anima Mundi* by the synonymous name of "collective unconscious," Jung would doubtless have been willing to subscribe to this bit of Cambridge Platonism offered up by Yeats—the more so since nest-building provided him with a favorite analogy for the instinctual-cum-archetypal functioning of the human psyche and since he believed that bees at least (and undoubtedly birds also) might reasonably be said to be virtually conscious in certain of their activities.

In his long essay on "Synchronicity," Jung tells how certain bees "not only tell their comrades, by means of a peculiar sort of dance [*that* would have delighted Yeats], that they have found a feeding-place, but . . . they also indicate its direction and distance, thus enabling the beginners to fly to it directly. This kind of message is no different in principle from information conveyed by a human being" (*CW*, VIII, par. 956). Now no one, Jung argues, would suggest that human beings are unconscious in conveying such information, "nor is there any proof that bees are unconscious." This leads Jung to speculate that the capacity for knowledge and communication of this sort, displayed both by insects without a cerebrospinal system and human beings with such a system, must derive not from the cerebrospinal system but from "a nervous substrate like the sympathetic system," which is common to insects and to man alike. Jung concludes—if his very Yeatsian presentation of a question as a half-statement should be called a conclusion—that "one must ask whether the normal state of unconsciousness in sleep, and the potentially conscious dreams it contains, can be regarded in the same light —whether, in other words, dreams are produced not so much by the activity of the sleeping cortex, as by the unsleeping sympathetic system, and are therefore of a transcerebral nature" (*CW*, VIII, par. 957). One could put this more simply, I think, by saying that all animate nature is akin in a state of conscious unconsciousness or unconscious consciousness, "when sleepers wake and yet still dream," when bees communicate with conscious intent and men move purposefully but unconscious of the instincts, the necessities, and the ends that guide them. "It might also be said that I built it in a kind of dream," Jung says of his tower at Bollingen. "Only afterward did I see how all the parts fitted together and that a meaningful form had resulted" (*Memories*, p. 225/214). Thus also with bees and their comb, birds and their nest: they are guided by the inherited instincts and, like Jung, are led on by a dimly perceived archetype— more a feeling, perhaps, than a thought—to create forms that are meaningful because they express the ages-old experience of their kind.

In Ireland, Yeats spent much time and effort restoring his tower, already possessed of "a meaningful form"—none other than the numinous and archetypal Jungian quaternity—and in so doing he joined Jung, the dancing bees, and weaverbirds in performing an intricate dance choreographed not by any individual consciousness but by those instincts inherited from "all dead birds and bees" and from all the dead of humankind. "The weaver-bird builds his nest in his own peculiar fashion no matter where he may be"—so does man build his tower whether near Gort or at Bollingen—"and just as we have no ground for assuming that he built his nest differently three thousand years ago, so it is very improbable that he will alter his style in the next three thousand" (*CW*, XIV, p. xviii). In an ingenious foray into Freudian territory, with the ways of his friends, the birds and the bees, as his weapon, Jung suggested in a letter to Henri Flournoy in 1949 that the Oedipus complex should be seen as "a psychic 'pattern of behavior,'" thus a potentially universal relationship drawn along the lines of specifically human instincts, and as the first discovered archetype—but by no means the only archetype, as Freudians would have it (though they would not, of course, call it by that tainted name). The Oedipus complex unquestionably grows out of a typical human situation, according to Jung, but, he continues: "There are any number of typical situations, each represented by a certain innate form that forces the individual to function in a specifically human way. These are the same as the forms that force the birds to build their nests in a certain way. Instinct takes a specific form, even in man. That form is the archetype, so named because unconscious thought expresses itself mythologically (*vide* Oedipus)" (*Letters*, I, 525-26). Freudians have not shown themselves overwhelmed with gratitude to Jung for "continuing what Freud began," as Jung chooses to claim he has done in this letter—written when Freud had been safely dead for ten years; and perhaps there is a certain amount of irony in his claim. The analogy of birds and their nests and human beings and the archetypes, however, an analogy that balances on the presence of an instinctual system and patterns of behavior in both, is too common in Jung to suppose that he was not altogether serious about that.

In the first of the *Two Essays on Analytical Psychology*, Jung transfers the word "archetype" across the analogical bond between animals and men, and draws the two into a vastly extended but closely bound kinship, when he says that "there is nothing to prevent us from assuming that certain archetypes exist even in animals, that they are grounded in the peculiarities of the living organism itself and are therefore direct expressions of life whose nature cannot be further explained" (*CW*, VII, par. 109). To try to explain these things, to attempt to work up a reasoned explanation of instincts and archetypes that express the nature of organic being and so explain themselves, would be a pointless and otiose exercise, the equivalent of interpreting that dance in which "image and meaning are identical." The kind of kinship between men and other animals that Jung envisions would imply that they must share those psychic propensities on which the existence of archetypes depends. Other animals besides man dream. Or, putting it as Jung does in his autobiography (and the basic idea of universal kinship, if not the ultimate Jungian elaboration of that idea, is Pythagorean, Empedoclean, and Platonic): "Because they are so closely akin to us and share our unknowingness, I loved all warm-blooded animals who have souls like ourselves and with whom, so I thought, we have an instinctive understanding" (*Memories*, p. 67/74). The understanding and the kinship that Jung imagines between man and animals with souls like our own is expressly "instinctive," and with good reason: the man who builds a tower "in a kind of dream" and guided by instinct should well understand "the young weaver-bird," dreaming his dream of weaverbirddom and directed by species instincts, that "builds his characteristic nest because he is a weaver-bird and not a rabbit" (*CW*, VIII, par. 435).

The source of our psychological "patterns of behavior" is to be sought in inherited psychic instincts, then, of which (as Jung never tired of saying) the archetypes are "self-portraits." But what is the source of instinct itself? Here Jung, shy of treading on metaphysical ground in the *Collected Works*, hesitated—but not Yeats, who happily rushed in to offer an ingenious old mummy truth that he no doubt had from a medium's mouth, or from the "dark night where lay / The crowns of Nineveh," since it occurred in a publication too early to have derived from his wife's automatic writing. "The dead living in their memories are . . . the source of all that we call instinct, and it is their love and their desire, all unknowing, that make us drive beyond our reason, or in defiance of our interest it may be; and it is the dream martens [*sic*] that, all unknowing, are master-masons to the living martens, building about church windows their elaborate nests. . . ."[2] All the dead bees and birds buzz and chirp about as the collective unconscious of beedom and birddom, and all dead martins, being a dream in the unconscious of living martins, provide the "dark impulse," the instinct and seeming foreknowledge of an end, that causes them to build their elaborate nests as they do. Jung hesitated, as I say, to give this sort of account in the *Collected Works*,[3] but he frankly acknowledged, on the other hand, that "all

---

2. *Myth.*, p. 359. Yeats's spelling has, I think, rendered up the wrong animal here: surely he intended the bird (martin) rather than the weasel (marten).

3. In a typical passage, Jung asks the question but leaves it up in the air: "What is behind these instincts viz., the sexual instinct and the power drive, which are certainly not the be-all and end-all of existence, but merely represent the limits of our understanding?" (*CW*, X, par. 312). Beyond the limits of our understanding, perhaps, but not beyond the limits of Yeats's imaginative vision—or of Jung's when he was in the proper mood and out of the *Collected Works*.

my works, all my creative activity, has come from those initial fantasies and dreams which began in 1912" (*Memories*, p. 192/184). And as he tells the story in his autobiography, the fantasies and dreams that shaped his psychiatric vision first forced themselves on him as the *Seven Sermons to the Dead*; and in that pseudonymous, half-disavowed text, Jung was more than willing to say that the dead are the source of instinct and to say further that instinct, like its twin the archetype, is something half-human, half-divine—it is, in psychological fact, a *daimon*. Take sexuality, for example: "The dæmon of sexuality approacheth our soul as a serpent. It is half human and appeareth as thought-desire. . . . The serpent is an earthy soul, half dæmonic, a spirit, and akin to the spirits of the dead. Thus too, like these, she swarmeth around in the things of earth, making us either to fear them or pricking us with intemperate desires." Thus sayeth Basilides, preaching the instincts to his congregation of the dead in the sixth of his *Seven Sermons*. It is scarcely surprising that the congregation should have reacted as it did to this sermon on the instincts ("With disdainful glance the dead spake: Cease this talk of gods and dæmons and souls. At bottom this hath long been known to us"), since "the spirits of the dead" are akin to the instincts, as Basilides has already said, or as Yeats phrases it, "The dead living in their memories are . . . the source of all that we call instinct." The old Preacher might as well expect to teach his grandmother to suck eggs as to teach his oddly constituted congregation about sexuality: "At bottom this hath long been known to us."

And yet, if the dead inhabit the unconscious, as Jung, in discussing the genesis of *Septem Sermones*, says they do—"the unconscious corresponds to the mythic land of the dead, the land of the ancestors" (*Memories*, p. 191/183)—then the effort to teach them something about themselves is neither illogical nor futile, since the condition of that which inhabits the unconscious is just that: it is unconscious. Yeats's phrasing is a little showier, but his meaning is identical to Jung's when he says, "All spirits inhabit our unconsciousness or, as Swedenborg said, are the Dramatis Personae of our dreams" (*Vision*, p. 227). Preaching to the spirited, instinctual dead about their own nature, therefore, and throwing the little light of consciousness into the great dark of the unconscious, is to do much the same sort of thing and produce much the same sort of effect and process as Yeats claimed to observe in the publication he called *On the Boiler*: "the emergence of the philosophy of my own poetry, the unconscious becoming conscious." What transpires in *Septem Sermones* is, again, much the same as what goes on in *A Vision*, where the Instructors—those spirits of the dead, dwelling in the Beulah Land of the unconscious—achieve conscious expression in the automatic writing of George Yeats and in the very careful, far from automatic reworking of W. B. Yeats. "The unconscious can realize itself only with the help of consciousness and under its constant control," Jung wrote to a correspondent in 1937 (*Letters*, I, 240). This, I think, is one good reason (though there are others) for Jung's fascination with the Gnostics and alchemists: they, like the dead of *Septem Sermones*—like the Instructors and spirits for Yeats—composed a part of his unconscious and the unconscious of the psyche of the West, and Jung conceived himself in the heroic role of the light of individual consciousness to their dark collectivity of the unconscious. As Jung imagined it, Gnostics and alchemists, in their highly symbolic and obscure writings, had projected the contents of the unconscious against the face of heaven and on to the physical universe, but those works had not been understood—they had been deliberately *mis*understood by the dominant Christian world—and so they had been pushed back below the surface of consciousness. "Gnosticism was stamped out completely and its remnants are so badly mangled that special study is needed to get any insight at all into its inner meaning," Jung writes of the effects of the campaign directed by Christianity against its arch rival. Nevertheless, Jung claims that as a psychotherapist he has observed symbols in his patients' dreams and visions (and in his own also) that can be traced right back under the surface of consciousness to that unconscious state to which Gnosticism was forced to retreat by Christianity seventeen hundred years ago. "But if the historical roots of our symbols extend beyond the Middle Ages they are certainly to be found in Gnosticism. . . . In spite of the suppression of the Gnostic heresy, it continued to flourish throughout the Middle Ages under the disguise of alchemy" (*CW*, XI, par. 160). So it remained for Jung to redo in our century what his alchemical and Gnostic predecessors had done four, eight, and sixteen centuries earlier—i.e., mine the depths and draw those contents back up from beneath the surface where history and individual prudence had forced them. It is as if the doctrines of Christianity alone were allowed to remain accessible to consciousness, and other "heretical" doctrines were forced into historical unconsciousness. (It is a bitter irony of history, as Jung pointed out, that until very recently the Gnostic writings were only known from quotations, put to polemical ends, in the writings of Christian enemies. This had the effect of drawing a double darkness over them.) Moreover, both alchemy and Gnosis—in addition to being, in Jung's view, really symbolic psychology rather than, respectively, embryonic chemistry and heretical philosophy—were quasi-mystery religions with secret doctrine for the ears and eyes of the initiated only. Hence they were very much like contents of the unconscious: mysterious, powerful, magical, ineffable, and unknown.

Hear, then, the ancient unconscious becoming conscious in the person of Jung, posing as the long-deceased but now resurrected Basilides of Alexandria ("where the East toucheth the West"), preaching to his unruly, even rather disrespectful, collection of the dead. In the beginning was the Pleroma, according to Basilides, which was both nothingness and fullness. Over against the Pleroma, which Jung elsewhere, speaking in his own voice, describes as "the sphere of paradoxical existence, i.e., the instinctive unconscious" (*Letters*, I, 61), and yet, while opposed to the Pleroma, also participating in it, is what the Preacher calls "Creatura": "Creatura is not in the pleroma, but in itself. The pleroma is both beginning and end of created beings. . . . We are, however, the pleroma itself, for we are a part of the eternal and infinite. But we have no share thereof, as we are from the pleroma infinitely removed. . . . Yet because we are parts of the pleroma, the pleroma is also in us " (Sermon I). There are, I believe, some readers who find the *Collected Works* obscure, but at least the obscurity is there thinned out by being spread over seven or eight thousand pages; when that obscurity is compressed into twenty-five brief pages, however, as it is in the *Sermones*, and so intensified several hundred times, I must confess that I too find it rather difficult to penetrate. But if the text is dark, the logic is bright, and the reason for the obscurity is perfectly clear: this is how the "instinctive unconscious" speaks, this is the way the dead express themselves, this is the language of Gnosticism itself brought dripping out of the teeming, paradoxical, and mad depths. In the "Red Book," where Jung recorded some of the fantasies that gave rise to the *Seven Sermons* (itself "a piece of automatic writing," according to R. F. C. Hull), and to the volumes of *Collected Works* that followed, Jung thus provided the rationale for his mode of expression: "The spirit of the depths took my understanding and all my knowledge and placed them at the service of the inexplicable and the paradoxical, or rather what must appear so to the people of these times. He robbed me of power to speak and write of anything that was not in his service, namely in the service of fusing together sense and nonsense."[4] So in this little text that does not pretend to be science, even though it contained the germinal experience that eventually produced the science of analytical psychology, the manner of expression is intended to do homage to that roiling unconscious where sense and nonsense are one—where indeed *everything* is one. (Readers baffled by the *Collected Works* will also find something of interest, and perhaps something of comfort as well, in Jung's description of the spirit that he served and the way he went about his service.) "As Plotinus says, things that are of one kind are unconscious," Yeats remarked in *A Vision* (p. 82); and of the collective unconscious, Jung wrote: "The indistinguishableness of its contents gives one the impression that everything is connected with everything else and therefore . . . that they are at bottom a unity" (*CW*, XIV, par. 660). The communications that Yeats and Jung received from the dead, dwelling in the depths of the unconscious, have seemed to many readers before now to offer support for Jung's notion that to serve the spirit of the depths properly requires a fusion of sense and nonsense.

For creatura (for which one could read "man-as-conscious-being"), however, "distinctiveness is its essence, and therefore it distinguisheth. Therefore man discriminateth because his nature is distinctiveness" (Sermon I). Preaching against the failure to distinguish as St. Paul preached against sin, Basilides threatens his congregation with the tenet that the wages of not discriminating are death (in that they are already dead, however, the threat may be supposed to lose some of its potency), which is to say, "We fall into indistinctiveness," and sink back into the unconscious: "We fall into the pleroma itself and cease to be creatures." His manner of expression may have been adopted from the unconscious and from the

4. Quoted from the "Red Book" by Aniela Jaffé, in "The Creative Phases of Jung's Life" (*Spring* 1962), p. 175. In a letter written less than a year before his death, Jung called *Septem Sermones* "a poem in Gnostic style" and "a poetic paraphrase of the psychology of the unconscious" (*Letters*, II, 571).

dead, but neither as Gnostic nor as scientist did Jung give his ultimate and undivided loyalty to the Pleroma. His science, according to Jung's own view of it, was a *natural* science and his reaction to the Pleroma a *natural* reaction, and as Basilides says, "The natural striving of the creature goeth towards distinctiveness, fighteth against primeval, perilous sameness. This is called the PRINCIPIUM INDIVIDUATIONIS." The question that faces the ancient preacher now is how, from the *massa confusa* that is the instinctive and collective unconscious or the Pleroma, this *principium individuationis* is going to set itself in motion. If the Pleroma (like Parmenides' Sphere) is "endless, eternal, and entire," as Basilides declares it to be, if it is "whole and continuous . . . , nowhere divided . . . , infinite and eternal," if there is nothing but the Pleroma and language has no reality apart from it, then how is consciousness, which is submerged and nullified in that whole and continuous oneness, ever going to precipitate itself out, stand off to one side, discriminate, distinguish, and become aware of differences? Parmenides asked Pythagoras and Heraclitus the same question—"Where, when, and how will movement, change, and separated consciousness commence if the Sphere is all and if thought is precisely coextensive with that One Being?"—Zeno rubbed the question in with his paradoxes, and they both sat back and smiled when there was no answer immediately forthcoming. Smile though he might, Parmenides locked himself up in that same logico-linguistic prison house to which he committed his philosophic antagonists. Empedocles, with his four-and-One key of the quaternity and the Sphere, tried to open the lock of Parmenides' One Being and so free the Eleatic Master (and Pythagoras too, since Empedocles shared with Pythagoras a love for the *tetraktys* and for the Orphic mysteries, and he was no doubt pained to see Pythagoras languishing in the jail of Parmenidean logic); and with his alternating cycles Empedocles reintroduced time—a cyclical time without beginning or end—into the universe and so temporalized the Sphere that Parmenides had declared endless, eternal, entire, whole, continuous, nowhere divided. Empedocles' solution, in fact, commended itself very strongly to Jung/Basilides and did so precisely by way of the Gnostic-alchemical tradition to which they both belonged and which, in its natural aspect, can be traced right back, through the *Timaeus*, to its quaternal roots in Empedocles' poem *On Nature*.

For the full systematic solution, however—a solution which comprehended the natural world and insinuated a supernatural one—Empedocles was not quite enough. It was necessary not only to provide for movement, change, and time in the natural world—in other words, to save the phenomena—as Empedocles, in response to Parmenides, had done, but necessary also to discover a supernatural model, an eternal paradigm, a One Being which that natural world and time itself, the inseparable correlative of nature, could be said to imitate or to symbolize. According to the completely elaborated answer to the dilemma—at least the answer as worked out by Plato and inherited from him by Neoplatonists, Gnostics, Hermetists, and alchemists alike—what is many here is One "There" (in the Yeatsian and Plotinian word for the other world in a two-world metaphysics), what moves here is still "There," what is *mythos* here is *eidos* "There," and what is sadly subject to time here is eudaimonically free in eternity "There." As a psychologist and self-proclaimed empiricist, Jung focussed his attention on the many, on movement, on his own myth and the myths of others, and on the unfolding of psychic processes in time; but that did not prevent him, as a man who only happened to be a natural scientists, from experiencing intuitions of the One, of stillness, of the *eidos* of human existence, and of the eternity that surrounds time and so mocks the efforts of time to become eternity. In an attempt to account for those intuitions, which have little enough place in a science of process, Jung had recourse to a psychology of the instincts. That is to say, he tried to explain the Pleroma by way of a tale of the birds and the bees.

"The collective unconscious," Jung wrote in his important essay on "Instinct and the Unconscious"—and I would mention again that by the Pleroma, Jung said he meant the instinctive or collective unconscious—"The collective unconscious consists of the sum of the instincts and their correlates, the archetypes" (*CW*, VIII, Par. 281). Now, if we throw this formulation of the Pleroma and the instincts together with Jung's remark in *Aion* that it is best "to explain as the 'will of God' the natural forces that appear in us as instincts" (*CW*, IX, pt. 2, par. 50), and join both of these to the typical observation, from the *Mysterium Coniunctionis*, that "sexuality does not exclude spirituality nor spirituality sexuality, for in God all opposites are abolished" (*CW*, XIV, par. 634), we shall be in a way to understand that Jung's Thirteenth Cone is the Pleroma, that the Pleroma is also God and the collective unconscious, and that God, the collective unconscious, the Pleroma, or the collectivity of the dead—we may choose whichever name pleases us, since they all come to the same thing—are instinct pure, unmediated, undifferentiated, unconscious of itself or of anything else. The jumble is nearly hopeless, but then so is the collective unconscious. What Basilides teaches his interested listeners is either that there is no sex for the dead (for how can there be sex where everything is one?); or that there is nothing *but* sex for the dead (there is certainly a good deal of confused mingling and blind groping in the Pleroma—and sex, Jung said, was a reversion to an "original condition of unconscious oneness": *CW*, XVII, par. 330); and further that these two antinomies—perpetual indulgence, perpetual abstention—are one and the same. So Swedenborg was right, then, about the sex life of angels and the dead, and so was Ribh, who maintained that when the bodies of the purified dead join:

> There is no touching here, nor touching there,
> Nor straining joy, but whole is joined to whole;
> For the intercourse of angels is a light
> Where for its moment both seem lost, consumed.

Or as Ribh, when "in ecstasy," has it:

> Godhead on Godhead in sexual spasm begot
> Godhead.

The sexual congress of Ribh's somewhat fevered imagination represents, I should think, either a tremendous fertility or a total sterility, but then, as Basilides had occasion to remark to the dead, "Nothingness is the same as fullness," and, "In the pleroma there is nothing and everything." Ribh/Yeats knew how to fuse sense and nonsense ("O what am I that I should not seem / For the song's sake a fool?") as expertly as ever Basilides/Jung did.

Yeats claimed to think that Ribh, except for a little heresy about the Trinity, was "an orthodox man"; and Jung, except for a little heresy about the Trinity (he thought it should be a Quaternity), probably imagined himself reasonably orthodox. Maybe so in both cases, but I am not sure of Ribh's scriptural authority for this:

> Natural and supernatural with the self-same ring are wed.
> As man, as beast, as an ephemeral fly begets, Godhead
>   begets Godhead,

For things below are copies, the Great Smaragdine Tablet said.

Nor do I know what scriptural authority Jung (preaching through his Basilidean mask) might have adduced for his lesson that spirituality and sexuality, which are inseparable in God, "are superhuman dæmons which reveal the world of the gods. They are for us more effective than the gods, because they are closely akin to our own nature. . . . But they possess and contain you; for they are powerful dæmons, manifestations of the gods, and are, therefore, things which reach beyond you, existing in themselves. . . . No man, therefore, escapeth these dæmons."[5] It would be very difficult, I think, to bring this enthusiastic doctrine of instinctual *daimones* into line with Christian teaching as we find it, for example, in St. Paul with his rather sour concession that it is better to marry than to burn. But Jung's orthodoxy, if orthodoxy it be, took its orientation from the Gnostic god Abraxas, who is a sort of personification (or deification) of the Pleroma; that deity has much less in common with the New Testament God than with the Old Testament Yahweh, whom Jung (in his "Answer to Job") characterizes as unconscious, amoral, bestial, insane, and a plague to man and himself. Jung's Yahweh and Basilides' Abraxas are really quite like the rough beast, its hour come round at last, of Yeats's "Second Coming"—savage, blank, pitiless, primitive, sunk in the unconscious and acting blindly out of it. Yahweh, Jung tells us, "is too unconscious to be moral. Morality presupposes consciousness"(*CW*, XI, par. 574); he has "an inferior consciousness," a "primitive 'awareness,'" and is what we should describe legally as "*non compos mentis*" (par. 638); he has "an animal nature," and this "explains Yahweh's behaviour, which, from the human point of view, is so intolerable: it is the behaviour of an unconscious being who cannot be judged morally" (par. 600). Yahweh does not, however, any more than Abraxas, represent all evil—or rather he does represent all evil but

---

5. Sermon V. In his edition of the *Odyssey*, W. B. Stanford has a note on the *daimon* that is apposite here: "δαίμων The word is used in H. of supernatural powers whose nature and function are vaguer than those of the θεοί (who are anthropomorphic in H.). . . . Usener defined a δαίμων as 'a momentary god,' i.e., one without fixed cult, function, or name, but simply the divinity of a single supernatural manifestation" (note on lines 134–35 of Book II). This is very much what Jung means by "dæmons" in the *Seven Sermons*.

he represents all good also; he is the deity of that paradoxical sphere of the psyche that is unconscious, the condition of pure potentiality in which all consciousness originates and in which all consciousness will eventually be again submerged.

Neither Yahweh nor Abraxas alone is enough, however: the unconscious, without consciousness, is simply a mess, and all mess *per se* is bad. Furthermore, as Basilides tells his audience or as Jung told his patients, the unconscious, when undirected by consciousness, spells destruction. Neither half of the psyche should be denied, neither the light nor the dark half, for they require one another if the psychic system itself is to remain healthy, vital, and balanced. The reason that Basilides preaches so much about Abraxas, or that Jung insisted on exploring the shadow, is that Christianity tries to deny the dark side of its deity (Jung was extremely vexed about the doctrine of evil as mere "*privatio boni*," for evil, he maintained, is not simply a negative but is as real and self-subsistent as good), and ego consciousness claims that it has no dark shadow but is itself the totality of psyche. "As long as Evil is a μὴ ὄν [non-being], *nobody will take his own shadow seriously*," Jung wrote to Father Victor White with emphatic insistence (the italics are his). "Hitler and Stalin go on representing a mere 'accidental lack of perfection.' *The future of mankind very much depends upon the recognition of the shadow. Evil is—* psychologically speaking—*terribly real*" (*Letters*, I, 541). The dead to whom Basilides delivers his sermons raise "a great tumult" and howl and rage when he preaches about Abraxas (nor was Father White apparently very pleased with Jung's preachments against the doctrine of evil as a μὴ ὄν or the *privatio boni*), "for they were Christians," as Basilides drily remarks at the end of the second sermon. (Here Jung's *Septem Sermones* fantasy gets rather confusing, since the congregation, if dead and therefore unconscious, should presumably be closer to Gnosticism than Christianity; but perhaps we should leave the contradiction with the observation that fantasy, too, can be paradoxical.) Jung's god, like Basilides' god, is the god of the entire human psyche, whether that psyche be Greek, Hebrew, Egyptian, or even Swiss. Jung would argue, I think, that his god is a fuller and more accurate expression of the psychic complex in which God takes his origin; hence, on any points where Jung differs from Christian doctrine, Jung would claim that it is he who is (psychologically) orthodox, the Christian church heterodox. Or as Jung says, after reading Father White the lecture against the notion of evil as the *privatio boni*, "I guess I am a heretic." It hardly needs saying that that is not a confession from a repentant sinner, nor is it the remark of a man who fears that he may be wrong.

How does the vital but mad swarm of the Pleroma, where everything is everything else, ever sort itself out to become that unique, separated, and individual self that Jungian psychology holds to be the ideal end (and paradoxically also the beginning) of all psychic process? Jung's first public answer to the question came in *Symbols of Transformation* (1912)—in the book's title as well as in its contents— and his last in the contribution ("Approaching the Unconscious") that Jung made to *Man and His Symbols*, completed within a few weeks of his death and published posthumously. In a letter of 1929 (the same one in which he wrote, "For my private use I call the sphere of paradoxical existence, i.e., the instinctive unconscious, the Pleroma, a term borrowed from Gnosticism"), Jung took hold of the question in terms that looked back to *Symbols of Transformation* and forward to *Man and His Symbols*: "The reflection and formation of the Pleroma in the individual consciousness produce an image of it (of like nature in a certain sense), and that is the symbol. In it all paradoxes are abolished. In the Pleroma, Above and Below lie together in a strange way and produce nothing; but when it is disturbed by the mistakes and needs of the individual a waterfall arises between Above and Below, a dynamic something that is the Symbol. Like the Pleroma, the symbol is greater than man. It overpowers him, shapes him . . ." (*Letters*, I, 61). The "dynamic something" that performs the Platonic and Hermetic task of first separating and then joining the Above and Below, the task of first differentiating and distinguishing realms of psychic being and then of uniting them in itself, is the equivalent of the *daimones* and mathematicals in Plato's two-world metaphysics, the equivalent of the symbols for evocation employed by Hermetic theurgists, and the equivalent of what Jung himself called the archetypes. The last of these Jung was accustomed to think of (and so was Yeats) in terms of image and emotion, the archetype or symbol being a formal representation, an image, likeness, or *eikon*, of an emotion, or an instinct, which is, as Jung says, "dynamic" but in itself formless. This is that same imposition of Limit on the Unlimited, of order on chaos, that Pythagoras and Pythagoreans have always assumed to be the "in the beginning" of the universe.

"Archetypes are typical forms of behaviour which, once they become conscious, naturally present themselves as ideas and images, like everything else that becomes a content of consciousness" (*CW*, VIII, Par. 435). How could an emotion or an instinct appear to consciousness unless it assumed some form? Formless, the emotion remains unconscious—certainly still powerful, but neither perceived nor understood and therefore the more dangerous. This is why, speaking of the visions, dreams, and fantasies that constituted his first direct encounter with the unconscious, Jung says, "To the extent that I managed to translate the emotions into images—that is to say, to find the images which were concealed in the emotions—I was inwardly calmed and reassured. Had I left those images hidden in the emotions, I might have been torn to pieces by them. . . . As a result of my experiment I learned how helpful it can be, from the therapeutic point of view, to find the particular images which lie behind emotions" (*Memories*, p. 177/171). Yeats was concerned with the source and nature of the poet's creativity rather than with the therapist's defense against the dangerous forces of the unconscious, but what he says of the emotional dynamism captured by the artist and contained in images points in the same direction as Jung's remarks about emotions transformed into images: "The old images, the old emotions, awakened again to overwhelming life, like the gods Heine tells of, by the belief and passion of some new soul, are the only masterpieces" (*E. & I.*, pp. 352-53). And elsewhere, echoing Jung's language about the "dark impulse" and the "pattern" or "plastic form" that it must discover before it can give effective force to the work of art or to the magical performance (the essay is the one on "Magic"), Yeats says that "surely, at whatever risk, we must cry out that imagination is always seeking to remake the world according to the impulses and the patterns in that Great Mind, and that Great Memory" (*E. & I.*, p. 52).

In *Man and His Symbols*, Jung explained—for about the hundredth time and, as it chanced, for the last time—the similarity and the difference between what Yeats calls "impulses" and "patterns," i.e., instincts and archetypes, and he took the opportunity once more to set his critics straight on what he meant by archetypes and their heritability. By the term "archetype," Jung says, he does not mean "definite mythological images or motifs," for those are "nothing more than conscious representations"; and he agrees with his critics that "it would be absurd to assume that such variable representations could be inherited." Nobody, Jung would say, inherits the contents of consciousness—but the patterns, forms, and tendencies of the unconscious we all inherit. Thus the archetype, which is *per se* irrepresentable, a part of the unconscious and so by definition that which is unknown and unknowable, is a reflection of psychic structure and heritable along with psyche itself. Can psyche get outside itself to become conscious of its own structure? Jung says no. Psyche is a dynamic process and cannot simultaneously *be* that process and *know* it. (Yeats in his last letter: "Man can embody truth but he cannot know it.") The archetype is not an image or a motif (for which Jung generally reserves the adjective "archetypal"—i.e., the likeness of something that cannot in itself be represented) but "is a tendency to form such representations of a motif—representations that can vary a great deal in detail without losing their basic pattern."[6] No more than Plato's Forms can Jung's archetypes ever be fully realized in images or *eidola* that strive toward the empty perfection of *eidē* and archetypes but will never achieve it. As to impulses and patterns, Jung writes in a passage that happens to face pictures of birds and bees (geese migrating in formation and bees dancing their cunning dance): "Here I must clarify the relation between instincts and archetypes: What we properly call instincts are physiological urges, and are perceived by the senses. But at the same time, they also manifest themselves in fantasies and often reveal their presence only by symbolic images. These manifestations are what I call the archetypes" (*Man and His Symbols*, p. 69). Impulses and patterns, urges and images, instincts and archetypes—all these paired terms represent attempts to describe a relationship that is indescribable because it reaches over the boundary between consciousness and the unconscious. The matter becomes more difficult when Jung (in an essay "On the Nature of the Psyche") refines—or obscures—the relationship by introducing a third term so that we must consider there to be a relationship not only between instincts and archetypes but also between what might be called emotional archetypes and intellectual archetypes. The "dominants of the collective unconscious," according to this dark clarification, "fall phenomenologically into two categories: instinctual and archetypal.

6. "Approaching the Unconscious," in *Man and His Symbols* (London: Aldus Books, 1964), p. 67. The original version of "Approaching the Unconscious" has now been published in *CW* under the title "Symbols and the Interpretation of Dreams"; the present passage is in vol. XVIII, par. 523.

The first includes the natural impulses, the second the dominants that emerge into consciousness as universal ideas" (*CW*, VIII, par. 423). It seems to me that Jung is inconsistent or at least confusing (but not for the first or the last time) when he distinguishes between instincts and archetypes but then, in the present passage, declares that the archetypes themselves are to be divided "phenomenologically" into those which are instinctual and those which are intellectual. Perhaps the inconsistency can be resolved by saying that though the dominants of the collective unconscious can be distinguished as to their phenomenological occurrence—the one apparently emerging into consciousness, the other not—so long as both remain unconscious they are not two but one: in the unconscious, instinct and archetype are two faces of the one same determining factor.

It vexed Jung when critics failed to penetrate his lavish explanations about the archetypes and the collective unconscious, or when they refused to see the clear light shining out from those explanations and understand that that light could illuminate so many dark places in the unconscious. He was also not happy that critics—sometimes the same ones who could not get through his difficult prose to seize the invaluable psychological concepts within it—accused him of personifying, "as mythology does," the contents of the unconscious; but the truth, according to Jung, is that "the personification is not an invention of mine, but is inherent in the nature of the phenomena" (*CW*, XIII, par. 61). Thus, when he wrote that "the anima personifies the collective unconscious" (*CW*, X, par. 714), Jung would defend himself by saying that this is no more than an empirical observation: in the thousands of dreams and fantasies that he had occasion to observe, the collective unconscious represented itself as a female figure. This, according to Jung, is how psyche speaks: It never talks of anything but itself—what is there for psyche to talk about except itself and its complementary twin, the physical universe, which is anyhow only known through psyche?—and what it says (which Jung claims not to have invented but merely to have overheard, like Yeats listening to the Instructors or Blake following the conversation of spirits in eternity) are such things as, "I am a woman" or "I am a serpent," "I am a hero " or "I am a shy animal," "I am the sun rising in the morning and setting in the evening" or "I am all oceans and rivers, 'a boy and a girl, a bush and a bird and a dumb fish of the sea' " (Empedocles commanded the language of psyche as well as anyone). "Being the science of the psyche, psychology is the sum total of what the psyche says about itself" (*CW*, X, par. 1065). Furthermore, the spirit of the depths that took the psychologist's understanding and all his knowledge and put them "in the service of fusing together sense and nonsense," could hardly be expected to exempt the voice of psyche from that same service. Jung confessed that when he first read the Gnostics and when he first took up alchemy—as when he first descended into the unconscious and gave himself over to the strange figures he there encountered—it all seemed an incredible jumble of nonsense with only very infrequent glimmerings of sense. So also with psyche itself, for the Gnostics and alchemists, like the analytical psychologist, were merely affording psyche the powers of speech that it desired and that were appropriate to it. What was needed, as Jung discovered, was adaptation to a very peculiar and very foreign, yet very familiar, language. Personification and symbolic imagery proved to be the major vehicles of communication for Gnostics, alchemists, and analytical psychologists for the good reason that they were also such for psyche itself.

"If it were possible to personify the unconscious," Jung said, with more hesitation than he was ordinarily wont to show and, in light of the mighty personification that follows, more hesitation than he had any need to show,

> we might think of it as a collective human being combining the characteristics of both sexes, transcending youth and age, birth and death, and from having at its command a human experience of one or two million years, practically immortal. If such a being existed, it would be exalted above all temporal change; the present would mean neither more nor less to it than any year in the hundredth millenium before Christ; it would be a dreamer of age-old dreams and, owing to its limitless experience, an incomparable prognosticator. It would have lived countless times over again the life of the individual, the family, the tribe, and the nation, and it would possess a living sense of the rhythm of growth, flowering, and decay.
>
> (*CW*, VIII, par. 673)

Having barely concluded this grand personification, Jung turns on his own creature (which is not unlike the visible living creature of the universe, modelled on the intelligible Living Creature, in the *Timaeus*[7]) to say that the collective unconscious is after all "not a person, but something like an unceasing stream or perhaps ocean of images and figures which drift into consciousness in our dreams or in abnormal states of mind" (*CW*, VII, par. 674). The personifications of Jung's psychology—or the personifications that, as Jung said, he did not invent but that psyche insisted upon—have much in common with the dramatization of Yeats's poetry. Jungian psychology and Yeatsian poetics both view psyche as a process and coming to consciousness as a drama, and Yeats significantly titled one volume of his autobiography *Dramatis Personae*.

> Her present image floats into the mind
> . . . .
> Lionel Johnson comes the first to mind
> . . . .
> On Florence Emery I call the next
> . . . .
> And I call up MacGregor from the grave
> . . . .
> All, all are in my thoughts tonight being dead
> . . . .
> Wherever I had looked I had looked upon
> My permanent or impermanent images
> . . . .
> They were my close companions many a year,
> A portion of my mind and life, as it were. . . .

---

7. Cf. *Timaeus*, 30c–d: "Let us rather say that the world is like, above all things, to that Living Creature of which all other living creatures, severally and in their families, are parts. For that embraces and contains within itself all the intelligible living creatures, just as this world contains ourselves and all our creatures that have been formed as things visible. For the god, wishing to make this world most nearly like that intelligible thing which is best and in every way complete, fashioned it as a single visible living creature, containing within itself all living things whose nature is of the same order" (trans. Cornford). The only difference that I can see between Plato and Jung is that Plato declares that the archetype that is the "visible living creature" is itself modelled on an Archetype or Paradigm (the intelligible "Living Creature"), while Jung delineates the archetype but will not speculate on whether that archetype is itself modelled on a superior Archetype.

Symbolic images, "as it were," or as Jung said, "figures which drift into consciousness" and float into the mind from the "unceasing stream or perhaps ocean of images" that is the unconscious. "[T]hese archetypes are of great stability and so distinct that they allow themselves to be personified and named," according to Jung (*CW*, XIV, par. 660); and according to Yeats (with Goethe as his authority), when he personified archetypes discovered in his own mind and named them Maud Gonne, Lionel Johnson, MacGregor Mathers, and so on, what he was doing was reshaping personal history in the light of the universal, mythological drama of psyche. "Are we not face to face with the microcosm, mirroring everything in universal Nature?" (*Ex.*, p. 144), Yeats asks, and we might add, "and vice versa." These figures that float into the poems are all parts and aspects of Yeats's mind, his thought, his consciousness, called up—like MacGregor from the dead—from his own unconscious where that merges and blends with a collective unconscious. "I have always sought to bring my mind close to the mind of Indian and Japanese poets, old women in Connacht, mediums in Soho . . . ; to immerse it in the general mind where that mind is scarce separable from what we have begun to call 'the subconscious' . . ." (*Myth.*, p. 343). Please, Jung might have responded, please call it "the unconscious," not "the subconscious," and I shall be happy to provide you with all the empirical evidence you need for your theory from my scientific observations of psychic activity.

The first bit of scientific lore that Jung would have passed on to Yeats would have been, I think, that where the personal unconscious reaches into the collective unconscious, or where the individual mind merges with the general mind, is where the great personification called the Anima takes shape, clothes herself in garments appropriate to this particular psyche, and thence exercises her great and sometimes baleful effect on the life of the individual. Yeats might not have been altogether delighted with this figure dredged up from the depths and given a scientific passport by analytical psychology, but he could scarcely have feigned ignorance or indifference, since he had been so endlessly tormented by his own Anima in the guise of Maud Gonne. Yeats's descriptions of Maud Gonne's personality and her effect on his consciousness sound like nothing so much as Jung's characterization of the Anima—just as Jung's descriptions of the Anima sound like nothing so much as a clinical analysis of Yeats's unhappy, confused, and half-mad relationship with Maud Gonne. As Freud gave a name to the relationship lived by Oedipus (and by millions of other sons), so Jung gave a name to the one lived by Yeats (and by millions of other lovers). Jung could also have told Yeats (but the latter had already intuited this from his own experience) that the relationship between consciousness and the unconscious is one of compensatory opposites, so that a masculine consciousness will encounter the unconscious in a feminine personification (the Anima) and a feminine consciousness will encounter the unconscious in a masculine personification (the Animus). We would do well to understand these figures for what they are, according to Jung, since if we fail to recognize that they are personifications of the unconscious that we all too readily project on to our sexual partners and opposites, then we will be little better than Yahweh, savage and amoral beasts thrashing around in unconsciousness, and thus, by our ignorance, we leave ourselves open to domination (and, so far as conscious life is concerned, to destruction) by the unconscious.

Though poets and psychologists of a more recent day might think otherwise, Yeats and Jung were agreed that men are different from women, and neither of them doubted that the difference was psychological and intellectual as well as physical and emotional. "Woman's psychology is founded on the principle of Eros, the great binder and loosener, whereas from ancient times the ruling principle ascribed to man is Logos. The concept of Eros could be expressed in modern terms as psychic relatedness, and that of Logos as objective interest" (*CW*, X, par. 255). Thus the psychologist on the parting of the ways, and he would doubtless have been all for the continuation of these sexual dichotomies on the Heraclitean principle that without warfare and the conflict of opposites life itself would simply collapse and cease. Yeats preferred for the most part to converse with women, as he several times said (not with all of the gender, however, and particularly not with "hysterical women" or with those that he was pleased to call "opinionated bitches"[8]),

---

8. The Old Man who introduces *The Death of Cuchulain*—hardly even a mask for Yeats, since he so clearly speaks for the aged playwright—ticks off in order all those vermin of the modern world ("this vile age") most despised by Yeats: "people who are educating themselves out of the Book Societies and the like, sciolists all, pickpockets and opinionated bitches. Why pickpockets? I will explain that. . . ." Evidently there is no need to explain "opinionated bitches." The implication is that in a happier age than the present one, women had no opinions and were not perverted from their proper feminine charm by education. Cf. *Letters*, p. 123: "What poor

because the "objective interest" of Logos will lead men into sterile dispute while the "psychic relatedness" of Eros can serve to encourage, increase, and complete a man's thought. "Of all the men I have known," Yeats remarked of the exception that proved the rule, Arthur Symons "was the best listener; he could listen as a woman listens, never meeting one's thought as a man does with a rival thought, but taking up what one said and changing it, giving it as it were flesh and bone" (*Memoirs*, p. 87). When, however, a woman is dominated by the masculine unconscious and when the Animus shows too clearly through her every word, then Jung cried "Beware!" and Yeats cried more dire warnings than that. Eros and Logos, the feminine and masculine principles, go wrong when they are unconscious yet dominant. A man becomes soft, moody, sentimental, "unmanly" (as Yeats said of "certain early works of my own which I have long abandoned," they show "a slight, sentimental sensuality which is disagreeable"—*Auto.*, p. 326); a woman becomes hard, opinionated, abrasive, "unwomanly." If he were to state briefly the difference between men and women, Jung says, he would put it this way: "as the anima produces *moods*, so the animus produces *opinions*" (*CW*, VII, par. 331). Neither moods nor opinions are to be encouraged, but there is little doubt that the male poet and the male psychologist were much more deeply offended by the latter than by the former. Indeed, it would be much, much better—or so Yeats and Jung both felt—if some way could be found to prevent women from having any opinions whatsoever; but of course no such way was to be found, since the unconscious of a woman is full to bursting with hateful opinions, and there are assuredly going to be women under the dominance of their unconscious just as there are going to be men under the dominance of theirs. "What comes to a woman from the unconscious is a sort of *opinion*," Jung said with a certain bitter emphasis (*CW*, X, par. 244), spitting the word out, in a very Yeatsian way, as if it were poison in the mouth; and though

---

delusiveness is all this 'higher education of women.' Men have set up a great mill called examinations, to destroy the imagination. Why should women go through it, circumstance does not drive *them*? They come out with no repose, no peacefulness, their minds no longer quiet gardens full of secluded paths and umbrage-circled nooks, but loud as chaffering market places. Mrs. Todhunter is a great trouble mostly. She has been through the mill and has got the noisiest mind I know. She is always denying something." Women should affirm, not deny: Eros should leave denials to Logos.

Jung goes on to say in the next paragraph, "Unconscious assumptions or opinions are the worst enemy of woman," it is unquestionably man, not woman, who suffers most immediately from the flaunting of those opinions: "they can even grow into a positively demonic passion that exasperates and disgusts men, and does the woman herself the greatest injury by gradually smothering the charm and meaning of her femininity and driving it into the background" (ibid., par. 245). It may seem odd that two men of such decided opinions as Yeats and Jung should have been so warm in their opposition to the holding of opinions by the distaff side of the race, but the apparent (perhaps unconscious?) assumption is that this is just exactly the difference between men and women—*vive la différence*, moreover, and now let us get on with our poetry and psychology, both of which are male activities founded on a principle that, when it occurs in a man, we properly call not "opinion" but "Logos." (Platonic philosophy, too, like Yeatsian poetry and Jungian psychology, scorned δόξα [opinion] as it envisioned the possibility of rendering a true—a good and masculine—λόγος.)

"Women, because the main event of their lives has been a giving themselves and giving birth, give all to an opinion as if it were some terrible stone doll." So Yeats declared in a language that Jung might not have allowed himself (feeling that discretion on "the main event" of women's lives is the better part of a psychologist's valor), however much he may have agreed with the sentiment. We men, on the other hand, Yeats continues, "we still see the world, if we are of strong mind and body, with considerate eyes, but to women opinions become as their children or their sweethearts, and the greater their emotional capacity the more do they forget all other things. They grow cruel, as if in defence of lover or child, and all this is done for 'something other than human life'. At last the opinion is so much identified with their nature that it seems a part of their flesh becomes stone and passes out of life" (*Auto.*, p. 504). That Yeats had learned this lesson from life and was not merely repeating textbook psychology (however close he may come to Jung's descriptions of opinion-loving, Animus-dominated women) is apparent if one considers "Easter 1916," where "argument" turns a woman's voice exasperating and "shrill" and where political opinion makes a stone of the heart. Or the depth of Yeats's experience and feeling is yet more apparent in his heartfelt prayer for a woman—the woman that his daughter was to become—which desires that she may grow into a womanhood, not like Maud Gonne's filled with opinions, politics, and anger, but like George Yeats's, whose "glad kindness" represents the truly feminine.

> An intellectual hatred is the worst,
> So let her think opinions are accursed.
> Have I not seen the loveliest woman born
> Out of the mouth of Plenty's horn,
> Because of her opinionated mind
> Barter that horn and every good
> By quiet natures understood
> For an old bellows full of angry wind?

This is the prayer of an affectionate father, no doubt; it is also the prayer of a man who feels that he has been in the grip of a mad dream of the unconscious for too long, has been demonically possessed and has projected his Anima on to a living woman whom it does not fit and who will not have it ("For each an imagined image brings / And finds a real image there"), and has at long last called the Anima home from its vagrancy for union with the right woman in a virtual *hieros gamos* where "Choice and Chance" are, as nearly as they can ever be, "at one" (as Solomon, speaking in Jungian accents, puts it in his exalted and edifying, postcoital—also, apparently, precoital: they were a randy pair—conversation with "the Witch").

For the Anima need not, always and inevitably, spell danger or destruction. Writing of Anima and Animus (fittingly enough, it was Emma Jung rather than her husband who gave exclusive attention to the latter in a paper that she called "On the Nature of the Animus"), Jung says: "These two crepuscular figures from the dark hinterland of the psyche—truly the semi-grotesque 'guardians of the threshold,' to use the pompous jargon of theosophy—can assume an almost inexhaustible number of shapes, enough to fill whole volumes. Their complicated transformations are as rich and strange as the world itself, as manifold as the limitless variety of their conscious correlate, the persona" (*CW*, VII, par. 339). Yeats would likely have felt "pompous jargon" to be an unnecessary and gratuitous thrust, since he adopted this (and even more inflated) language to describe the personifications that hover about in that crisis "that joins [the] buried self for certain moments to our trivial daily mind." And who is Jung, anyway, to talk of "pompous jargon" when he has just been going on at length about "Anima" and "Animus"? Be that as it may, Yeats, from his theosophical learning and private experience, confirms the Anima/Animus doctrine of Jungian psychology when, immediately after the passage about joining consciousness to the buried self, he writes, "There are, indeed, personifying spirits that we had best call but Gates and Gate-keepers, because they bring our souls to crisis, to Mask and Image . . ." (*Auto.*, p. 272). Of course, Anima and Animus are not the only "guardians of the threshold," not the only "Gates and Gate-keepers," not the only "archetypes of the collective unconscious." There are also, for example (and note psyche's tendency to personification), the Wise Old Man, the Shadow (called by Jung the "inferior personality"), and the Self, which latter is capable not only of various personifications but a number of schematizations as well (most notably by way of circles, spheres, and, of course, the numinous and ubiquitous quaternity). The special peculiarity of Anima and Animus is that they are always of the opposite sex from the person who dreams, envisions, or otherwise experiences them, and this is because every man has in his psychological makeup a feminine aspect (which remains largely unconscious), as every woman has a masculine aspect (which remains largely unconscious). "My dear, my dear," as Yeats wrote to Dorothy Wellesley, and one scarcely knows what transpired in the situation he refers to, "My dear, my dear—when you crossed the room with that boyish movement, it was no man who looked at you, it was the woman in me. It seems that I can make a woman express herself as never before. I have looked out of her eyes. I have shared her desire" (*Letters*, p. 868). Lady Dorothy become "boyish" and Yeats become womanish—it sounds like being a very remarkable commerce of realized Animus and Anima. What Yeats further claims about himself suggests that he succeeded, to a fuller degree than most people, in bringing the feminine aspect of his personality into consciousness—as, indeed, copious personal testimony about Jung would indicate was true of him also.

Having looked deep into the psychic well until a sketchy face forms before the mind's eye (though we are seldom aware of what we are about), we choose for sexual partner and marital *daimon* that person who seems to answer most completely to the image that we see reflected there, but of course that which we see can only be an image of psychic energies from the unconscious no more than dimly perceived by consciousness. Formless energies and imageless instincts, they still urge us to seek those forms and those images that they desire. Such, at least, is the teaching about the Pleroma of Jung/Basilides of Zurich/Alexandria and such the doctrine of the sometime "Patron" of the Dublin Astrological Society. The lore is esoteric and the myth is Biblical, but what Yeats says in *Estrangement* about the woman that a man is compelled to love adds up to the same thing as Jung's clinical and psychological discoveries about the Anima: "There is an astrological sense in which a man's wife or sweetheart is always an Eve made from a rib of his body. She is drawn to him because she represents a group of stellar influences in the radical horoscope" (*Auto.*, p. 480). There is also, as well as the astrological sense, a *psycho*logical sense in which this is true, which should tell us, as it told Yeats and Jung, as it told Plato, and as it has told philosophical astrologers of all time, that there is an intimate correlation between the disposition of the stars and psyche's destiny. "My evenings are taken up very largely with astrology. I make horoscopic calculations in order to find a clue to the core of psychological truth." Yeats or Jung? It could well be either, but chances to be the latter (*Letters*, I, 24). Jung would doubtless have been unwilling to come out of the astrological closet by accepting to be Patron of any such society as Yeats's (Jung did, however, acknowledge that he had horoscopes drawn up in cases where the psychological diagnosis presented special difficulty), but he nevertheless felt, as did Yeats, that it was possible to achieve psychic insights, and profound ones too, through "horoscopic calculations." If we can discover the "stellar influences" that make a man's Eve to be as she is, then, according to Yeats (and certainly according to the Zurich astrologer also), we possess an invaluable key to his character and his destiny as well. "These influences also create an element in his character, and his destiny, in things apart from love or marriage." A man's character is his *daimon* and his destiny—Yeats knew the Heraclitean dictum perfectly well. "Whether this element" in his character and his destiny "be good or evil," Yeats goes on to say, "she"—his spouse, his sweetheart, his Anima or his Eve—"is therefore its external expression. The happiest have such horoscopes that they find what they have of good in their wives, others must find what they have of evil. . . . All external events of life are of course an externalization of character in the same way, but not to the same degree as the wife, who may represent the gathering up of an entire web of influences" (*Auto.*, p. 481). When Yeats abandoned the role of unrequited lover to Helen of Troy and assumed the wiser and more mature, but no less passionate, relationship of Solomon to Sheba—entering that marriage bed that is "the symbol of the solved antinomy" and almost, by the ecstatic effort of the married couple, more than symbol ("O! Solomon! let us try again")—it is as if, through a genius virtually superhuman, he had recast his entire horoscope, completely remodelled his Anima, and turned his destiny right around from evil to good: *eudaimon* now rather than *kakodaimon*.

A man's Eve is the external expression, in Yeats's phrase, of a hidden element in his character, the externalization of dark impulses, "the gathering up of an entire web of influences"; in other words, she is his Anima—one of those archetypes that channel and give expression to powerful, blind, and formless energies of the personal and collective unconscious. What goes on at that psychic level where an instinctual charge limns itself as an archetypal image can never be described in the rational and discursive language of consciousness because once the process enters consciousness it ceases as a phenomenon of the unconscious. The process may go on between consciousness and the unconscious, and we may observe it, but then it must speak, and we must understand, a language of myth, symbol, and archetype, not a language of concept, reason, and logic. The poet of the depths and the psychologist of the depths —which is also to say the poet of antique truths and the psychologist of the Pleroma—must be skilled in the act of fusing sense and nonsense (nor would a sense of humor—the gift of consciousness to the silliness of the unconscious—come amiss in either case), for that is the way things are there, at that transformational depth, where old mummy truths have been laid to rest but only to rise up as the figures of our dreams, as revenants incapable of lying quiet in the tomb, as the voices of those dead whom we have "thrust back in the human mind again," whence they address, in ghostly tones of nonsensical sense, the living and waking consciousness. But those truths must find their proper voice and must dress themselves in the appropriate garments of dream-figures, else they remain mere dark impulses, pure instinct, invisible, intangible, undifferentiated—they remain, that is to say, unconscious, effectively dead, swallowed up and lost in the Pleroma.

Now in the Pleroma, nothing is distinguished or differentiated from anything else. Thus it was that Jung, our only modern scientist of the Pleroma, argued for what he called "the energic point of view"—the view, that is, that the unconscious is a kind of storehouse of energy that is determined quantitatively but not qualitatively; that psyche is a process whereby this originally undifferentiated and unconscious energy is transformed into conscious psychological capacities that are directed to specific ends; that the process of psyche is a closed system in which the quantity of energy remains constant—it is differentiated and transformed but suffers neither increase nor decrease; and that it is the symbol that effects the transformation, making what was undirected directed and differentiating that which was undifferentiated. Let us, Jung said, call this hypothetical quantity, this psychic energy, by its classical name of "libido," and let us not ascribe any specific form or direction to this old/new concept of "libido." Let us, in other words, try to undermine the Freudian position that neuroses have an exclusively sexual aetiology by redefining libido and by denying that it must necessarily have a sexual reference. There are, according to Jung, other things than sex that cause people to go crazy,[9] and libido, consequently, is best understood, not as the equivalent of sexuality, but "as an inclusive term for psychic intensities, and consequently as sheer psychic energy" (*CW*, VII, p. 53, n. 6). Jung had to choose some term to characterize the copious psychic facts he had observed, and so he chose "libido," but "libido" is only a word, after all, and changing the word will not change the facts. What if, instead of call-

---

9. Jung's progress from a Freudian to a Jungian position can be traced with particular clarity by comparing what Jung says on "love" and the "erotic" in the first and last versions of an essay that he published under various titles and heavily revised, in 1912, 1917, and 1943 (all versions are to be found in *CW*, VII). In the original version, Jung claimed that "in point of fact it [the erotic conflict] always is" the cause of neurosis (par. 423); in the final version he denied this outright, saying, first, that love, which often causes neurosis, is much broader than sexuality, and, second, that "There are other ways of becoming neurotic" (p. 18, n. 10). Once free of Freud, Jung went very far in the other direction. Addressing a "Pastoral Conference" in 1932, he said: "Among all my patients in the second half of life—that is to say, over thirty-five—there has not been one whose problem in the last resort was not that of finding a religious outlook on life" (*CW*, XI, par. 509). According to Yeats, "spiritual excitement and the sexual torture . . . are somehow inseparable" (*Letters*, p. 731)—but Yeats, so far as I know, was never invited to address a Pastoral Conference.

ing psychic energy "libido," we were to rename it "the Pleroma," or "the White Light"? Could we not then say something like this?— "The White Light is in itself an undifferentiated energy, and receives its differentiated impulse from the symbol that collects it." Saying this, we would have not only the warm best wishes of Jung behind us, but would be speaking word for word as Yeats spoke to his fellow adepti of the Golden Dawn when he addressed the inner circle on the question, "Is the Order of R.R. & A.C. to remain a Magical Order?"[10] Yeats, of course, devoutly wished that it remain so and that it not disintegrate into "a society for experiment and research" (p. 11)—which, to him, would be "an ignominious end" (p. 15). And it was the symbol—nothing else—that gathered magical energies, differentiated them, and put them into the wonder-working hands of the magicians. (If we recall that Leda was "laid in that white rush," and suggest further that the white rush and the White Light are doubtless something alike, we will be in a position to see that Yeats would have shared Jung's view "that though the term 'libido,' introduced by Freud, is not without a sexual connotation, an exclusively sexual definition of this concept is one-sided and must therefore be rejected" [*CW*, V, par. 185]. While the swan came down on Leda with—in the Freudian sense—libidinous intent, it would be needlessly irreverent to suggest that the magicians of the Golden Dawn hoped to exercise their symbols to such ends.)

"The psychological mechanism that transforms energy is the symbol." When Jung says this (*CW*, VIII, par. 88), he may appear to be removed from Yeats and the Golden Dawn by all the discretion that he imagined himself to exercise as an empirical scientist; but if we observe that it was the psychologist, not the Rosicrucian, who elsewhere said, parentically and as a kind of throwaway, "'Magical' is simply another word for 'psychic'" (*CW*, VII, par. 293), then must we not feel that Jung, whether for good or bad, is hoist with the same petard as Yeats and that it is in fact Jung's own petard? "The magical mechanism that transforms energy is the symbol." Yeats would not have cared much for the word "mechanism" in this context, but he was as committed to the content of this statement as Jung was. Symbols, in Jungian terminology, are

---

10. "Is the Order of R.R. & A.C. to remain a Magical Order?" was a privately printed pamphlet (1901); the quotation is from page 18. The pamphlet has been reprinted in George Mills Harper's book, *Yeats's Golden Dawn* (London: Macmillan, 1974).

"libido analogies" (*CW*, V, p. 146)—images, as it were, of dark impulses and thereby also an expression of those impulses—and the purpose of symbol-formation "is the transformation of libido" (*CW*, VIII, par. 93), "so we have every reason to value symbol-formation and to render homage to the symbol as an inestimable means of utilizing the mere instinctual flow of energy for effective work" (ibid., par. 90). The last step in the argument of Jung's pleromatic psychology, as also in Yeats's theory of poetry and magic, is the observation that we do not make up or invent symbols, archetypes, or libido analogues. We may, and we do, discover symbols, but we can never invent them, for they go farther back in time and farther down in the unconscious than the inventive capabilities of consciousness could ever reach. Symbols are the natural creation of aeons of human experience and so give effective body to the energies accumulated and passed on during that time; they would be incapable of transforming any of that undifferentiated energy of the collective psyche if they were the mere invention of ephemeral consciousness. It was Jung's special addition to Yeats's notion that we inherit energies and symbols alike from the dead of the ages to say that the inheritance is a psychological fact that can be observed empirically and demonstrated scientifically. Jung maintained (nor can there be any doubt that Yeats would have concurred with him) that we inherit our psyche, not the conscious contents of psyche but psyche itself, an inheritance which is not only from parents, ancestors, and nation but from the entire race, and moreover, that along with psyche we inherit psyche's symbols, which are, so to say, a picturing, in undrawn lines or in ink that becomes visible only through experience, of the structure of the psyche. According to Jung's science, the psyche, because it includes both the ages-old unconscious and the consciousness of today, creates symbols that "are always grounded in the unconscious archetype, but their manifest forms are moulded by the ideas acquired by the conscious mind. The archetypes are the numinous, structural elements of the psyche and possess a certain autonomy and specific energy which enables them to attract, out of the conscious mind, those contents which are best suited to themselves" (*CW*, V, par. 344). By turning this notion of psyche as a symbol-maker—*the* single, great symbol-maker—to religious questions, Jung contrived, in this same volume, to offend both believers and nonbelievers. Calling "God" a "psychic fact," Jung explains that "the God-image"—which "must necessarily be regarded as representing a certain sum of energy (libido) which appears as projection"—is a spontaneous creation of the unconscious psyche as it pictures itself, and so, although produced by human creativity, "it has a reality independent of the attitude of the conscious mind" (*CW*, V, par. 89 and n. 29). To nonbelievers, it was a scandal to talk of "God" at all, with or without the cautious dress of inverted commas, in a scientific work; to the devout, it was plain blasphemy to speak of a "God-image" as if God were a minor subjective toy—one of the archetypes, and as such not even *primus inter pares*—rather than the greatest objective truth. The offense given and taken seems not to have bothered Jung greatly, however, since, like Socrates, he continued "to say the same things about the same things" from the time of this early work right through the *Mysterium Coniunctionis*.

"The individuation process," Jung wrote in an essay that first appeared exactly midway between *Symbols of Transformation* and *Mysterium Coniunctionis*, "subordinates the many to the One." This is not at all surprising in a text on psychological processes, their nature and their goal, and except for the quasi-technical term "individuation process," the sentence states a principle that is surely basic to all varieties of psychotherapy. What follows, however, is surprising in the highest degree and is the sort of offhand comment (albeit posing as quasi-paraphrase of patristic literature) that has proved too much for some of Jung's readers: "But the One is God, and that which corresponds to him in us is the *imago Dei*, the god-image" (*CW*, IX, pt. 1, par. 626). In becoming an individual, as Jung has it, each of us conforms himself to the *imago Dei* archetype discovered within himself and thereby becomes—perhaps it would be safest to insert "as it were"—God. The psyche is a dichotomous and (we can be sure) a quaternal system in Jung's view, but it realizes itself as a process the goal of which is the highest and most intense unity. It is something of a paradox (on which Jung and the Pleroma thrive alike) that the individuation process commences in oneness, for the Pleroma represents a wild and woolly unity, and it concludes, after all the travail of dissociation, separation, and differentiation, after the "principium individuationis" has asserted itself and run its full course, once again in oneness, for the self is a union of all the contraries that go to make up psychic experience. From the destructive oneness of the solely unconscious to the highly creative, constructive oneness that joins consciousness and the unconscious, two unities unified—such is the individuation process of analytical psychology. It is almost, in that finest phrase of Plotinian mysticism, a question of "a flight of the alone to the alone," although Jung would of course ordinarily prefer to consider the process in its natural and psychological aspect rather than in its supernatural and mystical aspect. The calculus of Jungian individuation goes like this: the unconscious is a "one" ("The unconscious is the universal mediator among men. It is in a sense the all-embracing One . . ." [*CW*, XI, par. 419]); consciousness discovers itself in the unconscious and separates itself out, then distinguishes a series of pairs of opposites, and thereafter the endless multiplicity of this world ("That was the first morning of the world, the first sunrise after the primal darkness, when that inchoately conscious complex, the ego, the son of the darkness, knowingly sundered subject and object, and thus precipitated the world and itself into definite existence . . ." [*CW*, XIV, par. 129]); and yet the curious end of this unfolding of the many out of the one is (in Eliot's phrase) "to arrive where we started / And know the place for the first time"—for the self that is the goal and the intention of individuation is a psychic entity more intensely unified than the unconscious, possessed of and by a oneness equalled only in its own archetype, the *imago Dei*, and in the presumed, objective referent of that *imago*, God.

"Old writers had an admirable symbolism," Yeats wrote some fifty years before Jung got around to *Mysterium Coniunctionis*, yet referring to a solar and lunar symbolism to be found *passim* in volumes XII, XIII, and XIV of Jung's *Collected Works*. "I myself imagine a marriage of the sun and moon in the arts I take most pleasure in; and now bride and bridegroom but exchange, as it were, full cups of gold and silver, and now they are one in a mystical embrace" (*Ex.*, p. 24). That Yeats happens to be talking about the arts here rather than about alchemical and psychological processes is of very little moment, since the symbolism he refers to, as Jung so copiously demonstrated, is capable of psychological as well as artistic elaboration; moreover, the marriage of complementary opposites that Yeats envisions in the arts could very well be taken as a reflection or a projection of a prior "mystical embrace," namely that *hieros gamos* that Jung calls "the self." If the sun and moon of consciousness and the unconscious have not celebrated their nuptials and so produced a more unified One, there can hardly be a unity about those arts that psyche creates to express, reveal, and delight herself. A poem will have Unity of Being only if the poet has (but we should remember that this unity expressly includes the unconscious, hence will not be a mere surface affair and will doubtless fail to be apparent at times in the poet's conscious, daily existence; in the unconscious consciousness of his poem, however, it must seem to be present as his persona—the unity of the poet as Poet). "Because the microcosm is identical with the macrocosm, it attracts the latter and thus brings about a kind of apocatastasis, a restoration of . . . the original wholeness," Jung says, speaking a language very like the language of Aristophanes in the *Symposium* (and borrowed by Aristophanes from Empedocles). Of alchemical processes, which are really psychological processes expressed in a strange symbolic tongue, Jung goes on to say: "The moral equivalent of the physical transmutation into gold is *self-knowledge*, which is a re-remembering of the *homo totus*" (*CW*, XIII, par. 372). *Homo totus*, "the ἄνθρωπος, the Son of Man, the *homo maximus*, the *vir unus*, purusha, etc." (*CW*, XI, par. 419)—they are all, Jung maintained (and he had both tacit and explicit agreement from Yeats), archetypes of the self, the beginning and the end of psychic process, an exercise of Platonic *anamnesis*, a memory of wholeness and an apocatastasis that restores wholeness.

There may not be quite the same boisterous (not to say scurrilous) humor about the Christian formulation of this symbolic figure as there is in the Aristophanic tale, but that Christianity, too, provided an archetype of the self, and would scarcely have got off the ground as a religion if it had failed to provide one, was quite obvious to Yeats and Jung alike. That this archetypal god-man was neither unique to Christianity nor original with it was equally obvious to Yeats and Jung; on the contrary, Jung would say, because it is an archetypal idea it is by definition universal in occurrence and capable of autochthonous revival, anywhere, at any time. Wherever there is psyche, there are archetypes, and wherever there are archetypes, the archetype of wholeness or of the self will be in the forefront—or more exactly it will be at the center, since the preeminent image of the self (when it is not a quaternity) is a mandala, i.e., a circle or sphere. "This archetypal idea is a reflection of the individual's wholeness, i.e., of the self, which is present in him as an unconscious image," writes Jung (*CW*, XI, par. 230); and in the next paragraph, with reference to the success of Christianity, he says: "It was this archetype of the self in the soul of every man that responded to the Christian message, with the result that the concrete Rabbi Jesus was rapidly assimilated by the constellated archetype. In this way Christ realized the idea of the self." Thus Christ represents the culmination of all psychic process, since, as Jung puts it on the following page, "the goal of psychological, as of biological, development is self-realization, or individuation" (ibid., par. 233). More starkly and more emphatically (the italics are his), Jung elsewhere says, "*Christ exemplifies the archetype of the self*" (*CW*, IX, pt. 2, par. 70). In Christ, who represents the symbolic ultimate in individuation, the many are entirely subordinated to the One, "But the One is God," as Jung has said. However much offense symbolic readings may give to fundamentalist Christians, we can hardly call this blasphemy; the real question, as other critics have urged, is whether we can call it science. Yeats, who carefully avoided any position that would leave him open to the sort of crossfire sniping suffered by Jung in this matter—Yeats avoided it by having little enough commerce with doctrinaire Christianity and less with science—works out the question of Christ and the self in a journal entry that begins with the remark that the "imitation of Christ" is supposed to be in some way different from "self-realization" (*Memoirs*, p. 138). Jung always maintained that the *imitatio Christi* should not be understood as a slavish imitation, or as an attempt to "ape his stigmata" (*CW*, XI, par. 522), but instead should be understood precisely as "self-realization." Yeats seems of the same mind when, immediately after the foregoing passage, he turns contentious and demands, "What of it? Christ is but another self, but he is the supernatural self." Not all Christians would warm to Yeats's notion, but surely all Jungians would, and so would all good Empedocleans and Platonists, who must believe in a transmigratory supernatural self—the *daimon* of Empedocles and of the *Timaeus*—for which, in Yeats's variety of Christianity, Christ stands as the exemplar, the paradigm, the archetype. To realize that self is to attain to the philosopher's goal in the highest degree and to ascend to the *eidos* of humanity: such is the meaning of Yeats's remark (and of his poetry), of Jung's psychology, and of Plato's philosophy. What is most important to observe here is that in the picturing or imaging of its own structure and process (as Christ, as Anthropos, as Primordial Man), psyche displays its intrinsic oneness; and furthermore, the unity-in-complexity that is so profoundly characteristic of psyche is of the very nature of system. Thus, psyche herself insists upon her systemic nature.

Yeats, typically enough, was quick to bring the supernatural into his psychological system: Christ "is the supernatural self." But obviously system must embrace the natural as well as the supernatural, and Jung (who nevertheless did not altogether eschew supernatural reference and explanation) provides most of our evidence for a discussion of psyche as a natural phenomenon. It is Yeats who, in a well-known passage in *The Trembling of the Veil*, tells how he was deprived by natural scientists (Huxley and Tyndall) "of the simple-minded religion of my childhood," and so was forced to put together a religion of his own that he might bring the supernatural back to a mystical embrace with the natural: a religion composed "of poetic tradition, of a fardel of stories, and of personages, and of emotions . . . , passed on from generation to generation by poets and painters with some help from philosophers and theologians" (*Auto.*, p. 116). I think that Yeats would have been more than willing to acknowledge that these archetypal figures—for that is what they are: images of emotions and instincts—could appear spontaneously to the artist's imagination, and so be recreated by him, as well as being capable of historic transmission "from generation to generation." For his religion, Yeats says, he "even created a dogma," and the language of his dogma could be adopted by any worshipper in Jung's Church: "Because those imaginary people are created out of the deepest instinct of man [Jung: archetypal figures are personifications of the instincts], to be his measure and his norm [Jung: archetypes are analogous to patterns of behavior], whatever I can imagine those mouths speaking may be the nearest I can go to truth." No Jungian has ever imagined that he could go nearer to the truth than by an attentive observation of the archetypes of the collective unconscious. Finally, in an added twist to Jungian dogma— but it is a twist that Jung himself was often inclined to give—Yeats says, "When I listened they seemed always to speak of one thing only: they, their loves, every incident of their lives, were steeped in the supernatural" (*Auto.*, p. 116). Those figures that rise up trailing clouds of supernatural glory from the Pleroma that is their home appear on the one hand as self-portraits of inherited instincts and on the other hand as a "measure" and a "norm" for the individual, factors that determine both the possibilities and the necessities of human life. "Man," as Yeats uses that word above—as Jung uses that word too, and as he also uses the word "psyche"—is simultaneously a collective and an individual noun: archetypes are created out of the deepest instinct of collective man to be the measure and norm of individual man. Psychologically as well as biologically we are compelled to live in ways that are not, and cannot be, so very different from the ways of our ancestors.

The archetypes (and according to Jung this is true of everything psychic) look both backward and forward: the creation and deposit of collective psychic experience, they are also the ground plan and inheritance of individual psychic experience. The kind of figure "in visible human form" (*CW*, V, par. 259) that Yeats observed, listened to, and made the basis of his "dogma" would not be, according to Jung, "man" as a creature of trivial, everyday existence, "but the superman, the hero or god, that *quasi-human* being who symbolizes the ideas, forms, and forces which grip and mould the soul. These, so far as psychological experience is concerned, are the archetypal contents of the (collective) unconscious, the archaic heritage of humanity, the legacy left behind by all differentiation and development and bestowed upon all men like sunlight and air" (ibid.). Everything that the "principium individuationis" has done in the human past by way of breaking up and separating out the confused oneness of the Pleroma, dividing and differentiating that *massa confusa* with the sharp tool of consciousness, is paradoxically added to that Pleroma and stored therein to become a heritable possibility for every individual who will in the future be instinctively driven to make his way out of the suffocating unconsciousness of pleromatic existence/nonexistence. Why the Pleroma should thus harbor its own enemy is perhaps inexplicable, unless one falls back on its mere paradoxicality as an explanation, but what Jung indicates is that the collective unconscious receives into itself and preserves all the achievements, necessarily inimical to the unconscious, of human consciousness. Powerful and paradoxical as it is, the collective unconscious, it seems, need not fear receiving something as apparently insignificant as the light of consciousness. Consciousness, on the other hand, has every reason to fear the blind, overwhelming might of that amoral beast which is the collective unconscious. The material produced in relatively benign neuroses, Jung says, "is mainly of a personal nature," but in cases of real insanity (Jung's clinical investigations into the nature of psyche began in his work with schizophrenics), "the personal sphere is often completely swamped by collective representations" (*CW*, XVII, par. 207). Given the nature of the collective unconscious, Jung was necessarily ambivalent in his attitude toward it—which is something that all too few readers recognize, supposing that Jung was head over heels in love with that to which he had given a name in modern psychology. In fact, Jung recognized that the collective unconscious was a destroyer as well as a preserver; and while he explored it almost endlessly, he never ceased to warn patients and readers against the danger of death by drowning. That collectivity that makes one layer of the unconscious so insidiously attractive—for, like the sea with its vast energies, it is as potentially creative as it is potentially dangerous—is a matter of inheritance (since we all inherit that layer of the unconscious, we are all bound collectively together) and specifically, according to Jung, a matter of inherited brain structure. "This impersonal layer of the psyche I have termed the COLLECTIVE UNCONSCIOUS—'collective' because it is not an individual acquisition but is rather the functioning of the inherited brain structure, which in its broad outlines is the same in all human beings, and in certain respects the same even in mammals. The inherited brain is the product of our ancestral life. It consists of the structural deposits or equivalents of psychic activities which were repeated innumerable times in the life of our ancestors. Conversely, it is at the same time the ever-existing a priori type and author of the corresponding activity. Far be it from me to decide which came first, the hen or the egg" (ibid.). Jung may say that it is far from him to decide this issue, but the fact is that in the three sentences that precede his disclaimer he has already decided it very emphatically: like Yeats, Jung decides in favor of both the hen *and* the egg. The archetypes are the product of our ancestral life, deposits of psychic experience, the foster children of instincts and slow time. On the other hand, there is an "a priori type" that determines the configuration of ancestral life and of psychic experience, and for slow time itself there is an "ever-existing" archetype which can only be eternity.

Does psyche create myth, or does myth shape psyche? Of the mythological (i.e., archetypal) battle in the poem called "The Valley of the Black Pig," and of many other, similar battles represented by this one, Yeats says: "[A]ll these battles are one, the battle of all things with shadowy decay. Once a symbolism has possessed the imagination of large numbers of men, it becomes, as I believe, an embodiment of disembodied powers, and repeats itself in dreams and visions, age after age" (*Poems*, p. 810). From its apparent origin in the subjective emotions of men, the symbol or the archetype assumes an objective life and power of its own, so that it is simultaneously both the product and the shaper of human experience. "I consider . . . archetypal patterns to be the matrix of all mythological statements. They not only occur in highly emotional conditions but very often seem to be their cause" (*CW*, XIII, par. 550). The creation of a work of art is without doubt "highly emotional," as Jung puts it, and Yeats, in his comments on dramatic art, points up the paradoxical, Janus-faced doubleness of the myth, symbol, or archetype that gives life to the work of art as to its creator. The figures of the dramatist's art, Yeats says, must seem "the creation of a new personality," themselves absolutely new, as if they could never "have existed before his day, or have been imagined before his day" (*Ex.*, p. 152); yet his is a creation not so much of intellect and consciousness, where everything is new and different, but of the unconscious, where all is immensely old and the same—"not a deliberate creation, but the creation of intense feeling, . . . and every feeling is the child of all past ages . . ." (ibid.). Art "in its highest moments," as Yeats phrases it here, discovers the archetype or the image within the intense feeling and so turns that emotional intensity to positive ends. Archetypes—which, according to Jung, "are typical forms that appear spontaneously all over the world, independently of tradition, in myths, fairy-tales, fantasies, dreams, visions, and the delusional systems of the insane" (*CW*, III, par. 565)—descend to us, along with those intense emotions and instincts of which they are analogues, from all past ages; and through participation in the archetypes, as the artist succeeds in realizing them in his work, we reascend to that unity that is symbolized in so many different ways and that we might call "the self"—Yeats and Jung called it so—if by that we mean the self of humanity, the *eidos* of our being.

"Delusional systems of the insane"—the phrase is an important and revealing one. Jung was one of the first psychiatrists to maintain that there is a system, largely private though it remain, behind the delusions of madmen. What the insane say and what they do is for them not at all meaningless but is interrelated and interwoven as part of a complete and significant world, a complex and articulated system. According to Jung, there is, literally, a mad logic about all that is said and done in the insane asylum, and we should do well to attend to that logic and try to piece together that system because we, too, however normal or otherwise we be, have our share in that same unconscious that has completely engulfed the insane and that has extinguished consciousness in them. "The human psyche, even when in a pathological condition, is a complex whole actuated not only by instinctual processes and personal relationships but by the spiritual needs and supra-personal currents of the time" (*CW*, X, par. 1046). The conclusion to which this near alliance of the sane and the insane (almost a Heraclitean interpenetration of opposed states: insane sane, sane insane, living the others' death and dying the others' life) leads Jung is, characteristically, a double one: in the delusional systems of the insane we should grasp something more of the systematic working of the unconscious in all men; and, on the other hand, the psychotherapist ought also to be a psychologist, for "just as the general practitioner is rightly expected to know the *normal* anatomy and physiology of the body he has to treat, so the psychotherapist will sooner or later feel constrained to know everything that is of vital importance to the life of the psyche. He will, in short, have to approach psychology as one of the human sciences" (ibid.). In the insane we see a darkened mirror image of the sane, and in the sane an image of that balanced system that the insane would attain to if they could ever succeed in bringing their unbalanced system out of utter isolation in the unconscious. "When we penetrate into the human secrets of our patients, the madness discloses the system upon which it is based, and we recognize insanity to be simply an unusual reaction to emotional problems which are in no wise foreign to ourselves" (*CW*, III, par. 339). The myths, fairy tales, fantasies, dreams, and visions that Jung coupled with the delusions of the insane achieve their meaning by reference to an unconscious system from which they arise, a system which they express and reflect, and a system which binds all together in a single collective whole. Dreams, for instance, Jung says, "are the visible links in a chain of unconscious events" (*CW*, XI, par. 53); and if we recall our dreams, then we gain for consciousness a view into what Jung imagines to be "a continuity of unconscious processes," for dreams are "symptoms of some consistent unconscious activity which becomes directly visible at night . . . , but only occasionally breaks through the inhibitions imposed by our daytime consciousness" (*CW*, VII, par. 273). In *Analytical Psychology* (the Tavistock Lectures), Jung gives an intriguing formulation to this same idea of continuous unconscious processes when he speculates that "we are dreaming all the time, although we are not aware of it by day because consciousness is much too clear" (*CW*, XVIII, par. 162); and, while the language is more Yeatsian, I think what we learn is entirely Jungian when, in the 1925 *Vision*, we are told, "In our dreams we communicate with the dead in their *Waking State*, and these dreams never come to an end though they are only known to us while we sleep" (p. 246). The only difference between normal dreaming and the delusional systems of the insane, in Jung's view of it, is that in madness the "consistent unconscious activity" is forever breaking through the inhibitions of daytime consciousness and nullifying its clarity—it is, in fact, of the very nature of insanity that in such a condition the unconscious destroys consciousness and takes over even in daytime activities where consciousness would ordinarily rule.

The important point in all this is that Jung always took the psyche to be a system—a natural system that, like everything in nature, is ultimately inexplicable, and so, while the system remains natural, it is nevertheless not without suggestions of the mysterious and the supernatural. "I have often felt tempted," Jung told the audience for his lectures on "Psychology and Religion" at Yale, "to advise my patients to think of the psyche as a subtle body in which subtle tumours can grow" (*CW*, XI, par. 36). Whether Jung resisted the temptation or not, I have no way of knowing; one might observe, however, that this is a lovely but dangerous sort of language to be using in a scientific text. Yet, what Jung was trying to do, if he did indeed give in to the temptation, was to appeal to patients who could think only in material terms but who might be led by way of subtilized matter to some conception of nonmaterial psyche. Nor is the proposed progress from material body to subtle body to bodiless psyche illogical, since both body and psyche are inherited systems that have evolved over an enormous period of time. After a long and eloquent personification of the unconscious as a collective two-million-year-old human being (some of which has been quoted above), Jung says, "it would be positively grotesque to call this immense system of experience in the unconscious psyche an illusion, for our visible and tangible body is itself just such a system" (*CW*, VIII, par. 675). Dreams and all the other manifestations of unconscious psychic activity Jung takes as symptoms or signs revealing the nature of the underlying system; or, to change the metaphor, they resemble visible flowers that can teach us what the invisible rhizome is like: "The symptom is like the shoot above ground, yet the main plant is an extended rhizome underground. The rhizome represents the content of a neurosis; it is the matrix of complexes, of symptoms, and of dreams. We have every reason to believe that dreams mirror exactly the underground processes of the psyche. And if we get there, we literally get at the 'roots' of the disease" (*CW*, XI, par. 37). Perhaps by this time it need not be said, but it will hurt nothing to say, that the metaphor that Jung adopts here to describe the contents and the symptoms of neuroses is equally effective in describing the contents, the processes, and the products of the healthy (and philosophic) mind in both its collective and its individual aspects. The unconscious corresponds to the rhizome underground, and consciousness to a flower blooming aboveground; the dream mediates between the two, pushing up the shoot that flowers, as the voices of the dead mediated, for Yeats and Jung, between the unconscious and consciousness, between the Pleroma and differentiated being, between all the old mummy truths and the mummy wheat laid in the grave on the one hand and the living minds that revived them, gave them expression, and brought them to flower in *A Vision* and *Seven Sermons* on the other hand.

Instinct on the one hand and archetype on the other are the connecting links that establish a universal kinship throughout animate nature and that bring psyche and the physical universe into conformity with one another. In the *Timaeus*, after the Demiourgos has created the World's Body ("smooth and uniform, everywhere equidistant from its centre, a body whole and complete"), he adds thereto a World-Soul and stretches it right the way around so that the Body and Soul shall be respectively the physical and psychic counterparts of one another ("And in the centre he set a soul and caused it to extend throughout the whole and further wrapped its body round with soul on the outside"), and he thus brought into being a most subtle body interfused throughout with soul, "one world alone," as Timaeus calls it, "round and revolving in a circle, solitary . . . and a blessed god" (34b; trans. Cornford). Neither Yeats nor Jung could claim to have been there when the Demiourgos created the lesser gods and then appointed them to create humankind and other living creatures in their turn, but like Timaeus (who was not there either except by way of "*mythos*") they were imaginative men both, and the story that their imaginations told them as they looked out on to the physical world and down into their psychological world carried pretty much the same news about the one psychic/physical cosmos as Timaeus delivered to Socrates and his friends. According to each of the tales, *physis* and *psychē* are interwoven—by the Demiourgos or by instinct and archetype—into a single *kosmos*. "'Instincts' or 'drives,'" Jung tells us in *Mysterium Coniunctionis* (and by this time he hardly needs to inform us that archetypes are "self-portraits" of instincts or drives), "can be formulated in physiological and biological terms"; but this is very far from being all that should be said about them, "for they are also psychic entities," in tune with the full, self-balancing system that is the psyche: "They are not just physiological or consistently biological phenomena, but are at the same time . . . meaningful fantasy structures with a symbolic character" (*CW*, XIV, par. 602). This could well be taken for a description of the way in which system creates meaning, weaving nature and psyche together by means of instincts, "for every instinct," as Jung goes on to say, "is linked *a priori* with a corresponding image of the situation. . . ." Dancing bees, birds that migrate in formation, and other birds that build elaborate nests offer good examples and analogies for instinctual, archetypal activities among their human brethren.

All these various points—the systemic character of the collective unconscious and its archetypes; the underground and aboveground doubleness of psyche; the relation between heritable archetypes and the structure of the brain; and the tie between *psychē* and *physis*—Jung spells out in an essay that he calls "Mind [or Psyche] and Earth" (*CW*, X). The Archetypes, in this version of an old story, are "the hidden foundations of the conscious mind, or, to use another comparison, the roots which the psyche has sunk not only in the earth in the narrower sense but in the world in general." That psyche sinks roots here while pushing up shoots elsewhere, and that roots and shoots are both really archetypes is nothing for us to complain about, since psyche embraces the totality of the rhizome and its flowers, and sends its archetypes both down and up to the depths of the unconscious and the heights of consciousness. To put it another way, as Jung does immediately after the passage quoted, the archetypes are both outward- and inward-looking: "Archetypes are systems of readiness for action, and at the same time images and emotions. They are inherited with the brain-structure—indeed, they are its psychic aspect. . . . They are thus, essentially, the chthonic portion of the psyche, if we may use such an expression—that portion through which the psyche is attached to nature, or in which its link with the earth and the world appears at its most tangible" (*CW*, X, par. 53). If archetypes are the psychic aspect of the brain-structure, then one might suppose that they are altogether time-bound, since the brain is presumably a creature of time—unless, indeed, the brain-structure itself is to be seen as that "most sovereign form of soul" which, according to the *Timaeus*, is "given to each man as a *daimon*—that part which we say dwells in the summit of our body and lifts us from earth towards our celestial affinity, like a plant whose roots are not in earth, but in the heavens" (90a). For it is this *daimon* which will, if anything can and if properly cultivated, make us immortal and divine and will establish for us a blessed relationship with eternity. The archetypes, in Timaeus' version of them, are rooted not so much in earth as in the heavens and show forth that heavenly paradigm that determines their existence. According to the *Timaeus*, this cosmos in which we are so deeply implicated, both as physical and as psychic beings, is everlasting, but it is not eternal. Eternity—whether we listen to Plato's Timaeus, to Yeats, or to Jung—eternity is just not natural; nor is nature eternal. Jung was chary of saying that the archetypes are modelled (or *were* modelled by a Demiourgos) on an Archetype, and he declined to make the Timaean declaration that nature was created at a certain moment and has evolved to its present state in the course of time as the image of an eternal paradigm. But this is no more than to say that Jung chose to remain (at least for the most part) a natural scientist busy at his work within a Platonic universe which, however, he had no way of observing from outside itself or from outside time.

Yeats, with the assistance of a fine story about Plotinus and invoking the authority of a very questionable passage in the *Enneads* (Ennead V, Tractate 7), tried to get around the thorny problem of archetypes and an Archetype, or of time and eternity, by asserting something that he would call "timeless individuality." The story is that an Egyptian mage "offered to evoke a visible manifestation of Plotinus' presiding spirit" and, having done so, informed Plotinus that his *daimon* was of no lower order of spirit but was a God. (Unfortunately, the mage's assistant, being for whatever reason overwrought, strangled the birds—apparently necessary to sustain the evocation—and so the apparition disappeared before the evokers had any opportunity to chat with it.) Certainly, if his guardian genius was a God, Plotinus was possessed of a "timeless individuality," and it was Yeats's belief (expressed in a rather muddled passage in the introduction to *Words upon the Window-pane*) that Plotinus maintained the idea as a central part of his psychology and his philosophy. "It is fitting that Plotinus should have been the first philosopher to meet his daimon face to face, though the boy attendant out of jealousy or in convulsive terror strangled the doves, for he was the first to establish as sole source the timeless individuality or daimon instead of the Platonic Idea, to prefer Socrates to his thought" (*Ex.*, p. 368). Yeats continues his exegesis of the Plotinian discovery with the following rather dark observations, couched in Jungian terminology, which would seem to point to a doctrine of metempsychosis: "This timeless individuality contains archetypes of all possible existences whether of man or brute, and as it traverses its circle of allotted lives, now one, now another, prevails. We may fail to express our archetype or alter it by reason, but all done from nature is its unfolding into time." Timeless individuality, devised by Yeats out of Plotinus (with more than a little of Plato, Empedocles, and Pythagoras added to spice the idea up), appears to be an Archetype of archetypes—or an Archetype containing sub-archetypes—which operates as a transmigratory *daimon*, itself always the same no matter how many different faces it takes on in the round of its incarnations. What Yeats says in the final clause—"all done from nature is its unfolding into time"—is entirely agreeable with Jungian pronouncements on the archetypes; nor would Jung have found anything wrong with the phrase "timeless individuality," since something very like that was the center and the goal of his psychology. In his essay on "The Psychology of the Child Archetype," Jung discusses such a timeless individuality as Yeats finds in Plotinus, and he indicates that, as with the Yeatsian-Plotinian archetype, the child archetype is stored up in some supertemporal (if not supercelestial) place quite beyond the experience of men. "The 'child' is therefore *renatus in novam infantiam*. It is thus both beginning and end, an initial and a terminal creature. The initial creature existed before man was, and the terminal creature will be when man is not. . . . Wholeness, empirically speaking, is therefore of immeasurable extent, older and younger than consciousness and enfolding it in time and space" (*CW*, IX, pt. 1, par. 299). Jung does not speak of metempsychosis, except metaphorically (each individual incarnating the archetype of wholeness and thus the collective soul of the race), but the child archetype, which is virtually timeless and a symbol of individuality, is otherwise perfectly consonant with what Yeats read out of Plotinus (and perhaps read into him as well).

Plotinus was not the only philosopher who could warm Yeats's imagination to a doctrine of "timeless individuality or daimon." Indeed, there seems to have been a certain period (the years between the two versions of *A Vision*—those years when Yeats returned to reading philosophy after the Instructors' injunction against such reading had been lifted) when every book Yeats opened spoke to him of "timeless individual or daimon." The notes that Yeats scribbled in the margins of various books—A. N. Whitehead's *Science and the Modern World*, Benedetto Croce's *Philosophy of the Practical* and his *Logic as the Science of the Pure Concept*, Henri Bergson's *Matter and Memory*, and others—indicate that the revelations of the Instructors had been revealed before (or were being revealed just then: *Science and the Modern World* was first published in 1926), though the revelations were not always in precisely the terminology of *A Vision* and therefore asked for marginal glosses by the Instructors' most recent spokesman and the latest expositor of their system. *Science and the Modern World* is dotted with markings like "C. M." (Creative Mind), "B. F." (Body of Fate), and "unity of being"; on page 222, Yeats remarked to himself, "Hence non moral nature of daimon"— which is a thoroughly Jungian and Basilidean comment; and on page 226, Yeats wrote in the margin, "daimon = the individual spatio-temporal continuum as distinct from particular individual occasions[?]." The last word is not certain, but one hardly needs it to see that Yeats found the same idea in Whitehead, of timeless individuality, archetypes, and their realization in time, that he had found in Plotinus and adopted in the introduction to *Words upon the Window-pane*. Again hunting for equivalents of the *daimon*, Yeats wrote at the top of page 239 of Croce's *Logic as the Science of the Pure or created Concept*: "Daimon = reality itself as ordered in all lives of its individual"; and at the bottom of the same page, he wrote: "God is all reality therefore we always think Him. He is the negation of mystery." On page 394, apparently with the same twofold idea in mind, Yeats glossed a passage that he had marked ("the truth, which is his thought itself, the thought which acts in him and in all men") with a question mark and his old familiar word—"? Daimons." Finally, at the top of page 215 of *Matter and Memory*, Yeats wrote, in a phrase that sums up much of his doctrine about timeless individuality: "Daimon = that which completes unity of being."

Because he was deeply attracted to the idea that there is a continuity of individual being or personality—a continuity surviving not only sleeping and waking and all the events of a lifetime but surviving even a succession of incarnations as well—Yeats had to formulate his doctrine of "the permanent self or daimon" (*Ex.*, p. 331). What he came up with, though the terms might again vary as they did in Whitehead, Croce, and Bergson, was a doctrine that accorded fully with Jung's psychology of the self, "the individuation process," and "the transcendent function." Yeats's "timeless individuality," conveyed, according to Jung, in archetypes of the self, is destined as it were to break down into sub-archetypes as it is realized in a series of incarnations and in the course of time. As to the latter, Jung was quite agreed, and he believed (with Yeats) that each man has his own myth—or if he does not, then he is in a very bad way—and that it is the proper role of psychotherapy to help him live his myth rather than to substitute for it the psychotherapist's myth. As proof that he practised therapeutically what he preached mythically, Jung cited his "countless experiences" with "people belonging to creeds of all imaginable kinds" who came to consult him. With a certain pride, Jung says he sent these people, individually, back where they belonged: Jews he returned to the Synagogue and Roman Catholics to the Church; once Jung even brought a Parsee "back to the Zoroastrian fire-temple" (*CW*, XII, par. 17), but this was admittedly a unique case—a bravura performance on the therapist's part—rather than an everyday occurrence or evidence of Jung's own Parseeism. Jung was not a Parsee—that was not *his* myth; but an essential principle of his therapeutic theory states that it does not take one to know one, and Jung claimed to know a Parsee when he saw one. The myth that one lives, be it Parseeism, Judaism, or Roman Catholicism, represents a sort of halfway house to "timeless individuality"; or, turning it around, "timeless individuality" is an eternal *eidos* that unfolds itself in time as an archetypal or a mythical life.

Speaking of myth in the more common sense of the word, Jung says that "the hero myth is an unconscious drama seen only in projection" (*CW*, V, par. 612). It is, as Jung declared many times, only natural that the hero should be at the center of myths from all cultures of all times, because in the hero the psyche is telling its own story and projecting its own structural being, in the form of drama, on to the looking glass of nature. "The hero himself," Jung continues, "appears as a being of more than human stature. He is distinguished from the very beginning by his godlike characteristics. Since he is psychologically an archetype of the self, his divinity only confirms that the self is numinous, a sort of god, or having some share in the divine nature" (ibid.). Yeats was rather more reckless here, abandoning the caution represented by "a sort of" and opting for an uppercase rather than a lowercase divinity—"for a God is but the Self" (*E. & I.*, p. 461)—but he was undeniably speaking a Jungian tongue, albeit in a discussion of Indian religion. Again, it was not in a psychological context but in an exegesis of Blake's symbolism (the chapter titled "Symbol of the Centre" in *The Works of William Blake*) that Yeats wrote this startlingly Jungian remark: "The Centre is itself the hero, as it were, of a myth. Its story is a paradox" (I, 403). Further along Yeats says that there is a false center, which is the equivalent of egotism, and there is a "true centre, the great mental opening which leads to the Unlimited in the world of Eternity" (I, 408). Jung might say, "I trust that I have given no cause for the misunderstanding that I know anything about the nature of the 'centre'—for it is simply unknowable and can only be expressed symbolically through its own phenomenology" (*CW*, XII, par. 327)—he might say this, and it was no doubt true, but little as Jung knew about "the nature of the 'centre,'" he never wrote about anything else. The Uroboros has its center, as does the cosmos, as do the quaternity, the mandala, the circle, and the sphere, as did Blake, as did Yeats, and as did Jung. "The concept of the centre was called by the Chinese Tao, which the Jesuits in their day translated as Deus. This centre is everywhere, i.e., in everybody, and when the individual does not possess this centre he infects all the others with this sickness. Then they lose the centre too. *Deus est circulus cuius centrum est ubique circumferentia vero nusquam!*" (*Letters*, I, 470-71). Not only did Yeats agree about God and the circle—his "meagre Latin" compelled him to put the aphorism in English, however: "God is a circle whose centre is everywhere" (*E. & I.*, p. 287)—but he, too, thought that the sickness of our time could well be expressed in terms of loss of a center. Perhaps the sickest of all, in Yeats's judgment, are journalists ("the shallowest people on the ridge of the earth"), and the proof, as well as the cause, of their sickness is that "they have ceased to be self-centred, have given up their individuality" (*Letters*, p. 83).

After all the terrors that he had passed through in his "Confrontation with the Unconscious" (as he calls it in his autobiography), an experience that eventually led him to the center, Jung was not likely to go the way of modern journalists and cease to be "self-centred." During those years when he was, by his own account of it, in dubious battle for his sanity, Jung drew mandala after mandala, until finally, he says, "I saw that everything, all the paths I had been following, all the steps I had taken, were leading back to a single point—namely, to the mid-point. It became increasingly plain to me that the mandala is the center. It is the exponent of all paths. It is the path to the center, to individuation" (*Memories*, p. 196/188). Jung learned in his own life—and this was in a sense the *meaning* of his life—what Timaeus explained in a more theoretical manner in Plato's dialogue: that we will enjoy psychic health only if we give proper care to the highest part in us, our *daimon*, and so conform the movement of our incarnate soul to the revolving, circling, centering movement of the heavens. Eventually, Jung says, he "began to understand that the goal of psychic development is the self. There is no linear evolution; there is only a circumambulation of the self. Uniform development exists, at most, only at the beginning; later, everything points towards the center. This insight gave me stability, and gradually my inner peace returned. I knew that in finding the mandala as an expression of the self I had attained what was for me the ultimate. Perhaps someone else knows more, but not I" (ibid.). Yeats, in "A Prayer for My Daughter," knew no more than this ultimate to which Jung had attained:

> Considering that, all hatred driven hence,
> The soul recovers radical innocence
> And learns at last that it is self-delighting,
> Self-appeasing, self-affrighting,
> And that its own sweet will is Heaven's will. . . .

Nor did Blake, Plotinus, Plato, Empedocles, Heraclitus, and Parmenides—reverencers of the sphere, all of them. God, as they all believed, moves in circular ways his wonders to perform.

Not that they all understood quite the same thing by "God." For Empedocles (and no doubt Parmenides), the sphere itself was "a most blessed god"; for Heraclitus, the *Logos* that rules all change in the cosmos approximates to God. In the *Timaeus*, God is the Demiourgos—Craftsman, Maker, Creator; in Plotinus, God is The One—absolute, unqualified Unity, beyond both being and intelligibility. As to Blake, we can let Yeats speak (and in representing Blake's ideas—in a chapter of the *Works* that he calls "The Symbolic System"—Yeats is certainly speaking for himself as well): "The mood of the seer, no longer bound in by the particular experiences of his body, spreads out and enters into the particular experiences of an ever-widening circle of other lives and beings. . . . The circle of individuality will widen out until other individualities are contained within it. . . . He who has thus passed into the impersonal portion of his own mind perceives that it is not a mind but all minds. . . . When once a man has re-entered into this, his ancient state, he perceives all things as with the eyes of God" (*Works of William Blake*, I, 244). In re-entering his ancient state, in recovering original wholeness and radical innocence, in discovering all minds in his own mind and in finding God there as well, the seer of Blake/Yeats achieves union with what Jung called the objective or the impersonal psyche, and Jung distinguished that objective psyche only occasionally and very imperfectly from God. For Jung, however, and for Yeats in this passage, God is seen more as the end of creation and of human achievement than (as he is in the *Timaeus*) as the beginning of creation and the shaper of human achievement. But on a circle the beginning and end are common, and Yeats and Jung would doubtless be delighted to join hands with Plato and Heraclitus to compose a squared, quaternal circle. "Our imaginations are but fragments of the universal imagination, portions of the universal body of God, and as we enlarge our imagination by imaginative sympathy, and transform with the beauty and peace of art the sorrows and joys of the world, we put off the limited mortal man more and more and put on the unlimited 'immortal man' " (*E. & I.*, pp. 138-39). It was to precisely this same "unlimited 'immortal man,' " a favorite figure with him, that Jung regularly referred in a "Talk with Students" at the C. G. Jung Institute in Zurich in 1958: he was "the Great Man, the two million-year-old man," the being in whom collective psyche is identical with individual psyche—"As if *we* know nature!" Jung exclaimed. "Or about the psyche! The two million-year-old man may know something" (*Spring* 1970, p. 177).

This old phylogenetic being, whose psychic development is recapitulated in each of us individually, stands, in Jung's eyes, very close to God; and when we dream the Jungian Big Dream,[11] it is not easy to say whether it is a dream of God or of the Great Man, since, for Jung, God is a psychic experience, present to us as an *imago Dei*, an archetype, and when the dream is an affair of two-million-year-old psyche, then the *imago* will be so infinitely expanded that it will be nearly indistinguishable from *Deus*. "All consciousness separates," Jung says, and then adds in language that echoes Yeats very clearly, "but in dreams we put on the likeness of that more universal, truer, more eternal man dwelling in the darkness of primordial night. There he is still the whole, and the whole is in him, indistinguishable from nature and bare of all egohood" (*CW*, X, par. 304). There is no way that it could have been this "doctor of medicine" that Yeats had in mind (on the contrary, it was unquestionably Freud and his followers) when, in "Anima Hominis," he wrote: "The doctors of medicine have discovered that certain dreams of the night, for I do not grant them all, are the day's unfulfilled desire, and that our terror of desires condemned by the conscience has distorted and disturbed our dreams" (*Myth.*, p. 341).

11. "Thus we speak on the one hand of a *personal* and on the other of a *collective* unconscious, which lies at a deeper level. . . . The 'big' or 'meaningful' dreams come from this deeper level" (*CW*, VIII, par. 555).

The last clause (with its restatement of Freudian doctrine of the superego, the dream censor, and disguised incestuous desires) identifies clearly enough the doctors whose dream theories Yeats finds incomplete and unsatisfying; moreover, in not granting those doctors all dreams, Yeats is at one with Jung. Dreams, in Jung's psychology, come not only from material that was once conscious and that became somehow unconscious, but also from material that never was conscious and never was a part of the dreamer's waking experience. This other, deeper and truer dreaming—Jungian rather than Freudian—becomes the same thing as vision, Yeats says, and in such dreaming we know what we have never known individually but what we have always known as two-million-year-old man. "But the passions [so close, for Yeats as for Jung, to instincts and archetypes], when we know that they cannot find fulfillment, become vision; and a vision, whether we wake or sleep, prolongs its power by rhythm or pattern, the wheel where the world is butterfly" (ibid.). Jung said this same thing often, but never better than Yeats says it here. Neither of them would consent to reduce all dreams to previous experience because they both saw in certain dreams a vision of the ideal (which is impossible of individual fulfillment, as Yeats says) and a prevision of the future. "As far as my knowledge goes we are aware in dreams of our other life that consists in the first place of all the things we have not yet lived or experienced in the flesh," Jung wrote to a correspondent in 1956, echoing Yeats in thought and expression: "Beyond that material we are also aware of things we never can realize in the flesh and not in this life. Things belonging to the past of mankind and presumably to its future also" (*Letters*, II, 341). Such dreams are not (in the Yeats/Jung view of it) from unfulfilled incestuous desires but go right to the bottom of the human condition, where we know that our frenzied searching in this world is doomed to failure because what we seek is not the mother or the partner in bed (either of which we are rather too likely to find) but a *daimon* of another realm, another mode of existence. According to this dream psychology, the world does not determine our vision; instead, our vision breaks the world and reshapes it in conformity with an image that comes from deep within and from far in the past. An instinct, as Jung would say, insistently forces its own self-portrait on us, and it is not, nor will it ever be, the portrait of anyone in the world; so that all our Freudian incestuous desires are deeper and other than the son's desire for his mother or the brother's desire for his sister: they are nothing less than the serpent's closing on his own tail, Antaeus returning to the earth, the self wedding the anti-self in a *hieros gamos*, Narcissus joined to his daimonic image, Leda's egg—the Cosmic Egg—turning inside out and outside in without ever breaking the shell.

If we should ever succeed in attaining to this blessed, eudaimonic union, how eternal would we find it? Only symbolically eternal, Yeats implies, a state something like eternity but not really eternal because time itself bears no more than a symbolic relationship to eternity. The Thirteenth Sphere is not, except symbolically—as the work of art, for example, symbolizes it—an experience of this world. Jung's answer, which intends to do proper homage to the complexity and paradoxicality of the psyche and its archetypes, is very subtle, not to say tricky—an expert performance in nonsensical sense—but it may be that if we sort it out it will come to somewhat the same thing as Yeats's answer—without, however, a final, metaphysical commitment about the real existence of eternity in the Platonic and Yeatsian way: and this latter is admittedly a very important qualification and a very significant difference between the two. "The collective unconscious," Jung says in a typical formulation, "being the repository of man's experience and at the same time the prior condition of this experience, is an image of the world which has taken aeons to form. In this image certain features, the archetypes or dominants, have crystallized out in the course of time. They are the ruling powers, the gods, images of the dominant laws and principles, and of typical, regularly occurring events in the soul's cycle of experience" (*CW*, VII, par. 151). They may be "gods" (lowercase gods, however, be it noted), but in Jung's description (they have "taken aeons to form" and "have crystallized out in the course of time") the archetypes have nothing of transcendence about them, and even Jungian eternity, as we shall discover, turns out not to be transcendent. The archetypes "are deposits of thousands of years of experience of the struggle for existence and adaptation" (*CW*, VI, par. 374), or, expressed otherwise, they are "the inherited possibilities of human imagination as it was from time immemorial" (*CW*, VII, par. 101). Except metaphorically, and with a hint of inverted commas, Jung does not describe the archetypes as timeless or eternal. Besides, as he implies in one passage, timelessness is nothing to yearn for, since it is merely the state in which the insane live: psychotic patients, Jung says, "never find their way back from their dreams. . . . For them the hands of the world's clock remain stationary; there is no time, no further development" (*CW*, III, par. 356). No time, no development; no development, no life—hardly a condition that the therapist would urge on anyone.

On the other hand, writing a letter of consolation to a pastor whose brother had recently been killed, Jung could refer, with a kind of hopefulness, to "a psychic nullification of time," and could speak of a state of "relative eternity"—which is a notion that is profoundly paradoxical but that is also thoroughly characteristic of Jung's mature thought: "It is very probable that only what we call consciousness is contained in space and time, and that the rest of the psyche, the unconscious, exists in a state of relative spacelessness and timelessness. For the psyche this means a relative eternity . . ." (*Letters*, I, 256). In a letter written about a year before his death, Jung talks about a "continuum outside time and space"—which sounds very like Plotinus' "There" and the other world of Plato's two-world metaphysics, as well as like the "spatio-temporal continuum" that Yeats noted for himself in *Science and the Modern World* —yet Jung says that "the forms of existence inside and outside time are so sharply divided that crossing this boundary presents the greatest difficulties. But this does not exclude the possibility that there is an existence outside time which runs parallel with existence inside time. Yes, we ourselves may simultaneously exist in both worlds, and occasionally we do have intimations of a twofold existence. But what is outside time is . . . outside change. It possesses relative eternity" (*Letters*, II, 561). And what is eternity, or eternality, relative to? The answer must be that it is relative to time and temporal experience, which puts the Timaean cart before the horse and implies that eternity derives its reality from time. In his *Answer to Job*, however, Jung urges us to believe that "'time' is a relative concept and needs to be complemented by that of the 'simultaneous' existence, in the Bardo or pleroma, of all historical processes. What exists in the pleroma as an eternal process appears in time as an aperiodic sequence" (*CW*, XI, par. 629). In theory there should be no more process in heaven than there is giving in marriage, so that Jung's suggestion of "eternal process" would again indicate that the condition of the Pleroma is one of "relative eternality." What one should say, I suppose, is that Jung imagines the other world (as a scientist must do?) entirely from his experience of *this* world—that other world is for him psychologically determined as much as this one is—and so his eternity inevitably bears the coloring of time. After mentioning a number of archetypes in religious literature, Jung writes: "The religious point of view, understandably enough, puts the accent on the imprinter, whereas scientific psychology emphasizes the *typos*, the imprint—the only thing it can understand" (*CW*, XII, par. 20). This may be all that psychology can understand, but through analogical imagination it reaches out to grasp something of that other world where the imprinter looks to the Forms on which to model a cosmos; and so the scientific psychologist can say that "the Forms 'stored up in a supracelestial place' are a philosophical version of" the archetypes (*CW*, VII, par. 388), and that "within the limits of psychic experience, the collective unconscious takes the place of the Platonic realm of eternal ideas" (*CW*, XIV, par. 101).

I think that a hint of a way to resolve this philosophical/psychological dilemma is to be found in an essay by G. E. L. Owen titled "Plato and Parmenides on the Timeless Present." Writing of the possibility of change in the Forms (which, if it could occur, would imply the equivalent of psychological process in the realm of the Forms), Owen says: "[I]f Plato can claim, as he does in the *Timaeus*, that even to have a history is to change, then to say that justice captured the attention of Jones yesterday is to report a change in the Form. For on such an account it is a sufficient condition of change that something should become true of the subject at some time that was not true before. . . ."[12] By their availability to human thought and their contact with human psychology, the Forms become implicated in time and process, even though they remain absolute, eternal, and immutable in their philosophic character of that which is alone perfectly knowable. The philosopher's Forms and the psychologist's archetypes are thus like two sides of a coin or like the divided

---

12. "Plato and Parmenides on the Timeless Present," *The Pre-Socratics*, ed. Alexander P. D. Mourelatos (Garden City, N.Y.: Anchor Press/Doubleday, 1974), pp. 291-92.

line in the *Republic*: Forms descend along the line to become the archetypes of our world; archetypes ascend along the line to be the Forms of the other world. Jung, I think, had something like this in mind when, speaking of "impressive ideas"—that is, archetypal ideas—he said: "Although they come into being at a definite time, they are and have always been timeless; they arise from that realm of creative psychic life out of which the ephemeral mind of the single human being grows like a plant that blossoms, bears fruit and seed, and then withers and dies. Ideas spring from something greater than the personal human being" (*CW*, IV, par. 769). *Idea* and *eidos* are, of course, interchangeable words in Plato meaning the same thing ("form"), and if we substitute "Forms" for Jung's "ideas" and "archetypes" we shall not be doing hurt to either Platonic or Jungian doctrine. Perhaps we would do well to leave this tangled question with the observation that there is a hen (or a swan?) and there is an egg; there is a rhizome and there are multifold blossoms; there is eternity (at least "relative eternity") and there is time; there are Forms that provide the paradigm on which the cosmos was created and on which its continued existence depends, and there are archetypes that have been precipitated out of human experience for aeons, and continue to be so precipitated out, and yet these archetypes are coextensive with our psychic existence and determine that existence. The Pleroma, whose service we all must do in these matters, forbids us to make any statements that would be harder, faster, more purely sensible, and less tinged with the nonsensical than this.

CHAPTER IX

System

systēma, noun — 1. *whole compounded of several parts or members, system*; of the *composite whole* of soul and body; 2. in literary sense, *composition*; 3. in music, *system* of intervals, *scale*; 4. in metre, *metrical system*; 5. in medicine, *the pulse-beats taken collectively. Systēma* first occurs in Hippocrates and Plato and comes from

synistēmi, verb — 1. *set together*; 2. *combine, associate, unite*; 3. *put together, organize, frame* (*zōon empsychon*: Plato, *Timaeus*, 91a); 4. of an author, *compose*.
Adapted from *Greek-English Lexicon* of Liddell and Scott

System is in bad odor these days. Say of a man that he has a system —or if he does not have a system that he desires one—or say of someone that he thinks systematically, and you are more likely than not to cause great offense. "I am thoroughly empirical and therefore have no system at all. . . . As I already told you, I object to the term 'system.' . . . I have no doctrine and no philosophical system, but have presented *facts*. . . ." Jung's angry disclaimers (from three different letters: *Letters*, II, 185, 192, and 245) are entirely typical—typical both of Jung and of his time. Nor was it only those unfamiliar with his psychology who, out of ignorance or malice, offended Jung by their empirically unclean language: even someone as deep in the inner circle of Jungians as Jolande Jacobi could earn a reproof from Jung for her use of bad language. "It is a very good presentation of my concepts," Jung wrote to Dr. Jacobi, apropos of her essay on himself and Freud; but then, as if he has burned his fingers, Jung quickly pulls his hand from the fire—"or rather of the names I use to express empirical facts." Jung then proceeds to give his standard explanation (with greater patience than he was always wont to afford, for Jolande Jacobi was an adherent, after all, not an antagonist), and with a little kick at Freud included for effect: "But I always stumble over the frequent use of the term 'theory' or 'system.' Freud has a 'theory,' I have no 'theory' but I describe facts" (*Letters*, II, 293). And so on, with much more to the same purpose, both in this letter and in others. Furthermore, in Jung's view of it, his former mentor not only had a "theory"—a dirty enough word and possession; no, Freud was even worse than this: he had a "system" as well.

In a recent essay that I take to be altogether symptomatic (there is no reason to identify the writer, the journal, or the person who is the subject of the essay, since it would be easy to duplicate the sense of the passage from a number of other sources by other writers on different subjects), we are told that the philosopher who is the subject of the piece applied "thought systematically"; but the writer immediately qualifies this seemingly extreme statement and backs right down off the offending word: "The word 'systematically' may be misleading." The truth is that almost no one today wants to be accused of having a system or of thinking systematically, and so, as in the present case, out of concern for our friends or respect for people we admire, we disavow all system on their behalf and on our own, we deny that we ever have thought or ever will think systematically, and we hint that it is only "they"—those others, Freud, our empirical enemies and intellectual contraries—who make systems and entertain theories. In the disavowal quoted above, the writer goes on to say that the subject of the essay "was not a system-builder." Rather, according to the author, the subject "sought to descry systems that were already *there*, inherent in the body of man's interaction with the world and with himself as subject." The notion that this implies about the "system-builder" seems to me positively astounding: such a perverse creature, if I understand the description right, when he is getting ready to conjure up a system, first shuts his eyes, stops his ears, goes into a trance, and then spins a mad web from within himself that never touches on anything outside. Far be it from *him* to descry systems already there. If this is an accurate description of system-building, then it is little wonder that so many people find system-building malodorous. But of course it is not accurate, and the lunatic implied by the description is little more than a strawman. What system-builder claims, or has ever claimed, to descry that which is not already there or to build on any other model than that which is descried? Surely this is the whole point of system-building? Where does anyone begin to build a system—where did Yeats begin or where Jung (for in spite of all his assertions to the contrary, Jung's entire life was no more than observation of a living system and recreation of that system in scientific terminology), where did Timaeus or Plato begin, where do you or I begin—except in that which is descried as an objective, given, already existent system *"there"*?

System-building has not always been in such bad repute, as the reference to Timaeus and Plato will indicate to anyone familiar with the intellectual history of the Middle Ages and the Renaissance. The most glorious and comprehensive system ever put together in the Western world—a system that embraced the esoteric with the exoteric, included ethics, physics, and physiology with theology, metaphysics, and psychology, and discovered its perfect voice in a merger of *mythos* and *logos*—is to be found in the *Timaeus*; and it was by the *Timaeus* that Plato and the ancient tradition were known, and virtually worshipped, for twenty millennia. But after that came the "three provincial centuries." To those three centuries (the seventeenth to the twentieth) I believe that we owe much of the scorn that is heaped on the system-builder today, for one of the chief accomplishments of those centuries was to sever mind from nature, to declare nature to be matter and all matter to be dead, and thus to create an unbridgeable gap between *psychē* and *physis*. Since that time, anyone who subscribes to this doctrine and yet goes about integrating mind with matter and *psychē* with *physis* is fastening himself not (as in Yeats's poem) to a dying animal but to a dead one —or not even to a dead body, a carrion corpse, but to that which does not live, never has lived, and never could live. When we hear of system, I fear that we think not (as we should do) of an organism but of a machine. I should imagine that the mechanistic view that prevailed for three centuries of neo-Dark Ages might well scare off temperaments that would otherwise be inclined to view the world (as Jung puts it) "with holistic judgment"—which is to say, systematically.

It has not always been so with system-building, not even during the bad three hundred years—there was Blake, for example, pretty near the center of the evil times—nor is it so in the view of everyone in the present century. I could (and shortly will) quote Jung more positively on system, but he can be found saying hard things about it too. Not so Yeats: he thought Blake's system a splendid creature, he desired a similar one for himself, and he foresaw (or at least yearned for) the glorious and triumphant return of system in our time. In the preface to the three-volume *Works of William Blake*, the two editors (Yeats and Edwin Ellis) tell how the former, "with his eye for symbolic systems," came to the latter "and asked to have Blake explained." Ellis was unable to give Yeats very much by way of satisfaction for his large demand—so the story goes—but "he [Yeats] needed no more to enable him to perceive that here was a myth as well worth study as any that has been offered to the world. ... He saw, too, that it was no mere freak of an eccentric mind, but an eddy of that flood-tide of symbolism which attained to its tidemark in the magic of the Middle Ages" (vol. I, ix-x). We would do well to pause here and to reflect that Yeats—who, in some accounts of the matter, is supposed to have taken to systems only after the Instructors brought him his very own in 1917—was as systemminded in 1893 as in 1933, and that there is an astonishing amount of *A Vision* already present in the commentary on "The Symbolic System" in *The Works of William Blake*. For the system that was Yeats's very own was also very Blakean and very traditional, and this is why one can only suppose that the Instructors bore some very familiar names indeed: "William Blake," of course, but also—from within Yeats and from within "William Blake," for that matter—"Plato," "Heraclitus" and "Pythagoras," "Parmenides" and "Empedocles." Yeats's heart's desire, both early and late, was for a system to explain the world and everything in it, and he thought that *A Vision* constituted just such a living creature, capable of satisfying the emotions as well as the intellect. What Yeats called the "symbolic system" that was *A Vision* (*Ex.*, p. 394) was not the creation of a moment; it was the fruit of a lifetime—very much there in the work on Blake, more there in "Swedenborg, Mediums, and Desolate Places," and yet more there in *Per Amica Silentia Lunae*—and not the fruit of a single lifetime either (or so Yeats at least believed) or of consciousness alone but the fruit of many lives and of many centuries, of consciousness and the unconscious balanced, opposed, and harmonized, the fruit of the Great Mind and the Great Memory.

"Read Whitehead," Yeats wrote to Sturge Moore, "and from that go to Stephen MacKenna's Plotinus and to the *Timaeus*. What Whitehead calls 'the three provincial centuries' are over. Wisdom and Poetry return" (Yeats/Moore *Correspondence*, p. 93). Yeats's affection for Whitehead among modern philosophers was altogether reasonable, for he was one of the last great system-builders in the ancient manner before philosophy fell into its analytical, critical doldrums; moreover, he was professedly, and through and through, a Platonist. (It was Whitehead who made the famous remark—for which he has been both reviled and applauded—that all subsequent philosophy is "a series of footnotes to Plato."[1]) Whitehead, Plotinus, and the *Timaeus*—they make a glorious trio; for all three, the universe—"this our *Kosmos*," as the final sentence of the *Timaeus* calls it—is a living system, a Living Creature, and we, our consciousness and awareness, are an integral part of the system, vital organs, as it were, that bestow consciousness on the Living Creature. Yeats later wrote to Moore (Yeats/Moore *Correspondence*, p. 149): "I feel that an imaginative writer whose work draws him to philosophy must attach himself to some great historic school." And as for himself, he goes on: "I must not go too far from the main European track. . . ." There may be no real need to give a name to this "main European track"; it is, of course, the Philosophia Perennis, called, in its Western form, "Platonism." When Yeats proclaimed the return of "Wisdom and Poetry" (notice the uppercase, antique grandeur and majestic stateliness of their joint return), he also proclaimed his belief in the living system of Platonism, which, though invisible, buried, and perhaps forgotten for three centuries, was far from dead: as the Philosophy is Perennial, so is the rhizome system connecting Whitehead with Plotinus and Plato, and all three of them with Yeats . . . and with Jung.

Jung can call system all the hard names he wants to, but it does not change the fact that he was himself more than half in love with system-making—not, of course, a mechanistic system grinding its evolutionary way forward in a world of material causes without ends. On the contrary, Jung's was the good old variety of system—the Yeatsian, the Plotinian, and the Platonic variety—that brought

1. *Process and Reality*, Part II, Chapter II, Section I. What Whitehead said, more precisely, was this: "The safest general characterization of the European philosophical tradition is that it consists of a series of footnotes to Plato."

order into the swarm of experience, implied its own teleology in the distinct, specific form that it displayed, and gave a meaning to individual life by locating it within a comprehensive human, natural, and superhuman/supernatural pattern. I suppose the reason that Jung got so heated whenever he was called a philosopher or was said to have a system was that in his psychology he was skating on some rather thin scientific ice, over some cold philosophic waters, and lest that fact become apparent, he raised his voice so that only his own proclamation—"I am an empirical scientist, no system, no philosophy, no *Weltanschauung*, no nothing"—would be heard over the gabble of smaller voices beneath saying such horrid things as "Jungian theory and Jungian dogma," "philosophic system," "unscientific and unempirical." The age demanded it, and Jung complied, but even while his voice was raised in angry denial of all system, Jung quietly—as it were beneath the scientific din—continued to build his own, modelling it, of course, not on airy nothingness but on "systems that were already *there*, inherent in the body of man's interaction with the world and with himself as subject." When he was not speaking publicly and not writing for the scientific community, Jung could be frank enough: "The psychotherapist must be a philosopher in the old sense of the word. Classical philosophy was a certain view of the world as well as of conduct. For the oldest authorities of the Church even Christianity was a sort of philosophical system with a code of conduct to match. There were philosophical systems for a satisfying or happy way of living. Psychotherapy means something of the sort too" (*Letters*, I, 456). Now, I am aware that Jung was forever distinguishing between psychology (an empirical science) and psychotherapy (not a science but a living encounter)—a distinction, however, that in Jung's own hands falls right apart, as I intend to demonstrate in a moment—and it might be supposed that it is on the grounds of this distinction that Jung can acknowledge and even glorify philosophical system. But was Jung himself not primarily a psychotherapist, whose psychological science consisted of recording facts of the psyche observed in the therapeutic encounter (as well as facts observed in the process of his own psyche)? Jung certainly claimed this to be the case. Why, then, should it so raise his hackles when Jung is said to be in possession of that which psychotherapy is all about—*viz.*, a philosophical system? Perhaps the answer is to be found in the fact that Jung was, by his own admission, "a philosopher *manqué*" (*Letters*, I, 194) and a poet *manqué* (ibid., II, 189): "Watch out, the scientific ice is thin there!" —and Jung's voice automatically goes up by several decibels. The philosopher and the poet, at least of the old and grand style, not only can afford the luxury of a system but, according to Yeats, positively need one in order to speak at all—which is the whole reason for their existence—about "ultimate things." Without system they are reduced to mere chatterers, sentimentalists, and—no doubt—scientists *manqués* (this is why, for himself, as Yeats said, to follow "the main European track" means "that I turn away from all attempts to make philosophy support science . . ." [Yeats/Moore *Correspondence*, p. 149]). Without system the psychotherapist will cure no one (himself least of all), and without system the psychologist—though Jung would doubtless deny this bitterly—loses the very subject and object of his science. In that condition he finds, like Othello, that his "occupation's gone," for psychology is a living of the system that is psyche.

"This sounds like religion, but it is not. I am speaking just as a philosopher. People sometimes call me a religious leader. I am not that. I have no message, no mission; I attempt only to understand. If we are philosophers in the old sense of the word, we are lovers of wisdom."[2] Jung seldom showed himself so willing to be thought a philosopher as he does here—but as the choice was between being thought a philosopher and being thought a religious leader, Jung chose wisely; besides, he was talking to his followers rather than to the world, and so might confess what he would elsewhere deny. But it was in the *Collected Works* that Jung remarked that the investigator of "the delusional system" of a psychosis will inevitably exhibit "a *Weltanschauung* of his own, which nowadays is considered a terrible disgrace. Confirmation of such a possibility is as bad as being unscientific" (*CW*, III, par. 421). This sounds like Jung directing irony at the attitude that he himself regularly offered up for public consumption. In the sentence that follows—"But everyone has a view of the world, though not everyone is aware of it"— Jung must include himself in the first clause if not in the second (perhaps he was fitfully aware of his *Weltanschauung*: aware of it when writing something like the above, unaware of it—yet probably

---

2. "Is Analytical Psychology a Religion? Notes on a Talk Given by C. G. Jung (1937)," *Spring* 1972, p. 147.

aware that he was being unaware of it—when it might cause him to seem "unscientific"). It was in a letter, rather than in a scientific text, that Jung said that analytical psychology had its "roots . . . in Greek philosophy" (*Letters*, I, 206), and in another letter that he remarked that "as soon as psychology becomes anything like useful and practical . . . it needs must be philosophical. What else is behaviourism and mechanism and all that than a sort of unsound philosophical prejudice?" (ibid., p. 80). This, as I have pointed out, is why system has a bad name nowadays: because it is vaguely, but mistakenly, associated in many people's minds with such "unsound philosophical prejudice" as behaviorism and mechanism represent. As Jung knew well enough how to dissect those two unsound, false, and inadequate philosophical systems, he should have seen the error involved in shying at the word "system" merely because it sounds in most ears like "mechanism." It was, I believe, more the *word* than the fact of system that made Jung nervous for his young science, and he often seems fully capable of straining at such a gnat as the word "system" after swallowing a full-grown camel such as the psychological-cum-philosophical system that he lays out in eighteen volumes of *Collected Works*.

What is this camel, the elaborate, complex system, that Jung swallows with such apparent ease? What Jung says of the psyche and of psychology is something like this (and here it is that the distinction between psychotherapy and psychology, as I remarked earlier, simply breaks down):

 1. Psyche is a system that, when healthy, is self-balancing, self-regulating, and teleologically organized—a closed, energic system that comprises the antinomic opposites of consciousness and the unconscious, that has a quaternity of functions (thinking, feeling, intuition, sensation) through which it is oriented to the world, and that is directed toward an end of individuation, wholeness, and unity.

 2. There is what may be called a collective or objective or impersonal psyche as well as individual or subjective or personal psyche, and psyche in either of its aspects is a systemic process in precisely the way outlined above—dualism and quaternalism resolved in the achievement of a psychic monism.

 3. The science of psychology is an experiencing of psyche and a subsequent description of that experience in a more or less adequate and coherent manner. (At this point, as I have argued elsewhere,[3] autobiography merges with psychology: thus the psychologist records the autobiography of a subjective and an objective psychic system.)

4. Therefore, the fact that psyche is endlessly paradoxical and contradictory, and that the psychologist's rendering of the story of psyche must also be paradoxical and contradictory—an "ingenious ambiguity" (*Letters*, II, 69) being the essential quality of both—all this does not mean that psyche and its portrait or its *logos* (= psychology) are any the less systems. On the contrary: this is an attempt to make the systematic description more comprehensive, more nearly adequate to the reality—more truly systemic—by including incoherence as an element of ultimate coherence, chaos as the twin-opposite of cosmos, and a-systematic irregularity as a part of a total, single system.

This merger of psychology with psychic process and of science with autobiography makes the science of psychology a thoroughly systematic construct, since, as Jung insists, "the psyche is a self-regulating system, just as the body is" (*CW*, VIII, par. 159). Not only is it a self-regulating system, it is a *pair* of self-regulating systems—the "ectopsyche" and the "endopsyche," as Jung explained in the Tavistock Lectures: "[T]he *ectopsyche* is a system of relationship between the contents of consciousness and facts and data coming in from the environment.... The *endopsyche* ... is a system of relationship between the contents of consciousness and postulated processes in the unconscious" (*CW*, XVIII, par. 20). What Jung describes is a pair of double quaternities, both yearning, in their twoness and fourness, toward the oneness of self. The *Collected Works* are an extended song of psyche and a hymn of praise—in a sense, self-praise—to its glories as a system. (The *Timaeus* has justly been described in somewhat similar terms.) "The psyche ... observes itself and can only translate the psychic back into the psychic.... There is no medium for psychology to reflect itself in: it can only portray itself in itself, and describe itself" (*CW*, VIII, par. 421). The psychologist *is* a system, he *describes* a system, and so, in a rather fearful paradox, "Psychology is doomed to cancel itself out as

---

3. In *Metaphors of Self*, Chapter III.

a science and therein precisely it reaches its goal" (ibid., par. 429). It is not well for rational intellect to consider these matters over nicely or over long, for they go quite beyond logic and reason. But if Heraclitus, Parmenides, Empedocles, and Plato—also Plotinus, Nicholas of Cusa, and William Blake—be allowed to reverence the circle and the sphere that signify the perfection of system, perhaps we may grant Jung the same right and allow him to admire, beyond all rational bounds, and to extol the circular beauty of a psychology that merges its subject with its object, ties up its beginning in its end, and transforms the scientist into his science. The heart—Jung's as much as any other—desires a system, yet it was only (or so Jung appears to have felt) by this desperate and tangled device that he could satisfy his heart's longing and still remain what he announced to the world that he was—an empirical scientist.

In the essay that he called "Basic Postulates of Analytical Psychology," Jung was willing to admit an "inner resemblance" between psychology and philosophy, which, he said, "consists in this, that both are systems of opinion about objects which cannot be fully experienced and therefore cannot be adequately comprehended by a purely empirical approach" (*CW*, VIII, par. 659). Analytical Psychology was Jung's "system of opinion," a projection of his own experience with psyche, just as Psychoanalysis was Freud's "system of opinion" and Individual Psychology was Alfred Adler's. But this raises a rather delicate question about all the "systems of opinion" that are so many psychologies and philosophies: What if all the observed archetypal images of Jung's science, all the observed Oedipal fixations of Freud's science, all the stellar conjunctions of the philosophy-science of astrology, and all the patterns of cosmological order of the *Timaeus*—what if the entire *Système du Monde* described by Pierre Duhem in ten fat volumes (and even then the project was left uncompleted at his death)—what if they are all no more than "projections"? What if they are merely something that the psychologist or philosopher intuits or desires within and then projects and imagines to exist also without? Jung had an answer, though I think it questionable whether he could have been speaking as a scientist—especially an empirical scientist—when he gave that answer. "I always say that if there is a projection there must also be a corresponding hook on which to hang it" (*Letters*, II, 443). So—God is an enormous hook (or Hook) for the *imago Dei*. Whether this would please either fundamentalist believers or clinical psychologists is doubtful. If the psyche is in itself a system, which therefore can only perceive the universe as a system—or, to put it in other words, if the psyche projects its own configuration on the cosmos—does this mean that there is a hook for it to hang on? Does psychic system imply a Psychic System? Yeats and Jung both, I believe, thought so, and the idea—or is it rather a faith?—can be traced back through the Neoplatonists to Plato and the *Timaeus* and back beyond Plato to Pythagoras. The Platonic tradition is itself a vastly extended system reflecting the minds of its makers and projected on to the heavens— which is to say that the system in question is a psychic system, an historic system, and a cosmological system all at the same time. When (in an essay significantly entitled "Analytical Psychology and 'Weltanschauung'") Jung describes the collective unconscious, it is seen to be just such an historic and a-historic living creature as this: "The collective unconscious is in no sense an obscure corner of the mind, but the mighty deposit of ancestral experience accumulated over millions of years, the echo of prehistoric happenings to which each century adds an infinitesimally small amount of variation and differentiation. Because the collective unconscious is, in the last analysis, a deposit of world-processes embedded in the structure of the brain and the sympathetic nervous system, it constitutes in its totality a sort of timeless and eternal world-image . . ." (*CW*, VIII, par. 729). Psyche and world, balanced against one another and reflecting one another, together create a "timeless and eternal worldimage" that is heritable as the analogue of mental structures and that realizes itself historically in such elaborate systematic groupings as the one that we call the Platonic tradition.

In his Introduction to *The Resurrection*, Yeats distinguishes two philosophic systems—Communism and Catholicism—at work in the modern world, and he remarks the adherence of both to a kind of faith, the first a faith in materialism, the second a faith in revelation. "Yet," Yeats says, "there is a third myth or philosophy that has made an equal stir in the world" (*Ex.*, p. 395). He then thoughtfully treats us to a description of this third myth, which—and this should surprise no one—turns out to be Platonism, especially in its aspect of an Empedoclean-Heraclitean conflict, reversal, and marriage of opposites. Ptolemy, who played a considerable part in defining this third myth, "thought the precession of the equinoxes moved at the rate of a degree every hundred years," and so he determined the length of the Platonic Year—"the thirty-six thousand years, or three hundred and sixty incarnations of a hundred years apiece, of Plato's Man of Ur" (as Yeats, with a mistaken air of familiarity, calls Er, whose myth is recounted at the end of the *Republic*)—and this calculation made by Ptolemy became received doctrine from then on down through the long course of the Platonic tradition. Now, Yeats says, it has been discovered in modern times "that the equinox shifts its ground more rapidly than Ptolemy believed," and so shall we not—we who subscribe to the third myth and who find it an infinitely more satisfying system than either of the other two—shall we not, as "somebody" suggests, be forced to "invent a new symbolical scheme"? There is no hesitation and no uncertainty in Yeats's answer: "No, a thousand times no; I insist that the equinox does shift a degree in a hundred years; anything else would lead to confusion."[4] It is not scepticism nor is it religion that frightens Yeats—and in this he is more of a system-builder than either the Communist or the Catholic—but the confusion and disorder consequent upon tampering with any one detail in the carefully articulated, highly elaborated, and beautifully concatenated system: like a house of cards, the entire structure threatens to come tumbling down if anyone touches Ptolemy's miscalculation. Confusion, as Yeats believed, and not error is the worst enemy of system.

4. *Ex.*, p. 396. The tenor of Yeats's argument is typical—and not very solemn. He presents his view as a quixotic and moderately humorous one and then, with that ironic attitude standing him in good stead, he proceeds to defend his view absolutely and vigorously. A couple of details in the presentation are particularly fine. Yeats speaks of "empirical evidence" for "the re-birth of the soul" and then quickly runs us through the conditions for experimental proof of theories in higher mathematics: "In a few years, perhaps, we may have much empirical evidence, the only evidence that moves men to-day, that man has lived many times; there is some not yet perfectly examined—I think of that Professor's daughter in Palermo. This belief held by Plato and Plotinus, and supported by weighty arguments, resembles the mathematical doctrines of Einstein before the experimental proof of the curvature of light." Whoever "that Professor's daughter in Palermo" may have been, there can be no doubting the acute and sage (as Yeats felt it to be) analogy between proof of Einstein's mathematics and empirical evidence for reincarnation. Yeats (wisely) preferred not to descend to particulars, but otherwise there is something of the same misplaced confidence in Yeats's estimate of his knowledge of Einsteinian mathematics as we frequently find in Jung—who admitted that he had no mathematics but proceeded to do a good bit of erroneous calculation all the same. I think that Yeats was having a humorous go at the science that terrifies all of us, while Jung, on the other hand, was doubtless quite serious.

If, to save the system, we must accept a simple physical or mathematical miscalculation, then we ought not, in Yeats's view of it, be over fastidious about scientific accuracy, for if we fail to save the system we shall not succeed in saving the phenomena, and in abandoning the phenomena along with the system we shall have failed to meet Plato's challenge to the Academy—*sōzein ta phainomena.* "'What then?' sang Plato's ghost. 'What then?'" When we have failed to save the phenomena, what answer will we give to that singing ghost?

On the one hand, order, pattern, organization; on the other hand, inclusiveness, completeness, totality—these are the great twin principles of system: that the net shall display a most beautiful reticulation and that nothing shall escape the net. The motives may be more emotional than they are intellectual, but whatever the nature of the motivation, there is a distinct tendency in every system-maker to imply universality or to claim total comprehensiveness for his creation. Empedocles' elements are the *rhizōmata pantōn*—the roots of *all* things; when Parmenides describes his *estin*—what is—he uses the word *pan* (all) so many times that we can only suppose this inclusiveness to be its essential and defining characteristic—"what is" is the all and the only existent (I count thirteen uses of *pan*, in various forms, sometimes in compounds, in Fr. 8 alone). The Pythagoreans, according to Aristotle, "thought the principles of mathematics were the principles of *all* things" (τῶν ὄντων ἀρχὰς . . . πάντων), and "they supposed the elements of numbers to be the elements of *all* things" (τῶν ὄντων στοιχεῖα πάντων). It was, indeed, just this "allness" and their failure to distinguish between mathematics and solid geometry, between an abstract and a physical world, between the realm of mind and the realm of senses, that so vexed Aristotle when he came to treat of "those who are called Pythagoreans." But the Pythagoreans are the original system-makers, for it is in their concept of *kosmos* (if the concept was Pythagorean) that we have the two invariable elements of system—order and inclusiveness—brought together. Heraclitus might attack Pythagoras and others for polymathy, but he was himself equally given to ordering all things as one. "*All* things happen according to this Logos," he said (Fr. 1); and "*all* things are one" (Fr. 50), "*all* things are in process" (πάντα χωρεῖ, from *Cratylus*, 402a), and "*all* things are *always* in flux" (ἀεὶ πάντα ῥεῖ). The word "all" echoes through these Pre-Socratics as if they were all of them so many Wordsworths writing a few miles above Tintern Abbey.[5] Likewise, Timaeus' account of the creation may be no more than a "likely story," but it nevertheless takes for subject nothing of slighter scope than "the all" (περὶ τοῦ παντὸς ... τὸν λόγον:91c), and he offers to tell how the Demiourgos—the archetypal system-maker of all time—fashioned "the all" (τὸ πᾶν:30b). "Let us," Timaeus says at the very outset of his probable tale, "Let us state the cause wherefore he the system-maker made a system of becoming and the all."[6] The world that seems so diverse to us—or worse than diverse: fragmentary, chaotic, painful, and meaningless—will never be a universe, will never be an ordered whole, except through a living system capable of discovering a unity in plurality.

The system implicit in any one of Yeats's poems achieves this, and so does the system of Jung's psychology (whether by that we mean the process of his psyche or the science he erected on observation of that process): both systems transform plurality, or they organize plurality, into unity. It is easy enough, at the beginning of "Among School Children," to distinguish the children and their activities from the Senator and his progress through the long schoolroom; but by the end of the poem, after Pythagoras and his *kosmos*, after Plato and his Ideas, after the archetypal Presences and all the heavenly glory that they symbolize—after all this, "How can we

---

5. A motion and a spirit, that impels
   All thinking things, *all* objects of *all* thought,
   And rolls through *all* things.
               . . . *all* that we behold
   From this green earth; of *all* the mighty world
   Of eye, and ear. . . .
Wordsworth doubtless had the *pan* of the Pre-Socratics and the Pan of the Greek woods and hills in mind when he wrote these lines from "Tintern Abbey."
6. 29d-e: Λέγωμεν δὴ δι' ἥν τινα αἰτίαν γένεσιν καὶ τὸ πᾶν τόδε ὁ ξυνιστὰς ξυνέστησεν. Cornford: "Let us, then, state for what reason becoming and this universe were framed by him who framed them." Lee: "Let us therefore state the reason why the framer of this universe of change framed it at all." Bury: "Let us now state the Cause wherefore He that constructed it constructed Becoming and the All." Jowett: "Let me tell you then why the creator made this world of generation." I am well aware that the translation in the text has less to do with English than any of these others; the point of that translation, however, awkward as it may be, is to demonstrate the relation of Plato's subject and his verb to *systēma* and *synistēmi*.

know the dancer from the dance?" From a most disjointed and random diversity, Yeats's poems make their way, through quaternities, trinities, and antinomies, to the most intense unity. The poetic act is an exact imitation of the Demiourgos' creation, fitting the many together as a unified image modelled on the single paradigm: a sensible living creature that is a likeness of the intelligible Living Creature. The poem is a realization of its own *eidos*, just as this, our cosmos, is a realization of the *paradeigma* that embraces all *eidē*, all "Presences," and all archetypes. Below each of Yeats's successful poems, before and beyond each of them, one feels the living form, the *eidos*, the invisible, intangible, incorporeal rhythmic body that makes this all one thing, unique and unrepeatable—"single in its kind and one," as Timaeus says in his final words; there is, as the very essence of each poem, an indwelling, systematizing presence that transforms the multiverse of experience into the universe of this poem. Yeats was talking about time and something beyond time, but he might as well have been describing his own poetics or Jung's psychology of individuation—self as the entelechy and the end of psychic process—in this sentence from *Per Amica Silentia Lunae*: "When all sequence comes to an end, time comes to an end, and the soul puts on the rhythmic or spiritual body or luminous body and contemplates all the events of its memory and every possible impulse in an eternal possession of itself in one single moment" (*Myth.*, p. 357). All sequence moves to its end and desires its end, and when time achieves its goal—when it closes itself in a circle, when the serpent bites its tail and the stillness of eternity prevails over time, its own moving image—then time also achieves its own destruction, since it no longer exists: time has had its end. All things, according to Yeats, yearn for their end, and so too—in fact, so preeminently—does time:

> Through winter-time we call on spring,
> And through the spring on summer call,
> And when abounding hedges ring
> Declare that winter's best of all;
> And after that there's nothing good
> Because the spring-time has not come—
> Nor know that what disturbs our blood
> Is but its longing for the tomb.
>
> ("The Wheel")

This is both fulfillment and extinction, completion and death, the gathering up of a sequential, pluralistic process into a static, unified beginning-and-end.

"*Telos*" (which gives us "teleology") means, among other things, "an end accomplished, the fulfillment of something, the end of life, initiation into the Eleusinian mysteries"; "*teleios*" or "*teleos*," the adjective corresponding to *telos*, means "complete, perfect, entire." Timaeus (at 33b) tells his companions (and no one hints any disagreement) that when the Demiourgos set about giving shape to his perfect (*teleon*) Living Creature, the One and All which is our cosmos, he made it into a sphere, "which is of all shapes the most perfect (*teleōtaton*)." The unfolding of unity into multiplicity and the return of multiplicity to unity can be seen as a dichotomous, twofold process, but it can also be seen as a unified, circular (hence perfect) process imitating the archetypal sphere that gives shape to our cosmos. "The unit," Jung wrote, "is necessarily the ἀρχή and the origin of multiplicity. Because it is *undifferentiated* the unconscious is a unit and hence the ἀρχή μεγάλη and indistinguishable from God" (*Letters*, II, 122-23). Not only is the unit the *archē* and the origin of multiplicity, it is also the *telos* and the conclusion of multiplicity, its completion, its perfection, and its grave. Moreover, as Jung frequently maintained, this relationship of the unit to multiplicity is, in an abstract way, very like the relationship between the unconscious and consciousness: the unconscious is the beginning and end of consciousness; it is the great, undifferentiated, and undying unifier and destroyer of consciousness, which is multiple and differentiated, a momentary phenomenon that is begotten, born, and dies.

Working out his thoughts on this same scheme of unity-multiplicity-unity as a circular process, and adding to that scheme a corollary notion that a hierarchy of archetypes obtains throughout the universe and makes of it a single, complex system of temporal and spiritual circles within circles, Yeats wrote in his usual hesitant-assured, tentative-conclusive manner: "We may come to think that nothing exists but a stream of souls, that all knowledge is biography, and with Plotinus that every soul is unique; that these souls, these eternal archetypes, combine into greater units as days and nights into months, months into years, and at last into the final unit that differs in nothing from that which they were at the beginning: everywhere that antinomy of the One and the Many that Plato thought in his *Parmenides* insoluble, though Blake thought it soluble 'at the bottom of the graves' " (*Ex.*, p. 397). I cannot see the slightest difference between what Yeats says here, unfolding a most elaborate and *teleion* system from the unit and then refolding that system back into the unit, and what Jung wrote about the unconscious which is undifferentiated, therefore both unit and *archē*, and its relation to the great unit, the great *archē*, another name for which (for whom?) is God. Get enough of Yeats's souls—"these eternal archetypes"—together, and, according to the logic of days into months into years into first-and-last unit, they will add up to God; or, to be more exact, abandoning Jung's terminology in favor of a more Platonic, Plotinian, and Yeatsian one, the gathered-up souls would compose the unified and unique paradigm after which they and this entire universe were created. Jung was forever analyzing the system of psyche in terms of opposites and quaternities; Yeats was forever analyzing his symbolic system in terms of antinomies and various fours (four faculties, four principles, four elements, four perfections, four contests, etc.—cf. *Vision*, pp. 100-104); but as often as they analyzed the whole into pairs and quaternities, they turned back to synthesize or systematize it in the sphere, which embraces, at beginning and end, and contains both contraries and quaternities. All dyads and all tetrads, their systematizing suggests, are comprehended in the monad, as all gyres and all squares are comprehended in that εὐδαιμονέστατος θεός, that "most blessed god," that is the Sphere.

Any system, whether philosophic, poetic, or psychic, is composed of parts, and many of them, even though unity be an essential aspect of system and of the system-maker's intention, and even though the *sine qua non* of a system be that it display an integral oneness. Some people may claim to find the chaos and confusion of everyday existence "one world," but they can do so only by a very drastic denial of a large part of reality. In psychological terms, there is immediately the contrast and opposition of subjective and objective perception: the latter never experiences things as one, and the former does so only by a denial or an overriding of the latter. "Judge by reason," Parmenides says, and never give credence to "thy aimless eye, thy echoing ear or thy tongue" (Fr. 7). In this way, perhaps, by closing our eyes, stopping our ears, and stilling our tongues, we will experience things as one, for it may be that the mind will discover its own unity superior to the plurality of the world and will be able to impose it effectively on that plurality. This is the only way to maintain an extreme monism, however, and it explains why few people hold consistently and continuously to a monistic vision. On the other hand, the monistic vision is possible intermittently and is moreover possible, is indeed common, as an alternating view balanced against dualistic, triadic, and quaternal visions: in the interplay of eye and world, things may arrange and present themselves, with a kind of Hopkinsian inscape, in alternating patterns of one and two, one and three, one and four. The monistic vision in itself is quintessentially the vision of mystic experience, but the mystic union is intermittent and momentary, so uncommon that it cannot even be termed alternating. This conjoining of the mystic experience and the monistic vision indicates that monism has its source and justification in another, radically different world from the one ordinarily delivered up to us by the senses. In "Vacillation," Yeats achieves the monistic vision momentarily (for "twenty minutes more or less"), and, sitting at a table in a Lyons café, he "was blessèd and could bless" the street he looked upon. But the street knew nothing of this, and the Lyons café was certainly unchanged in its hysterical pluralism. The monistic home is not here but "There," not in this Heraclitean world of process but in that Parmenidean world of pure homogeneity and absolute stasis. It was one of the greatnesses of Plato to take a system asserting the One, and a system asserting the many, and make of them a system asserting the One and the many.

If the extreme monist is naïve, however, and if his desire for oneness is so intense as to cause him to discard the world and his senses so that his mind alone may prevail, all manner of pluralists share this same yearning—though they are perhaps less obstinate about it—for unity. Antinomists, Trinitarians, Quaternalists, it makes no difference, all of them try to discover unity in their favorite archetypal number. The first talks of a *complexio oppositorum*, the second of a tri-unity, the third of a squared circle of wholeness, and each of them would return all pluralities to the One and would return himself to rest again in the achieved perfection, the *teleios telos*, of unity. The antinomist turns his line of opposition into the diameter of a circle, the trinitarian circumscribes his triangle, the quaternalist circumambulates his four corners, circles his square and squares his circle, in each case so that, like the child that the *Sophist* encourages us to imitate, he may have it both ways: reality is double, it is triple, it is quadruple—and it is One. Thus too with system, which, being itself one, affords us a way of perceiving plurality *sub specie unitatis*, and so allows us to save the phenomena while satisfying our need (which, if not divine, is very human) for unity, which is to say our need for order, which is to say our need for meaning.

After he had finished his work on Blake and had discovered in his writings all the system that he had surmised beforehand was there, Yeats wrote to Elkin Matthews describing what he and Edwin Ellis intended to do in their book. First, he says, they will present a "general account of system" that will run to some one hundred and fifty pages, this to be followed by forty pages or so dealing with each of the prophetic books. "The indolent," Yeats declared, "will find all they need for an understanding of the main system of Blake in these accounts and in the general account of system in the first 150 pages of [the] book." The upshot of their work would be, Yeats thought, that "no one . . . will ever again say that [Blake] was mad unless they are also prepared to say as much for every other mystic who ever lived." The more he worked at Blake, the more Yeats came to feel "that hardly any fragment of his poetry can be understood as he understood it, by any reader, until his system is also understood. . . . His lyrics even will seem more beautiful when they have taken their place in his general system."[7] On page 257 of the first volume of the book that Yeats and Ellis eventually produced, we are presented with a schematic version of Blake's system—or a corner of the system that reproduces the organization of the entire system—that looks like the accompanying diagram.

This diagram obviously corresponds to the antinomic opposites and to the four faculties and the four principles of Yeats's *Vision* (still more than thirty years in the future) and equally obviously to the introverted/extraverted oppositions and the four functions of Jung's *Psychological Types*. One hesitates before the muchness of it all: where does one *not* find nearly identical quaternities whenever some visionary—Blake or Yeats or Jung, Boehme or Paracelsus or Timaeus —sets about drawing out the whole scheme of the world or of real-

---

[7]. This letter to Elkin Matthews is in the Robert H. Taylor Collection, Princeton, New Jersey; quoted by kind permission of Mr. Taylor.

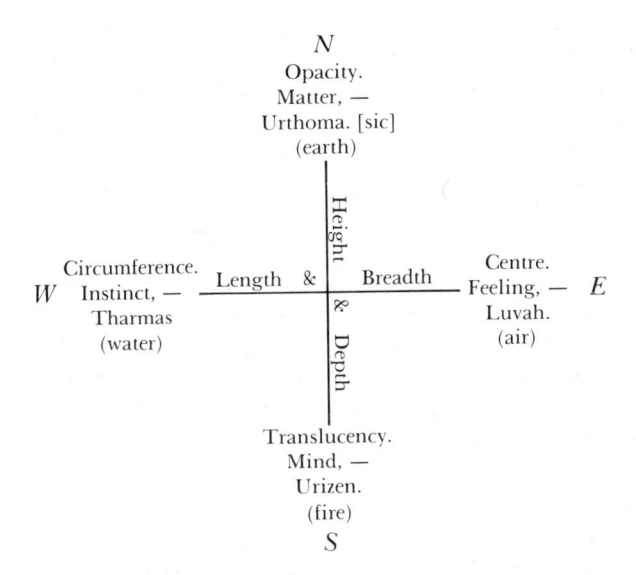

```
                          N
                        Opacity.
                        Matter, —
                        Urthoma. [sic]
                         (earth)
                           │
                           │ Height
       Circumference.      │
   W   Instinct, —  ── Length & ──┼── Breadth ──  Feeling, —   E
       Tharmas              &                     Luvah.
        (water)             │ Depth               (air)
                            │
                            │
                       Translucency.
                         Mind, —
                         Urizen.
                          (fire)
                            S
```

ity? It seems as if, in the division of experience, the investigator could not *but* come up with quaternities—they appear to be in his mind as much as in the world, but in the world as much as in his mind. It is clear that the mind cannot know any other reality than the one it is fitted out to know—as Blake put it, a cup cannot contain more than its capaciousness—but that reality that is proper to it, or configured to it, the mind *can* know: a cup can be filled to capacity, and what it holds is no less real for being of just that volume.

In a letter of 1926, written to Olivia Shakespear, Yeats referred to "those more remote parts of the System that are hardly touched in *A Vision*" (*Letters*, p. 715), implying by what he says and how he says it, as well as by the uppercase honor conferred on "System," that there is the system of *A Vision*—in itself coherent and sufficiently complete, but in a certain sense subjectively determined by his and his wife's joint *daimon*—and that there is also, outside and beyond *A Vision*, an objective System, uppercase, altogether complete, *teleiōtaton*, a perfect marvel of coherence, integrity, and comprehensiveness. To the same correspondent Yeats wrote in 1929: "Four or five years' reading has given me some knowledge of metaphysics and time to clear up endless errors in my understanding of the script.

My conviction of the truth of it all has grown also and that makes one clear" (ibid., p. 768). If the receiver, redactor, and transmitter of all that ancient knowledge did not himself understand everything that was given to him and that he passed on as best he could, and if, as the years passed and he learned more and so became capable of understanding more of the truth of it all and did in fact perceive that it was "true"—if these "ifs" hold, then how could anyone doubt (Yeats wondered) that there was a System behind his system and behind Blake's system and behind the systems of numerous other men going as far back as Pythagoras and his contemporaries in the "fibrous darkness" of ancient Greece and ancient psyche? To put it another way: What other system could the Instructors have given Yeats? What other system, worthy of the name, is there? Communism or Catholicism?—no, they wanted to do, and did do, better by their child than that.

In a little book called *Before and After Socrates*, F. M. Cornford tells a charming and impressive story about Pascal (which he glosses with the remark that "If this anecdote is not true, it is enough . . . that it might conceivably be true"—he is telling, in other words, an *eikota mython*, a likely story). The story is that Pascal's father forbade his tutors to teach the boy any mathematics or geometry, but that Pascal, determined to taste this forbidden fruit, took a piece of charcoal to his room and there traced out figures on the floor—"the shapes of triangles and parallelograms, whose very names he did not know." This desire to learn the divine sciences in which Pythagoras, Timaeus, and Nicholas of Cusa's Idiot were so proficient (and in which Yeats and Jung were about equally deficient) might be taken for a common human trait, but we are not all of us Pascal, and few or none of us would get as far as he before he was discovered—in Cornford's description: "He was not yet twelve years old when he had made out the definitions and axioms he required; and he had reached the 32nd proposition of the First Book of Euclid before he was detected and forbidden to discover the rest of geometry."[8] There are a number of different lessons in this probable story. Cornford presents it as confirmation of the teaching of the *Meno* "that knowledge of mathematical truth is *a priori*," and he sees in it a sort of analogue to the experiment that Socrates performs with the young

8. F. M. Cornford, *Before and After Socrates* (Cambridge: Cambridge University Press, 1932), pp. 72-73.

slave in that dialogue. Another lesson the story teaches is that there is but the one geometrical system; hence Pascal—given the fact that, alone and unaided, he had the genius to discover a system—could have discovered none other. Pascal found the same truths of geometry individually, and in the same way, according to the same systematic logic, as the human mind has discovered them collectively. If all the discoveries of Euclid were lost tomorrow, would not another Euclid or another Pascal appear in the fullness of time to reconstruct the whole system first set down by Euclid, found coherent and adequate—i.e., true—by generations since, and rediscovered by Pascal? As to our system: If there had been no Pythagoras and no Heraclitus, we should have been forced, not to invent them, but to discover them and to produce them out of our deep mind, for they exist there as well (fortunately) as in history, and they are essential to the human effort.

One of the first occurrences of the word *systēma* (according to the Liddell-Scott *Lexicon*) is in the *Epinomis*, which is either Plato's final work or the work of a close associate in the Academy. Wht the Athenian Visitor is in the process of saying in that dialogue when he has recourse to the word *systēma* is that (as Timaeus also declared) the highest, most divine knowledge of which humans are capable (and which it is consequently their most solemn obligation to pursue) is to be found in study of those gods that are the heavenly bodies, and the most essential science, therefore, is astronomy; but astronomy is founded on a knowledge of geometry, which is founded on a knowledge of mathematics, which is founded on a knowledge—a sort of mystical intuition—of number. Everything from the order of the cosmos to a melody played on a syrinx or a psaltery is determined, in this view of things, by those pure, perfect numbers reverenced by the Pythagoreans. From a system of pure numbers to constructions of plane and solid geometry to forms and patterns projected into bodies and played out in time and space—this is the necessary progression of learning urged by the aged Plato in the guise of an Athenian Visitor. "To the man who pursues his studies in the proper way, all geometric constructions, all systems [*systēmata*] of numbers, all duly constituted melodic progressions, the single ordered scheme of all celestial revolutions, should disclose themselves, and disclose themselves they will, if, as I say, a man pursues his studies aright with his mind's eye fixed on their single end" (991e; trans.

A. E. Taylor). A system of numbers lies at the center of things and it gives its order to a series of concentric systems that extend to the furthest reaches of the cosmos. What the Visitor promises to anyone who proceeds from system to system in the proper way, tracing from the center out and from the circumference back in, is that he shall himself become that integer that is simultaneously a number and not a number and that is both the beginning and the end of all number: he shall become one within himself and one with the order of the universe. As such a person "has reduced the manifold within himself to unity," the Athenian says, "so will he be happy, wise, blessed, all in one" (992b). It is not hard to see that what Plato urges so passionately here is no odd corner of learning or an idle pastime but the organizational principle of all system and the highest good to which men can aspire. All varieties of system—whether philosophical, psychological, theological, cosmological, aesthetic, musical, or poetic—are all, by their structural order, hierarchical imitations of the prevailing harmony that is the creative principle behind and throughout the universe.

"Now," Socrates says to his companions in the *Phaedo*, just before going to bathe himself in preparation for his death, "to affirm confidently that these things are as I have told them would not befit a man of good sense; yet seeing that the soul is found to be immortal, I think it is befitting to affirm that this or something like it is the truth about our souls and their habitations" (184d; trans. Hackforth). What Socrates has been telling all the while has been no more than a likely story, but as his story finds the soul to be immortal, he implies, it is more likely than those myths that would deny the soul's immortality. The case is the same with system-making: neither Timaeus nor Timaeus' creator—neither Socrates nor Socrates' perpetuator—would affirm confidently that everything, in every detail, is exactly as his *mythos*, on its way to becoming a *systēma*, declares it to be. But from all knowledge and all evidence, both internal and external, the tale is likely—very likely: as likely as Socrates, Timaeus, and Plato can make it. And it is important that it be likely, because we must be able to believe in it. As Socrates says of his myth and of belief in it, "I think it is a belief worth risking; καλὸς γὰρ ὁ κίνδυνος: for the risk is a noble one." System is a likely story in the same way, a noble risk in the same sense.

"Plato's *Timaeus* . . . was a sacrosanct authority for medieval science—and rightly so!" Jung's reasons for thus warmly endorsing the attitudes of medieval science bring us back to that which was in the beginning and to that which is essential to system and to order of every sort: "Our modern attempts at a unitary view . . . do indeed lead to the question of the cosmic demiurge and the psychic aspect of whole numbers" (*Letters*, II, 352). So the question is rather larger than a question of science, medieval or modern; it is a question of psychic and physical *kosmos*, of the union and identity of the two *kosmoi*, and of the numerical organization that determines *kosmos* of all varieties and at all levels. To another correspondent, Jung wrote: "Number, like Meaning, inheres in the nature of all things, as an expression of God's dissolution in the world of appearances" (*Letters*, II, 302). When Jung thus draws Number and Meaning together we can observe how noble he feels the risk to be, for one of his deepest insights is that "meaning makes a great many things endurable—perhaps everything" (*Memories*, p. 340/313)., The individual discovers meaning in discovering a system—a myth, a likely story, a noble risk, call it what we will—that he can believe in. This is what Socrates said at the end of his life, Plato at the end of his, Yeats and Jung at the end of theirs. "Man can embody truth, but he cannot know it"—this is Yeats's formulation in his last letter, but it might as well have been Jung's, and it is the whole logic on which the art of Plato's dialogues proceeds. Socrates never knew the system which Plato had him embody. A system represents the individual's adaptation—Socrates', Yeats's, Jung's—his personal adjustment, to the order that he observes or intuits in the cosmos; it is his creation of a unified order within himself—a unified order which *is* himself—and an attunement of that order with the environment and universe surrounding him. A system is not a mechanical or a fixed thing but is a balance and a *harmonia* forever renewed and forever coming into being, a process which seems to have an end but whose true end is the whole process itself: there is a *telos*, but that *telos* lies not in the conclusion but rather in the whole shape of the life lived.

The philosophic-poetic system for which Yeats speaks and the philosophic-psychic system for which Jung speaks are to the comprehensive historic-philosophic-psychic-poetic system for which

Plato, his predecessors, and his successors speak as flowers to a perennial rhizome. One peculiarity about a rhizome, as the dictionary tells us, is that "it produces shoots above and roots below," which is indeed the case with Platonism, the *tertium comparationis* in which Yeats and Jung find their peace, a common ground and a meaning; for Platonism is rooted below in the Pre-Socratics, its *rhizōmata*, and in the unconscious of mankind, and it produces shoots above in just such latter-day adherents as Yeats and Jung. It is a truly complex system of a rhizome, its roots and its shoots. In Yeats and Jung, the individual mind, *anima hominis*, elaborates its necessary system just as the collective mind, *Anima Mundi*, has been doing for so many centuries, an ontogenetic recapitulation of the phylogenetically developed *imago mundi*: a reflection in the individual and collective psyche of the cosmos without. And so with our system, the system I have tried to trace and in tracing to recreate—it is a vast and intricate *imago mundi*, an elaborate and complex yet coherent *systēma tou kosmou*. "And now at last"—if I may presume to adopt the final words of the *Timaeus* for my own:

> And now at last we may say that our account of the universe has reached its end. For having received creatures both mortal and immortal and been filled up by them, this our Cosmos has become a visible living creature embracing all that are visible, a perceptible god that is a likeness of the intelligible, most great and good, and most beautiful and perfect, this Heaven single in its kind and one.

INDEX

Abraxas, 302-303
Adler, Alfred, 62, 355
Æ. *See* Russell, George
Aetius, 70
Africanus, Leo. *See* Leo Africanus
Allt, Peter, 277*n*
Alspach, Russell K., 277*n*
Anamnesis, 273. *See also* Memory
Anaxagoras, 103-104
Anima, 214-15, 310-18
Anima hominis, 207, 246, 370
Anima Mundi, 118, 184, 189, 207, 246, 248, 253, 291, 370
Antaeus, 342
Anthropos, 181, 221
Aquinas, St. Thomas, 117, 238
Archē: four elements as *archai*, 46-47; *archai* of Pre-Socratics, 49-50; number as, 62, 361; of modern physics, 205-206
Archetype(s), 7, 261-265; archetypal ideas, 11; physiology of, 19-21; Pre-Socratics as, 21, 26; Pythagoras as archetype, 27; and number, 62; and *archē*, 63; emptiness of, 64-65; in Yeats, 66-68; of quaternity, 69-70; of self, 117-19, 142, 178, 186, 266-67, 323-25; in Plato, 131; in Parmenides, 131; in Plotinus, 144-45; and *eidos*, 209; and time, 229-32; Jung on, 229-33, 305-308, 342-45; Yeats on, 249, 273, 309-310, 334-35; and instinct, 252-53, 281-82, 289-303, 305-308, 326-28; Christ as, 323-24; of collective unconscious, 325; inheritance of, 332-33
Archimedes, 68
Aristophanes, 105, 179, 220*n*, 323
Aristotle, 25, 33, 37, 63, 105, 167, 358
Arnold, Mathew, 271
Augustine, St., 12, 16, 59

Beans, Empedocles' warning, 182
Benchley, Robert, 60

371

Index

Bergson, Henri, 335-36
Blake, William, 11, 75, 105, 113, 166-67, 236, 249, 254, 261, 267, 273, 337, 348-49, 362, 364-65
Boehme, Jakob, 11, 236, 364
Bohr, Niels, 204
Bonaventura, St., 142
Bowra, C. M., 10 and *n*
Buddha, 177
Burnet, John, 29*n*, 63, 64*n*, 89*n*, 103, 118, 130*n*, 133, 135, 139, 153 and *n*, 160, 244 and *n*
Byzantium, 247-50

Callimachus, 64
Cameron, Alister, 27*n*, 76*n*
Center, 337-38
Cherniss, Harold, 120
Chōrismos (separation of realms), 30, 33-34, 48-49, 145
Christ, 75, 176-77; as mythic figure, 190; and Unity of Being, 266; and self, 323-24
Cicero, 154*n*
Clement of Alexandria, 36
Coincidentia oppositorum, 104
Coleridge, Samuel Taylor, 262
Collective unconscious, 12-13, 184, 253-54, 298; and *Anima Mundi*, 291; Jung's personification of, 308-309; and consciousness, 326-27; Jung on, 342-44; as system, 356. *See also* Unconscious
Complexio oppositorum, 105, 113-14
Concord, 170-71, 177-78
Cornford, F. M., 29, 76*n*, 89, 232, 366-67 and *n*
Corpus Hermeticum, 221
Correspondence, 75-76, 78
Cratylus, 37-38, 125
Crespi, Angelo, 116*n*
Croce, Benedetto, 335-36
Cusanus. *See* Nicholas of Cusa

Daimon, 7, 34, 39, 117-19, 189; and Pre-Socratics, 26; of Empedocles, 47-48, 168, 180, 181-83; and myth, 209-211; in Plato, 213-15; soul as, 217-18; and *eudaimon*, 217-19; of Yeats and Mrs. Yeats, 241-44, 248-49; and Yeats's Instructors, 242-44; of artist, 261-62; and instinct, 216-17; 295, 302; and

soul, 333; of Plotinus, 334; Yeats on, 335-36; and Unity of Being, 336
Dante Alighieri, 75, 135, 265
Demiourgos, 141
Democritus, 205
Diels, Hermann, 89*n*
Diogenes Laertius, 26
Diotima, 105, 146, 213-14, 216, 222, 260, 279
Discord, 170-71, 177-78
Dodds, E. R., 156 and *n*, 181*n*, 219
Dolmetsch, Arnold, 76
Donne, John, 271-72
Dreams, 331, 340-42
Duhem, Pierre, 10-11, 355

Edelstein, Ludwig, 191*n*
Edinger, Edward, 207*n*
Eidos, 193, 199; and archetype, 209; and myth, 221-22; Platonic, 231-32; of Man, 262
Elements: as *archai*, 46-47, 164; in Heraclitus, 99-100; in Empedocles, 205-206; in *Timaeus*, 205-206
Eliot, T. S., 173, 250, 322
Ellis, Edwin, 349, 364
Empedocles, *150-183 passim*; character of, 28; reincarnations of, 44; contribution of, to Platonism, 44-48; as Parmenidean, 44-45; on time, 44-45, 151-52; as Pythagorean, 45; on *rhizōmata*, 45, 163-65; on Love and Strife, 46-47, 158, 167-72; *daimon* of, 47-48, 168, 180, 182-83; presence of, in Yeats, 150-51, 158-62; Yeats's knowledge of, 152-55; as shaman, 155-57; as archetypal figure, 156, 167; palingenesis in, 157; on Great Year, 158-59; as nature poet, 159-60; doctrines of, 160-63; presence of, in Jung, 163-70; and mandalas, 165-66; on sphere, 167, 169-72; as prophet, 172-77; full cycle of, 179-80; and beans, 182
Enantiodromia, 90, 106-107, 110-111, 122, 152, 173-75
Eros: in Plato, 213-17, 219-221, 269; Jung on, 215-17, 219-221; and memory, 259-60; and women, 311-14
Eudemus, 79-80

Farr, Florence, 76, 275
Fire, symbolism of, 101-103, 178-179
Fitzgerald, Roger, 5*n*
Flournoy, Henri, 292
Form(s), 36, 37, 47, 51-52, 187-88, 227, 286-87; of Beauty, 67-68, 268-70; in Yeats, 249, 261-72; Jung on, 344
Freud, Sigmund, 26, 62, 186, 292-93, 318*n*, 340, 346-47, 355
Friedländer, Paul, 131 and *n*, 188 and *n*

Galen, 17-18*n*
Gnosticism, 296-97, 302-304
God: as sphere, 142, 338, 362; nature of, 339-40
Golden Dawn, Order of the, 77-78
Gonne, Maud, 65-67, 83, 214-15, 220, 267, 268, 286, 310-11, 314
Gosse, Edmund, 280-81
Great Mind. See *Anima Mundi*
Great Year, 109-110, 158, 357
Gregory, Lady Augusta, 237, 272-73, 280-81
Gregory, Robert, 280-81
Guthrie, W. K. C., 36*n*, 89, 118, 155, 156, 199, 233, 261*n*, 272
Gyres, 179-80

Hackforth, R., 188 and *n*, 198
Harmonia: Pythagorean doctrine, 58; in Yeats, 75-76
Harper, George Mills, 5*n*, 6, 319*n*
Hecataeus, 85, 88
Hegel, G. W. F., 123 and *n*
Heisenberg, Werner, 203-206, 205*n*
Henn, T. R., 6*n*, 15*n*
Henry, Paul, 144*n*
Heraclitus, *86-124 passim*; character of, 27; contribution of, to Platonism, 35-40; on *Logos*, 35-36, 98-100, 130; on perpetual flux, 35-37, 95-98; opposed to Parmenides, 36-37; *daimon* of, 39, 117-19; on Pythagoras, 84-85; presence of, in Yeats and Jung, 87-93; doctrines of, 94-95; and process philosophy, 97; on *palintropos*, 97, 112; circle in, 99-100; and four elements, 99-100; on fire/water symbolism, 100-103; on opposites, 104-107; paradox in, 113-14; doctrine of unity-in-plurality, 120-21

Hermes Trismegistus, 73, 217
Hesiod, 84-85, 88, 123, 130
Hippocrates, 78
Hippolytus, 105
"Hodos chameliontos," 127-28, 142
Homer, 123, 275
Hone, Joseph, 245, 268*n*, 276*n*
Hopkins, Gerard Manley, 36, 159 and *n*
Hopper, Vincent, 69*n*
Hull, R. F. C., 297-98

Iamblichus, 57, 77
Idea(s) (*eidē*), 29, 37-38, 132; of Maud Gonne, 65-66
Images, 16, 22
Imago Dei, 321
Imitatio Christi, 324
Individuation, 120-21, 178, 321-22, 360; Jung on, 181
Instinct(s): and *daimon*, 224-25, 302; and archetype(s), 252-53, 281-82, 289-303, 305-308, 326-28; and memory, 259-61; in Yeats and Jung, 288-303; and the dead, 294-95

Jacobi, Jolande, 346
Jaffé, Aniela, 298*n*
James, Henry, 275
Jeffares, A. Norman, 100
Jesus. *See* Christ
John, Augustus, 284
Johnson, Lionel, 310
Joyce, James, 97
Jung, Carl Gustav: knowledge of Yeats, 5*n*; Yeats's knowledge of, 5-6; ideas in common with Yeats, 6-7; on Pre-Socratics, 10; sources of his ideas, 13-14; on *Timaeus*, 14, 369; mathematics of, 55-56; and quaternity, 56-57, 59-60, 68-70, 163-67; on numbers, 59-60, 68-70, 73; on opposites, 61-62, 105-107; as monist/pluralist, 61-62; on correspondence, 78; on metempsychosis, 81-84; reincarnations of, 84; and Heraclitus, 88-93; and Heraclitean flux, 95; on *Logos*, 98, 108-109; on fire/water symbolism, 100-103; on enantiodromia, 110-111, 173-175; on the self, 114, 142-43, 178, 181-82, 322-25; on

daimon, 119-21; on individuation, 120-21, 181, 321-22; on sphere, 141-43, 164, 169-70, 220-21; presence of Parmenides in, 142-43, 150; on pleroma, 146-47, 296-301; on symbol, 147-48, 251, 299-300, 319-20; presence of Empedocles in, 157-58, 163-70; on libido, 168-69, 318-21; as prophet, 172-76; on National Socialism, 173; and myth, 186-91, 193-94, 199-202, 337-38; on Eros, 215-17, 219-21; on archetypes, 229-33, 305-308; on time and eternity, 229-33, 342-45; on memory, 232-33; on rhythm, 250-53; on instinct, 288-303; his tower, 292; on unconscious, 295, 298, 307-310, 342-44; his Thirteenth Cone, 300-301; on evil, 303-304; on Anima, 310-18; on men and women, 311-14; and astrology, 316; his "energic" view, 318-21; on magic, 319; on *imago Dei*, 321; on origin of archetypes, 327-28; on dreams, 331, 340-42; on the Great Man, 340; opposed to system, 346-47; philosophy in, 350-53; system of, 353-56
—*Works Cited*: "After the Catastrophe," 175n; *Aion*, 120-21, 142, 201, 216, 300; *Analytical Psychology*, 55n, 330; "Analytical Psychology and 'Weltanschauung,' " 356; "Answer to Job," 302, 343; "Approaching the Unconscious," 304; *Archetypes and the Collective Unconscious, The*, 195-96; "Archetypes of the Collective Unconscious," 98, 100; "Basic Postulates of Analytical Psychology," 355; "Child Development and Education," 100; *Collected Papers on Analytical Psychology*, 6n; Collected Works, 75, 88, 191, 202, 230, 354, and *passim*; "Commentary on *The Secret of the Golden Flower*," 6n; "Epilogue to 'Essays on Contemporary Events,' " 175n; "Fight with the Shadow, The," 175n; "Flying Saucers," 121; "Instinct and the Unconscious," 300; *Letters*, 17, 19n, 55n, 83, 102, 148, 206-207, 231, 293, 297, 303, 304, 316, 338, 341, 345, 346, 347, 351, 352, 355, 361, 369; *Man and His Symbols*, 305, 306; "Meaning of Psychology for Modern Man, The," 100; *Memories, Dreams, Reflections*, 10, 72, 73, 78, 84, 112, 146, 157-58, 166n, 174, 200, 201, 202, 227, 230, 254, 294-95, 305, 338, 369: *Mysterium Coniunctionis*, 24n, 88, 95, 100, 142, 201, 300, 321, 332; "On Psychic Energy," 168; "On the Nature of the Psyche," 306; *On the Psychology of So-Called Occult Phenomena*, 254; "Psyche and Earth," 332-33; "Psychological Approach to the Trinity, A," 60n; *Psychological Types*, 21, 61, 90, 240, 364; *Psychology and Alchemy*, 100, 232, 237; "Psychology and Religion," 330; *Psychology and Religion*, 98, 164, 181, 220-21, 237: "Psychology of the Child Archetype, The," 335; "Role of the Unconscious, The," 113, 175n, 207; "Schizophrenia," 20; *Septem Sermones ad Mortuos*, 4, 61-62, 112, 128, 146-47, 288, 293, 296, 303; "Structure of the Psyche, The," 201; "Study in the Process of Individuation, A," 164-65; *Symbols of Transformation*, 100, 186-87, 196, 201, 228, 304, 321; "Synchronicity," 291; "Talk with Students, A," 340; *Two Essays on Analytical Psychology*, 108, 174, 216, 253, 293
Jung, Emma (Mrs. C. G.), 314
Jung, Franz, 5n

Kant, Immanuel, 147-48
Kelly, John S., 6
Kirk, G. S., 36n, 86, 87, 101n, 106, 120
Kosmos: in Pythagoras, 70-73; in Yeats, 71-72

Leo Africanus, 241
Libido, 168-69, 318-21
Likeness, 135-37, 140-41, 195-97, 203
Living Creature (*Timaeus*), 140-41,

170-71, 261, 350; compared to collective unconscious, 309
Logos, 98-99, 108-109, 130; and *mythos*, 184-86, 191-95; and men, 311-14
Love, 170-71, 177-78; in Empedocles, 46-47, 158, 167-72

MacKenna, Stephen, 140, 151, 350
Macrobius, 154n
Mandala(s), 121, 165-66, 338
Mannin, Ethel, 107, 175
Maria Prophetissa, 69, 166, 167, 238
Markievicz, Constance, 96
Mathematics, of Yeats and Jung, 54-56
Mathers, MacGregor, 259, 310
Matthews, Elkin, 364 and n
Mayer, Robert, 232
Memory: in Yeats, 226, 285-86; in Jung, 232-33; and instinct, 259-61; and Eros, 259-60. *See also* Anamnesis
Metempsychosis, 80-84
Michelangelo, 264
Mill, John Stuart, 27
Monism, 74-75, 362-63; and pluralism, 18-19, 40, 122
Moore, T. Sturge, 212n, 350
Moore, Virginia, 6 and n, 15n, 241n
More, Henry, 291
Mourelatos, Alexander P. D., 344n
Music, 76-77; of the Spheres, 68
Myth: in Plato, 184-87; and *logos*, 184- 87, 191-95; in Pre-Socratics, 184-85; in Jung, 186-91, 337-38; in Yeats, 189-93, 214-15; as psychic drama, 194-95; as symbol, 195-97; of Yeats and Jung, 199-202; and psychology, 202-203; in *Timaeus*, 202-205; and *eidos*, 221-22; and immortality, 221-23, 225-26; of soul, 221-22, 307-308, 328-29

Napoleon, 177
Narcissus, 342
National Socialism, 173
Nevinson, H. W., 5 and n
Newman, John Henry, 95, 270
Nicholas of Cusa, 11-12, 58-59, 74, 105, 113, 121, 147, 171
Nietzsche, Friedrich, 89, 132-33, 267

Nous, 74, 103-104, 105
Number(s), 16-19; as archetype(s), 18; in Plato, 17, 59; Pythagorean, 18, 32, 56-58; in Jung, 59-60, 68-70, 73; in Yeats, 58-60, 238; as *archē*, 62, 64-65, 361; basic to system, 367-68

O'Casey, Sean, 215
Oedipus, 26, 292-93
Oeri, Albert, 55, 60
Olney, Richard, 20n
Opposites: in Pythagoras, 60-62; in Jung, 61-62; in Heraclitus, 104-107; of psyche, 311-12
Ouroboros, 141
Owen, G. E. L., 344

Palingenesis, 157
Palintropos, 112, 122
Pan, 126, 359n
Paracelsus, 11, 236, 288, 364
Paradigm, 265; in *Timaeus*, 136-37, 229, 333; in Yeats, 249
Paradise Lost, 147
Parkinson, Thomas, 71, 116n, 285
Parmenides, *125-149 passim*; character of, 27-28; as logician, 27-28, 130-31; contribution of, to Platonism, 40-44; opposed to Heraclitus, 40-42; "Way of Truth," 125-26; "Way of Seeming," 126-28; presence of, in Yeats, 128-29, 133-36, 242-43; on *logos*, 130; Nietzsche on, 132-33; denial of likeness, 136-37; presence of, in Jung, 142-43; and symbolism, 148-49, 228-29; monism of, 362-63
Pascal, Blaise, 366-67
Pater, Walter, 90-91n
Pauli, Wolfgang, 205n
Penfield, Wilder, 19-21 and n
Perennial philosophy, 24-25, 350; its beginnings, 10-11; psychic determinants of, 12; Yeats's belief in, 237-38
Phidias, 173
Philosophy: its immortalizing effect, 35, 260-61; Yeats on, 234-38; and the unconscious, 237-38; and symbolism, 238; Socrates on, 272-73; in Jung, 350-53

Physics: of *Timaeus*, 202-206; language of, 204-206
Piero della Francesca, 82-83
Plato, *184-233 passim*; character of, 28-30; his use of Pre-Socratics, 29-30; and *chōrismos*, 30, 49-50; and Pythagoreanism, 32-35; and mathematical objects, 34, 51; union of Heraclitus and Parmenides, 42-44; synthesis of Pre-Socratics, 48-52; *archai* of, 49-51; number in, 59-60; myth in, 184-87; *logos* in, 184-85; system in, 190-91; on *daimon*, 213-15; on Eros, 219-21; Primordial Man, 220-21; on memory, 226
—*Works Cited: Apology of Socrates*, 119-201, 202; *Cratylus*, 30, 34, 35; *Epinomis*, 29, 34, 225, 367-68; *Epistles*, 290n; *Gorgias*, 34, 189, 197, 277; *Laws*, 29, 34, 35, 189, 225, 274; *Meno*, 34, 226, 233, 261, 366; *Parmenides*, 30, 130-31, 143, 189, 362; *Phaedo*, 29, 34, 35, 39, 47, 187, 189, 190, 191, 192, 198, 208, 213, 219, 222, 225, 226, 261, 277, 278, 368; *Phaedrus*, 30, 39, 47, 189, 192, 193, 194, 198, 201, 208, 222, 225, 226, 259-60, 261, 262, 268, 274, 278; *Philebus*, 34, 35, 39, 189, 225; *Republic*, 29, 34, 35, 37, 39, 47, 96, 98, 143, 189, 192, 208, 213, 219, 222, 225, 231, 261, 265, 272, 274, 277, 345; *Sophist*, 29, 30, 42-43, 131, 189, 364; *Statesman*, 30, 47, 177, 189; *Symposium*, 35, 47, 52, 105, 144, 146, 179, 181, 189, 213, 216, 219, 221, 225, 261, 279, 323; *Theaetetus*, 30, 35, 38, 42, 131, 189, 225; *Timaeus*, 28, 30, 34, 35, 39, 43-44, 45, 47, 51-52, 98, 136, 137, 167, 170, 185, 189, 191, 195, 198, 202-206, 213, 217-18, 226, 229, 230, 231, 233, 258, 261, 265, 276, 309, 324, 333, 339, 344, 348, 359, 369, 370
Platonic Man, 151-52, 181, 199, 220-21, 264
Platonism: as *tertium comparationis*, 8, 369-70; as historical tradition, 9, 52-53; in Yeats and Jung, 15, 236-38; its sources, 15, 24-25; as a story, 25; its teleology, 31, 48-49; its *rhizōmata*, 52-53; as psychic system, 53; as system, 350, 356-58
Pleroma, 128, 132-33, 146-47, 296-301, 304, 326-27, 345
Plotinus, 12, 16, 18, 59, 67, 119, 140, 143-45, 151, 236, 298, 335, 343, 350; on symbolism, 144-45; on archetypes, 144-45; *daimon* of, 334
Pluralism, 74-75; and monism, 18-19, 40, 122, 363-64
Porphyry, 100, 101n
Pre-Socratics: Jung on, 10; as psychic determinants, 13, 29; as archetypal figures, 21; as mythic figures, 26; and myth, 184-85; and Yeats's Instructors, 243-44
Process, 120
Prophecy, in Empedocles, 172-77
Psyche: structure of, 18; and *physis*, 20-21; as *daimon*, 217-18, 333; language of, 307-310 inheritance of, 320-21; as system, 324-25, 330-31, 353-54; and myth, 328-29
Ptolemy, 356-57
Purohit, Shri, Swami, 5n
Pythagoras, *54-85 passim*; his character, 25-27; legendary accounts of, 25-27; as first philosopher, 26; reincarnations of, 26-27, 35, 84; as archetype, 27; contribution of, to Platonism, 31-35; and Music of the Spheres, 32; on number, 32; Table of Opposites, 60-62; and *kosmos*, 70-73; presence of, in Yeats, 71-73; music in, 76-77; correspondence in, 78-79; metempsychosis in, 80-84; Heraclitus on, 84-85

Quaternity, 16, 56-57, 61, 68-70, 163-67, 170, 292, 338; Christian, 69; as archetype, 69-70; and *rhizōmata*, 163-67
Quinn, John, 239

Raine, Kathleen, 15n, 259n
Recurrence, 79-80
Reincarnation. *See* Metempsychosis
Rhizōmata, 163-65; of Platonism, 24-25, 52-53; of Empedocles, 45, 52-53; in Yeats, 236-38
Rhythm, Yeats on, 249-52
Ribh, 301-302

Ross, W. D., 29n, 131 and n, 198n
Russell, Bertrand, 54-55
Russell, George (Æ), 83, 102, 270

Salkeld, Cecil, 245
Salter, Emma Gurney, 114n
Schwyzer, Hans-Rudolf, 144n
Scopas, 65
Seiden, Morton Irving, 15n
Self, 114, 142-43; "incorruptible self," 115-16; archetype of, 117-19, 178, 186, 266-67, 323-25; Jung on, 178, 322-25; Yeats on, 180-82, 223, 260-61, 266-67, 284-87, 322-25, 337-38, 360
Shakespear, Mrs. Olivia, 6n, 239, 364
Shakespeare, William, 265
Shaman, 155-57
Shelley, Percy Bysshe, 153n, 238, 271
Shorey, Paul, 147-48 and n
Simplicius, 36, 105, 170
Skemp, J. B., 165n
Socrates: his personality, 28-29; on universals, 37; Plato's use of, 185-91; his "autobiography," 187-89; as mythic figure, 188-89, 198-201, 208-209; character of, in *Apology*, 199-201; on philosophy, 222-23, 272-73; in *Phaedo*, 368
Soul, and myth, 221-22. See also Psyche
Sphere, 151-52, 164, 178, 181; in Empedocles, 46-47, 167; in Parmenides, 140; in Yeats and Jung, 141-43, 146, 220-21, 224-25; as God, 142, 338, 362; of eternity, 228-31; and cycles, 229-31; as beginning and end, 362
Stallworthy, Jon, 283
Stanford, W. B., 17n, 276n, 302n
Steinach, Eugen ("Steinach operation"), 78, 271 and n
Stewart, J. A., 221-22
Strife, 170-71; in Empedocles, 46-47, 158, 167-72; in present age, 174-75; and hatred in Yeats, 180-81
Swedenborg, Emanuel, 11, 59, 149n, 236, 238, 301
Swinburne, Algernon Charles, 116n
Symbolism, 136-41, 195-97, 224-25; etymology of, 145-46; and Parmenides, 148-49; and time, 226-29;

and philosophy, 238; Jung on, 251; Yeats on, 273-75; in Platonic tradition, 299-300; and energy, 319-20
Symons, Arthur, 312
Synchronicity, 7
Synge, John, 272-73
Syrianus, 33
System: in Yeats, 240-41, 349-50; of psyche, 324-25; behind insanity, 329-30; Jung's opposition to 346-47, 350-53; in *Timaeus*, 348; mechanical view of, 348, 353; in *Le Système du monde*, 355; *kosmos* as, 356; of Platonism, 356-58; order and inclusiveness of, 358-59

Table of Opposites, 60-62
Tabula Smaragdina, 73
Taylor, A. E., 39n
Taylor, Robert H., 364n
Taylor, Thomas, 10, 33n, 77, 90
Tertium comparationis, Platonism as, 8, 369-70
Thirteenth Cone (Sphere), 117, 132, 182-83, 222, 224-25, 228-33; in Jung, 300-301
Time, 137-38; in Empedocles, 44-45, 151-52, 183; in Plato, 50-52; and history, 151-52; and myth, 226-29; and symbolism, 226-29; archetype of, 229-32; in Jung, 230-32
Timon of Phlius, 94
Tynan, Kathleen, 209

Unconscious: personal vs. collective, 207-209; and philosophy, 237-38; and *A Vision*, 241-42; locale of dead, 295; in Yeats and Jung, 294-96. See also Collective unconscious
Unity of Being, 7, 75-76, 115-16, 119, 178-80, 279, 323; and Christ, 266; in Yeats's poetry, 286-87; and *daimon*, 336
Uroboros, 112, 338

Valentinus, 288
Valéry, Paul, 138-39
Van der Post, Laurens, 77
Vico, Giambattista, 236
Villiers de l'Isle Adam, 117

Villon, Francois, 265
Virgil, 71-72, 80
Voltaire, 20n-21n

Wall, Richard J., 5n
Water, symbolism of, 100-103, 178-79
Watkins, Geoffrey, 4 and n, 5n
Wellesley, Lady Dorothy, 105, 200, 234, 315
Wheelwright, Philip, 90, 106
Whitaker, Thomas, 5n
White, Father Victor, 303
Whitehead, Alfred North, 137-38 and n, 146, 335, 336, 350 and n
Whole-natured forms (*oulophyeis typoi*): in Empedocles, 151-52; and Unity of Being, 178-80
Wilson, F. A. C., 15n
Wordsworth, William, 235, 359n

Xenophanes, 85, 88

Yahweh, 302-303
Yeats, Anne, 239
Yeats, George (Mrs. W. B.), 239, 241, 242-44, 296, 314
Yeats, John Butler, 75
Yeats, Michael, 239
Yeats, William Butler: Jung's knowledge of, 4-5; knowledge of Jung, 6n; ideas in common with Jung, 6-7; sources of his ideas, 13-14; like Empedocles, 28; mathematics of, 54-55, 58-60, 238; as mystic, 56; knowledge of Pythagoras, 63-64; and *kosmos*, 71-72; on Unity of Being, 75-76; on correspondence, 78-79; on metempsychosis, 80-83; presence of Heraclitus in, 87-88, 105-107; knowledge of Heraclitus, 90-93; his "Heraclitean fragments," 93-94, 152-55; and Heraclitean flux, 95-97; on *logos*, 98-100, 108-111; on fire/water symbolism, 100-103; on opposites, 105-109; on Great Year, 109-110, 158, 357; *enantiodromia* in, 109-111; on the self, 114-17, 180-82, 223, 260-61, 266-67, 322-25, 360; *daimon* of, 118-19, 181-83, 248-49, 335-36; and *hodos chameliontos*, 127-28; presence of Parmenides in, 128-29, 133-36, 139; on sphere, 140, 146, 169-72, 224-25; on symbol, 146, 273-75, 319; presence of Empedocles in, 150-51, 157; knowledge of Empedocles, 152-55, 158-62; as nature poet, 158-60; as prophet, 172-77; on gyres, 179-80; on hatred, 180-81; myth of, 189-93, 199-201, 209-211, 214-15; on proof of spirit world, 210-212; on "blessedness," 218-19; and Daimonic Man, 218-19; his metaphysics diagrammed, 233-35; on memory, 226, 259-61; and philosophy, 234-38; his family and poetry, 239-40; and psychological types, 239-40; his "centric myth," 240-41; his system, 240-41; on natural and supernatural, 244-46; on Byzantium, 247-50; on rhythm, 249-52; and tradition, 253; on spirit world, 254-59; on immortality, 260-61; on Forms, 261-72; on Christ, 266; on Beauty, 270-71; anamnesis in, 273; on archetype(s), 273, 309-310, 334-35; his reading of verse, 276; movement of his poems, 277-87; self in his poetry, 284-287; memory in his poetry, 285-86; on instinct, 288-303; his tower, 292; on unconscious, 295; on the dead, 295-96; and Anima, 310-18; on men and women, 311-14; his reading in philosophy, 335-36; on journalists, 338; on dreams, 340-42; enthusiasm for system, 349-50; his Instructors, 349
—*Works Cited*: "Acre of Grass, An," 235; "All Souls' Night," 107, 245-46, 250; "Among School Children," 71-72, 107, 116-17, 140, 220, 225, 270, 284-87, 288, 359; "Anima Hominis," 127, 340; "Anima Mundi," 98-99, 223-25, 269; *Autobiographies*, 9, 57, 65, 75, 114, 115, 116, 200, 210, 265-66, 271, 281, 312, 313, 315, 317; "Before the World Was Made," 227; "Blood and the Moon," 107, 255; "Broken Dreams," 267; "Bronze Head, A," 267; "Byzantium," 107, 247-48, 250; "Choice, The," 209; "Choice and Chance,"

314; "Circus Animals' Desertion, The," 277n, 281-83; "Conjunctions," 239; "Coole Park and Ballylee, 1931," 100; *Countess Cathleen, The,* 282; *Death of Cuchulain, The,* 311n; "Deep-Sworn Vow, A," 267-68; "Dialogue of Self and Soul, A," 107, 129, 214-15, 218, 255; "Dolls, The," 129; *Dramatis Personae,* 309; "Drunken Man's Praise of Sobriety, A," 101-102; "Easter 1916," 95-97, 108, 279-81, 313; *Essays and Introductions,* 66, 75, 96, 114, 139, 141, 182, 209, 212-13, 248, 249, 250, 254, 257, 258, 260, 264, 266, 274, 279, 287, 291, 305, 338; *Estrangement,* 316; *Explorations,* 54, 58, 65, 66, 67, 79, 82, 88, 100, 106, 117, 121, 172, 189, 191, 192, 201, 237, 240, 266-67, 270, 322, 334, 349, 362; "Fergus and the Druid," 159; "Fragments," 253-54; "Gift of Harun Al-Rashid, The," 242-44; "Gratitude to the Unknown Instructors," 239-40; "Gyres, The," 170, 175-76; "He and She," 240; *Herne's Egg, The,* 249; "High Talk," 282; *Ideas of Good and Evil,* 213; "In Memory of Major Robert Gregory," 103, 270; "Is the Order of R. R. & A. C. to remain a Magical Order?" 319; *King of the Great Clock Tower, The,* 234, 263n; "Lake Isle of Innisfree, The," 102; "Lapis Lazuli," 200-201, 283-84; "Leda and the Swan," 16; *Letters,* 56, 82, 102, 105, 107, 120, 123, 135, 146, 175, 200, 209, 215, 234, 239, 260, 270, 274, 315, 338, 365; "Long-legged Fly," 264; "Magi, The," 129; "Magic," 256-57, 305; "Meditation in Time of War, A," 108, 135; "Meditations in Time of Civil War," 290; *Memoirs,* 73, 77-78, 83, 115-16, 211-12, 258, 281, 312, 324; *Michael Robartes and the Dancer,* 74; *Mythologies,* 99, 114-15, 127, 176-77, 180, 181-82, 218, 222-25, 235, 248, 249, 271, 279, 310; "Needle's Eye, A," 149 and n; "Old Stone Cross, The," 275; "On a Picture of a Black Centaur by Edmund Dulac," 244-45; *On Baile's Strand,* 102, 282; *On the Boiler,* 65, 88, 106, 234, 235-36, 296; *Oxford Book of Modern Verse, The,* 282 and n; "People's Theatre, A," 272-73; *Per Amica Silentia Lunae,* 84, 133, 135, 288, 349, 360; "Phases of the Moon, The," 97; *Poems,* 67-68; "Prayer for My Daughter, A," 103, 180-81, 270, 314, 339; "Prayer for Old Age, A," 234-35; "Quarrel in Old Age," 268; "Results of Thought, The," 269-70; *Resurrection, The,* 89, 109, 191, 356; "Sailing to Byzantium," 107, 129, 135; "Second Coming, The," 103, 173, 175-76, 302; "Statues, The," 63-66, 76, 82; "Summer and Spring," 219; "Supernatural Songs," 141, 301-302; "Swedenborg, Mediums, and the Desolate Places," 212n, 254, 349; "Symbolism of Poetry, The," 228, 250, 273-74; "There," 141; "To be Carved on a Stone at Thoor Ballylee," 278; "Tower, The," 107, 108, 256; *Tower, The,* 177; "Tragic Theatre, The," 276-77; *Trembling of the Veil, The,* 210, 281, 325; "Two Songs from a Play," 80; "Under Ben Bulben," 66-67, 82, 107, 112, 250, 260-61, 262-63, 264, 265; "Vacillation," 107, 108-112, 134, 182, 218, 256, 279, 363; "Valley of the Black Pig, The," 328; *Vision, A,* 16, 21, 59, 68, 75-76, 81, 93, 103, 105, 116, 117, 122, 128, 138, 139-40, 148, 151, 157, 163, 165, 173-74, 177, 179, 191, 223, 226, 238-39, 241, 245, 247, 298, 349; 1925 *Vision,* 4-5, 71-72, 153-55, 168, 176, 179, 191, 241, 290, 330; *Wanderings of Oisin, The,* 282; "What Then?" 235; "Wheel, The," 360-61; *Winding Stair, The, and Other Poems,* 177, 238; "Woman Young and Old, A," 227; *Words upon the Window-pane, The,* 334, 336; *Works of William Blake, The,* 337; "Young Man's Song," 269

Zeno, 133, 138-39

Designer: Al Burkhardt
Compositor: Freedmen's Organization
Printer: Thomson Shore
Binder: Thomson Shore
Text: Compugraphic Baskerville
Display: Typositor Zapf Book Light and Demi
Cloth: Holliston Roxite A 50365
Paper: 50 lb. P & S Offset B 32